DRUM
DISO...

by Bill Hayes

EXBOURNE TO AUSTRALIA

First published July 2001
This paperback edition published July 2001

Published by Fairfax Business Pages
Reply Paid 70388
Kings Cross
New South Wales 2011
Australia

Telephone: 1300 666 683
Facsimile: 1300 303 355
Email: pacificmediaworldwide@hotmail.com.au

100 Chad's Creek Road
Strathewen
Victoria 3099
Australia

Telephone: 61-3-9714-8213
Facsimile: 61-3-9714-8205

ISBN   0 9579033 0 8

Typeset by Thu-za-Nwe
Printed by Galloping Press, Sydney, Australia

Cover Photograph of Bill Hayes the Author
in his office, June 2001

BILL HAYES

spent the first twenty three years
of his Life in the village of Exbourne
near Okehampton in Devon

Bill played Rugby Union for
North Tawton and Okehampton
and was well known in the local farming community

Having spent many years in Australia,
he returned to Europe and took a Year Out
in Paris, France, where he wrote this Book

Today, he is a successful Breeder of Racehorses

"Drunk & Disorderly" is subject of a forthcoming
Movie and Television Mini-Series

Photograph by Sam Shao, Maroubra, New South Wales
December 2000

AUTHOR'S NOTE

Dear Readers,

Welcome to my world as I take you from Exbourne my small village in Rural Devon in the days of the Horse and Cart on a trip to Ireland, South Africa, Zimbabwe, Tanzania, Holland and back to England.

We then go from England to Portugal, Australia and back to Ireland eventually concluding the story in Paris early in the year 2000.

I would like to pay special thanks to Jane Mays, the Literary Editor of the "Daily Mail" in London whose constructive criticism and helpful advice assisted me in putting this book together.

I have spoken publicly at many Dinners about various incidents in my life, equally, I have mentioned others to my Family and Friends on various occasions. However, this is the first time I have catalogued the whole chain of events that brought me to Paris today.

I would also like to thank John Morris who is mentioned in the early pages of this Book for his constructive criticism and also correcting me on certain facts relating to the village in the early Fifties. John privately recalled conversations he had with my Father in the late Forties and early Fifties which went a long way to explain the attitude and actions of my Father in those days. I refer to some of these facts in the Appendix at the end of this Book.

Each Chapter could have been a story in itself yet I felt for the first Edition of my life story, it was paramount to cover the period of 50 years in general form without going into great detail.

I would like to take this opportunity to thank many of the people mentioned for being a part of my life and apologise to those people who I failed to mention. As for people who crossed my path with the intention of doing me an Injustice, they will know for themselves that I have documented the events as impartially as possible without Malice.

If my Book prevents even one suffering Alcoholic avoiding my path and stops them from walking the road I had to walk, then my Book was not in vain.

I hope my story Benefits my children by allowing them to know who their Father really is. I feel confident my True Friends will accept me as I am today. The man who has found what he was looking for through the Bottom of a Glass.

Everyone who has heard part of my story has said, "Bill, you should write a Book". So eventually on the advice of all those people, the Book has been written.

Frank Guy from my Village who is now in his eighties read the draft of this Book and said to me, "Billy, I noticed you never once said you are Sorry in the Book". I have done Steps Eight and Nine of Alchoholics Anonymous and attempted to make amends to those people I have harmed except when to do so could have hurt them or others.

WILLIAM HAYES

Paris, France 13th November 2000

DEDICATION

To My Burma Girl A'Sitting
I know she thinks of me
(Pictured Below)

Without her Love, Blind Faith and Dedication,
this book would never have been recorded.
30 September 2000.

APPERITIFF

Lagos was the worse place I have ever been in my life. Being drunk didn't help matters much. Thank God I was wearing all my gold. The customs checked all my baggage and took whatever that they fancied. When I complained they put a gun to my head and they were not joking. This was very, very frightening.

Page 184 Paragraph 5

I rang the prison bell and said "I am back". The one condition of the Home Leave was no returning intoxicated. Here I was at three o'clock in the morning ringing the bloody bell requesting to be put back in prison. I must be the only bloke in the world guilty of attempting to break into a prison.

Page 194 Paragraph 3

At this point we all knew the most northerly prison in England is Durham Top Security Prison. This was the prison in the film "McVicar" with Roger Daltrey and Adam Faith. "The End of the Earth" for everyone on the bus. My mother was born in County Durham.

Page 195 Paragraph 5

I got the bus to London. I knew that in Smithfield Meat Market I was still a legend. I went to Darringtons, Gee and Webb, David Andrade. These people had known me thirty years from being a little boy. I will never forget Peter Andrade telling me no. I said "Peter, just lend me Five Pounds". He said "No". I was so ashamed of what I had become as now I was a beggar, living on a Park Bench.

Page 207 Paragraph 5

I was taken to Perth Police Station and remanded in custody to await the arrival of Gover. My first morning in the prison I was borrowing a cigarette from one of the officers. He said, "Surely Bill, you can afford a cigarette with all of your money?". I thought it strange or perhaps, he was just a Friendly Screw as he gave me a packet of cigarettes. At lunch time I saw the "West Australian" newspaper and the headlines of "$7 million Fraud". There was my photo and a photo of Pat Mullens and David Gover, the Victorian Uniformed Police Sergeant, who had got the extradition on the basis of $7 million fraud.

Page 279 Paragraph 3

CHAPTER ONE

I came into the world on the Twelfth of July 1947, six weeks late and feet first. Difficulties with the pregnancy and the birth caused my twenty seven year old mother to be crippled for a time after my birth. My brother Bruce was born eighteen months later in December of 1948 completing the Hayes family of Barbara the eldest, Bobby the first son, myself and Baby Bruce. Being christened William, I was always known as Billy or Bill so the Hayes children all shared the same initials of *BH,* none of us having a middle name. My father, Robert, who was twenty six years old had spent the last six years as a Royal Marine Commando during World War II and was a Butcher by trade.

My parents moved to a Twentieth Century country house and farm in the village of Exbourne, Devon in August of 1947 and this was to be my home for the next twenty three years. The village was nestled between Dartmoor and Exmoor in the heart of Devon and one of several small villages and hamlets all within two or three miles of each other connected by small winding country lanes with very high hedgerows. These high hedges are peculiar to Devon, Cornwall and being made of soil topped with trees, they are a blanket of colour all the year round, starting with the white snowdrops, yellow primroses in Spring and purple violets in Summer all bedded in the lush green Devon grass.

The village was a Hive of activity built around the village square which consisted of a blacksmith shop, baker's shop, butcher shop and village hall. The horse was just going out of fashion being replaced by tractors, yet all the farmers kept teams of two or four cart horses or work horses as well as hunters and thoroughbreds. There was no shortage of business for Tom White, the village blacksmith and every morning he could be seen at his smithy shop shoeing horses and talking to the old men of the village who sat around the square. Many of these old men lived to great ages. I recall Granfer Madge who lived to be ninety-nine. Tom White himself lived to be one hundred, after the smithy was closed when the horses disappeared, replaced by Tractors.

Guys, the village Bakery, was the biggest employer in the village with a bake house, shop and a fleet of vans delivering bread and pasties to all the surrounding villages and farms on a daily basis. The baker's shop sold everything for the home with the exception of meat and vegetables as rationing was still in place from the war, all the village ladies had rationing books to purchase such things as meat, butter, sugar or fruit. Very little money changed hands in the shop. Everyone had an order book. The shop assistant would tick off the items in the book and enter the price and the accounts were settled on a weekly or monthly basis.

Across the square was Mr Chapple's Butcher Shop which again was mainly deliveries in vans to surrounding farms and villages. This business was eventually taken over by my father and amalgamated with his own butcher's shop at the house. The Village Hall was always known as Chapple Hall as it was owned by Butcher Chapple until the Coronation of 1953 when the village purchased the building and changed the name after a stone laying ceremony to commemorate the Coronation. Every Tuesday the National Provincial Bank took over the Village Hall and offered banking facilities for the village people and local farmers.

There was a village pub, the Red Lion in the High Street which had two petrol pumps for the village needs yet there were few cars in the village in those days. Joe Skinner, the landlord, also ran a taxi business in a large green Hillman car as the only transport was the village bus three times a day. Across from the pub was the post office which again carried a big staff of six or seven men, every morning delivering mail to all the outlying farms by bicycle. One could set one's clock by the postman and all mail was delivered to the village and the farms by nine o'clock every morning, with a second delivery in the afternoon. There was a garage and mechanic in the old Chapel in the High Street known as Guys Garage. Frank Guy, the owner, was a genius with body work and engines, and also serviced all the bakers and butchers' delivery vans as well as tractors.

There were numerous farms in the village itself, that

used to milk cows twice daily all these farms had milk stands outside the gate which were the same height as the milk lorry that collected the milk in churns every morning for the Ambrosia Creamery. The village farmers all had land outside the village which usually consisted of one or two fields in one direction and one or two fields in another. This complex web of fields was caused by the selling of fields over the years. The average field would be no more than five or six acres. A ten acre field was very unusual in our village. All farmers had milking cows, sheep and pigs and at harvest time they would all help each other getting the hay in or the corn harvested. There were no balers in those days and the hay when ripe was piked by hand into ricks which were to then thatched. The corn was cut with a binder and the sheaths of corn stacked to dry in the sun, then man handled also into ricks to be thrashed later in the year. Thrashing was a huge job requiring the services of twelve to fourteen men. This today is all done by one man on a combine harvester.

There was a village contractor, Hawkins Madge who had ten or twelve men that would go around at harvest time as he was the only man with the mechanical machinery and a thrasher. Morley Guy was the local haulage contractor with two cattle lorries that collected livestock weekly to go to the local cattle markets at Okehampton, North Tawton or Hatherleigh. As I have said, it was a hive of activity in the agricultural sector.

There was a beautiful Norman church in the centre of the village with a Church School and a Methodist Chapel at the bottom of the village. The Manor House and village cottages made up the balance with a population of two hundred and eighty souls. The village church was never locked and the electoral roll was kept in the church porch on a notice board.

There was, of course, a Parish Council, Church Council to administer the annual activities and requirements. This consisted of organising the local village carnival every November which was a torch lit procession of floats on horse and carts or tractors and trailers. The church fetes in the Summer, Sunday School outings to the seaside and various concerts in the Village Hall. There were no television so people only had the radio and village activities to occupy their leisure time. One of the main events of the year was the Harvest Festival where the church would be decorated in sheaths of corn, various fruits and vegetables, followed by a church service and Harvest Tea in the Village Hall.

Every house, farm and cottage had its own vegetable garden and all vegetables were home grown. There were orchards attached to most of these gardens. In Summer, you could fill buckets with wild blackberries, elderberries as well as mushrooms growing wild in the meadows. Rabbits were also in abundance and we had a village trapper known as Trapper Madge. Hubert Madge would set traps or gins in the fields every night and send the rabbits to London once a week from the railway at Sampford Courtney, three miles away. There was no shortage of labour as there were still camps left from the war *Displaced* persons mainly Ukranians and Polish who were taken around to farmers in lorries each day as casual labour.

Tumbles House, the family home was built in 1163 A.D. by the Rev. Tumbles, the Norman vicar of the village. It was the oldest standing house in the village. There was a list of vicars in the church from its building to the present day, Rev. Tumbles being the third Norman vicar in the church after its building in the Eleventh Century. The house was situated just off the village square with the rear of the house and fields backing onto open country as far as the eye could see. On a clear day from the top of the village you could see Dartmoor and from the back of our house you could see the Hills of Exmoor in North Devon.

Tumbles was a beautiful three storey house with a thatched roof, stables, and farm buildings. There was a gate lodge cottage in the yard as you enter the two iron gates, approaching the house. Then a large court yard with the stables and a privet hedge surrounding the front lawn complete with privet arches going over the footpath. At the rear of the house were the farm buildings, slaughter house and two walled vegetable gardens along with an orchard and meadows for grazing.

The interior of the house was very spectacular with giant oak beams running through the ceilings, oak paneling on the walls and large black oak settles on either side of the fire place. The fire place you could stand in. There were hooks coming down the chimney for the curing of bacon and ham. The top story was never used and the house was so large the space wasn't missed. We used to call this floor the attics. We were banned from going there as children as the floors were very unsafe. This meant, of course, we always went up there. The staircase was ten feet wide with a landing half way up where it divided into two separate sets of stairs, one to the first floor and one to the attics.

At the rear of the house was a wash room or laundry room known as the back kitchen. This room was filled with a giant cast iron mangle to wring out clothes, ten gallon boilers to boil clothes and all the equipment to make mince meat and sausages for my father's butcher's shop. This mincing machine alone was the size of a small car. There was always a lovely smell of soap and spices. The spices and rusk was for the making of sausages. This kitchen backed onto the back garden where my mother kept hens for eggs and geese for Christmas holiday fare.

The farm was all converted into piggeries and my father fattened pigs for bacon. They were collected weekly in a big green lorry to go to the Harris Bacon at Totness. We had two cows for milk, *Daisy* and *Buttercup* and two large boars for breeding with the sows called *Billy* and *Bruce*. We used to ride the two boars like donkeys as they were so quiet, which is unusual. Boars can be quite ferocious. This was caused by them one day fighting and boars will fight to the death. My father took them into the slaughterhouse and hung them up by their back legs and beat them with a broom handle. He then proceeded to put both boars in one pen, where they lived, one on one side, one on the other side. When the sows or gilts come into season the boars would both serve the sows resulting in split litters, half black and half white as Billy was a white boar and Bruce a Saddleback black boar. The office walls were covered with rosettes for prizes for my father's pigs at the local Shows.

We also had a pony called Jessie who was a Dartmoor Pony and we all learnt to ride from an early age. Hunting was very popular in the village with several hunts having a Meet in the Village Square each year. This always started out with the stirrup cup being given to the *Master of the Hounds* which was either Brandy or Whiskey, then off they would go. Every November/December the various Hunts held a series of Hunt Balls at various Village Halls which were lovely events, all the farmers in Black Tie and dress suits, and the ladies in long gowns.

There was very little money around in those years just after the war. People would darn socks, patch trousers and shirts, things unheard of today. We had a village cobbler who would repair shoes, several village ladies who would make, alter and repair clothes and a village bicycle repair shop as this was the main means of transport. Having said there was little money around, there was a great camaraderie in the village with concerts, Whist Drives, football and cricket teams which most of the villagers took part in. Village cricket is always very glamorous with all the men in their starched shirts and crisp white trousers and white shoes as opposed to the dowdy way they dressed for the every day work mainly on farms or in the bakehouse.

One of my earliest memories is my mother crying in the middle kitchen then taking Bruce and myself for a long walk in the push chair. I had to stand on the foot stand whilst Bruce rode in the seat. We went for a couple of miles to the next village and back again. I realise now this must have been caused by my parents having a row.

I remember going to Aunty Louis in the cottage in the yard very regularly then her husband died and she moved away and was replaced by Aunty Tancock. These aunts were of no relation just the wives of agricultural workers who we called aunties. I remember when Aunty Louise left. I asked the new lady if she would be my aunty and, of course, she agreed. Lena Tancock was her name. How I came to call her Aunty Tancock and not Aunty Lena I have no idea, as her husband was Uncle Tom.

I remember her running across the yard in 1952 telling my mother the King was Dead. I knew what a King was from Fairy Tales and assumed *the King was Dead in the Cottage.* I recall being excited and frightened going to the cottage to see this Dead King to be told by Aunty Tancock the King was in

London and she had heard the news on the wireless.

There was another cottage on the other side of the yard called Willow Cottage where a Mrs Morris lived with her three sons, John, Cyril and George. I spent many many hours in there with Mrs Morris and the boys or rather young men as they were.

She always gave me cake with icing and drinks of lemonade. Apparently I used to crawl there before I could walk but I have no recollection of this.

Some days I would go with John Morris in his van and he was a contract electrician servicing local farms and houses. They were a nice family.

Every Wednesday morning a big lorry would arrive with the meat for my father's shop for the week. The drivers were called Paddy and Geordie. I was always very afraid of them as they were covered in blood from carrying beef, pork and lamb over the yard to the shop.

As these were rationing days all meat had to be purchased from the Ministry of Agriculture until 1954 when meat came off ration. Due to sugar rationing we only had sweets once a week usually on a Friday when we would count out either Dolly Mixtures or Liquorice Allsorts and divide them amongst ourselves. This usually being the job of Barbara, my sister.

We always had nannies to take care of us. I remember Phyllis Downs as being my first nanny, then Pamela Rice as the next one. There was an awful lot of work to be done each day with over three hundred pigs to be fed twice daily and then the farrowing of the sows.

My father delivered meat every day to the neighbouring villages and farms. These were called the Meat Rounds. As children we would very often go with him to deliver the meat all wrapped up and labelled for each house or farm. Then he would always be ages talking to the farmers or going to look at their livestock while we are waiting in the van. One Christmas at the village of Jacobstowe, I was alone with my father on Christmas Eve and he was in Locks farm talking as usual. I knew it was late and was terrified if he was much longer I may miss Father Christmas coming with all my presents, so I knocked on the door telling him I needed to go to the toilet and could he take me home. Another evening at the village of Broadwoodkelly, he asked me to take the meat into the farm and he called me *"Cock Sparrow"*. I have remembered that night all my life as the only time my father had shown any real affection towards me.

My father was a giant of a man with a terrible temper. Although he never physically hit us, I was always terrified of him. Despite this, I would do anything to gain his approval and followed him everywhere, hoping he would notice me.

What stands out in my mind in those years was the lack of touch by my parents, hugs, kisses, and cuddles. I have learnt over the years children needs this so very desperately if they are to grow up in a normal way. In the years that were to follow, I have been addicted to the touch of a woman and have no pride or shame in touching people I am fond of. *"Yesterday is another country, they do things different there!"*.

My first day at school was in January 1952. It was snowing and I had to hold Barbara's hand until I arrived at the school. Barbara would have been nearly nine years old and I was four and a half.

The village school comprised of two classrooms, one for infants, four to seven years old and one for Juniors seven to eleven years old.

At the age of eleven you took your Eleven Plus and depending on if you passed or failed, you either went to Grammar School or Secondary Modern School.

My first teacher was Miss Greenslade who came to school on an auto cycle, which was an ordinary bicycle with an engine on the back wheel.

Every Sunday we attended Sunday School which was fun and we were always playing tricks on the teachers, either hiding in the church or intentionally giving wrong answers to questions.

Barbara and Bobby were always putting me up to answer these questions such as who was Abraham's son? My hand would go straight up and the teacher would say *"Yes, Billy?"* thinking I knew the answer and I would then tell her the name of a local farmer. Another of these questions and my hand going up first and I answered *"Nick Nack Paddywack, give a dog a Bone"*.

The teachers were young village people and it was all great fun.

After Sunday School we would go on walks down the country lanes on down to the little brooks then ran near the village and pick flowers to take home to Mum.

There was always a Sunday School outing each Summer to one of the local seaside towns, usually Bude or Torquay, Painton and Dawlish.

A bus would be hired for the day and all the kids, teachers and some of the mothers would go along with several old ladies from the village who were either spinsters or widows.

Every Mother's Day we would have flowers blessed at the alter and then give them to our mothers, as Mum had four of us she just took Barbara's flowers and we all gave ours to various village ladies. I always gave mine to Aunty Bobbie who was my Godmother and a local nurse.

Saturdays were the worse days of the week as we had to deliver meat to all the people in the village. We all had a big basket and would take one joint at a time, which meant going up and down the village all of the Saturday morning while other children were playing Cowboys and Indians or riding bicycles.

One Saturday, I had delivered the meat to the post office and Margaret Crocker, the post mistress, always gave me a penny for myself. On my way home I started to play Conkers with David Denford, a boy of my own age.

The result being I became so engrossed in collecting Conkers and filling my pockets that I forgot where I put Croker's money for the meat. My father was furious when I go home and sent me back to find it but I had no idea where it was.

Saturday lunch time my father would set off to deliver the meat to neighbouring villages in the van. One Saturday as we got to the bottom of the village we saw Bruce waiting with his basket at the local Telephone Exchange, which was a small house like building with an automatic exchange in it.

My father stopped the van and asked Bruce what he was doing, and he replied *"Delivering Mrs Cawker's meat"*. Poor Bruce who was new on the deliveries being the youngest, had been directed there by Bob as a trick, and the poor little fellow had been waiting there for hours. Children can be very unknowingly cruel to each other.

It was around this time when I had just started school that Mum was going into hospital and Bob and myself were to stay at a farm in the village on Bonleigh about five miles from home.

This was a marvellous time living on the farm and being thoroughly spoilt.

They were a lovely devout Plymouth Brethren family with two sons who worked on the farm and two teenage daughters, Fiona and Josephine.

We spent all day on the farm milking the cows, feeding the pigs, riding on the tractors and when my father came to take us home one Friday evening, we refused to go home. The Bedford family said it was okay and they would deliver us on the Saturday evening.

I knew we would be in trouble as this meant we didn't have to deliver meat on the Saturday morning and my father had to do it himself. When we got home we were indeed in trouble. My father refused to speak to us and my mother chastised us for not helping my father. This was the first time I realised that the working each Saturday was very unfair on children as young as we were, yet work wise, the worse was to come as the years went on.

Sundays were always good days with enormous Sunday lunch of Roast Beef and Yorkshire Pudding, mushy peas, roast potatoes and gravy.

The village bake house used to leave the ovens on and all the ladies in the village carried the roasting joints, surrounded by potatoes to the bake house at ten thirty Sunday mornings. Then go to church or chapel and collect the cooked meat at twelve thirty in the afternoons. It was a ritual in the village.

Sunday Teas were also grand occasions with fancy cakes on a silver cake stand and lovely enormous teas. Sometimes we would be invited out with our parents to local farms for tea to neighbouring villages. This was usually after Sunday School and meant getting all dressed up and taken in the meat van, the children riding in the back and my parents in the front.

These were wonderful occasions going to the farms of

George Brooks and Broadwoodkelly or the Bedford family. We would all sit around the farmhouse table with Bread, Butter, Jam, Scones, Cakes and Savoury pies.

My father would usually then go and look at the livestock on the farms. The farmers always wore their Sunday suits, the evening would culminate in going to the local church or chapel for evensong.

I was also in a few scrapes in those early years. Once the chamber pot broke in my bedroom cutting the cheek of my bottom from side to side and being rushed to hospital. I still have the scar.

Another time, I got a wooden meat skewer stuck in my nose, then it broke off and couldn't be removed, again taken to the hospital. I went to my father's shop one day and took all the silver coins out of his drawer, that acted as the Till. I took the money to the village shop and put in on the counter and asked for an ice cream. I remember ice creams were only Three Pence. I must have put several Pounds on the counter.

Mrs Guy put all the money in an OXO tin and took it back with me to my parents, giving me the ice cream first. I was in serious trouble that day.

Bob had to go to hospital to have his tonsils out. This was a big adventure, Bob being in a hospital in Exeter some twenty miles from home.

We could visit him but not go into the ward that had these giant Teddy Bears. Bruce and myself were so envious of him getting all the attention.

Mrs Kettle, a lovely lady in the Village gave my father a giant Easter Egg to take to Bob in hospital and as we were in the van he put it under my seat.

Whilst he was doing deliveries I broke the paper and the silver foil and ate some of the chocolate. It must have been a very long morning because as we got home my father sent me back to the van for the Easter Egg. All that was left was the silver paper as I had eaten it all. I was promptly sent to bed for the day, the worse punishment of all.

My father always kept his cigarettes in a drawer in the office. They were Players Medium Cut. One day I took off the cellophane paper from the pack, removed the silver paper from the cigarettes thinking, if I put it all back smoothly he wouldn't notice. Well, as you can imagine, he did notice and went mad *as there was not only a thief in the house but a Smoking Thief!*

There was a small kitchen attached to the village school where school dinners were cooked. Previous to this we used to get our school dinners delivered from the school in the neighbouring town of Hatherleigh four miles away. I noticed Mrs Bird, the school cook, had a big tin of cooking chocolate in the kitchen that looked delicious. I used to dream about this chocolate at night.

One Saturday, Larry House, my friend and I broke into the school by climbing in the window, got into the kitchen and ate as much chocolate as we could digest. We left our teeth marks all over the chocolate which was in metal tins. Ruling out mice as being the culprits.

We never got found out despite the *Stewards Inquiry* by Mrs Trethewey, the Headmistress, I think everyone knew it was Billy Hayes.

Despite all the pleasant things in those years of the late Forties and early Fifties, there was also a Down side. The main one being TB. There was no known cure for TB so people if they were lucky, were sent to a Sanatorium in the hope fresh air would clear their lungs or at least make breathing easier. There was a large Sanatorium at the village of Moretenhampstead some fifteen miles from our village with over one thousand beds for victims.

The main spread of TB was put down to cow's milk and in the early fifties all herds of cows had to be T.T. Attested. This meant the cows were checked for TB and the farms were cleaned up with the milking shippens having to be made with concrete floors and washed daily as opposed to bedding the cows in straw and more straw to cover the dung.

This took several years to bring into practice and the results were incredible. You never hear of TB today. I often wonder how much TB was, in fact, Cancer as the word Cancer was never heard of in those days and the symptoms are very similar.

Mental illness and suicides was also a big factor in village life. There was a mental hospital at Exminster near

Exeter that was a city within a city complete with its own village for the staff, farms, abattoir, shops and some seven thousand patients.

There was a lot of inter-marriage of cousins and second cousins in rural Devon mainly caused to keep properties and farms intact in the families. There were many people who spent their lives waiting for someone to die so they could inherit. We had a boy at school who was Barbara's age and he owned the farm his mother and father worked on, inheriting it from an Uncle. There were also bitter family feuds going on in the village that lasted from generation to generation. Sadly when I went back to the village in 1999, there was still a family feud going on to the present generation of a family over inheritance.

There was a family in the farm next door to us called the Finnemores. They were intelligent people and good farmers yet they were all alcoholics. The word alcoholic was never used but the results to this family were horrendous. The eldest son, Harold, hung himself. The youngest son, Harry or William Henry, went to prison for stealing a milk cheque to get money for booze and eventually took an overdose. The old man lost an eye to one of his cow's horns trying to milk the cow Drunk. He was eventually pushed on the fire by his wife drunk suffering severe burns to the head and hands. They tried to treat the burns with cow's udder cream to avoid a police investigation.

He died and it was all kept very quiet. The village policeman, Fred North, was a good man and a very understanding man. It was a criminal offence to attempt suicide in those days and Harry could have been charged with attempted suicide before his attempt eventually succeeded. Equally, Jane could have been charged with attempted murder after the death of the old man. Eventually Jane died in hospital when the liver gave up.

They were a great Horse family and I used to ride our pony Jessie to go and collect their cows in the evening for milking. I was always very afraid of them and the stories I had heard. Many times I have thought of that family not knowing my own destiny in life.

Adultery was also rampant especially amongst the Methodists. Whether this was to compensate for not drinking or smoking I don't know. In our own village the more pious the Methodist was, the more skeletons he seemed to have in the cupboard.

In the small village of South Zeal there was an American army camp during the war. In 1945 six Black children were born in the middle of normal white families. These poor unfortunate children all went to senior school with me but they stood out only because they were Black. This leaves one to question how many white children are cuckoos in the nest, as there is no way of telling by the colour of the skin. There were six or eight men, women and children in our small village whose parentage, according to popular rumour was in doubt.

Everything in our lives carried on as normal until 1954 when meat came off the Ration and then my father was allowed to open the slaughterhouse and go into the wholesale meat business. Whilst our childhood was far from normal, it was heaven compared to the years that were to follow.

The Coronation in 1953 was the last relatively normal year of my childhood. There was only one lady in the village with Television and she had her house full of people on Coronation Day. John Morris, the electrician mentioned earlier, hired a small nine inch television for the day, erected a temporary television aerial so the Morris house was also full for the day.

All I can remember seeing is lots of snow (caused by bad reception, not the weather), and vague pictures of the Coach and Horses and the Abbey. The following week it was on at the local cinema in Okehampton and, of course, everyone went.

There was a competition in the village for the Best Decorated House. We spent hours putting up Red, White and Blue Bunting Paper all over the house, the garden, the stables. Then half an hour before the judges came it rained *cats and dogs* and spoilt it all. Making matters worse, the judges only peered over the gates as it was so wet so we got no prize.

That evening in the Village Hall we had the choice of a Bible in a Box with the Queen's photo or a mug commemorating the day. We all chose the Bible.

In the same year, my mother took Barbara and Bobby

to London to visit one of the Billy Graham crusades. This was with a trip organised by the Plymouth Brethren family Bob and I had stayed with.

When Bob came home and told us about the London Underground and the moving staircase plus the electric doors on the train we could natter to him for hours in excitement about his adventure. There was a photo of Mum, Bob and Barbara in Trafalgar Square feeding the pigeons. Bruce and myself were in awe of it all. London to us was as well to be America or Timbuktu, it was just so far away. Today, of course, it's only three hours in the car.

CHAPTER TWO

Meat De Control in 1954 meant a team of builders came to the farm to bring the slaughterhouse up to date for the re-opening. This meant digging drains by hand for long distances taking down walls, plastering walls and building pens to hold the livestock.

Finally all was completed and the Opening Day arrived. The first cows to be slaughtered were the two house cows, Daisy and Buttercup who were past their used by date as milk cows. When slaughtered, Daisy was so riddled with TB the carcass was deemed unfit for human consumption. This was a shock on two counts, financially for my father and the fact we had all been drinking the milk for years off a TB infected cow.

My father started going to the cattle markets buying sheep and cattle, then decided to go into wholesale meat full time. For a while my mother took over doing all the meat rounds, learning how to drive, on the meat van. Father employed a TB victim called Bill Windrum. His job was to ride with my mother who had "L" plates until she passed her driving test. Once she had passed, Bill went to work as an odd job man on the farm, building yards, painting, etc. He was a very good carpenter and built many sheds for cattle and sheep. Eventually the TB got the better of him and he had to return to the Sanatorium. God Bless him, he was a relatively young man who had spent many years in a Sanatorium for TB all his life.

Financial things were good. We all had bicycles and our first television which was one of three in the village. When the numbers of livestock increased and we were all made to work in the slaughterhouse before school and after school.

Initially we had to clean the guts and bag the feet and heads, then gradually to learn how to skin the sheep. This highly skilled job meant as schoolboys we could earn the wage of Thirty Pounds weekly, when the average farm worker's wage was only Eight Pounds weekly.

We would go to the cattle sales with my father and I realised in those early days this was the life for me, buying in the cattle sales.

I still recall all he other meat wholesalers, Dan Stevens of Copplestone, Bill Yeo from Barnstaple, Tom Tucker of Holsworthy, Fred James, Halwil, Frank Allen from Bude, Sam Lendon of Winkleigh, Harold Jasper from Launceston. All these wholesalers had their own abattoirs and used staff to kill the animals paid at the piece work rate of Two Shillings per sheep. They killed sheep by the thousands and all made fortunes. Harold Jasper is alive and ninety six years old, still buying sheep with his son and grandson.

My father would buy sheep in the same numbers as these men and send them home. Then attempt to kill them all himself with us boys as *slave labour.* He was probably successful for a while but eventually was losing thousands of Pounds. The sheep my father would send home would be standing in the pens for up to one week losing weight, thus losing money. Then he would go and buy similar numbers again. It was never ending. So when everyone made fortunes, my father was losing a fortune.

All the meat went by rail to London. The railway container came every morning at eight o'clock in the morning to load all the lambs for the train. It took my father six months to realise the train didn't leave until six o'clock in the evening so all the late nights and early mornings were a complete waste of time. We would work until ten p.m. most nights then go to school and the same again the following day. This went on for two years until 1956 when my father went Broke.

The ironic thing is he was getting seven days credit from the auctioneers and getting paid the following day from London, all he had to do was get the sheep killed. My father never seemed to learn any of this elementary business procedure and was convinced his way was right and all the other wholesalers who were making money were wrong. The result was that in 1956 the auctioneers all came for their money.

Sheep were always breaking out of the meadows at home. One day my father bought a load of lambs from a farmer called Littlejohns only to be told the following week he had bought his own sheep back that had escaped our meadows.

I recall Jack Gregory, the local Transporter, coming for

his money and my father couldn't pay him one Monday evening. Then the following Saturday, Mr Vick, the local auctioneer came for his cheque with the same result. Mr Vick gave us children all Two Shillings and Six Pence each and Barbara a One Pound note, then took our pet pony in part payment. We all was very angry over Vick's actions until 1967 when he showed me a letter from my father saying he would pay the debt of One Thousand and Seven Hundred Pounds when we children were grown up. Joe Vick held me liable for that debt in 1967 and I paid it reluctantly, yet I could see his point as my father gave up and made no effort to repay his debts.

Things went from *Bad to Worse*. I recall my parents cancelling the papers as they couldn't afford them. The shop had already been closed and the business picked up *Free of Charge* by other local butchers. The van was gone and for the first time in our lives we had no transport of our own. My mother made the decision to move back to Manchester and Bruce and myself were to go as the *"Advance Party"* and stay with my grandparents.

This came as a *Shocking Blow* to me as I wanted to be a Dealer, Farmer and Wholesaler. I had this fantasy about restoring the farm and even cleared out a stable in the piggery complete with bedding in the stable for when I got my own horse again.

I had collected hay and straw on a trolley Bruce and myself built and hiding it all in the old stables for when I grew up. I had a store of fifty bales I had accumulated one at a time from what farmers left in their fields at Harvest time. Leaving the village and our home, as well as my Best Friend, Larry House, was out of the question.

Larry was a farmer's son who lived about one mile from the village. I spent all my spare time with him on his farm, bird's nesting, fishing, swimming in the river. He was a wild boy but knew all there was to know about animals, pets, birds and fish. His father was a very poor farmer financially and drove around in a ram shackled van with only one back door. Some Saturdays, his parents would take us to the local cinema in Okehampton to see a movie. We were very close friends.

However, my grandparents took Bruce and myself to

Manchester on the Steam Train. Most of the trains were then steam driven and the railways ran right through Devon, both sides of Dartmoor down to Cornwall. The journey to Manchester took all day, yet the whole trip was very exciting for us as two little country boys.

Grandad was a coal miner having moved to Manchester from Co. Durham during the Depression of the twenties. My nanna, Rebecca, was a tiny little lady and took only a Size Two shoe. She was Jewish by birth and very Psychic. We were thoroughly spoilt at home but the school was awful.

Having been used to our small village school where everyone talked the same as us then transferring to a large Town School, was *quite a culture shock.* However, there were many benefits, like going to the cinema every Saturday afternoon for the matinees, taking a big bowl to the Fish and Chip shop to collect chips for lunch, riding on Trolley Buses and ordinary Double Decker buses, we soon settled down.

I have no idea how long we stayed there but it was several months. Then, one day, my parents appeared and told me things were now good at home in Devon.

My father was in business doing contract slaughtering for a Mr. Reed and Mr Rattenbury and the Slaughterhouse had re-opened. I was told things were going to be different and we would all get a wage each week so I went home whilst Bruce stayed with grandparents.

I had mixed feelings about going home. I often thought to myself, if only my father was like the other Wholesale Butchers and employed a staff to do the work. It all made no sense to me. I knew at that early age I was being taken home for my abilities with a knife, being able to skin sheep. The idea of getting a wage by way of half crown saving stamps appealed to me, yet that was not money I could spend.

The village had gone through quite a lot of changes in the previous couple of years. The village Blacksmith was closed as the tractor had replaced the work horses. The shop of Butcher Chapple in the Village Square was now the Post Office. Frank Guy had built a new garage as the village crossroads at the top of the village complete with petrol pumps. Joe Skinner, the taxi driving landlord of the pub Red Lion had retired and there was a new landlord to the Red Lion. More people in the village were now driving cars also.

School was easy to settle back into and Larry House had not changed at all. My brother, Bob, had passed his Eleven Plus exams and was going to join Barbara at the local Grammar School who had passed two years earlier. I was the only Hayes at the village Primary School. I still spent all my spare time with Larry House when the opportunity arose.

The slaughterhouse was very busy killing sheep for Mr Reed and calves for Mr Rattenbury. The busy days were Monday to Wednesday and all weekends. There was a cattle market at Okehampton every Saturday, so this meant we had to work every Sunday morning from four until lunch time. The rail container used to arrive at twelve noon as the trains were earlier on a Sunday.

Things continued as usual on all fronts and eventually Bruce returned home several months after my return. This was in 1956 and the Russians had invaded Hungary causing a flood of refugees to come to England. We had a Hungarian Refugee Fund in the village school to raise money for the victims.

Barbara, my sister and Michael Daniels, her friend arranged for a village concert to raise money for the refugees. We all had to do a recital or sing a song and we managed to raise £9-7/6, which was a lot of money for young children to raise alone. Cyril Lang, one of the village farmer's sons was dressed as Santa Claus with a cotton wool beard. His beard caught fire on the candles of the Christmas tree whilst he was going on stage. Other than that, the event went down very well.

The church fetes were always held at the Rectory in the summer with Fancy Dress, Sports, Tug-of-War for the men and the usual Three-legged Races and Sack Races. There were always Hoop-la stalls and Lucky Dips and the whole afternoon was crowned with delicious Devon Cream Teas, with real clotted cream. The carnivals were still held in November which were torch lit processions of Brass Bands and tableaux of Tractors and Trailers on Horse and Cart, where people would have either a comedy event on a topical event. There was always a Carnival Queen and her attendants along with a Carnival Prince and Princes. The evening would rounded off with a dance in the Village Hall.

I sat for my Eleven Plus in 1957 which was a two part examination. The first part I passed along with another boy called David Denford. We were always the top two in our group at school. For the second part we had to go to the senior school in Okehampton. I took it as elementary I would pass and never thought any more of the exam.

Miss Trethewey, the village Head Mistress, came to the slaughterhouse at half term. Whitsun of 1957 to tell me I had failed. I couldn't believe it. We were busy working in the slaughterhouse and I knew very well how to hide my feelings. I couldn't wait for the day to be over and go to bed and be alone. I was devastated yet pretended I didn't care. It was considered soft for boys to cry but I can still remember holding back the tears and carrying on with my work. The Secondary Modern School had a green uniform when the Grammar School colours were Black and Gold. I considered the Secondary Modern Blazer the *"Green Blazer of Shame"*. All the Riff Raff and Idiots went to that school and I was to have to spend the next five years in their company. My mother was very comforting but my father never said a word. I didn't think at the time my six months away from the local school made any difference. I believe, in hindsight, I just took it for granted I would pass and never took the exam terribly seriously.

So in September of 1957 I went to Okehampton Secondary Modern School. I was placed in the "A" stream as I had past the first part of my Eleven Plus exams. I rebelled for the next two years. I was rude to the teachers treating them with contempt, fighting at school, refused to do any work or any homework. My mother didn't know what to do with me. My School Reports were as appalling as my behaviour and I was put into lower and lower classes. *I thought I am a Failure so I will act like one.*

At the end of my Second Year at school we had a new Form Mistress called Mrs Labrum and she paid special attention to me. She was a *very classy lady* and I would have done anything to please her. One day she pulled me to one side and asked what my problem was. She had read in the local paper, my father had been charged with having his three sons

21

unlawfully working in a slaughterhouse under the age of fifteen. The result of her faith in me was that I began to work hard, was back up to the "A" stream and for the rest of my school days was in the top three of the class every year.

Homework was always difficult as we had to work in the slaughterhouse until eight to nine o'clock most evenings but it was not impossible. I realised if I took my "O" Levels I could then go to the Grammar School to take my "A" Levels and be where I wanted to be albeit five years later. I settled for this.

The case in the local Newspaper was caused one Sunday morning by my father. Fred North, the Village Constable, would call to the slaughterhouse once a week to check the Pig Licenses as all pigs had to be moved on a Police permit so that in the event of Swine Fever, the pigs could be traced. We were all loading the railway truck with lambs and there were a couple of drivers in the yard. My father was in one of his rages of temper and told Fred North to *"Fuck Off"* regarding the licenses as he was busy. Rather than leave matters alone, my father pushed his luck by seriously abusing Fred and the job he was doing, a waste of Tax Payers money, etc.

Had we been alone just us Boys, it would have gone no further. However, because of the drivers in the yard, Constable North was made to look Foolish. Fred said, *"You will regret this Bob and you will pay for it"*. Constable North must have been seething at the needless Public Humiliation. There was a Devon By-Law stating that *no person under the age of fifteen was allowed in a slaughterhouse* so my father was charged on three counts, one for each of us.

With great bravado my father claimed he was not concerned and would go to prison rather than pay any fine, etc, etc. My father had a way of justifying any of his actions when he obviously knew he was in the wrong.

The result was he was fined Three Pounds for each of us and the matter was concluded. The local papers made a piece on it for all our school teachers to read along with our classmates.

This was the point in my life where I could no longer hide the Shame and Embarrassment my father caused me. He was a *Self Righteous Bully*. There is no other way to describe him. Men are supposed to be tough, don't show feelings, don't cry. This was fine for him, an ex Royal Marine Commando who was physically big. He had no compassion for anyone else who didn't reach his own expectations.

The reality was he was dependent on my mother to safeguard his feelings. He had no friends, only my mother. We boys were treated as slave labour and the older we got the more he had to rely on us. This may not have been quite so bad had he succeeded in his business but failure after failure was to follow.

A couple of months after this incident with Fred North, my father had been constantly abusing Mr Reed the owner of all the sheep we were killing. Eventually Mr Reed had had enough. He took his business to Tiverton Abattoir. So my father once more in 1958, was without an income. However, he was still justifying himself that he was in the right.

My mother had to then go to work. I recall my father's Balance Sheet in 1957/58. He had made Two Thousand Two Hundred and Fifty Pounds profit which was amazing in those days. His accountant was a Clown and, of course, he paid tax on the full amount. The banks didn't want to know him because of his track record and he had succeeded in alienating all his benefactors. Mother initially got a job as a cashier in a butcher shop in Okehampton. Then she worked as an Auxiliary Nurse followed by becoming a cook in the school canteen, eventually taking over the village Primary School Canteen. My mother had an exceptional brain and was a very astute, educated lady. Today, I realise she could have been anything she wanted in life. She chose to be the nursemaid of my father.

Father was so used to being a Big Fish in a small pond and always getting his own way. He had lost all touch with reality.

He got jobs as a slaughterman in Launceston, Winkleigh, Chard, Copplestone, but they never lasted more than one week. He would walk out as things were not being done *"His Way"*. He eventually stayed home and did nothing. We used to kill four to five cattle, and six pigs each week for local butchers and this was his only work. My mother was keeping the family.

My father, rather than get off his butt and clean up his slaughterhouse, let everything fall to wreck and ruin. The yards were never cleaned, any painting or white washing I used to have to do myself. He would brood and meditate all day and took up yoga and writing letters to the local paper that were usually published each week.

The pressure on my mother must have been immense at this time. I recall her working nights at the Hospital and we hardly saw her.

After about one year of this very uncertain life for us children, my father obtained the contract to slaughter sheep for a Mr Hawke who was a wholesale butcher based in Cornwall. So we were again back to late nights, early mornings and even more sheep to kill. The one benefit of the previous year, was we didn't have to work as children, now it was back to square one, with a vengeance. However, my mother never gave up her job, so despite all the Free Labour of us boys, my father still couldn't make ends meet. I have to this day no idea where the money went. We three boys could have earned Thirty Pounds a week each anywhere in Devon, so my father was Four Thousand Five Hundred Pounds per annum ahead of the game before he began, along with my mother's wages.

I had taken a great interest in the meat business, not I may add the way my father was doing things. I would ride on the Fat and Bone lorry to visit other slaughterhouses in the area. I would also ride on the meat lorry to London and visit Smithfield meat market. All the meat was being transported by road now and the railways were coming to an end.

I can recall going to the Smithfield show in 1956 with father and Bobby. I was taken up with Smithfield from day one. By the time I was twelve years old, I knew the names of every stall holder at Smithfield and I also knew who handled the meat for each abattoir in Devon and Cornwall, Somerset and Dorset. I really loved the business and wanted to be like Mr Hawke as opposed to my father.

Mr Hawke never had to kill the sheep himself and drove around in a Mark 10 Jaguar keeping Racehorses. My father's attitude was, without hard work you get nowhere. Sadly, he took this to extreme, so all carried on as normal until the fire in 1960.

I was twelve years old and on reflection, a strange little boy, but always kept my feelings to myself. I was a Romantic Dreamer. I continued to believe in Father Christmas until I was eleven years old. I knew in my heart it was not true but I so desperately wanted to believe in the fantasy. I recall so well seeing a picture of a white horse at the village primary school and deciding I was going to have one. I cleared out a pen in the piggery and even had water in the trough and hay in the racks for when my horse arrived. My secret store of hay and straw was eventually discovered by Bobby, my brother, who told my father and my father promptly used it all for the cattle pens. It had taken me two years to collect it all to be taken from me in three days.

I knew as I was very strong and being left handed, I could pack a punch but I would never hit anyone in the face. I was afraid that if I lose control I would be capable of killing. I had a fight with Bruce at this time and he beat me fair and square. I just lay there whilst he punched me in the face never once returning the punch.

Much as I loved my father, I had built up a gigantic resentment against him, his failure, his lack of get up and go. On reflection, the poor man and all his failures in life had caused him to give up, as I later learned.

From being a little boy I would day dream about older women. I would always have somebody special and one day I was going to have a girl friend just like her. These fantasies were well before my puberty and all going on between my ears.

I recall having a brown peddle car when I was very young and pretending it was cattle lorry. I would go on the telephone, book in the cattle and sheep and then go off on my peddle car to haul them. My party piece when my parents had guests was to be an Auctioneer. This was still in my head from going to the cattle sales with my father and I could do it very well.

Whilst I was always acting as Billy, the boy who couldn't care less, I noticed everything around about me. I still recall when my parents were fighting praying they would stop. My mother would often go off to a separate bedroom and I would pray that she would move back, knowing that if she did, the Trouble and not talking to each other would stop. I seemed to take in all my parents' problems and troubles on my own shoulders.

My biggest fear was always my mother leaving home. She left a couple of times to go back to her parents. In retrospect I cannot blame her at all. She had it very tough. It used to devastate me inside, yet I could always keep up the outward appearance that it didn't hurt. The first thing I would do coming home from school each day was go to the cattle yards to see if there was any livestock in. I knew if we had stock, we had money.

I was very sensitive and because of this, ashamed that I was so sensitive. Today I realise this was quality that should have been *nurtured* and not crushed. Things didn't seem to affect my brothers and sister yet they alone know how they felt during those years. I can only write my story as I saw it and am well aware my siblings' story of their same events may be totally different.

The fire was on the Sixth of June 1960. My grandparents were staying with us and my parents had gone out to buy a new car at Okehampton. We were all in the parlour watching the *"Lone Ranger"* on television and my Nanna was already in bed. Bruce came running into the house calling *FIRE*. He was screaming. Bob and myself went out to the yard and saw all the straw in the stables was on fire.

We grabbed a hosepipe from the slaughterhouse and couldn't get it on the tap in the yard, so I phoned the Fire Brigade. Within minutes things looked very bad and the flames were going through the loft of the stable and through the roof.

The Fire Brigade arrived and couldn't find the water hydrant to get water. Apparently the council when re-surfacing the village roads had covered the manhole with asphalt. The fire got onto the beams of the stable and spread to the roof of the house. Within fifteen minutes the roof of the house was ablaze. Eventually the water was found by the three fire engines but by this time could not stop the fire spreading.

The whole village turned out and were marvellous and most of the furniture was saved. Percy Denford carried my

Nanna out who had been awoken from her sleep and she was fighting poor old Percy telling him to put her down. It was all like an awful dream. Around eight o'clock that night my parents arrived home and the house was just a shell, the walls and the chimney. The chimney alone weighed over one hundred tonnes. It was a tragedy and that night we all stayed with various people in the village. I stayed initially with the Denford family eventually moving to Guys farm across the road.

Danny Twining, our local doctor, appeared and told my mother it was not a doctor she needed but the W.V.S. (Women's Voluntary Service), who gave aid during the war. Danny became a good friend of my wife in later years and I could appreciate his humour. My parents, however, took great offence at this remark. The next forty eight hours were a complete turmoil of salvaging, cleaning, then preparing what we were going to do. The insurance was the next problem to be solved.

It came to light after the fire the property was not owned by my father. It was, in fact, owned by a retired butcher called Len Bannister who lived in Portsmouth. Uncle Len as we knew him had purchased the property in 1947 for my father to manage, so all the pigs we kept were, in fact, the property of Uncle Len also. He had recently died so the estate was being managed by his wife Aunty Minnie. I remember so clearly their visits to us as children having no idea they were, in fact, my father's employers.

There had been a difference of opinion when my father turned wholesaler in 1954. Len Bannister would have no part of the wholesale business instead it was agreed my father would purchase the property from him. This being agreed, the payments were to be made over a twenty year period. The insurance money for the house Aunty Minnie said she would keep in return my father could have the land, slaughterhouse and farm buildings *Free of Charge*. This was not a Bad Deal for either party yet meant my father had no money to re-build the house.

There was no question of re-building a country house the size of Tumbles. At best, we would only be able to re-build a Bungalow. This caused a lot of bad feelings between my father and Minnie Bannister, while my father did all his complaining at home, he said nothing to the lady concerned, Minnie herself. So a team of demolition experts were employed to remove the shell of the house and clear a site for the Bungalow.

In the meantime, my father converted the old Granary into a small house, then built a series of extensions on this so we had temporary accommodation. Making the best of a bad job, it was livable but that was just all. Once more my father proceeded to spend far too much money on this temporary accommodation, leaving no money in reserve to build a new house.

Whilst the fire was no particular one's fault, it was an awful way for us to have to live and we spent the next three years living in this temporary accommodation. People had forgotten the fire and Tumbles House and strangers assumed we had always lived this way. This was another example of my father not being able to get off his backside and do anything constructive.

Making matters worse, there were new regulations coming into force on the Licence of Slaughterhouses. They all had to be re-built to conform with these new regulations. All the local abattoirs has the choice of conforming or closing. My father, despite having a good business, decided to close. I have no idea why he took this choice. It still makes no sense but close he did. So there we were in 1962 once more with no income only my mother's wage working in the school canteen.

Three months after the closing my father decided he would re-open the slaughterhouse again. So along come teams of builders and we re-built the slaughterhouse that was now called Exbourne Abattoir.

The local authorities made my father dot his I's and cross his T's in every way to conform to the new regulations. My father soon learnt because he had let the Licence go, it was not going to be easy to get it back again. Had my father done this work when the abattoir was still open, he may have been ok. The net result was he had to spend thousands of Pounds on the abattoir until July of 1962 it was finally open again.

I remember one day all of us boys having to stay off school to dig by hand a septic tank which was four metres deep five metres long and four metres wide. This we had to do with shovels and picks rather than my father hire a JCB digger for the day. My father's philosophy of hard work is the only way to succeed.

I was invited to sit down with Mr Castle, the Builder and make my contribution to the design of the new abattoir, cooling rooms and pens. Even the glass slatted windows were of my design. I was very proud of my achievements and after school at night built the cattle pens on my own with galvanise sheets and timber. So at fourteen years of age I used all the ideas I had seen in other local abattoirs to re-build Exbourne abattoir.

Bob, my brother got a motor scooter in 1961 when he was sixteen and in the school summer holidays went to work for the Vestey organisation at Exeter. Bob was like all of us, a very good slaughterman. I was extremely jealous as he came home with £14 each week which was a lot of money in those days. One Saturday morning he was playing Rugby so I offered to go in his place. Bob took me on the back of his scooter and dropped me some twenty three miles up the road.

As I was only fourteen years old the Vestey Management couldn't believe their eyes when they saw me perform. All the slaughtermen told me to slow down as I was going so fast I was setting precedents they couldn't maintain. The net result was Mr George Downes, the Vestey Manager for the South West of England, collected me every Saturday morning at five o'clock and returned me home at lunchtime for the next two years. I was flattered, honoured and delighted to be the Prodigy of Mr. Downs. I was paid Five Pounds every Saturday morning as well as being chauffeured back and forth in his large black Woseley.

I got to know George Downes very well and the Vestey organisation. At this time, Lord Vestey was the *World King* of the *Meat Business* with operations in all continents. They had fifty separate meat, shipping, leather companies in England with some three thousand Butcher shops and sixty abattoirs. Vesteys controlled the meat business in Argentina, Australia, New Zealand, Brazil, Uraguay and Paraguay. They also owned the Union Castle shipping line, Union cold storage, Union cartage,

Ffyfes Bananas, Donald Cooks canned goods.

The whole operation was run from Weddel House in Smithfield, London and controlled by Lord Vestey himself. Sam Vestey, the present Lord Vestey as a boy was sent out to New Zealand to learn his trade on the slaughter house the same way I had been taught. This meat empire was taking very good care of me, little Billy Hayes, their youngest employee. Every large town in England and Wales had an Eastmans or Dewhurst shop which was Vesteys, so they had all the profits from the Farm to the Plate of Beef, Pigs, Sheep as well as the leather business. They controlled all the meat imports to England through the Weddel organisation. It was a massive operation.

Mr Downes always wore a black suite, grey tie, black overcoat and bowler hat. This city gent attire was the standard dress of all Vesteys top executives. The managers of the three thousand Butcher shops had to return a 33% gross profit on the shops each week. Any profit over this the Manager could keep. Having said all of this, Vestey was a very discreet operation.

Sid Perry the Cattle buyer for South West England lived in the farmhouse at the abattoirs and everyone assumed it was his house and farm. Equally, none of the many operations traded under Vestey name so no one really knew how much they owned until 1970.

The *"Sunday Times"* did a *"Boots and All"* expose of the Vestey organisation in 1970. This showed all the Vestey companies were registered offshore and paid no English tax of any kind. Yet, the expose failed to mention the seventy thousand employees all paid English tax and the money was generated from Vestey. When meat was nationalised in the Argentine in 1966 Lord Vestey paid £4 million to have his three top Executives released by kidnappers. Vestey had farms in Australia the size of Belgium and Holland.

School was going well during these years and I was always in the top three of my form during exam time. I only had one close friend at school, a boy called David Willis. His father was the Police Sergeant at Hatherleigh a village four miles from homes. I never told any one at school about my Saturday mornings going to Vesteys at Exeter.

On Saturday afternoons I would always meet David

Willis in Okehampton and we would go to a coffee bar and in the evenings to the cinema usually with a couple of girls from school. My father was very generous with pocket money and we were always given a Pound note each to spend which was more than double what our friends receive. I always played Rugby for the school on Saturday afternoons during the winter months.

Work at home was the same every night until eight to nine o'clock. and Saturday mornings for Bob and Bruce as I went to Exeter. Sunday mornings were the busiest days. We began work at four o'clock in the morning never finishing until about two o'clock in the afternoon. Bob had successfully passed nine 'O' Levels G.C.E. Certificate despite all the hours of work, so anything was possible. My father's moods and tempers seemed to have become worse as the years went on.

My mother was still working and there seemed very little hope of ever getting a new house built. Life was very tough at home. My mother, I believed, suffered most of all as she wanted so much for us boys. Barbara had been able to get away to college and she was living in Torquay except for holidays.

Business wise for my father the abattoir was in full production by Christmas of 1962. I was going to Manchester for my school Christmas holidays so I could revise for my 'O' level G.C.E. trials. If I was successful in June of 1963, I would be going to the Grammar school to take my 'A' levels. At the school Christmas party some boys and myself went down to one of the town pubs and had some beers and whiskeys before the party and were seen leaving the pub by one of the school staff.

The following day I had to stay home from school and work, so I missed *all Hell breaking loose* over the Drinking scandal. As this was the last day of term I had to wait until the new term in January for my punishment. I was a School Prefect, the House Captain and House Rugby Captain, also played for the school First XV at Rugby. The other boys caught leaving the pub were all stripped of the Honors and Badges.

I took all my homework for revision and went on the train alone to Manchester. This was a great journey as I could smoke, drink in the buffet car and act like a grown up. I was fifteen and a half years old. My Aunt and Uncle both went to work and I became very friendly with the girl who lived next door. We spent all our days together and in the evenings went to the cinema or to traditional Jazz clubs in Manchester as traditional jazz was all the rage.

January of 1963 was the worse weather on record in Devon. There were snow drifts of several feet and our village was cut off. This meant I couldn't get home and my holiday was extended by a further two weeks. I had no complaints as I was having a lovely time with Margaret, the girl I had met. Her situation was the same as mine. She had also failed the Eleven Plus exam and was going to Grammar School after she had taken her 'O' levels. When my time came to leave, her father drove me to the station and we agreed to write to each other every week so home I went.

For many months since I became fifteen, my father used to complain daily it was my duty to leave school and help him. I fought him on this and refused. However, the first day back at school I learnt I was going to lose all my Badges and Honors over the drinking incident. So I went to the local bus stop and went home. It was mid morning and I took my father a cup of tea and said *"I have left school"*. That day was fine but from the next months all he used to say was that I was no use and should go back to school. I never told him the real reason for my leaving. I decided I would build the business, build a new home and eventually marry Margaret and become a Livestock Buyer and Wholesale Butcher.

Mr Downes of Eastmans, the Vestey group, gave me the contract to slaughter Sows and Pigs for them. We had a new contract with a company called Nichols in Cornwall as well as all the sheep from Mr Hawke. We began to take on staff at the abattoir and by May of 1963 work had begun on building the new house. My Darling mother was able to give up work for the first time in five years and stay at home doing the accounts and making endless cups of tea for all the people coming to the abattoir on business. Every week I received a letter off Margaret and life was pretty good.

My father was a very cruel man and very insensitive. When we were alone in the abattoir every day I grew to hate him and all he stood for, yet as we had been taught, I treated him with great respect never answering him back but he was quite insane. When I think of some of the names he used to call me, some of the things he used to say to me. It was really quite wicked. As I never retaliated and said anything, no one knew how much resentment was building up inside me. It was very unhealthy.

I bought a motor scooter on my Sixteenth Birthday and used to go to college every Monday afternoon in Exeter doing a course in Meat Technology. This always caused problems when we were busy. I used to meet a girl who was nineteen every Monday evening and that relationship lasted twelve months, the length of my course. Diane was her name and she shared a flat with one of Bob's girlfriend in Exeter. I played Rugby every Saturday for North Tawton, a local town and every Saturday evening went to the local dance. My life was very good socially yet the work was very hard and I received no wages only my pocket money.

My father then began on Bruce that he should also leave school. Despite my being home the volume of work was such that Bob and Bruce still had to work after school as well. I have no idea what finally persuaded Bruce but he also left school and came into the business. The moment Bruce left school my mother agreed we should have a wage of Five Pounds weekly. I asked about the previous year I had received no money but that was never mentioned again. We had built up a good business but my father was still offending the clients with his rudeness, temper and arrogance. He also foolishly spent money on wasteful things in the abattoir. No matter what money we earned my father would find a way to spend it.

Bruce became a better slaughter man than me. He was really quite exceptional. On Friday nights we would go to an abattoir at Copplestone and kill one hundred and twenty to one hundred and fifty sheep at Two Shillings each. This was very good money, then be home to do our normal work on a Saturday. My father would be happy to go to Copplestone and kill sheep rather than develop our own business. I used to become so angry and frustrated with him as he was always on the *short road to nowhere*. When I think back to how Bruce and myself put up with him, it amazes me.

On my Seventeenth Birthday I passed my Driving Test and was able to use the company mini van for my social occasions.

Sometimes I could take my father's Humber. Bruce and myself were both playing Rugby for Okehampton and drinking beer by the gallon. I would have a Date most nights of the week and take out various girls. Devon was full of beautiful quaint little villages with country pubs, restaurants and there were always dances, Hunt Balls, and Rugby Balls so socially life was really the Tops. I had many serious girlfriends and was very Happy with my life.

Now that I was able to drive I thought I had better have a look at the livestock markets and see if I could realise my dream of being a Livestock Buyer. I can still remember my first auction and the first livestock I purchased.

I went to Newton Abbot Market and the sheep all seemed very expensive, however, I bought two ewes for Ten Shillings each. When I got home one of them escaped whilst I was unloading it from the van and was never seen again. The second one realised Thirty Shillings so I knew I was onto a Winner. I used to go to Newton Abbot every week and buy thirty to forty sheep, twenty to thirty pigs, kill them and sell the meat on Smithfield. I was making a good little living.

I then took on a Buyer called Norman Hines to buy Calves for me and a buyer called John Lancaster to buy anything that was cheap, cows, sheep or pigs. I began going to the Moor Sales on Dartmoor, Chagford and Ashburton and buy cattle. I had my own transport company that collected all of my meat from the abattoirs and life was really pretty good. I was a very cautious buyer as it was my own money. The village farmers then began to sell me their lambs, John Guy, Morley Guy, Morris Sage and Bill Clarke. So I was now accepted as *"The man to do business with"*. I could not have been Happier. I met a girl called Doreen Webb who had just begun at Leeds University. She was a blue eyed blonde and beautiful yet when she was away at college I had many girls to choose from and they remained friends for many years. I was making a couple of hundred Pounds per week and still paying my father the full rate to kill my animals, despite providing the labour.

I had become involved with a girl called Helen Smith who was in Bob's form at school. Bob was now away at Manchester University. This was in March of 1966. On the Sixteenth of March I had taken Helen out for the evening. She had been working as an Au Pair girl in Italy. On my way home I was hit broadside by a Bedford van. I recall seeing lights and the next thing I was lying in the gravel on the road. I put my hand to my face and my lips were severed and hanging on my chin. My legs had no feeling but were at a strange angle. I felt no pain only the thought *"My God, what has happened"*. That was my last memory for several days.

When I woke up I saw Reverend Preston, the village vicar and white walls. I couldn't move so I assumed I was in Heaven. The next thing I saw was a nurse who I later learned was called Sister Loosley. I was in Intensive Care with tubes to do everything, my legs in splints. I couldn't talk as I had a Tracheotomy on my throat. I didn't realise how ill I was. I came and went drifting between conscious and unconscious. I then saw my father holding my hand and crying and it was several more days before I became conscious.

When I came around I was put into a general ward with my legs in splints. Then I saw my face for the first time. My head was twice the normal size and black and blue. All my right cheek was one big scar. My teeth was wired together as my jaw was broken and I was in a mess. The face was the biggest shock to me as I had always been quite vain about my looks and they were all gone.

I received over one hundred and fifty Get Well cards. People came from miles to see me. Margaret from Manchester, Julie Vernon from Lemmington Spa and everyday the daughter of the owner of the local brewery came without fail, Jackie. As there were so many visitors they were given five minutes each in groups of four people. The phone never stopped ringing at home. I never realised how popular I was but it was very flattering.

My main concern when I came around fully was my small business, and the new extension on the abattoir I had organised with my father, which was going to be very expensive. My mother and father assured me all would be okay, yet I knew in my heart without my being there, it would not be. My father persuaded me to sign my cheques each week for the auctioneers and he would keep my business going. My mother came to see me twenty three miles every single day for the next fourteen weeks.

I signed the cheques hoping and praying my father would do the right thing by me. I was powerless and strapped to my bed because of my legs, knowing full well I had lost out on so many things.

Eventually in July of 1966 it was time to go home. I was fitted with an iron caliper on my leg and with the aid of a walking stick went home. The first thing I learnt was my father had been killing two hundred to three hundred pigs a week and three hundred to four hundred sheep per week in my name, John Lancaster doing all the buying. I knew that I couldn't make money on these numbers myself as Ewes and Calves were my business. When I did the books I found out I was in debt to the tune of *Forty Thousand Pounds.* My father had lost all of this in fourteen weeks and making matters worse, in my name. I was barely nineteen years old.

I didn't know what to do. The auctioneers were giving my father seven days credit in my name. We were getting paid the day after sale but the reality was, the debt was there. I spoke to Bob about this and we agreed we couldn't let my father get into trouble I would have to *Carry the Can.* This was the biggest mistake of my life. I should have gone to the Police in July of 1966 and reported my father. All the hate that had been building up over the years came to the surface. My parents thought the accident had changed me. This was not the case. My father's ignorant cruel blunder changed me. Here I was with my face all scarred, my leg in irons, I had worked night and day for the previous four years to see my father destroy it all. Then he was not man enough to admit his mistake. He always hid behind my mother. I could have quite easily killed him on that day coming home. Instead I turned to whiskey and began to drink for oblivion from that day.

What was I going to do? I couldn't trade myself out of a debt of that magnitude, I was lost. All I know about Limited Companies was what I had learnt at school about the *South Sea*

Bubble. What I didn't realise was that being a Minor, only nineteen, I couldn't be held liable for these debts. Yet, my name would have been ruined just like my father's. I investigated Limited Companies and came up with a compromise.

I realised if I had a limited company I could transfer the debts and then liquidate the company. Bob had taken a year off from University and our only concern was to protect our father. My father never ever took responsibility for his own actions at any time that I can recall. We were *Bullied* and *Brain Washed* into a service of loyalty to him. We floated a limited company with Bob as the only one who was twenty one. He had to sign all the papers. I then began to trade as Exbourne Meat Company, hiding the debts of Forty Thousand Pounds. The only way I could hide this was obtain more credit and get paid quickly.

We approached Barclays Bank to borrow the money to purchase the abattoir, house and farm from my father. The Bank Manager met my father then laid down one condition. He would only advance the money if my father left the business and the home and had no dealings in it at all. This we agreed.

We floated a second company R. W. & B Hayes, the three brothers and purchased the place Lock, Stock and Barrel from my father. My father was so very resentful yet six decks down he must have realised his own guilt caused this *awful situation*. So we had all the assets in one company and continued to trade with the other company. All very lawful and done without any form of legal advice, it all came from our heads.

At least I managed to get something quietly organised but I knew that it was not the way I had wanted things to be. I was not able to drive my car as my legs were in irons so Bob used to drive me to the cattle sales every day whilst Bruce took care of the abattoir. In hindsight, we did the whole thing wrong but it appeared to be the only way at the time. My father made no effort to leave despite us owning the property and carried on as though *everything in the garden was rosy*. It was not a happy period.

My father must have been deeply wounded by my attitude towards him. I was so very bitter, yet he was so thick skinned and I couldn't find any compromise. I used to go to the cattle sales at Week St Mary every Saturday, whilst buying my sheep, look over my shoulder and there was my father bidding against me. The sheep that would be too expensive being knocked down to me. Without a public scene I was powerless to stop him. The good thing was that was the only market where he didn't owe money so he never come to any of the other markets.

My father always said and believed to make money in London you had to buy *Small lambs and Small pigs*. The reality was the case of the only way to make money was *Heavy lambs and Heavy pigs*. Bless him, he really did not have a clue. There was a vast difference between the Best Meat and the Best Profit. Lord Vestey specialised in all his shops the Worst Quality Meat at the Best Price for the consumer. My poor father's attitude was the same as Hard Work, if you don't deal with quality meat, then it is no good.

I began to drink on a daily basis. I would have my whisky every morning before the cattle sales then again when the cattle sales were over. There was fortunately no breathalysers in those days. Every night of the week when the last lorry left for London, I would be off to the pub. My London buyers would start calling on the phone at about six o'clock each morning and my life settled down into some sort of routine. I was still writing to Margaret and in February 1967 decided to go and visit her at College.

I should point out here that my father had a very Bad War in the Royal Marine Commandos. He was on the Norwegian landings and the Normandy landings. This, my mother believed, had a very serious effect on him especially his mood swings. He also suffered a fractured skull at Canterbury during the war in a motor cycle accident leaving him unconscious for a long time. I mentioned this because there was no such thing as Trauma Counseling in those days. You only have to look at the effect of the Vietnam Veterans when they came back from the war. My father was a trained killer, martial arts expert, who was at the very spear head of all the wartime landings. He went from Corporal to Sergeant to Sergeant Major in one week because his comrades were all killed. I have said he was quite mad and I believe totally insane at times. Yet I do, as a man today, have great pity for my father and also realise his mistakes against me were not done from malice.

Having defended my father, I must also say the most cruel thing I ever heard him say was about Education. My father always purported to be very anti-Education. I believe he had a complex over my mother who was highly academically educated. He never once assisted or helped us with our school work and to the contrary all the work at home made our school life very difficult.

I heard him saying one day that Gilbert Daniels must be very proud of his three boys all passing the Eleven Plus exams. This was a local farmer whose three sons had all gone to the Grammar School. My father made this remark knowing full well I was within his hearing and I was deeply shocked that he thought this way, meaning that he was not very proud of Bruce and myself who Failed.

The only kind words he were said to me were at the village of Broadwoodkelly, he once patted me on the head and called me *"Cock Sparrow"*. I was elated that I was in his good books. He wrote me a long long letter after my accident in 1966 telling me if God gave him the chance and I survived how he would make things up to me. Unfortunately this was like his letters to the auctioneers in 1956 telling them he would one day pay them. Just *words* on a piece of paper.

I decided to spend a weekend away with Margaret and visit her at her College in the Midlands.

Margaret was at St Paul's College, Newbold Revel near Coventry in the Midlands of England which was a lovely drive on the *"Foss Way"*, the old Roman Road. I arrived on the Friday evening and arranged to meet Margaret in her local pub, *The Plough Inn*, where she had arranged my accommodation. I stood at the bar positioning myself where my right cheek was in the shadow as I was very self-conscious of my face.

The first thing Margaret did with tears in her eyes was turn my face around and kiss all my scars then touch them with her fingers and told me, *"Never be ashamed of those Bill, they are a part of you now"*. I felt very humbled and we then discussed old times. It had been one year ago exactly when

Margaret last came to Devon and spent the weekend with me just three weeks prior to my accident. I had met a girl at a party who was in the same college, as she came to Devon several times a year and gave Margaret a lift.

Margaret was immediately concerned at the rate I drank whiskey and water as I was a very Hardened Drinker by now. I took her back to the college and we arranged for me to collect her in the morning. This was the first time I had been away from my business in nine months and the break was so welcome to me.

The following day after showing me around the college we went for lunch to the village of Meredon which is supposed to be the very heart of England. There is a super old pub in the village called Bull and an Oak Tree in the car park. The Tree itself is supposed to be the exact centre of England. It was all very Romantic and nice.

The two things I noticed about myself then was that I could talk freely and I forgot the scars on my face. Margaret proceeded to tell me that I had hurt her very badly when she came to Devon two years previously as I was involved with many other women. She also said on her last visit she saw little change in me as a terrible womaniser. She told me my letters from hospital and since were full of *"Self Pity"* and this was not the Bill she knew.

This most certainly put me in my place and I said to Margaret, *"when I am twenty eight and can no longer play Rugby, if you are still single I would love to marry you"*. I said it quite flippantly. Margaret looked me in the face, I noticed I didn't turn my face away as usual and she said *"if that's the case Bill, we will get engaged now"*. I very nearly fell off the chair. We were both nineteen and approaching twenty years of age and I realised she was very serious.

Margaret even know the ring she wanted, a Solitaire Diamond. She also told me when she was fifteen she had seen a solicitor's sign with the initials J & H, Jackson and Hayes and she wanted this on her wedding cards. We went to Coventry and bought the ring and that evening went to a party at the college. I rang my parents and told them the news. They didn't seem surprised and were highly delighted.

The Sunday morning as was correct I decided to drive Margaret to see her parents when I could officially ask for her *Hand in Marriage*. The parents had always been very nice to me on our previous meetings. The result was her father *"went spare"*. He said it was a waste of time getting his daughter educated to then go off and marry me. We explained it was going to be a long engagement but her father would have none of it and I left Margaret at home travelling back to Devon.

That evening she rang me and told me that her father had tried to take the ring from her finger without success. He was threatening to make her a *Ward of Court* and send her off to an Aunt's until she saw sense. The result was Margaret went back to college and in defiance of her parents came to Devon every weekend.

I had told Margaret all about my business problems caused by my father. This made her cry for me. She also arranged with my mother for me to see a Plastic Surgeon to get my face repaired.

So off I went to Bristol to a Private Clinic and had my old scars taken out and replaced with micro-surgery new scars. I felt very guilty at the Hospital as all the other patients were young children born with harelips and cleft pallets or one nostril and here I was having *cosmetic* surgery.

Margaret stayed with one of my friends Sally Jones, a local doctor's daughter who was a nurse in Bristol and the operation was a great success. So by Easter of 1967 I was getting well physically. My leg had also repaired and Margaret decided that Easter Holiday to give up college and come and work with me in the business. This was a monumental decision for her and totally against her parents' wishes. All I can remember of those days were how wonderful it was to be loved so very much by another human being. We placed an announcement of the engagement in the local paper and I gave up my *wild ways* and chasing women. However, my drinking did not slow down rather increased.

To all intents and purposes I appeared the epitome of success. My own business, my trucks to carry my meat, my Humber car and my beautiful fiancee. I loved to dance and at school when it was raining and we couldn't play cricket. David

Willis and myself used to go to dancing classes with the girls. All the other boys were too shy to go but we loved it so I learned to Quick Step, Fox Trot, Barn Dance, etc.

Socially we had the Hunt Balls, Rugby Balls, Jockey Club Balls with Victor Sylvester and his Band. It really was the *"High Life"*. I was always asked to Judge the Lambs at the local Agricultural Shows and I loved the way I was living. We had racing at Newton Abbott, Taunton and Devon and Exeter and I introduced Margaret to the Racing World. Despite all of this, I was carrying the terrible burden of my Forty Thousand Pounds deficit and was, in actual fact, insolvent because of my father.

I had secured many livestock contracts, as well as the abattoir business. I was buying lambs to export to France for Doug Clay who was the biggest exporter in England. I was buying live cattle for Hughs of Chelmsford and live cattle for Ivanhoe Meat Company in Buckinghamshire. All in all, I had become a very Big Operator. We had a staff of thirty at the abattoir and were the biggest employers in the village and the area. All this could and should have been so good only for my dreadful secret of the missing money.

Margaret lived in the family home having her own room and my parents absolutely adored her. Margaret got on very well with my father and did something to Bridge the Rift between us yet I could find no forgiveness for him. Having said this, Margaret made me look at his point of view. It was done from ignorance and not malice which was very true. Life was good but we still had to wait until we were twenty one before we married.

My greatest pleasure in the evenings was to go around my cattle yards and check the livestock I had purchased. My men began work at five o'clock in the morning every day and daily we would handle two hundred pigs, twenty to thirty cattle and three hundred to four hundred sheep. My men worked a six day week with Thursday being the only day off. On Thursday I would bring in outside men just to kill cattle for the South Coast of England to be delivered every Friday.

Early one morning in May of 1967 the phone went as usual from the London buyers and my father answered it, then went to my bedroom to call me. Finding my bed unslept in he knocked on Margaret's door. When I appeared he allowed me to take the phone call, then said to me *"Take that girl home to her parents. If she was my daughter I would kill you"*. He was very calm, cool and collected and went on to say he felt responsible for Margaret whilst living in the family home. For the Period, this was not an unusual reaction and also showed he had a great respect for Margaret. Whilst I am sure sex before marriage was not unknown it most certainly was never spoken of.

To say I was angry was an understatement. I was furious. It was my house, my business, all paid for in full. I recalled the promises of my father when I left school, he said *"You don't need a wage as one day this will all be yours"*. Well yes, now it was all mine, paid for at the market price, with money I had borrowed from the bank. All my years of free labour went for nothing. The reality was we worked and paid for our own upbringing. We worked and paid for our father's life style and in the end he had lost all of my money. I was again being treated like a small boy by my father who had been living off me for the last five years.

Once more, as I was taught, I was respectful and agreed to do as he asked. Then when he saw that I was not going to argue, pushed the point that it had to be *now*. This was six thirty in the morning and the *last straw that broke the camel's back.*

I called Margaret. We packed our bags and told Bruce I didn't know if I would be back or when I would be back. Bob was away at University. That would have been a very good time to walk out on everything and start all over again somewhere else. I left Bruce the cheque book and allowed him to continue.

We drove to Somerset and called into see the Cobden Family who were very large Cattle Exporters and spent the day with them. I took Margaret to Chedder Caves, then we visited all my clients from Bedford to London looking at their abattoirs and factories. We eventually ended up at Stratford-upon-Avon and booked into the Swans Nest, a lovely five-star hotel in the town. Margaret loved the Theatre, so each night we went to the Theatre followed by drinks with all the actors at the Black Swan known as the *"Mucky Duck"*.

Margaret had been a regular Theatre goer from her school days and all through college had made time to go to

Stratford on a regular basis.

Anthony Quayle later Sir Anthony Quayle was the Theatre Director in those days. Margaret knew Diana Rigg well from her days in Rep at Stratford. The lovely Jean Anderson was playing Mrs Hardcastle in "She stoops to Conquer" by Oliver Goldsmith. This was the school play in which I had played Tony Lumkin many years earlier. Drink and Theatre go hand in hand so I was very much at home with these people.

I rang Bruce daily and he was coping very well. My father would answer the phone and all I would say is *"Can I speak to Bruce please"*. After about two weeks my father came on the phone and said to me *"I told you to take that girl home"*. I told him that as long as she was with me she was home. I also told him what I thought of him and he could carry on and spend another Forty Thousand Pounds of my money as I no longer cared. Margaret and myself had a lovely holiday and all was well. I forgot Devon, forgot the business and it was good for me.

We eventually drove to Margaret's parents to test the water on their reaction to us. They were ice cool yet polite and made it quite clear they would never accept our getting married. I had a long talk with my mother who said my father was very upset and we should come home. I said *"No way without Margaret"*, Mum said she would clean out the caravan in the yard and Margaret could live in the caravan as then no one had any grounds to complain. We were not living under the same roof. This being agreed we finally went home. My father was all over me and treated me like the prodigal son returning. I had my Margaret in my business and all was well. Margaret learnt the office from my mother and took over all the books, cattle payments, auctioneers payments and would usually go with me to the cattle sales.

I used to go to the auctions six days per week which also involved a lot of drinking. I was the youngest buyer in the area as well as one of the biggest buyers, so I was mixing socially with men of forty to sixty years of age. I was only nineteen. They were all very seasoned heavy drinkers and loved to talk of the old days, the Black Market during the war and I, of course, loved to listen. They all made a great fuss of Margaret as this was strictly a men's world and she was the only lady at that time who went to the auctions with her man. All in all life was very good.

My parents decided to take a holiday in July of 1967 and go to Majorca for three weeks. This was their first holiday since their Honeymoon twenty five years previously, a weekend in Blackpool. We had just celebrated their Silver Wedding. So off they go and everyone is happy. On the way home my father had his first heart attack on the plane and had to be taken from the airport direct to hospital. He was suffering from Angina. He was told to slow down, take things easy, so at least we thought we can now get him to leave, in accordance with the instructions of Barclays Bank.

My father returned from hospital worse than ever if anything. He insisted on working in the abattoir and was constantly complaining about the standards of all my employees. My staff were very good and very loyal to me and they just let him carry on as though he wasn't there. His favourite trick was to roll forty gallon drums full of water all over the floor. These minor tidal waves would soak anyone who was in their path. He would be shouting all day to himself about Meat Inspectors, the staff, his ungrateful sons, it was all very embarrassing.

I had some very important cattle people coming down from London one Wednesday morning. They had given me the job of buying their live cattle. When they arrived having showed them around the abattoir and yards, I took them into the house for morning tea. My father was sat in the kitchen in his underpants and vest, with his Dirty working clothes on the floor and refused to speak to them. I was so bloody embarrassed and ashamed it was awful. I realised that day if I couldn't get the old man to go then I would have to go. I just couldn't take any more of his oppressive behaviour.

When we were at school he had not one good word to say about any of our friends. They were all spoilt or lazy, etc. My father believed all normal parents were wrong and he was right. *His Sons were going to be Men.* Whilst it may appear I am labouring this point, I must say in my defence that listening to this kind of talk every day for the whole of my life it, of course, had a great effect on me. We had been taught or brain washed to listen to this man and respect all the nonsense that came from his actions, words and deeds. My father was a Dictator in his own little world and protected from reality by my mother. There was a very sadistic streak in him, I am sorry to say.

One example of his madness and bravado bearing in mind we were always made to do as we were told. My father kept greyhounds and used to race them at Exeter, Torquay and Taunton. One Thursday when the sheep arrived from the cattle market at North Tawton, the dogs got out and attacked the sheep. There were, maybe five to six adult dogs and four to five puppies. My father, of course, blamed us for not closing the stable door properly and told Bob to shoot all the dogs as they had tasted blood. Bob seemed to have no fear of my father and promptly shot all the dogs.

Well, my father then went insane. We had killed his Beloved greyhounds and we were wicked and cruel, etc. etc. My father went to bed for two days not eating or drinking and never spoke to anyone for a week. This was only one instance of this type of behaviour.

Bob was a very *Modest, Great Achiever.* He became Head Boy of the Grammar School and I only found out from one of my school friends, he was selected to play Rugby for Devon, then South West Counties and again we only found out second hand. Even when he got on England School Boy Rugby Trial he never boasted of his achievements. He was the first pupil from our village primary school to go to University. I was very very fond of Bob and he had been my hero for many years. Bob never escaped the snipes or jibes of my father. If anything he got it as bad, if not worse than us but it seemed to have no effect on Bob. My father hurt me considerably. My sister Barbara could do no wrong in my father's eyes but Bruce I believed suffered as greatly as myself and perhaps, Bruce suffered most of all.

In September 1967 Margaret informed me we were going to have a baby. I was elated and we told my mother of our situation. Margaret returned home to Manchester to get her parent's permission to marry. They reluctantly consented but refused to come to the wedding and *disowned* her. Margaret also went to her local Catholic Priest to perform the ceremony and he refused to marry us. He told Margaret *"You will live to Regret it"*. They were very cruel words, so we agreed to get married in the village church and David my brother in law would give Margaret away.

There was a cottage in the village called *"Rose Cottage"*. It was a beautiful small Fourteenth Century cottage with a modern extension on the rear consisting a bathroom, dining room and kitchen.

This cottage was the summer home of a London couple who came to the village only once a year. I negotiated a lease on the cottage and we both loved it. It was at the North end of the village so at last I was going to be free away from my father and be my own man. I was twenty years old.

Margaret and my mother planned the wedding and did all the invitations. We had the J & H on the cards as Margaret had seen when she was fifteen. We had three hundred guests consisting mainly of business people, Auctioneers, Farmers as well as all of our London clients, some friends of all the family and Margaret's friends from college. Margaret had six Bridesmaids and all the dresses were made by a lady in Crediton who had also done my sister Barbara's wedding.

The reception was to be held in the Plume and Feathers Hotel in Okehampton and we decided on a three week Honeymoon on the Island of Malta. So the date was set for Fourth November 1967 and the Banns were duly called three weeks prior to the wedding from the local church. This was the event of the year in our village.

By the autumn of 1967, I had built a good team of cattle buyers. Morley Guy the village man who used to own the cattle lorries was now working for me. Walter Luxton a Dealer from Halwil in West Devon, Bruce and myself would also cover the auctions. Every day all the local farmers from the surrounding villages brought the livestock to the abattoirs as opposed to going to the cattle sales. Whilst I was losing no more money, I couldn't redeem the Forty Thousand Pounds that was still short.

The morning of the wedding I went to purchase cows from a dealer at North Tawton, who as well as being a cattle Dealer also kept a pub and so I was drinking whiskey in his pub at one thirty in the afternoon on the Saturday having bought the cattle and getting married at three o'clock. The abattoir had been closed for the day giving the staff a holiday as all the staff and their wives were invited to the wedding.

At three o'clock the time of the wedding the *Heavens opened* with and thunder and lightning and the rain just poured down. The wedding ceremony over we had to have all the photos taken inside because of the rain. The reception was a *"Hoot"* with champagne flowing by the gallon and at seven o'clock Margaret and myself took a car to Exeter, where we caught the London train. We stayed in the Washington Hotel in Curzon Street, Mayfair that night and flew to Malta the following day.

Meanwhile back in Devon, the celebrations went on all Saturday evening and all day Sunday coming to a conclusion Sunday evening when everyone returned to various parts of the country. We only heard about this upon our return from Malta. Brother Bruce was in charge of everything during my absence. Bruce was very young and not good at handling the personnel but he was honest and a very hard worker and a loyal brother so I felt calm in leaving him in charge.

The honeymoon was marvellous in the small town of Sleima on Malta. We stayed at the Castle Dragonora which was a casino and hotel as well as a night club all in one. Every morning I had the Barber give me a hot shave then he would rub my face with a block of ice. It was marvellous.

Margaret and myself had time to sit and plan our future. I had everything in place to put the liquidation into motion and absolve the debts. The only stumbling block was *my father refusing to leave* and if he stayed, he would surely be caught up in the *"fall out"* from the liquidation. So even at this point, I was protecting my father in exactly the same manner as my mother. My brother Bob is the only other person who was party to my plans and he had given his agreement and consent.

Margaret wanted to have six children and retire when I was thirty. This was very conceivable at the time. She had became very involved in the village life. She had a lot of time for old people and children and they seemed to love her as much as she liked them. We went back excited about the cottage as we had never lived as man and wife until now, on our honeymoon. We had so much going for us that our love seemed to have no boundaries.

We arrived home at the end of November and I received a letter from Mr Vick the auctioneer who had taken our Pony as children. He had newly opened an abattoir of his own and was desperate to remove me as competition. He sent me a copy of my father's letter claiming that my father would pay the One Thousand and Seven Hundred Pounds owed, when his boys had grown up. Vick was now claiming the money from me.

I didn't want to embarrass my father by showing him the letter but I paid the money. To make matters worse, after I had paid, Vick insisted I pay for my purchases on the day of the sale and I was no longer given seven days credit. This I also had to swallow. This was not a pleasant home coming as Hatherleigh, only four miles away, was my main source of supply of livestock.

I organised a meeting with Joe Vick but to no avail. He wanted my business in his abattoir so very reluctantly I began to slaughter some of my animals at Hatherleigh to keep the peace.

The cottage was marvellous just so snug and homely in those winter months with a coal fire and Margaret and myself. Most evenings Morley Guy would call in on his way home and we would have long evenings talking about his childhood in the village, his dealings in the cattle trade. I became very fond of him and looked upon him as a father figure. He had no shame in telling me all of his business affairs, his near bankruptcy with the Tax man and I believed, he was in awe of me. His was the man I used to pretend to be when I was, as a child in my peddle car, now working for me.

Morley's father, Norman Guy, was the local miller and had a reputation as a great Ladies man. Morley was the eldest son. Before the war Norman arranged finance for Morley to purchase a forty acre farm at the north side of the village called Brooklyn and Morley built a successful agricultural contracting business along with two cattle lorries.

When war broke out Commodore Smythe Osbourne, the Squire of the next village, Monkokehampton, gave Morley the job of being his driver in the R.A.F. Morley's wife Mary was the daughter of Joe Skinner the village Pub landlord and there were rumours of a liaison between the Commodore later Sir Percy Smythe Osbourne and Mary Skinner, Morley's mother-in-law.

Whilst Morley was not a big farmer he would always graze the farms of men who were in financial trouble. I suppose on reflection, Morley was rather like a vulture. I recall him grazing the farm of Larry House's father, Wally. Also Bill King's farm at Cadham. Bill had a very large family and money was always short.

Morley also befriended a Mrs Taylor in the village of Samford Courtney and actually inherited the right to purchase the farm at the Fixed Price in Mrs Taylor's Will. The family were outraged.

Morley's finest hour was in December 1967. There was a lovely farm called *Woodhall* on the edge of the village owned by the Hatherleigh family. When Mr Hatherleigh died the widow ran the farm with her very Shy, Backward son. Morley again took the grazing of the farm and came to my cottage one night telling me he had purchased the farm of one hundred and twenty acres for a knock down price.

Morley sold the house as a Country House and retrieved the cost of the whole farm. He then had one hundred and twenty acres *Free of Charge*. This farm is in the hands of Morley's family today. Perhaps I should have seen a warning light then of Morley's attentions towards me.

Socially life was marvellous. We held the Jockey's Benevolent Fund for Disabled Jockeys, who had been injured riding in races. This event was a Beara Court every year and there were always two to four bands from Jamaican Steel bands to Victor Sylvestor's Dance Band as well as Rock & Roll. It was a marvellous event with all the leading trainers, owners and jockeys of the day. Josh Gifford, David Mould, Dave Dick, Bobby Beasly, Fred Winter. These events along with the Hunt Balls kept us very busy on the winter nights.

We had our first Christmas together at Rose Cottage and everything in the garden was Rosy, *pardon the Pun*. I knew I had to make plans on the liquidation in the New Year but that seemed a lifetime away. I savoured every day as it come to me.

Margaret was involved in the flower decoration at the church as well as the local library and she was very pregnant and very content. I had the J & H from the wedding card made in gold and put on a gold chain one for Margaret and one for me. They were quite lovely and peculiar to her dreams as a fifteen year old girl.

Margaret started bringing me home library books each week and I began to read every night. Thomas Hardy was her favourite author. When at school she always associated his works with her dreams of me in Devon. This was very *Romantic* and here she was living in Devon fulfilling her dreams. We became very close to my sister Barbara and David, her husband and many weekends they would come down to Devon to stay with us. This usually resulted in David and myself drinking all night. When we returned from dinner or a party, then going to Guy's bake house in the early morning getting a fresh loaf of bread and having breakfast. So my drinking while still under some control was far from normal. I drank in great excess.

Our favourite haunts were the Dartmoor Inn at Lydford and the Highwayman Inn at Sourton. John (Buster) Jones is still the Landlord. We were always given a Royal welcome and I had a charge account at all the local pubs. I would settle up by cheque once a week. I bought Margaret a new mini car for Christmas in 1967 so she was now under her own steam in regards to transport rather than waiting for me to come home to take the Humber. There was still no sign of my father leaving the house so I just let matters go for a while in the hope of a small miracle.

In January of 1968 the local council decided I must put a new drainage system into my abattoir. This was a very big expensive operation. I thought if I am going to have to close to do this I will rebuild the whole plant. So that's what I decided to do. I organised this through several local building and excavation companies.

My plan was to do as much work as could be done with the plant in full operation. This close for two weeks and by working twenty four hours a day completing the interior without too much delay on my production. For the two weeks of closure I would move my whole operation to Haterleigh Abattoir. This being decided I set my plans in motion. This was all to be financed by the Trading Company with the asset belong to my Holding Company. I found a clause in my copy of Articles and Memorandum which stated *"The Company can spend what money it deems fit if the outcome is to improve the Prosperity of the Company"*. I took this to read that by improving my plant my Trading Company could operate faster and more efficiently.

I came home from Holsworthy market the first Wednesday in January to find my plant closed. All my staff were waiting for me in the Mess Room. My father had gone insane, sacked all the men and we had two hundred pigs in the pens awaiting slaughter. I could hear him in the abattoir rolling the bins of water, his favourite forty gallon drums. He had all the taps going. I had some very big very tough men working for me and out of the thirty men no one would dare go near him. At least, they had waited until I got home.

I went into the abattoir and asked him what was he matter. He replied *"These men can't do the job properly, they are not slaughter men, they are only knacker men"*. I said *"Dad, its none of your business. I pay the wages, I own the livestock"*. He went totally bananas and I thought he was going to kill me. Then he said the fatal words *"You can fuck off, this is my slaughter house"*. So many times over the years he had said this to me. So many times he had taunted me as a young boy, young man and now grown man. All the hate, temper of ten years came out of me. At once I told him, *"This is not your slaughter house. It is mine. I paid for it and you took the money. Now you fuck off!"* I was raging. He came for me raised his hands to hit me, then when he saw I was not going to stand down, he walked away. He took off his knives and walked into the house.

I got all the men to start work again and went home to Margaret and told her what had happened. I drank a half bottle of whiskey and calmed down. I dreaded going back to the abattoir. Bruce came up to see me and said the old man had gone to bed. I can't remember everything I said to my father but I know I got all the years of anger off my chest.

When I went back to the abattoir, all was well. My men were working hard to catch up on the day and the following day my father left for Bournemouth. He went to stay with my sister Barbara, no goodbye or apology. It was over and my father was gone. I was so relieved yet even after all he had done he left me with a feeling of guilt. Things could have been so different. My father could have bought a nice cottage in the village and come to work part time. He could have gone to the farms and judged the livestock, all I knew was that he could not be around at the time of the liquidation. The news travelled fast that father was gone.

When anyone asked me where he had gone and why he had gone, I merely said it was his heart and he had to rest. My father was only forty six years old and things could have been so very different for him and for me.

The building work was completed by March of 1968 and I received a new license for the abattoir. My impending liquidation was the best kept secret in Devon with only Margaret and myself being aware. I had not even told Bruce.

The *"modus operandi"* was to liquidate my Trading Company with debts of One Hundred Thousand Pounds, hold onto my Holding Company with assets of the family home, the abattoir, the farm and the cottage in the village which I kept as an office. This would leave me with a beautiful plant I had designed and built myself. Legally owing nothing and the chance to start again alone, with no family around me just Margaret and myself. Given the choice, I would have turned back the clock to 1966 and my Forty Thousand Pounds but this was not possible.

I contacted a firm of accountants in Exeter called Simkins and Edwards and appointed my own liquidator. I *Pulled the Plug* on the Wednesday, Twenty Eighth of April 1968. I had to let go thirty good men and found them all jobs with other abattoirs. My men were so grateful, I got my office manager, Frank Heap a job with a local transport company. I only retained my two best slaughter men and Stanley the local Village Idiot as he was not employable by anyone only me. All my men shook my hand, wished me luck and thanked me. I thought that was hard, now I had to deal with the creditors.

I was so very fond of Stanley. He was the mentally slow son of a large family a couple of miles from the village.

His brother John who inherited the farm was instructed by his father to always keep a home and job for Stanley.

However, John sold the farm for £1,200, a lot of money in those days and left Stanley with the new owners. They got rid of Poor Old Stanley once they had secured the farm and he was Homeless at the age of forty.

Stanley was very similar to the character played by John Mills in the movie, *"Ryan's Daughter"*. Tony Walker, our very first employee when I left school saw Stanley crying in the village Pub and took him home.

My father gave Stanley a job and this was how I had inherited him. He could be so very charming yet equally cantankerous. Many times in rage I would sack him and he would look me in the eye and say, *"I have as much right to be here as you, Boy"*. He was so funny that I could never stay angry with him for long.

I learned many years later he fell off his bicycle in the snow and got frost bitten and had to have his toes amputated. He later died in a home in Plymouth. Stanley loved a drink also, especially at weekends he could put the Beer away.

I was aware all the auctioneers carried credit insurance so they caused me no concern. I had made sure all *my local accounts were paid*. Morley Guy my main Buyer was paid with cheques from my clients that I had endorsed, so he was in fact a *preferential creditor*. The whole county was in a state of shock and the village seemed like a graveyard as opposed to a hive of activity.

We arranged a Creditors' meeting on the Fourteenth of May 1968 at the Village Hall. The receiver presided over the meeting. I had to sit at the table on the stage and face all of my creditors. I only wished I could have told them the true story, how my father had caused all of these problems. The result was a Committee of Investigation was formed from the creditors, to work with the receiver and liquidate all the money they could.

The meeting was over and I went home to Margaret. She was not at home. Mary Guy, Morley's wife had very kindly called down and taken her off for the afternoon. I drank a bottle of whiskey and Margaret came home. The relief was enormous, it all being over having taken me two years since I came home from hospital yet I knew I would have great difficulty starting again.

Two days later, my son William was born weighing 8 lbs 8 oz with a mop of bright red hair just like his Nanna. We were going to call him Paul Mason Hayes but Margaret took one look at him and said *"He is another William"* and that's his name. We were both so Happy we had on one hand lost so much and yet the miracle of a child a healthy child over shadowed everything. There was a painting of a Punch & Judy Show that Margaret loved, hanging on the wall of a local pub. I had purchased it weeks before and had it hanging in the house for when Margaret came home with our Baby.

CHAPTER THREE

I was twenty years old and on paper a wealthy young man despite the fact I had lost credibility. Margaret and myself moved into the Family Home with William and I spent the next few weeks making a lawn for the baby whilst my men cleaned and painted the farm and abattoir.

Morley Guy came to see me and proposed that we continue the business under his name and do the killing at Hatherleigh. When things had quietened down, we would move the operation back to my abattoir. This was a very tempting offer and I accepted. I did all the marketing and Morley purchased the livestock. However, he never moved the business back to my yards. I had given Morley the Best of my markets and clients for the meat, skins, casings and offal and he took it all. He left me *High and Dry*. I had nothing in writing, only the gentleman's agreement. Ten years later, Morley died a millionaire having sold this business of mine to Bridgeman of Devon for a large amount of money still being retained as the Buyer.

Margaret always told me I gave people too much and that I was too generous with my staff. So I had now to find a way to set up in *competition* with my own business, with the disadvantage of not being able to go to the cattle sales. The scandal and rumours began to die down with a few exceptions. Margaret went to the village shop one morning for a loaf of bread to be told *"Mrs Hayes, you will have to pay cash from now on"*. We had an account there for the past twenty years. Frank Guy at the village garage brought my first monthly account to the house and asked me to pay cash. It was for Thirty Pounds. I had been paying him Six Hundred Pounds per month for the previous two years for my lorries and cars and he had been paid in full. Another preferential creditor like his brother, Morley.

The pub in the next village Samford Courtney had received the business of my thirty men every lunch and every evening. We also took our London clients there to stay when they were visiting Devon. The landlord Alf Ward closed my account immediately. There were several people like this who jumped on the bandwagon. *People like to cut down a Tall Poppy.*

By August of 1968 I had persuaded several local dealers to back me. Roger Seccombe, Sam Lias, Walter Luxton and John Ross, the Managing Director of Lord Vestey's Hide and Skin Company in Exeter and I was away again in Full Production. The local farmers began to come back, the first one being Richard Bendyshe. Richard had a country mansion in Jacobstowe as well as six hundred acres. He owned the whole village. This property now belongs to Noel Edmunds, the BBC personality. Once people saw Richard bringing all his sheep to me they were very quick to follow. This was the local Squire giving his *Seal of Approval to my operation.*

The committee of investigation had decided to invite the Fraud Squad from Plymouth to investigate the liquidation. No one knew how I was able to hold onto all of the properties legally. This gave me no concern at the time as the real cause of the liquidation was well hidden.

Margaret was pregnant again with our second child and there was going to be a thirteen months age difference in our two children. So we were well on the way to our six children and retiring. I made the Peace with my father who had purchased a small butcher shop in Bournemouth and my parents were living in a flat quite close to my sister, Barbara. The sad thing was the shop, like all my father's ventures, was non-profit making and my mother had yet again to go back to work. I was powerless to help as I was busy competing with Morley Guy to rebuild my own business.

Two or three individuals came after me legally on a personal basis. We used my father's solicitor, Bill Sutton who had a reputation for being a *"Straight Talking Tough Yorkshire Man"*. Whilst he was this, the poor man used to stutter with Nerves when he appeared before a Judge. The longer the case went on the worse he stuttered. Having lost the first case, I sacked him. I found a young man called David Bickford who was an excellent advocate to take care of all my affairs. I had learnt at an early age to succeed in business, you need a good accountant and a good solicitor.

David used to come to the village Pub on Sunday lunchtimes with his wife and have drinks with Margaret and myself. David's wife was the daughter of the Chaplain to the Queen and he was a Roman Catholic. His wife caused great alarm in her family by converting to Catholicism to marry David.

This was, of course, the reverse of Margaret becoming Protestant in order to marry me. David eventually took a post as Government Legal Adviser to a small Caribbean Island and went off to a magnificent life style. I had played Rugby with him for many years.

Life was getting back to normal. I was free, married and the business was beginning to grow. Poor Bruce got a very raw deal on reflection. I had arranged for Bruce to go to London the day after the liquidation and meet Gee & Webb's John Brewster and get a job on Smithfield. I thought the contacts he could make in London would eventually help us in Devon. I learnt that he was, in fact, staying in Okehampton with his girlfriend and not taken my advice.

My brother-in-law, David had purchased a restaurant in Bournemouth and gave Bruce the job to manage this with a self-contained flat over the restaurant. So Bruce moved to Bournemouth. This didn't last long. I have no idea what the row was over but the next thing I know Bruce was working at Millers Bacon Factory in Poole, Dorset and living with my parents. I had never put Bruce fully in the picture yet having said this, he also had spent the previous two years living on the fat of the land complete with MG Sports car. We went short of nothing in the previous two years with charge accounts and the run of the cheque book. However, *with justification*, Bruce is very bitter over this period of his life.

My brother, Bob, came home from University in June of 1968 and moved into the family home. Whilst Bob worked very hard for no wages it was not what I wanted. I wanted to be alone with my wife and my baby and enjoy the new baby when it arrived. I asked Bob to get off his backside and do something with his Degree. Bob had been on a four year course at University including the year he had taken off, so he had been lucky enough to get away from the hell of my father. Bob then moved to my sister in Bournemouth and eventually began a career as an Insurance Broker. The story of Bob from humble beginnings with nothing, to his retirement as a Tax Exile before he was forty years old is another story in itself that one day should be written.

By Christmas of 1968 we had turned the corner and my life was very organised. The plant was going well. I kept a very small staff and worked in the abattoir daily myself. Margaret ran the office and every Monday evening all my Buyers would come, the youngest being sixty years old and the oldest being seventy. We would go to the village pub, I would work out the figures for the week and pay them by cheque. Margaret would entertain their wives at the other side of the bar. This ritual every Monday built very firm friendships with these men and their families. The whole evening would wind up about midnight every Monday.

We had a new landlord in the village pub the Red Lion, a man called Eddie Potter who was from Deal in Kent. I took all my business there after the incident with the landlord at Sampford Courtney. After my liquidation Eddie became a very valuable friend to me in more ways than one.

Whilst only twenty years of age I was a very old man in all my ways. I had a very old head on young shoulders. I always dressed very traditionally with Calvary Twills and Brogue Shoes and Sports Coat for the village, Tweed Suit and Brogue Shoes for the Races or visiting farmers and my evenings at the pub. Then a Blue Pin Stripe Suit for going to the city, my Bankers or London, to see my clients. I remember one Sunday David Willis my school friend calling to see me after many years. I found I had nothing in common with him or anyone of my generation. I was content with my people who were a generation older than myself.

My world was my Margaret, my son and all the Babies that were yet to come, as well as my business, my livestock and my farm. My home really was my Castle.

Two months after my liquidation Mr Vick the local auctioneer who had built the abattoir at Hatherleigh went into receivership. This was followed by Bill Yeo a very large firm of second generation meat wholesalers. These two very large liquidations took all the pressure off my liquidation and I was no longer news.

When William was born all the village ladies had knitted clothes for him. Now with the new baby on the way, the wives of all my dealers were busy knitting again. It was really quite lovely. Margaret continued doing the alter flowers in the church and I continued reading each night until June of 1969 when the baby was due in a matter of days.

We had been invited to a Dinner Dance at Launceston, a market town on the Cornish border. It was to be quite a formal affair so Margaret decided to make a cocktail dress. It seemed pointless to buy a dress so close the end of the pregnancy. The dinner was on Thursday the Twelfth of June 1969.

We arranged for Michael Macdonald to babysit for the evening. Michael was the eldest of a large family of children and worked for me in the abattoir. We drove to Cornwall in the early evening for dinner at eight o'clock.

The evening was marvellous with good music and dancing. We danced all evening and at the end of the night when the bar was closed I remember getting a *treble whiskey* and water, one for the road. The last words of our hosts was *"Will Bill be okay to drive, Margaret?"* to which Margaret replied *"He always get me home. He needs me!"*. She took my arm and we went off to the car.

I remember seeing lights and that was all. I woke up and put my hand to Margaret. She was moaning. I put my hand on her knee and felt a very large cut there and passed out. At the time of the impact with a lorry I think Margaret said *"You Bloody Fool, Bill"*. I say I am quite sure of this but not positive.

I woke up in hospital the next morning at Plymouth. My face and nose once more a mass of cuts and bruises. There was a very good looking young doctor, who was South African and he said to me *"Mr Hayes, I have some bad news for you"*. I knew immediately what he was going to say. Margaret was dead along with the baby.

It later transpired that Margaret was dead in the car so she was only taken to the local hospital in Launceston. The impact has caused the baby to rupture her liver. The previous day she had just had all her hair cut and looked so lovely at the dance. Radiant with the pregnancy and blessed with good health. Now she was lying dead in a strange hospital. It was a baby daughter, who would have been thirty one years old today, the Sixteenth of July 2000.

CHAPTER FOUR

My parents arrived at the hospital with Barbara and David and I was given bottles of whiskey. I discharged myself on the Sunday and returned home. Barbara had taken over the house and looking after William. She had a son of her own, Bradley who was only five months older than William, so Barbara's nanny took care of both babies.

My brother Bob made all the funeral arrangements for Wednesday, Eighteenth of June 1969. I buried Margaret in her wedding dress along with all of her jewellery. I refused to go and see her body and it was not until going into the church on the Wednesday afternoon I realised she was dead. I was surprised that so many people came to the funeral from all over the country. It was a great tribute to a most wonderful lady.

My cattle dealers, Walter and Roger and John Ross the Vestey man, along with Captain Simmonds carried my wife to the grave. These four men she loved dearly. The captain was a retired Army Officer who had a local farm. Very much a *confirmed Batchelor* he would come to the abattoir with a very unruly bunch of flowers and always give them to Margaret. He always called me "Hayes" like one of his men in the officers mess. Margaret just had this way of bringing out the Best in everyone. As the coffin was lowered I threw the J & H that I was wearing around my neck into the grave.

When I arrived home the house was full of family and guests, along with Margaret's parents. The first time I had seen them in two and a half years. It was the first time they had seen their grandson, William. It was all very tragic. William was playing happy, not knowing the event that was taking place. I went into our bedroom which still smelled of Margaret an saw all the hand knitted baby clothes people had made for the new baby.

My paddocks were full of sheep that had built up since the accident, so on the Friday I opened the abattoir again. Bruce came home to take over the management. I began to drink for total oblivion. I had no interest in anything only drink and William. Barbara employed a nanny for me, a girl called

Virginia. She was a lovely girl but very heavy handed. Within a week all the lovely hand made clothes of Williams had been shrunk and the colours run with the washing machine. She was as clumsy as Margaret was gentle, yet she loved William and was good to him. Barbara was a brick to me spending many weeks in Devon helping me and we got to know each other very well and I loved her dearly.

The inquest recorded an accidental death. Yet I was charged with driving without due care and attention and fined Fifty Pounds. The amount I had to drink that night never came to light and the guilt I have carried alone ever since. I had no interest in the business. People brought in the livestock, I paid for it, and sold the meat and just went through the motions. In my business this is fatal as the prices fluctuate daily. No matter, I was in the village pub every day at eleven o'clock until three o'clock in the afternoon, then home to load my lorries for London and back in the pub at six o'clock at night.

On my way home from the pub at night I would call in the churchyard and sit down by the grave and talk to Margaret. This was how it went on for the next six months, my business getting deeper into debt. My drinking escalating. I refused to change anything in the house. All Margaret's clothes, make up, etc. remained just as though she was going to come home. William was now walking and I became a danger to William as well as to myself.

In December of 1969 I was informed the Fraud Squad were going to prosecute me under the *1948 Companies Act* for:

(1) Trading whilst insolvent
(2) Failing to keep Correct Records.

The insurance money on my car paid double in the event of death. So I had a cheque for Four Thousand Five Hundred Pounds. I paid this to David Bickford my solicitor to fight the case. Making matters worse, Bruce was also going to be charged. This was the price we had to pay for my father's negligence in 1966.

To hear my father talk in those days, *"Bruce and myself had brought all of this on ourselves"*. My father was playing the role of the Wronged Father, whose sons had not listened to his advice and according to my father, the whole problem was caused by us bringing in staff to do the work and not do it ourselves. How *seriously deluded* my father was but luckily for him, the Fraud Squad also believed his version of events.

My trial was a Devon Assizes in January 1970 and we fought the case. When the prosecution was over, I gave my Defence. The Judge, Justice Seabag Shaw intimated to my counsel, James Black, if I changed my Plea I would keep my liberty. I was informed of this during the lunch time recess and followed my counsel's instructions and changed my Plea. James Black was accepted in the New South Wales Bar in 1986, around the time I came to Australia, and was made a Circuit Court Judge in New South Wales in August 2000.

The Jury Foreman got up and said *"Your Honour, what if the Jury think the verdict is Not Guilty?"* The Judge said, *"Now the Plea has been changed, the Jury has to be dismissed"*. I was given Nine Months Suspended Sentence on the first count and Six Months Suspended Sentence on the second count. It was all over. On my way out of the court the Jury Foreman came to me and said *"We would have found you Not Guilty, Bill. I am so sorry"*.

This was a lovely thing of the Jury to say but at that time of my life I was so addled with alcohol it didn't really matter. However, in years to come that verdict and the start of my criminal record was to come back and haunt me time and time again. I was the *Walking Dead*, alive but not alive.

I went for a Holiday to the Canary Isles with Barbara and David and left Bruce to run the abattoir. I met a Danish girl who was very kind to me and to some point returned me for a while to the human race. At home, I always had ladies to escort me to the Hunt Balls and Rugby Balls but no one was ever serious in my life. I took love where I could get it.

I decided it was time to engage a full time live in nanny and placed an advertisement in the English *"Sunday Times"*. I interviewed several ladies at the Royal Clarence in Exeter and selected a girl called Margaret Sweeny who was twenty seven years old. I was approaching my Twenty Third Birthday. Having outlined her duties she was moved into the family home and William became very attached to her. Margaret's father was a drinking alcoholic and I believe in those days she was aware I had a serious drinking problem.

My house was no longer a family home rather it was Open House. When the pubs were closed people would turn up for drinks. There were always parties drinking, music, people assumed I had soon got over my wife's death. I was lost, like a ship without a rudder. Only for William I had no reason to go on. *I used to go to bed at night and pray that I wouldn't wake up.* Then, of course, I always did so I would drink and drink some more.

I had one attempt at suicide driving into a Norman Bridge at the bottom of Exbourne Hill. All I succeeded in doing was to put more scars on my face and very nearly lost my right eye. I was several days in hospital and banned from driving for two years. This made me very dependant on Margaret, the Nanny, to take me around locally. The local landlord's daughter also used to drive me until she went to University in Paris.

By June of 1970 I decided to sell out, give up. I should have offered the place to Bruce or may be even stayed myself but I had no heart in the business or the home. The cattle dealer who had the pub in the next village made me an offer. He would buy the business and clear all of my debts with the Bank. In return he would employ me as the Managing Director on a salary. I could retain the family home as it was and advise him on the meat business. This seemed a good way out of all my responsibilities so I accepted.

Within three weeks of the takeover, Bill Speake, the man who bought me out dismissed me, evicted me from the family home and laughed in my face. Once more like Morley Guy, I had nothing in writing. With the knowledge I have today, I could quite easily have had the sale made invalid. I really didn't care. I just wanted to get drunk, stay drunk and end it all. I gave up without any fight.

I realised years later the common denominator between Joe Vick, Morley Guy, Bill Speake and Richard Leventhorpe, was a solicitor called Peter Brown.

Brown was the sone of the local Coroner, Lt Colonel Brown and a very *Vicious Homosexual* who took it upon himself to put Bill Hayes in his place.

Today I shudder when I think how *Innocent* and *Unprepared* I was to take on these people who had Brown as their Knight in *Horn Rimmed Glasses!*

I burnt all of Margaret's clothes, put my furniture in a removal van, put William's toys and bicycles in the car and told Margaret that I could no longer pay her wages. She refused to leave me and we drove to Cambridge where I got a job as a slaughter man with an export meat company. I was one month short of my Twenty Third Birthday and left my village in Devon in June 1970.

CHAPTER FIVE

The company chairman, Mr Radcliffe, in St. Neots, Cambridge, was well aware of who I was and treated me so very well. I was given a new three bedroom house and paid piece work to kill sheep and pigs five days a week. On Saturdays I went to Bedford market and bought the pigs for his company.

This was my first time not living in Devon and I soon got to know the local pubs. Margaret settled into the house and William was as happy as a pig in muck. I was earning very good money and no responsibility of any kind.

I was then head hunted by Cliff Playle, the largest private pork wholesaler in England. Playle's operation was at Royston in Herts. The job was Two Thousand and Five Hundred Pounds per annum plus a four bed-roomed farm house so I joined Playles.

Before I could move into the house I was once more head hunted by a man called Stanley Jackson. This man was a pig dealer from Cheshire who had just purchased an abattoir in Leicester. He offered me the job of running the abattoir with full control, doing the livestock buying as well as selling the meat at a salary of Three Thousand and Five Hundred Pounds per annum plus expenses. I could not refuse this wonderful offer.

We obtained a house in Nuneaton and I began at the abattoir on the Second of November 1970. My first job was to staff the plant, then build the business. My home was only six miles from Margaret's old college so quite often I would go off to the Plough Inn where I had stayed when I got engaged to Margaret. I began living in my past at this point and drinking for oblivion.

I began going to the cattle sales at Rugby on Monday, Melton Mowbray on Tuesday, Leicester on Wednesday and Banbury on Thursday. My lifestyle was again good and I was once more back in the meat trade with a vengeance. My drinking had escalated to enormous degrees which caused many problems at home.

There is no doubt I had one of the *Best Jobs* in the

country with my expenses and kickbacks from the dealers and skin merchants. I was earning One Hundred and Twenty Pounds weekly. Margaret came to work in the office and we employed a nanny for William. Stanley Jackson, my boss, had lost his wife in similar circumstances to mine and been left with two little boys. He was only forty years old, had remarried and was a very successful businessman. Stanley only came to the plant one day a week and left me to my own devices, as long as the figures balanced each week and we made profit. I really could not have asked for more. I was a hundred kilos in weight and still very old fashioned in my ways. Margaret, my nanny, used to ridicule me and call me a *country bumpkin*, which I suppose I was.

I hated the fact that I had to employ someone to replace my first Margaret. I hated myself for causing her death, *to hide all of this I drank more and more*. I became very violent in the home as well as things I hated in my father and other men, I became. I was out of control, having a good team of men at the abattoir my work never suffered but my private life was Hell. There was a pub actually attached to the meat factory called the Three Bells. I would be doing most of my business in the pub. The operation was so small compared to Devon I could run it in my sleep. This, of course, left me more time for drinking.

My parents came to stay and of course did not approve of my relationship with Margaret. My mother knew better than anyone I was using people. This was not only unfair on Margaret but a short road to nowhere for me. Margaret left me several times during this period mainly caused by rows over her friends and one particular friend who was a Methodist minister in the North of England. I hated myself, hated Margaret yet was so dependant on her for William and myself.

I remember meeting my brother Bob at Twickenham, London for the Middlesex Rugby Seven Aside in April of 1971. On the Sunday after the Rugby we all went for a beer on the Thames. I was a beautiful spring day in London. All the people seemed so happy. Bob was with Brenda who later became his wife. All the couples in the park enjoying themselves, families with children were playing together. I had never been so *lonely in my life* as I was that day. There is a song by Kris Kristoffsen called *"Sunday Morning Coming Down"*, that was me. I had a wonderful job, nice home, partner who loved me and I was miserable and wretched inside. It was awful.

Christmas of 1970 Margaret realised she was pregnant and I wanted her to keep the child. Margaret refused unless we got married. The last thing I wanted was marriage to anyone. Margaret made all the arrangements to have the pregnancy terminated. On Christmas Eve I said, *"If you go and get all the papers, I will marry you"*. Margaret duly did this and we were married on the Second of January 1971.

The baby was still born in April of the same year, a little boy. I felt trapped, deceived and all the self-pity in the world was within my heart. My drinking became worse and so did my violence. I eventually crashed the car drunk. So I was up for drink driving and driving whilst disqualified. I gave my name as Bob's and thought I had got away with it. I phoned Bob and told him what I had done.

Bob came to court and I admitted who I was so I was also charged with giving a false name. I was very lucky and fined One Thousand Pounds and banned from driving for a period of five years. We left the court jubilant to celebrate, however, six weeks later I was recalled to Devon Assizes as I had breached my suspended sentence from the Assizes in January of 1970.

I got the best legal advice available and it seemed a good idea to re-engage James Black as my barrister. I was to appear at Devon Assizes on the first Friday of July 1971 one week before my Twenty Fourth birthday.

I told the men what to do at the factory for the day and I would be back on Saturday morning. It was a two hundred mile drive to Devon. I spent all night drinking and decided that Margaret take William to my parents if the worse come to the worse. I was very confident I would be okay as there was no similarity in my case at Devon Assizes and drink driving. Veronica, our nanny, took care of William and we set off for Devon at five o'clock in the morning.

The Assizes were at the Castle in Exeter the same as my previous case. On going into the court I met the Sergeant from the Fraud Squad who had investigated my liquidation. The penny didn't drop at the time that he was the one who asked the

Judge to recall me.

I confidently appeared before the Judge with no concern about the outcome. The Judge then said, *"Mr Hayes, you are obviously a very intelligent man and knew you were breaking the law by driving. I find no alternative other than to impose your suspended sentence. You will go to prison for nine months and six months consecutively making a total of fifteen months. Take Him Down"*. I nearly died.

I had never been in a police cell or prison in my life, now I was facing ten months in prison of a fifteen month sentence. I had not even told Stanley Jackson I was going to court. Sandy, my foreman, was expecting me at the plant the next day. I could see Margaret was in a state of shock. This was awful as I was led to the cells below the Castle at Exeter. Billy Hayes arrives back in Devon after one year being away, as a prisoner of Her Majesty.

CHAPTER SIX

I had driven past Exeter Prison thousands of times, going shopping, going to the bank, going to Exeter cattle market each week never dreaming I would end up as a client. The place was very gloomy. I was stripped of my clothes and weighed. I remember I was two hundred and sixteen pounds or ninety eight kilos. I was then given a prison uniform of blue overalls, blue shirt and pullover as well as jacket.

I was then put in a cell with two other inmates and classed as a *Star Prisoner* which was a first offender. What amazed me was how the other prisoners just accepted their lot. I was like a caged animal locked up. I had no idea as to the value of freedom until now and I thought I would go insane.

I was sent to work daily in a mat shop where I sat at a loom making doormats all day. It was soul destroying. We weren't allowed to speak and the minutes dragged let alone the hours. I counted every minute and just made it very hard for myself. We were given a wage of Thirty Five Pence per week enough for half ounce of tobacco, papers and matches. We were allowed to write only two letters a week and entitled to one half hour visit every twenty eight days. I believed this was going to kill me. While we had access to library books the lights were turned out at nine o'clock at night. I had plenty of time to reflect on my life. What was now going to happen to William, I didn't really care about the business.

I was allowed my first visit the following week called a Reception Visit and Margaret came to see me. She had followed my instructions and moved all the furniture into store and taken William to my parents. She refused to leave me and asked me if she could move to Exeter with William to be near me. I agreed and Margaret moved to a caravan on a farm near Exeter. I was to be moved to an open prison in six weeks and her caravan was half a mile from the prison gate. Sandy, my foreman, had been marvellous in helping her make the move from our home in Nuneaton but Stanley Jackson was furious and wouldn't believe that I knew nothing of my being sent to prison. On reflection, I can't blame him as I was still in a state of shock.

One of the prison warders was an ex client of mine called Bill Holmes who used to own a fishmonger's shop and he treated me very badly. There were three prisoners who had been ex employees of mine. It was a very humiliating and humbling time for me. After the mandatory six weeks, I was moved to an open prison ten miles from Exeter. This comprised of a group of huts very similar to a prisoner of war camp in the movies.

There was a choice of work, one the scrap yard stripping plastic from electric cables or two the prison farm. The third choice was being able to go to work on civilian farms so I opted for the third choice. My first job was on a farm picking potatoes. This farmer used to graze sheep for me in the winter. I was so ashamed of myself and I had lost much weight I pretended to be my brother, Bruce. We had many conversations on Billy Hayes and what a great man he was.

The second farm I was on was the brother-in-law of one of my client farmers from Okehampton. He also had a guest house and Diana Rigg was staying with them as she was appearing at the Northcott Theatre in Exeter with Keith Michelle. I had met Diana first in Stratford-upon-Avon with Margaret and, of course, she knew me. She was and is a very classy lady and kept me in cigarettes.

As I mentioned earlier in the story, Margaret introduced me to Diana at Stratford and we had several wonderful evenings together. She was a striking Lady of nearly six feet in height and must have felt a great pity for me in my reduced circumstances. I kept the programs of Diana in Repertoire from 1963 to 1964 that Margaret used to keep in her Treasure Box.

The visits to the open prison were two hours every three weeks which was better. Margaret used to bring William *who called the prison "Daddy's Farm"*. We then used to meet during the day on the farms when I was working and have picnic lunches with William.

I became a Roman Catholic and used to go to mass each week at the Estate of Lord Clifford at the village of Chudleigh. Only twelve prisoners used to attend and Margaret and William would be sat beside me, even though we couldn't talk. The prison officer used to sit at the back of the church. All of this continued until Christmas Eve 1971 when I was caught one lunch time returning from a picnic with Margaret. I was then sent back to the closed prison at Exeter.

I had got over the first six months of the sentence and lost one week's remission for going *AWOL*. Several evenings I had actually got out of the prison and met Margaret in the woods. This was all very romantic but a great strain on my nerves as the risks of getting caught. If I had been caught, I would have been charged with attempted escape.

I was put back in the mat shop but after one day complained about the dust in my lungs and was given a job in the laundry. I was still in a three men cell but my cell mate John Dennis was a sheep farmer who was in prison for stealing sheep and it was bearable. I left the prison in Mary 1972 weighing nine and a half stone or one hundred and thirty pounds (sixty kilos).

Margaret had by this time got a small flat near Exeter and had been busy writing letters to secure me employment. She wrote to every meat company in Ireland and from the six replies we selected two to go and see once I had got myself together again. Margaret had proved to be very loyal, very loving and a great wife and friend. William absolutely adored her so we had our wedding *blessed* in the Catholic Church at Exeter.

This was the girl who had joined the meat executive for a career in Devon looking after a small boy. She ended up travelling all over England living in a caravan and visiting me in prison. As I had lost so much weight Margaret arranged with the prison governor to send a tailor into the prison to measure me for a new suite. This was duly done and when I got home and tried the suit on, the sleeves came up to my elbows and the trouser legs came to my knees. I didn't care about the suit but felt so sorry for Margaret who had tried so hard to please me.

During my ten months in prison whilst reflecting on my life I had not come to terms with my drinking problem. Poor Margaret even had a half bottle of wine for me with my breakfast on the morning of my release. So my drinking continued exactly where I had left off, too much, too often with no concept of the word alcoholic.

I have a very clear memory on that first day of Margaret putting on her make up, sat at the dressing table in our bedroom. She had given up so much for me and now here she was so very happy just like a little girl at Christmas. All she ever wanted was me and William. I felt an awful chill and tremendous guilt. There was no way I was ready to love anyone, only my dead wife. I was full of guilt, remorse, self hate and yet I owed this girl so much. I became like an actor on stage from that day, hiding my real feelings, never being able to speak of how I really felt only on a surface level. I was going to do my best to please this girl who had given her life to my son and myself.

CHAPTER SEVEN

I had been invited to Ireland by three companies, the main one being M. J. Lyons of Longford in the midlands of Ireland. So in June of 1972 we took the car on the ferry from Swansea to Cork and drove the length of Ireland to Longford.

This was a lovely journey and reminded me so much of Devon when I was a boy. There were horses and carts taking the milk to the creamery, small farm cottages, and they still had the cattle sales in the streets called *Fairs*. Half way to Longford we got a puncture and I had to get a lift on a Donkey and Cart to the next village for assistance. William wouldn't leave my side from the time I came home from prison. It always gave me a warm glow to think that I was coping in bringing him up.

Poor William apparently turned to Margaret in the car as I was riding off on the donkey and cart and cried his heart out. He thought I was going back to my Farm, of course, meaning the prison. I returned with help and we changed the wheel and were on our way.

I had changed considerably, no longer the stable country boy but now ten stone in weight and a twenty eight inch waist. I had my hair cut long going over my ears. Modern flairs in my trousers and quite the trendy man about town. Yet this facade didn't change the man inside who was now drinking daily to cope, full of anger, bitterness and guilt at my failures in my short years. I was still a *walking corpse* so full of self hate it wasn't possible to love anyone, only my son.

We arrived in Longford and were taken to the family home of Matt Lyons. He was a man in his early seventies and had six factories in Ireland. Three Meat factories, Pet Food factory, By-Products factory as well as his own Hide and Skin Factory. Matt had six sons all running a business each. The seventh son Michael was an architect in charge of all developments. He also had considerable farming interests.

The job offered to me was running the main beef and lamb factory in Longford as well as assisting on the marketing with the other factories. Albert Reynolds, who later went on to become the Irish Prime Minister, was the partner in the newly

William Henry Mason my grandfather, Rebecca my nanna and
Muriel my mother 1925. My grandad played the banjo, the piano
and could also knock out a tune on the Spoons.
Rebecca was the seventh daughter of a seventh son.

Muriel Hayes (nee Mason), my Darling Mother
who was always there for me, aged 14
at School Christmas Party in 1933

Bob Hayes, my Father as he arrived in Devon in 1947
fresh from the War. My brother Bob said at his funeral,
"No man ever worked so Hard for so very Little"

*Eggesford Hunt outside family home,
Exbourne 1948. Muriel and Bob behind
Huntsman's left shoulder*

*Me dressed as Little Boy Blue at the Village
Fete. Rebecca, my Nanna with arms folded.
Bruce is the other little boy. 1953.*

*Sunday School trip Teighmouth.
Me on horse, Barbara and Bobby 1950*

*Dave Willis (my School Friend)
in Exbourne 2001*

*My Grandad. I need Haircut.
Bob, Bruce and Barbara. 1949.*

*Most of Exbourne Village
Barbara's Wedding 1963.*

Bob, myself and Barbara 1948

*Barbara's Wedding. My parents and
David's Father and Sister 1963*

William, my Son, 1970

*My parents with Barbara, David
Bob, Bruce and myself, 1963*

My Mother in Australia 1996

My Father feeding Pigs, Devon 1948

My father in North Wales 1932

*Bob, my Father and Uncle Dick
In the Slaughter Yard 1933*

My Father feeding the Pigs 1948

The Slaughter House in Devon 1955

My Father as he arrived in Devon 1947

My Father's Shop in Bournemouth 1968

My Parents when Courting 1939

Nanna, Grandad, Mum, Cousin Billy Mason
Bob, Barbara and myself, 1950

My Parents in Majorca, 1967

Mum and Friend before Bikinis
were recognised 1947

Nanna, Grandad and Mum 1927

Mum as a Young Girl
soon to be a Young Lady

Grandad, Mum, Bob, myself and my cousin Kevin (the Policeman in the book) who is standing beside the Tiger's head

Myself dressed up as the Queen of Tonga Fancy Dress at a church fete, 1954

The four of us dressed up in winter clothes to go cutting logs, 1952

Barbara, Bruce and myself with the two children from Primary School in front of "Tumbles" House, 1953

Grandad and Mum having a cup of tea at Exmouth, 1951

William in 1970 before we left Devon

Bob as a Teenager 1963

Grandad and Bruce with Pigs 1950 with his

Bob looking Cool as a teenager,
dressed for work in the abattoir

Dad and Mum in front of Chalet
after the Fire 1961

Uncle Bill and Aunty Jane
The man who loaned me the Miner's Boots

Mum with Bruce and myself in front of
Tumbles House 1951

1963	1974	1987	2000
The Man *Takes the Drink*	*The Drink* *Takes the Drink*	*The Drink* *Takes the Man*	*Recovery*

May 2001 - At the Grand Hyatt Hotel, Melbourne with
Amy and Priscilla

built Pet Food Factory. This was a wonderful opportunity as the Irish Meat Plants were so large there was nothing in England to compare with them in any way.

We were taken to Cork for the weekend to meat Willy Lyons who ran a Bacon Factory there, and were generally shown Ireland, wined and dined. All the sons were very heavy drinkers so I was in my element. We were found a small house to move into, however, initially it was agreed we would stay at the local hotel. I was asked what salary I required, I replied *"I will work for my expenses for one month. If all goes well, I will name my salary. If I tell you my salary now you will be frightened"*. Everyone laughed and admired my confidence.

We returned to the UK to finalise things and pack up our furniture and while Margaret was doing this in Exeter I went to London. I called to see Sainsburys, Safeway, John Mansons, the Vestey organisation and told all my clients that I was moving to Ireland and persuaded them to buy my beef and lamb. I then went to Forest Gate in the East End of London and met my Indian clients who also agreed to buy from me. So I knew I was going to Ireland with a full order book of the Best jobs in London. The Irish plants at this time were all selling to English meat wholesalers, I was cutting out the wholesalers and going direct to the retailers.

I spent a day with Bob who was becoming a very successful Insurance broker. He had been kind enough to take out an Insurance Policy against me, so William would be protected if anything ever happened to me. I never paid him back with either thanks or money.

I then went to Bournemouth and saw my parents staying with Barbara and David, who lived a very high jet set life in those days with parties every day. I recall Barbara saying one evening, *"You are foolish to take Margaret Bill, you will never stay with her"*. Barbara had observed me flirting at a party with one of the guests and she knew that I would never be capable of being faithful.

I took the plane from Bournemouth to Dublin and Margaret was to follow in the car on the ferry. Arriving in Dublin, *free, able to drive again, fit* and *healthy,* I became a great womaniser. I was just the same as I used to be prior to my first marriage. I loved the Irish ladies and sadly for Margaret could not keep my hands off them. I knew Barbara was quite right, I should have come alone with just William, yet owed Margaret so much, I couldn't just drop her.

We moved into our small house and within two months I had agreed a salary of Eight Thousand Pounds per annum plus my expenses. We then moved to a large detached house with chickens in the garden and a large vegetable garden. My work went perfectly and in a short space of time I was the talk of the country. Two meat wholesalers were overhead to say *"Hayes knows every town in England"* to which the second one said *"He knows not only the towns but every bloody street!"*.

I pioneered *Direct Selling* of meat to the UK and as Matt Lyons sat on the Board of the Irish Meat Exporters he was always boasting about his young Englishman. I had taken the plant from sixty Cattle and six hundred Lambs per week to six hundred Cattle and three thousand Ewes per week. As the Irish prices were so much lower than the English, it was not difficult to sell to my people. I was very *Hands On* all the time.

Having got the English market sewn up, John Lyons and myself began on France, Italy, Norway, which meant a lot of travelling to the continent always *"First Class"* and the Best Hotels. The Bacon Factory sent a parcel of Bacon, Sausage, Pork fillets every week. The Lyons shop in the village gave us Salmon and the best cuts of Beef every week. We lived off the fat of the land and life had never been better.

I was playing Rugby for the local town and secretary of the Round Table. Margaret became pregnant in October of that year and all was well. My drinking was serious, every Friday night the Lyons brothers and ourselves would go out for drinks then go back in turn to one of our houses. These sessions never finished until five o'clock Saturday mornings. They were great nights. The ladies drinking as much as the men. The Irish most certainly knew how to enjoy themselves. I was drinking gin in those days.

I purchased some farm land to build a new house, arranged with all the local farmers to set up co-operatives to market all their lambs through Lyons. I organised two contracts for Albert Reynolds at the Pet Food factory. The first one with

Pedigree Pet Foods of Melton Mowbray and the second one to Brand Label for Sainsburys. These two contracts were the start of *C & D Pet Foods* where Albert eventually made his fortune. This was all done *Free of Charge* as part of my brief with old Matt Lyons. The only downside to all of this is when I finished work in the evening, I didn't want to go home. I always went to the local hotel.

I was involved with several women, one from my bank, my dentist receptionist as well as one of the girls in the office. I was living the life of a single man, then going home.

Having said this, I would come home every lunch time and was very good at deceiving Margaret. I was in fact living a double life. I would go off to play Rugby on a Sunday and so many times Margaret would turn up to take me home drunk. The whole town was one large social event every week. There were dances, Balls, Parties and Margaret always came with me to these events so she really had no idea of my double life. I was a drinking alcoholic in the company of many other heavy drinkers and alcoholics. We were all *riding on the crest of a wave*. I had all the usual trimmings, a new Mercedes car, dozens of suits, I would get my hair washed and blow dried every morning in the town. I became a very self-centered, arrogant man but I was very good at my job.

Margaret and myself went to a funeral in the North of Ireland in early 1973. One of my sheep buyers had been killed in a car crash, leaving a widow and two small children. Una the wife was six months pregnant. I was very fond of this man, Des Connolly. This was our first time to the North in the height of all the troubles.

Poor Des had died intestate and all of his creditors who he owed money to tried to clean the Estate. John Lyons and myself owed Twenty Thousand Pounds for sheep so we paid this money in cash direct to Una, the widow.

Una was a *Beautiful Lady* and I was Godfather to their beautiful baby daughter born four months after the death of Des. Desiree, my God-daughter is twenty seven years old today and I have not seen her for many years. Something else I must do in my future life, God willing.

Coming back, we called into the border town of Clones

and I saw the magnificent meat plant. I had heard of the plant run by a man called Tunney. Rumour said it had been financed by Charles Haughey when he was the Minister of Finance. As I sat at the gates looking in, I said to Margaret, *"I want to be a part of this, and I will be"*. We drove home to Longford.

I was getting an amazing amount of publicity in the Irish Press, *"The Independent"*, and *"The Times"* were always doing articles on M J Lyons and Bill Hayes. The English *Meat Trades Journal* sent over their editor, Tony Pike, who stayed with me for one week then wrote a six page spread on old Matt Lyons in the 1920's and Bill Hayes in the 1970's. There were five photos of me in that article. Brother Bob rang me one day as he had read an article in the English *Sunday Times* about me and he wondered if I knew it was there. This was always a huge *"Ego Trip"* for me. I remember Doug Wilkins, the previous Manager of Haterleigh abattoir ringing me asking if I had got any jobs going for him. This was the man who with Morley Guy had *stolen* my business. Stanley Jackson rang me to do business again and I made my peace with him after my sudden departure from his factory the day I went to prison.

My parents came to stay and fell in love with Ireland. My poor old father's shop was at a stand still and mother was still working. I recall the first night of their visit, the bed collapsed under them in the middle of the night. It was hilarious being woken by my father's laughter and mother's giggling.

I took my father to the Irish Grand National at Fairyhouse and we had dinner on the way home. He was a different man so much more mellow. He had never dreamt of a plant as large as my plant in Longford let alone seen one. I asked him would he consider coming to Ireland to live and he said *"I would come tomorrow"*. I most certainly was not going to do anything in a rush as I was still very apprehensive of him. One of his tempers in Longford would again have destroyed all I had built. I sent my parents back to the airport in a chauffeured car and at least I had made my peace.

My daughter, Edwina, was born in June of 1973 in Dublin. She was a fine healthy little girl but Margaret became very possessive over her. This was Margaret's baby, her own baby. I had no say in her name or say in anything. The local cattle dealers did the same as Devon, all brought knitted clothes and all put luck money in the cot to wish the Baby well. Margaret chose the Godparents and Edwina was christened in Longford Cathedral.

I had been approached by Tunney to join him at a salary of Twelve Thousand Five Hundred Pounds per annum. This salary was unheard of in 1973 in any business. This meant my driving sixty miles a day to Clones as I did not wish to leave Longford. I accepted the offer and joined Tunney in July 1973. I was twenty six years old and at the top of the tree.

CHAPTER EIGHT

Hugh Tunney was forty four years old, married with four children, the youngest one James being the same age as William. The eldest daughter, Nuala, was Seventeen and had a crush on me. Hugh reminded me of myself in Devon, Tweed Suits and Brogue Shoes, has short hair and when he went to Dublin, the Blue Pin Stripe suit.

We floated a company called THM Exports Limited. Tunney, Hayes and Mackle. Eamon Mackle was the Managing Director of Clones and had been inherited from the previous owners of the plant. Mackle was on a salary of Five Thousand Pounds per annum which was good money in those days. THM were to continue my buying meat from other factories and sell at a profit. The profits being divided three ways.

My main brief was to sell the cattle from Clones who were killing six hundred Cattle per week. The first week I sold one thousand three hundred Cattle at good money. The second week I sold one thousand five hundred cattle and we could only kill one thousand four hundred and fifty cattle so I began with a bonus and immediately became Tunney's right hand man. I was increasing the profit margins by Ten Pounds per head on the cattle so we were in profit from day one.

I was *Very Arrogant, Very Confident* and dressed each day in a *Very Flamboyant* manner with pastel colored suits, white suits, and always had my hair washed and blow dried. The last thing I appeared to be was a Butcher or meat wholesaler yet now I was in a very big way of business.

There were so many meat executives in those days who had no idea of how to use a knife. So my first day in Clones I went down onto the kill floor and worked on the line. That really secured my position and took away any doubts of who this *"Dandy"* was, because I looked like a Dandy even to myself.

I controlled the Irish cow market with my contracts for Birdseye, Findus, Ross Foods and J. Lyons, as well as my French contacts in Viandest in Metz and Soviex in Paris. I took over the contracts of Gregory Shapiro in the South of France and everything I touched turned to gold.

At the end of 1973, I negotiated a contract with the military government in Portugal and agreed to ship sixteen thousand Cattle in eleven weeks. This gave me control of all the cows in Ireland. The Portuguese Minister of Agriculture spent the weekend with me at Longford with two of his agents, by the end of the first night, I had him Greek dancing in my drawing room as drunk as could be. This was the biggest contract for Beef ever undertaken in Ireland. This also meant my flying to Lisbon every Thursday for the next eleven weeks to see my beef unloaded. All this meat was paid for *up front* by Irrevocable Letter of Credit and at the end of the contract, I salvaged eleven containers of rejected meat which had been paid for and sold them in Belgium for the sum of Eighty Thousand Pounds, a *nice little Bonus.*

I spent every night in Lisbon at the night clubs drinking and womanising. In those days it took up to one/two hours delay to book a phone call to Clones in Ireland and after many attempts at getting Hugh and missing him, Hugh made me promise never to leave the hotel until 10 p.m. each night.

Lisbon is the most Beautiful City of Palaces and Flowers, yet the Poverty was awful. The average monthly salary in those days was less than Fifty Pounds per month. In all my years I have never seen such a city for night life and available women with perhaps the exception of Dar es Salaam.

I was spending a lot of time in Dublin going to and from the airports, also meeting my overseas buyers. I became involved with several girls in Dublin and was very much part of the Jury's Hotel and Royal Dublin Hotel scene.

The sixty mile drive twice a day became a handicap, especially going home at night after my drinking all day. Margaret was not happy about my being with Tunney and preferred the security of my life with the Lyons family. Margaret was very attached to Matt Lyons, the old man and would often drive him to Dublin for his various meetings.

Old Matt Lyons used to take Margaret to all of the Irish Meat Exporters meetings and introduce her as his very Good Friend, leaving the impression Margaret was his *Kept Woman.* He really was a character and one day took Margaret to the hotel owned by one of his daughters and introduced Margaret as his daughter, Theresa's new mother or rather, stepmother.

Matt Lyons was a Beautiful, Intelligent, Lovely Old man, full of Irish wit and poetry. He could recite verse after verse for hours of the most beautiful prose. He had been very close to his wife Helena, building his empire with her for the twelve children but was a very sad lonely man when I met him, yet retained his lovely Irish humour.

My marriage was in ruins and Margaret was even more possessive over Edwina. William had started school and was blooming into a nice little boy.

Some nights I would stay in Monaghan town at the Four Seasons Hotel. This hotel would have dancing every night and was owned by the Provisional IRA. Monaghan was the Paris of Ireland. People would come over the border from the North each night to get away from the troubles. I met a nurse called Bernadette who was from Armagh in the north. Her family had had great problems with the English soldiers and her brother had been interned by the British, and was in jail without trial.

The relationship became so serious I considered getting divorced and marrying Bernadette and told Margaret of my position. Margaret agreed that she would go back to England and start again. That evening I went to see Bernadette to be told she had been talking to Margaret on the phone and what a *Bastard* I was, etc. etc. I was asked to leave her little village under the threat of physical violence at gun point, so that was the end of that. Margaret wanted a new start with me, so again, we decided to it one more try.

Christmas came and went in 1973 and the Portuguese contract was over. Hugh had purchased a half share in a £3 million project in Northern Ireland in the town of Enniskillen, driving there one morning the week of the opening he decided to sack his Manager and install me as the Managing Director. We agreed terms in the car on the twenty mile drive. There was a brand new house to go with the plant and this was mine *"Freehold"* if I took the position, so I agreed.

My brief was to complete the building over the next two years. Buy the cattle, sell the meat and generally run the plant as my own plant. I told Margaret that if she really wanted a new start I would give her a cheque book to go and furnish the house in anyway she wished. We would try again so we agreed to give it a go.

We moved into the Killyhevlin Hotel in Enniskillen in the suite next door to the owners, Raymond McCartney and his wife. Margaret spent all her days with Decorators, painters and furniture shops and totally furnished the house from scratch and a credit to her, she did a lovely job. The house was palatial inside. Margaret soon became pregnant again and we moved into our new home.

Northern Ireland was very dangerous in 1974 with the troubles, especially as I was representing a company from the South. I purchased a farm of one hundred and thirty acres, ten miles from the town and settled down to running my plant. I had the idea if I got rid of the partners, the Ulster Farmers Mart, this would be a good place to settle with Tunney and myself as equal partners. I then began to put my plans into place to achieve this goal. My drinking was very serious by now.

I became very friendly with a young barrister from Belfast called Peter. Peter had a drinking problem about the same as mine. However, despite this, Peter went onto become the youngest High Court Judge in England. Peter came down most weekends and I also became very friendly with a local solicitor Jack Taylor who had a practice in the town.

Jack had been a School Teacher in Belfast and married Daphne, another school teacher. At the age of thirty six he realised that no children were going to come as a result of the marriage . Jack had always wanted to be a solicitor so he went back to college as a mature student graduating at the age of thirty nine.

Daphne, Jack's wife, continued to work as a teacher and financially supported them both. They were a lovely couple and we became very close. I can say today Jack Taylor was the only man in my life I trusted 100% as a *Friend, Confidante and Advisor.*

I had intimated to Hugh how we could get rid of the partners but he thought the risks were too great. I had no doubt I could pull it off. The result was I ran the plant at a huge loss for several weeks. I had money owed to me intentionally all over

England. Then I resigned. I decided on the Friday to leave on the Saturday, the following day.

The partners were horrified as the Plant was *me*. I booked a month's holiday in Monte Carlo and on the Sunday, Margaret and myself flew to Monte Carlo leaving the children with Margaret's sister in England. My clients in Nice sent a stretch limousine to collect us from Nice Airport and drove us to Monte Carlo. We were treated like *Royalty*.

In June 1974, there was the opening of the new casino and sporting club in Monaco which was actually built under the Mediterranean. It was a beautiful building. Frank Sinatra, Sammy Davis Jnr and Lisa Minnelli were there to do the Cabaret for the opening. I recall sitting in the bar of the Hotel de Paris and it was full of these very small insipid men. Their wives with diamonds the size of golf balls. We later learnt this was the Heads of the *World Wide Mafia* all invited for the opening of the new casino.

Lisa Minnelli was then living with Jack Haley Junior and they were always in the bar of the Hotel de Paris. Muerell, my client, used to have the Mercedes 600 at my disposal with driver to go anywhere I wished.

I kept in touch with Tunney daily and to my dismay the partners had decided to have a go at the running of the plant themselves. So my plan of them leaving didn't seem to be working, yet confident, I had the holiday of my life.

I had brought my brother Bruce to Enniskillen early in the year of 1974 with his wife and two children. Bruce became the General Manager of my plant. A couple of weeks prior to the attempted takeover, I had secured Bruce a position in Clones so he was safe if all backfired.

Bruce and myself devised the plan that he would go to Clones at seven o'clock one morning and tell Hugh Tunney he was leaving Ireland because of his fear of the *Troubles*.

I gambled on the assumption that Tunney would not let Bruce go. This was quite a gamble to take in retrospect but it worked. Bruce arrived at Hugh's office and within fifteen minutes he was given the job of Production Manager of Clones along with house and company car. Within twenty four hours Bruce was settled in Clones and we had achieved what we set out to do.

I could always predict the reactions of men, if I knew them well. Equally, I can predict how to set up situations to my choosing, Crawford Scott once told me I could make people *Dance to my Tune.*

The other member of the Tunney team was Crawford Scott. Crawford had previously been Tunney's partner and was now on a salary of Fifteen Thousand Pounds per annum to purchase all the cattle for both plants. Crawford could not read or write and was totally *eccentric* in all ways. He would wear silk suits and crocodile shoes and be covered in cattle shit. He was just so clever he bounced on a hairline between madness and genius. I absolutely adored him. Margaret was equally fond of him as he was a great *Ladies Man.* Years earlier he had been involved with Christine Keeler from the *Profumo Scandal.* Crawford has a string of racehorses and was also a compulsive gambler.

Hugh Tunney was born in 1928 in the small farming village of Trilick in County Tyrone, mid Ulster. He was the eldest of five sons and four daughters, born to an Alcoholic Catholic Cattle Dealer and his wife. For any Catholic family in recently annexed Ulster as part of the British Empire after the Irish war of Independence followed by the Civil War, these were very tough days. Hugh's father was a very clever man and an excellent judge of cattle with his sharp wit, and a *Good Eye* and had no problem making a comfortable living as a dealer. However, alcohol was his *Achilles Heel* making any success short lived and the children grew up with a constant fear of insecurity. Making matters worse, he was a very violent drunk which made the boys all turn away from their father and towards their mother.

It was agreed that at the age of fourteen Hugh would leave school and be apprenticed to the local butcher in the next village of Irvingstown. This was normal for the war years of 1942. Hugh had no fear of hard work and took to the job as a Duck to water, learning how to buy the live animals, slaughter them and then cut them up in the butcher shop. His sharp brain and natural easy going wit made him very popular with the town housewives doing their weekly shopping in the butcher shop.

The butcher McGirr had a son of the same age as Hugh but it was settled that Gerry, the son, would stay at school and become a professional person when he left. With his apprenticeship completed Hugh was running the whole business at a very low wage. However, it was understood upon the retirement of McGirr that Hugh would takeover the business and become the natural *Heir Apparent* for a nominal price. With this goal in mind Hugh worked night and day building and expanding the business until 1954 when he was twenty six years of age. McGirr the butcher eventually died with Hugh having the business but nothing was ever put in writing.

Gerry was the apple of the widow McGirr's eye and he had failed miserably in any attempts at academic and professional career. Despite being a very bright young man he had a taste for the high life and was partial to heavy bouts of drinking, getting trouble and going nowhere. The widow decided it was only fit and proper that her Gerry take over the business and with this in mind gave Hugh notice one Saturday in 1954 with no severance pay, no week's wages, just finished him. So after twelve years of building up the business Hugh was left high and dry and there was no chance of employment in the local area as a qualified butcher. This bitter lesson in life was to haunt Hugh for many years to come. In the following week, like so many young Irish men in those days, he took the ferry to England to try his hand in London.

Having never left Ulster this was a *Big Step* for the small village country boy. On the ferry he had his ticket but not the price of a decent meal. Telling his tale to one of the ferry stewards he was treated to a meal and a cup of tea by this kindly steward which put him on good stead for the train journey from Liverpool to London.

London in 1954 was just being re-built after the war and meat had come off rationing. So the meat industry was booming. Hugh had no problem getting employment in various butcher shops, each move of job slightly bettering his pay and prospects but he was always known as Paddy. Paddy had to do all the lifting of the heavy meat, equally, all the cleaning of the shop at cease of business. This only made him more determined to succeed and fuelled his already very *anti English* feelings that had begun in his home village being a minority catholic in what was considered occupied Ireland. Hugh eventually ended up working for Lyons Findus in a factory in London, EC1, boning beef on piecework. The money was good, he was paid for what he produced.

Socially he loved to go dancing yet never took to drinking with so many bitter memories of his father. The times he did drink he found he could very easily lose control of himself and was then haunted by the memories of his father. One Saturday whilst living in Camden Town, he met a Belfast girl at a dance in Wembley and after a brief courtship they were married. Irene was a nurse in London and a very beautiful graceful girl. They set up home in a basement flat between Camden Town and Kilburn. They only problem with the flat was everyone who walked past in the street could look into the living room. The best day of their lives was when he had enough money for Irene to put up some new curtains leaving their lives private from the eyes of passers by. They were goods day and happy days. The work was hard but the ambition was strong. Hugh always bought the Meat Traders Journal and the Farmer & Stockbreeder keeping up with the current trends and prices in the industry. One week in 1956 he read about George Lonsdale, a successful meat baron who was buying cattle in England and exporting them live to France. This piece in the Farmer & Stockbreeder was to change Hugh's life forever.

George Lonsdale's offices were in Smithfield, London ECI where he ran a large wholesaling business, had stalls on the Smithfield market and was involved in all aspects of the meat industry. Hugh made a telephone call to go and see Lonsdale one Wednesday in 1956. This was the only day he had time off as Wednesday was his half day. Washing, shaving, putting on his only suit, Hugh went to see George Lonsdale at Lonsdale House, London, EC1. Hugh purported to have made the journey direct from Ireland and not around the corner from his basement flat. Explaining to Lonsdale the availability of Irish cattle far cheaper than English, he persuaded Lonsdale to buy a load of six hundred Cattle from Ireland to be shipped to France. Lonsdale was impressed with the young man and Hugh left his office like *a dog with two tails.*

When he got back to his flat it was time to share the story with Irene who was pregnant with their first child and work out how he could put together six hundred Cattle with no money. The first choice was his father but the old man could never bankroll an operation of this size. The Mollaghan Brothers of Longford in the Midlands of Ireland were the biggest dealers in Ireland in those days, so the following Saturday after work Hugh set out for Ireland again on the ferry, this time to Dublin and went to see the Mollaghans.

The two brothers were greatly interested in this new contract for France as prior to this time all Irish cattle were sold to England. The prices were acceptable but even the Mollaghans were not prepared to bankroll six hundred Cattle at One Hundred Pounds per head or Sixty Thousand Pounds. They could not do an order of this size especially to a complete stranger from the North of Ireland. Hugh, being modest and naive agreed to work for One Pound per head in Commission so Mollaghans were getting all of the profit. Despite this they declined.

The following Wednesday back in London, he was too embarrassed and ashamed to go back to George Lonsdale and tell him that he could not deliver the cattle but after a long talk with Irene decided it was the decent thing to do. He was warmly received at Lonsdale House. The young man from Northern Ireland told George the problems over finance. Lonsdale said *"How much do you need?"* and Hugh said *"Sixty Thousand Pounds."* George Lonsdale called his secretary and asked her to bring his cheque book then asked Hugh who to make the cheque out to. Hugh answered *"the Mollaghan Brothers"* and Lonsdale gave him Sixty Thousand Pounds on the spot. Hugh went back to the flat and told Irene, gave up his job and flew to Dublin with the cheque for Sixty Thousand Pounds for the first six hundred Cattle. His commission was Six Hundred Pounds or six months wages as a Butcher in London.

Hugh somewhat in *"awe"* of the Mollaghans and their reputation duly gave them the cheque for Sixty Thousand Pounds and he was in business. The first load of six hundred Cattle took ten days to put together and it was arranged for the French buyer to fly in to inspect the cattle. The six hundred Cattle all in Mollaghans yard outside Longford were beautiful

Hereford cattle and perfect for the English market. However, they were too fat for the Continental trade and the buyer didn't want them. As the buyer could not speak English, young John Lyons was sent for, the son of the owner of the local meat factory as John could speak French. The result was the buyer didn't want the cattle, only leaner plainer cattle suitable for the French market. As no one had previously shipped cattle to France this was a new exercise for all parties. The Frenchman left in disgust, John Mollaghan went to bed and sulked for twenty four hours. Hugh was devastated. It was agreed that Hugh would sell the six hundred purchased cattle to England and the Mollaghans would buy six hundred Leaner Cattle. This accident was very fortuitous as Hugh contacted numerous abattoirs in England and sold the cattle by weight. It equally showed Mollaghans a good profit. So he was in business at One Pound per head selling six hundred Cattle per week to France and a further six hundred Cattle per week to England. Life had never looked better and Hugh purchased a house in London and based himself there selling cattle on behalf of Mollaghans.

After a couple of successful years as the agent for Mollaghans, Hugh got to know all the other livestock buyers who were shipping cattle to the UK and came into contact with Crawford Scott who used to purchase cattle for Mollaghans in Northern Ireland. Crawford was a legend in his own lifetime having been bankrupt on several occasions and was the *Al Capone* of the cattle business. Crawford who couldn't read or write had a photographic memory and could recall the cost of an individual animal many months after purchase despite handling thousands of cattle per week. It was agreed that Crawford and Hugh would go into business together and base their operation in Belfast rather than London so Hugh purchased a house in the Antrim Road, Belfast and they formed UK Meat and Livestock.

Crawford was doing all of the livestock buying. He was second to none. Hugh was selling the cattle to the English abattoirs on a deadweight basis when they met Gregory Shapiro.

Gregory was the original city gent. Pin-striped suit, grey tie, waist coat and he had great connections in the south of France as well as Paris for the sale of live cattle. His main clients being the company Muerel of Nice. Gregory went to meet all the auctioneers in Ulster with Crawford and it was agreed that Shapiro would buy the cattle in his own name and Crawford was appointed the agent. It took one year for Gregory to catch the Ulster auctioneers for over £1 million despite keeping up his first class lifestyle in Victoria, London, complete with original paintings, houseboy and maid.

Gregory had lost a lot of money on the gambling tables of Monte Carlo and London Casino's which caused his bankruptcy. It was agreed that Gregory now bankrupt would act as an agent with all his connections in France for UK Meat and Livestock. After about twelve months, Gregory had taken Crawford and Hugh for Sixty Thousand Pounds.

Hugh heard that Gregory was in Dublin staying at the Gresham Hotel so he got Crawford into the car and said *"Let's go to Dublin, I'm going to throw Shapiro out of the hotel window"* to which Crawford replied *"Hugh, let's please get the Sixty Thousand Pounds first and then throw him out of the window!"*. Gregory eventually paid in dribs and drabs over the next ten years and the writer actually collected the last payment in 1974 and acted as the peacemaker between Gregory and Hugh. Gregory once more became the agent of Hugh for a couple of years in the 1970's after this peace making mission. Gregory, without doubt, had the connections. He could and would have been a great *Meat Baron* in his own right but for his weakness. *compulsive gambling*. When the writer brought Gregory back to the Irish meat trade in 1973, it was the talk of the country, however, he was a wise old man in his mid seventy and only wanted a chance to prove he could still perform, and perform he did with excellence.

When UK Meats had cash flow problems in the early 1960's, Hugh had to go to the Banks alone as Crawford by his very name was a sure way of being refused by the Banks. Despite the fact Crawford was over his most recent bankruptcy and travelling very well financially, business just went on improving until 1968 when Wilson Coulter came on the scene and wanted live cattle to go to Libya. This was just prior to the Gadaffi coup. Today the Libyan Market is recognised as one of the best in the world. Despite all the political sanctions of the last twenty five years, Libya takes ten thousand Live Cattle every week from Ireland and now Australia. During the fuel crisis of 1974 Libya kept Ireland supplied with oil in exchange for cattle.

Coulter was one of those men with the most amazing connections but never had the ability to trade himself. When the Libyans were due to arrive in Belfast he said to Crawford *"Be very careful what you say. I told these men you are the Biggest cattle man in Ireland"*, to which Crawford replied, *"You told the Arabs right, I AM the Biggest Fucking Cattleman in Ireland!"* Crawford went on to ask Coulter how he was getting to the airport to meet the delegation and Coulter informed him he was going on the bus. There Coulter was, pulling off one of the biggest cattle deals to ever come to Ireland and he couldn't afford a car.

Crawford and Hugh took over the negotiations and the deal was set up and Coulter paid his commission. They heard no more from Coulter until one day he made contact wanting to supply Pots and Pans to Abu Dhabi. Crawford and Hugh had no interest but no doubt there was a second fortune to be made, one only has to look at Mohammad Al Fayed to realise the monies involved and profits to be made brokering for the Arabs.

Coulter eventually fronted for a Merchant Bank and purchased Moy Meats, one of the largest plants in Ulster and was kept on the Board as Managing Director. He retired a very wealthy man which goes to show *"You can't judge a book by its cover"*. Although late in life, Coulter made it in the end.

The cattle were going every week to Libya. One Sunday morning Hugh was relaxing at home in Belfast when he heard on the radio there was a military coup in Libya. He nearly died as there was one boat in Tripoli unloading, one on the way and one due to leave Greenoar. The next day, this loss would have broken Hugh and Crawford.

Crawford was dispatched to Tripoli taking Homer, his eldest son, when Hugh finally got hold of him on the Sunday evening. He asked Crawford *"How are things out there Crawford"* and which Crawford replied *"There's an awful lot of sand out here, Hugh"*. Hugh, totally at his wit's end was overhead to *say "Fuck the sand, Crawford, what about the money?"*. Crawford quietly said in his broad Belfast accent,

"The Wee Man is alright. We will get paid", and get paid they did via Russia. All Letters of Credit were honoured, which goes to show first hand who was behind the coup and placed Gadaffi where he is today. This also accounts for the political resentment the U.S.A. have held against Libya for the last twenty five years. Despite all his failures, Gadaffi was a good man for his people. Unlike other African States, you don't see *Beggars, Homeless or Poor People* in Libya. There is no *Starvation*. Needless to say Hugh and Crawford ceased dealing with Libya – too much aggravation!

Hugh and Crawford had Buyers in all parts of Ireland, North and South but the live cattle trade was coming to an end. Owen McWilliams was the Buyer in Co. Derry and he was the uncle of Charles Haughey, the junior Minister of Finance in the Jack Lynch's government in Dublin. Haughey had a farm at Ashbourne, County Meath. And Owen put the store cattle in and Hugh used to sell the finished animals.

There was an abattoir in Clones, Co. Monaghan with a very chequered history once owned by Archie Watson of Moy Meats, then owned by Ian Magahy of Lagan Meats. Hugh and Crawford, along with Tom Hennigan and Gerry Tierney floated a company and purchased the plant. They only put in Five Thousand Pounds each for the purchase in 1969 so they could now slaughter their cattle in Ireland. Hugh could sell the carcass to the UK and Europe as opposed to live cattle.

They had inherited a Plant Manager from Archie Watson, a man who had worked his way up from loading lorries at Newry called Eamon Mackle. Hugh realised the potential in the plant immediately and with his contacts now in Dublin could get IDA grants to expand the plant at no cost to himself and all to the government. First of all he had to get rid of the partners. This prize was too big to share. With that knowledge and connivance of Mackle, they ran the plant at huge losses for several months with Crawford and Hennigan taking their money and moving on. Crawford became the buyer of Irish Meat Packers in Dublin and Export Controller for Frans Buitilaar of Boston and went onto better things. Hennigan never forgave Hugh and also went onto Irish Meats Packers as a Buyer. However, his son, Mossy, became the biggest meat wholesaler in Dublin. Gerry Tierney left to join the Northern Bank Finance and left with enough profit to make the parting very sweet.

By 1970 Hugh had a £1 million Meat Plant but at the cost of the government and the contract for all the TB and Bruecelosis Reactor cows in the twenty six Counties of Ireland. His cup was overflowing when Charles Haughey was taken to court for smuggling arms and guns into Ireland for the I.R.A. Charlie lost his cabinet post, however, contacts were made and the I.D.A. and the Finance Office of the government continued to support Hugh. Charles, of course, made a come back as Prime Minister of Ireland.

Hugh most definitely did not fit in with the established Irish meat trade and no matter what he did, the Department of Agriculture would not give him a licence to export to the U.S.A. Eventually the department had to concede as Clones was a show piece of an abattoir. When granted the licence, Hugh did not have the capital to fill the stores with meat for the U.S.A. market. There were no containers in those days, all the meat went by Frozen Hold in lots of two hundred to three hundred tonnes.

Hugh told his tale of woe to Monty Guerenz, the Managing Director of Illinois Beef Company. Monty, like George Lonsdale fourteen years earlier said *"How much do you want, Hugh?"* And true to his word, Guerenz bankrolled the first shipment of beef to the States and paid for the storage and shipping. Hugh could always get good men to run with him.

Thomas Borthwick was one of the largest meat wholesalers in England and Roy Thompson who later became Chief Executive, was a Northern Ireland boy. He arranged for a *"small price"* to pay Hugh for his beef on a telexed copy of invoice before the meat left the plant. So every Monday, Borthwick would T.T. funds into the Clones account to 95% of full value, the balance was settled at the end of the week. Hugh had also learned in the early Seventies the French were so desperate for cheap Irish beef they would pay F.O.B. by Irrevocable Letter of Credit. So again, the cash was rolling in. In 1972 my name came to the attention of Hugh and a marketing team second to none was born.

Hugh had purchased a magnificent granite built manor

house in Clones for Three Thousand Five Hundred Pounds as Clones was a ghost town prior to the evolution of the meat works, situated on the border at the beginning of the troubles in 1969. No one in their right mind wanted to be there. Using his natural flair and what he had picked up in hotels throughout the world, he transformed this into a palatial home restoring all the wood panelling, built stables for his horses and even had the drive illuminated with all the old Belfast Gas Lights that were replaced in Belfast with electricity. The house, if in Dublin today, would make £3 million.

As well as increasing the business, my influence on Hugh caused him to lift his own personal image and exposure in the trade. I introduced Hugh to Swifts and had him made an honorary member of the Institute of Meat. I decided with Hugh we should bring Irene into the business coming into the office once a day. We then liveried the trucks in Hugh's colours. When I was in Portugal, Hugh rang him one night at midnight and said *"Bill, I am tired of everyone saying my plant is Charles Haughey's, equally tired of everyone thinking Mackle is the Boss. I am going to change the name to Tunney Meat Packers. What do you think?"* I was all for the idea so all the livery on the trucks was changed again to Tunney Meat Packers. Any contractor who wished to pull meat from the Clones plant was made to paint his trucks in Tunney's livery. This is quite common today with Coca Cola, Schweppes, etc, but unheard of in 1973 when I made the rule. Times were good and better to come with the EEC beef mountain and intervention.

In 1974 with the government buying the beef the profit was One Hundred Pounds per head and Clones was killing three thousand Cattle per week. My brother, Bruce Hayes, was the Production Manager and against impossible odds made the plant really tick for the first time. Killing three thousand Cattle with the same staff that were pushed to kill one thousand five hundred Cattle. The result of Bruce in increased production meant profits of Three Hundred Thousand Pounds weekly with a future as long as one could see. In 1974 Clones made £8 million clear Tax Free on all exports. This was now an empire with farms of one thousand acres, feedlots for two thousand Cattle as well as Enniskillen with projects costing a further £2 million. Tunney

Meat Packers was now a force in the Irish Meat Industry. Hugh was the first *IRISH MEAT BARON* and I was his *Right Hand Man.*

On my return home I had a meeting with Crawford and Tunney and it was decided I would go to London and persuade all my clients to return their business to Clones and *"Boycott"* Enniskillen. This being done the partners were now feeling the pressure of running the plant themselves. The one thing I could not allow was for them to know I was working with Tunney. One of my secretaries from the factory was keeping me daily informed of what was going on. Sadly while Margaret was in England collecting the children, I got into a very bad local scandal with the girl.

She had stayed the night at my house, not informing her parents or fiancée that she would not be home. They informed the police that she may have been kidnapped or murdered which was common in those years of the 1970's in Northern Ireland. The police came to my home in the early hours of the morning, finding me drunk and Betty naked in my drawing room. All would have been okay only for the fiancée being with the police and witnessing the whole scene. Making matters worse she was dismissed from the meat factory the next day for fraternising with the enemy, me.

By August 1974 we decided to tell our partners they could buy our 50% of the factory for the price of One Hundred Thousand Pounds. We were tired of losing money. They had a meeting and said we could buy *their* 50% for One Hundred Thousand Pounds. We gave them a cheque there and then on a Thursday evening at eight o'clock and went back to my house. We had purchased a $3 million asset for One Hundred Thousand Pounds.

I became the Managing Director. Hugh the Chairman and Irene Tunney, Hugh's wife the secretary. The first thing we did was take down all the signs and change the name to Tunney Meat Packers, Enniskillen. This was Hugh's hometown and everyone wants to go back to their home town as a success. My *"Coup"* had come off and I had got rid of all our partners. I felt ten feet tall and bullet proof. Then sadly Margaret lost the baby.

I had no written contract with Hugh. Everything we did

was on the shake of the hand. Having said this, I was unlimited in my expenses. I had accounts at all the best hotels, for my petrol, for my airline tickets, etc. I never needed money or cash. My cheque used to go in the bank each week and never get touched. The only real conflict we ever had was over my farm that I bought very cheaply off a relation of Hugh's, that was the first time he cried *"foul"*.

I purchased a large beautiful Tudor Mansion sat in one and a half acre of gardens in Enniskillen and Hugh asked me if I ever left or sold the house, could he buy it off me. The house was magnificent and now I was a king with a castle. My life was just getting better and better.

Oscar Wilde went to Pretora School in Enniskillen and when the "Great Hall" at Pretora was rebuilt, the paving stones or floor slabs were all taken to my house the *"Byways"* to make paths on the lawns and in the garden.

The *"Byways"* was steeped in recent history and just a lovely peaceful, tranquil place to live. I have always had a great admiration of Oscar Wilde and his natural wit and turn of phrase.

CHAPTER NINE

The day to day running of my plant began to bore me. All the dreams of a boy having my own plant, my own farm I had achieved with great results. I could have put my whole Devon operation in the corner of the yard at Enniskillen and it wouldn't have been noticed. My home was the best in the county, yet I was unhappy. So *wretched, restless* and *unhappy*. I was no longer the country boy with principles and dreams. I was known as the George Best of the Meat Business. I lived for *Booze and Fun*.

My bank refused to advance me money to buy cattle for my farm which I thought was very strange. They eventually gave me half of what I had asked. I later learnt that Hugh had given the instructions to my Bank, not to facilitate me in anything outside company business. This was a very painful blow to my ego and Plans.

Hugh loved to control people to the point of being quite Sadistic. I could never be controlled. I recall Jason Graham saying in Enniskillen, *"Hayes is like a Wild Horse. He would be a great Horse and win any race if only you could get a Bridle on him"*. This, of course, frustrated Hugh immensely.

Hugh had gone on a spending spree in the Republic buying Hotels and also was negotiating with Lord Vestey for the purchase of Abbey Meats in Belfast. This was the biggest meat operation in Europe at the time. I was becoming more and more restless and decided what I really wanted was to be a Broker. I envied the overseas brokers that came to our plant with their jet set lifestyle and beautiful secretaries. This was the life for me, a *Play Boy*, I suppose for want of a better word. I still had the problem going home. I never wanted to go home, not like Devon in Rose Cottage where I couldn't get home fast enough.

I had two children I loved to death. I took them out for Sunday lunch, took them to the farm with me. I adored my kids but was very unhappily married. This was no fault of Margaret. No person could have tried harder. This was all in between my ears. *The grass was always greener.* I became very violent at home when I eventually got there. I was a cruel wicked bastard of a husband. We had a lovely lady who took care of the children, Mrs Spratt and everyone knew I was a wild drunk. The only one who couldn't see how bad I was, *was me.*

I recall in 1974 two men coming to the mansion. They said they were from AA and could they talk to me. I went mad. Kicked them down the drive and abused Margaret for her cheek inviting them. I never gave them a chance to tell me what AA was all about. I drank gin by the bottle. Lunch time I would start then when I finished at the plant go to the hotel and drunk until ten to eleven each night, solitary *drinking on my own.* I would make any excuse for a trip to Dublin and go off with my various women. I was out of control totally.

I could only get a 50% mortgage on the *"Byways",* my mansion, so I paid the rest in cash. I had been killing some of my own cattle and selling them to a company in Fleetwood to raise the extra capital. I never even told Margaret what I was doing. Hugh found out from his network of spies what I had been doing and hit the roof. The net result was I went to Clones and after a blazing row, *I walked out.* This was in February 1975.

Ross Reid boasted to me a couple of years later he was, in fact, the informant. I had introduced Ross to Hugh Tunney when I did my Portugeuse contract. *"You can take the Boy from the Gutter but you can't take the Gutter from the Boy!"*

I told Margaret I was going to Devon for some time to myself and would ring her. I went to Devon taking Anne Carolyn, a girlfriend of mine and the travel agent rang Margaret to confirm the tickets on the Thirteenth of February 1975. Margaret realised I was not travelling alone. My marriage finished that day and I was free at last. I spent a week in Devon then returned home to live separate lives in the same house. No more deceit, no more lies, I was free to do as I pleased.

So by March 1975 I was drinking in the morning to get out of bed. Going to the hotel at lunch time and arriving home at three o'clock drunk as a skunk. One day Tunney came to the house and could make no sense of me. I returned home another day and Crawford was there. I again was legless. Hugh and Crawford would have done anything to get me well and so would Margaret but I was beyond help. Making matters worse I had plenty of money to drink as much as I wanted. I was twenty seven years old approaching twenty eight and a *useless, worthless drunk*. I lived from drink to drink. We had separate bedrooms and Margaret still tried to bring the children up normally. I didn't realise drink was my problem.

I was like a child in a sweet shop. After all the years of work, all the years of responsibility now I just gave up. Keeping my big house, my Jaguar and Mercedes cars, drinking to wake then drinking to sleep, it was awful. I was living in the same house as my wife and children yet so *Lonely, Guilty*, full of *Self-Pity*. Even now writing about those days makes me very sad. The damage I must have done to my children and my wife. I was helpless and hopeless.

I crashed my Twelve Thousand Pound Daimler Sovereign by hitting a tree whilst drunk. I left the car in the ditch and took a taxi home. Margaret said *"Where is the car, Bill?"* and I said *"I have put it up a tree"*, to which Edwina said *"Oh, you are a Clever Daddy, putting a car up a tree!"*.

My insurance was only Third Party so it was a total loss. This was five years pay to one of my men in the factory and I didn't blink an eye lid only sat down and had a gin and tonic. I then began to go everywhere by taxi if I was very drunk. Belfast, Dublin, one hundred miles by taxi and home again.

Insanity was not the word for my behaviour, no one could help me.

As opposed to being one of the most popular men in Devon, I was now without a doubt one of the most *Hated Men* in Enniskillen. I was a violent wife beating drunk. One of the contractors came up to me in the Killyhavelin who had done the central heating in the house said *"Bill, when are you going to pay me?"* I said, *"Fuck Off"*. He promptly belted me all around the bar. I was too drunk to fight back.

Margaret called the police several times and I was charged with assaulting her on two occasions. This, of course, was in the local papers so everyone knew of our problems. I had no idea what to do until one morning I woke up and still had to a half bottle of gin left. Drinking this so early in the morning made me as high as a kite. I then found the answer. I would go to South Africa and become a *Meat Baron* there. This was the place to go. I think I must have got the idea from a Wilbur

Smith book but the following day I was on my way to the Carlton Hotel in Johannesburg, sunny South Africa. This was going to be different.

My travel agent was used to me making trips at a minute's notice. I agreed Margaret keep the *"Byways"* and I would be in touch with her from South Africa when I had some plans. It was sad leaving the children but I was no use to anyone myself included and, of course, the children were seeing me drunk, falling all over the place as well as my violence to Margaret.

I recall an evening the wife of one of the Swifts executives coming to our door at the *Byways*. She said her husband was so drunk that she is in fear of her life and could she stay with us. I was quick to call this American Meat Executive a Callous Brute and a Drunken Fool yet I was worse than he knew how to be.

CHAPTER TEN

I had a hire car waiting for me at the airport courtesy of my travel agent. Then I was in the city of Johannesburg. I drove to the city centre and booked into my hotel. The Carlton at the Carlton Centre. This was the best hotel in town. I had a lovely suite. As this was late in the afternoon I was just in time for cocktails known as *Sundowners* in South Africa. All the office staff and business people meet up for an evening drink, prior to going home. So I was soon well pissed and alone in a new country.

The Hotel Manager was very obliging to me mainly because I always attracted a big crowd in the bar. I was the life and soul of the party. He arranged me introductions to the South African Meat Commission and several of the largest players in the South African Meat Industry. Anyone who stayed in the hotel connected with meat or farming were directed to me including Ian Smith, the former Prime Minister of Rhodesia who wanted to export cattle semen to Australia and New Zealand.

Ian was down in Johannesburg for a Rugby match at Ellis Park and wanted me to handle the export of cattle semen from Rhodesia on a worldwide basis.

The White regime in Rhodesia was coming to an end and Poor Ian was now clutching at straws to get what revenue he could for the country's white settlers.

I had met many colonial men like Ian Smith who fled to Devon and Cornwall after the Mau-Mau uprising in Kenya in the Fifties. Sadly, there was no compromise between Black and White. The White Colonials considered themselves *The Masters.*

South Africa at this time was a large exporter of meat to the rest of the African continent as well as the Middle East and Israel. Sadly, today they are dependant on imported meat. This was also the world's second largest exporter of wool.

I was offered two very good positions, one with Cyril Huruitz to manage his plant at Krugersdoorp killing five thousand Cattle per week. The second one with Andre Mouton running a new plant of smaller capacity at Heidelberg, sixty kilometres south of Johannesburg.

I became very friendly with a man called Bill King, who was a gold prospector. He had spent his life taking teams of miners around the country prospecting. He was obviously very successful as he had just purchased a new Rolls Royce from Jack Barclay, London and flown out the salesman from London with the car to have a holiday at his expense. This man Bill really was a character and a very heavy drinker.

Richard Burton and Liz Taylor were staying on the same floor as myself. They left the hotel to marry for a second time on a Game Reserve in Botswana and came back to the hotel. Life was one big party.

I became involved with the Mayor of Johannesburg's secretary, Lisa Livesey, a Jewish girl of my own age. She eventually moved into my suite and went to the office direct from the hotel at eight o'clock each morning. Lisa had no doubt of my drinking problem as I was going into alcoholic blackouts and had no recollection of the evening's events, the following day.

Only for Bill King and the Burtons, I might have taken up one of the opportunities offered to me, however, it was lunch time each day when I surfaced, straight to the bar and I was off on the merry-go-round again. When my money ran low, I rang Jack Taylor to telex me more. Jack, my solicitor, thought all the money was going into a business. It was going on my expenses. Jack sold my farm of one hundred and thirty acres and I spent all the proceeds during those months.

Paddy Ryan, the Irish Consulate to South Africa became a very Good Friend of mine and would call in for a Sundowner every evening on his way home. Paddy was a Limmerick man and had a *Wonderful Easy Going* manner.

He reminded me of Alec Guinness playing *"Our Man in Havanna"*, the Graham Green film. All day with nothing to do so one had to go through the motions of appearing busy. There was no trade between Ireland and South Africa in those days. Today, Ireland supply twenty thousand tonnes of Beef a year to South Africa.

I was very taken with Lisa and made all sorts of promises of a life together when I settled down in South Africa, yet when Bill King and the Burtons left the hotel, it was never quite the same.

I met a lady in Australia many years later who was working in the Carlton during this period and she knew me straight away and laughed about our antics which were the talk of the town. I decided I had had enough and would go back to Ireland, sort out Margaret and the house and return to Africa when my house was in order.

CHAPTER ELEVEN

I got as far as Belfast and stayed with a girl called Mary McGowan who I had met through Bruce. Bruce was now the General Manager of Abbey Meats in Belfast and had the top position in the European Meat Industry. I was several months in Belfast with Mary, who believed I was divorced. Then one day a private detective came to the house to seek grounds for Margaret's divorce. I invited him in, gave him a drink and he told me it was the simplest case he had ever undertaken. I was furious with Margaret as it was just a waste of money.

Mary was a very Black Protestant and her father and brother were both in the RUC.

We had some wonderful parties that were open house to both sides of the political divide.

I recall Trevor Hanna, the reputable Belfast journalist who would call around many evenings. John Hume who later went onto receive the Noble Peace Prize, was a very good friend in those days.

Religion and Politics went out of the window at our many parties.

I am sure Mary went onto make some man a wonderful wife. She most surely was a fine lady of the *utmost integrity*.

So I decided to move back to my big house in Enniskillen. This was not comfortable with Margaret yet great to be with the children again.

I was offered a position with Golden Vale Marts in the South of Ireland. They had built a giant meat works in Rathdowney, Co. Tipperary and offered me the position of Managing Director. This was a Farmers Co-op with Farmer Shareholders and it was an excellent opportunity.

I met the Company Secretary at Doncaster Races and Horse Sales in the autumn of 1975 to finalise things. I bumped into Peter Blackburn from Devon at the Sales. Peter had an abattoir at Chard in Somerset specialising in manufacturing cows. In 1970 Peter sold 49% of his business to Broole Bond Leibig, the makers of Fray Bentos and OXO for One and a Half Million Pounds. Peter now sat on the Brooke Bond Board of

Directors and after Lord Vestey, he was the most powerful meat man in England.

I had no dealings with Peter when I was in Devon but used to meet his father Tom at Launceston market on a Tuesday. Peter had just built a Seventy Thousand Pound House in Chard made from the Norman Granite Bridges that were being taken down in Devon and Cornwall in order to widen the roads. He was the most charming man and knew all about me so I introduced him to Michael Quade, the secretary of Golden Vale Marts.

I was to start at Rathdowney on the Monday and had agreed to sell my plain cows to Peter in Chard. I arrived at the local hotel in Rathdowney on the Sunday afternoon having again agreed Margaret keep the *"Byways"*. I would pay the mortgage on the house and give her Thirty Pounds weekly to take care of the children. Everyone was happy with the deal financially. My salary was Twenty Two Thousand Pounds per anum plus my expenses and 10% of net profit.

Matt Lyons Jnr had been involved with Golden Vale at the building of the plant which was formerly the old Guinness Brewery. Matt's wife, Peggy was the doctor in the village. I remember drinking in the bar of the hotel and nothing more until the next day. It was midday Monday, when I woke up. I should have been at the plant at seven o'clock in the morning. I was in the worse withdrawal of my life so had a couple of drinks, a *Hair of the Dog*.

For the first time drink didn't work as it always had in the past. I thought I was going to die. I drove to Peggy Lyons, the doctor, to see what was the matter with me. She told me I was in acute alcoholic withdrawal. She telephoned a taxi immediately and sent me ninety miles to St John of God Hospital in Dublin. I have no memory of my first week in hospital only the second week. I was taking these pills full of liquid called Heminevrin. They made me as high as a kite. They are used to wean you slowly off alcohol.

Feeling better, I discharged myself against advice of the doctors and took a taxi to Rathdowney. I went straight to the office of Michael Quade and apologised for being late. *I was ten days late*. Michael Quade told me they could no longer use my services. I had made such a spectacle of myself in the hotel. The word had got back to the Directors of the Co-op that *I was a Madman as well as a Drunk.*

Michael had done a deal with Peter Blackburn that Peter would put in a management team from England and market all the meat. The deal was done. However, he kindly told me he would always sell cattle to me, *if the price was right.* So my tail between my legs, I drove back to Enniskillen.

Basil Dean, the Manager of Hatherleigh Abattoir, four miles from my village, became the new Manager of Rathdowney. He was a nice Somerset man of my age and a pupil of Peter Blackburn from Chard.

Margaret must have been able to see what I couldn't see. I was on the slippery slide to nowhere. I had become unemployable by anyone.

John Lyons rang me one day and told me he had some Italian Buyers who wanted to buy calves in England for live shipping to Italy. I met the men in Dublin and made the arrangements to take them to England.

I drove them down to Devon and Somerset and we met Frank Patton, the biggest calf dealer in the South West England. It was agreed we would fly one plane load a week of two hundred and forty Calves to Italy. I chartered a plane from Manston Airport in Kent and flew across with the first load. I made Two Thousand Five Hundred Pounds profit. The Italians spending two days with me had no doubt I was a drunk and after the second load I ran the business from Ireland.

The result was by the third load they dealt with Patton direct and cut me out. I had Five Thousand Pounds for two days work and just let the business go without any concern, throwing away Five Thousand Pounds weekly.

Margaret had come to the end of the road by Christmas 1975 and decided to move back to England. I was angry when she left and refused to allow William to go. So William and myself were alone in the big house. I took William with me on all my drinking tours.

Things were so bad I was asked to leave hotels in Dublin as I was making a spectacle of myself. I was driving around the country drunk with William in the car. I would take

William to the races and never leave the bar. It really was pitiful. I was still involved with Mary McGowan. She helped me somewhat but I couldn't take care of myself let alone my seven year old son.

I decided for Christmas of 1975 it would be nice for William to go to Bob's for a holiday. At least he would be with a normal family. I bought him clothes all modern with flairs the same as my own along with platform shoes and put him on the plane. Poor William, I thought he looked so good. Years later he told me how embarrassed he was the way I dressed him. I was now living in the *"Byways"* on my own.

The police turned up one morning over a cheque for One Thousand and Two Hundred Pounds I had given to a man for sheep, *"Postdated"*. I was very rude to them and they charged me. Jack Taylor said *"There is no Jury in Enniskillen will convict you, Bill"*. Making matters simpler, I pleaded guilty and was given a nine month suspended sentence. I didn't realise then that this would cost me dearly in years to come by adding to my criminal record, yet again!

I didn't know what to do by the New Year of 1976. Jack told me I should sell up, dry out and start again. Jack arranged a private sale of the house. I sent all the furniture and paintings to Margaret except my Punch and Judy painting from Devon. Jack took care of this. I took the money from the sale off Jack in cash and purchased a new Lotus sports car. I left Ireland with all my clothes in my car and very little money. The car was just a pointless extravagance. I was a poser, *Jack the lad*, with flashy clothes and flashy car and no substance.

I called to see Bruce on my way out of Ireland and crashed my car into the congregation of his village church coming out of mass. Thank God no one was hurt. My new car was fibreglass it spoilt the look of the car and I had to get it repaired taking the balance of my money. Bruce lent me money and I gave him the deeds of my land in Longford where years earlier I was going to build my new family home. So I drove on the ferry to England and went to see William who had started at the local school in Bob's village.

There I was in the Spring of 1976 nearly twenty nine years old and I was already a *"Has Been"*. William told me he missed Margaret and Edwina and wanted to be with them. I rang Margaret and the next day met her in London and handed William over. When I saw the two children together, I knew it was the right decision.

Bob was very angry with me at the time. However, give Bob his due. He arranged with his local doctor get me in a private clinic to *dry out.* I went through all the motions of the interview then as opposed to going into the clinic, chose to leave Bob's home and go my own way. Bob washed his hands off me that day as I would not take help when it was offered. I still couldn't see that drink was my problem. Today I realise my behaviour was nothing to do with *moral fibre* I was suffering from a very serious disease, alcoholism.

My plan was to go back to killing sheep on the slaughterhouse floor. I always knew I could get a day's pay. I was so used to the high life *"Champagne drinker's tastes now with a Beer drinker's income"*. I went to Lamberhurst in Kent and worked two days, Hastings in Sussex and worked two days and eventually ended up at Walton-on-the-Hill with Curly Bell, who had been a guest at my wedding, working on the kill floor.

Curly Bell was the Partner of Doug Clay. Doug was the biggest and most wealthy cattle exporter in England. I had bought lambs and cattle for Doug from being a Boy. Clay was a total extrovert like Crawford Scott, bounced on the very fine line between Insanity and Genius.

Doug was always being exposed on TV and in the Press for Cruelty to Animals in the live shipping days. This was caused by the Animal Rights people. I recall seeing him once on camera chasing these Protesters away from his boats at Sheerness in Kent. Doug waving his stick and swearing.

Doug called into Rolls Royce in Camberley, Surrey, one day to collect a new Rolls. The Manager said, *"Mr Clay, there is a two month waiting list for a new Rolls"*. Doug left, came back two hours later, sacked the Manager and took the Rolls from the Showroom. He had bought the Garage.

Doug had two homes and two families. One at Battle near Hastings, Sussex and one at Gloucester. He always told me to wear a hat in cold weather to keep my *Brains Warm.* He was quite serious.

Bob Burkett, Curly Bell's foreman, was working in Brussels for Doug and received a phone call one day to go to Brussels airport and take the suitcase out of the Mercedes that Clay kept in Belgium. Bob got to the airport, the car was not locked and he took the suitcase out of the boot. He placed it in the Mess Room at the abattoir in Brussels and forgot all about it. Three weeks later Doug arrived in Brussels and asked Bob where the case was. Bob got it from the Mess Room and gave it to Clay.

Bob was flabbergasted when Clay opened the case as it contained One Hundred Thousand Pounds in used Ten Pound Notes. This was in the 1960's, at least a couple of million on today's values.

Curly ran the meat end of the business and supplied the British Embassies with meat in all parts of the world. They had built a high-tech abattoir at Walton-on-the-Hill in Surrey, close to Epsom Downs.

Arthur Pitt, the successful Horse Trainer at Epsom, is a son-in-law of Curly. Between the two of them, Clay and Bell, milked the Brussels Subsidy *Gravy Train* for every Penny they could before the rest of England realised it existed. They were very clever men doing things well before their time.

I told Curly I was my brother, Bruce, as I was only ten stone with hair on my shoulders. I bore no resemblance to Bill Hayes of Devon, a fifteen stone Country boy. I was earning Two Hundred Pounds weekly and spending Two Hundred Pounds weekly. I stuck it out for a couple of months until I had to go back to Enniskillen for a Court case. Margaret was suing me for Maintenance. I spent a week in Blackpool borrowing Five Hundred Pounds cash off one of my clients in Fleetwood, then returned to Ireland for the day for my case.

When I arrived at Court the Bailiff seized my car as Maintenance for Margaret and the court sentenced me to three months in prison, for failing to pay Maintenance. There was consideration given to the fact Margaret had all the furniture. I had paid her weekly into her bank, the only person who could get me out of trouble was Margaret. I wrote to her from prison and she wrote back and told me to *Go to Hell.*

Margaret had made William a *Ward of Court* in

conjunction with my parents-in-law. Now she was getting her *revenge* on me. There was no one going to benefit by my being in prison. Jack Taylor, my solicitor, never forgave Margaret and there I was in the Crumlin Road Prison, Belfast, with no Right of Appeal.

In 1976 it was the height of the political problems in Northern Ireland, so most of the prisoners were IRA or UVF. There were very few English men there only a couple of English soldiers, who were on Protection. There was an awful time each day we had to work in a wood yard, splitting these giant tree trunks by hand and chopping them up for firewood. It really was soul destroying. My father had been very ill in hospital with a perforated ulcer and the only person who wrote to me was my mother.

I eventually got a job as a cook in the Officer's Mess and it was quite bearable. There were some very sorry cases in Belfast jail at this time on both sides of the Political Fence. The whole prison was guarded by the British Army with loaded guns.

I was there out of spite of my ex-wife who had just taken my car. Yes, I was a Bad Husband, yes I was a Drunk, but I don't believe I deserve to be locked in prison for any of my behaviour. I was in prison for a Debt. I was a very sickman with a disease that was killing me.

There was a famous escape from Crumlin Road during my time there. Many Ballads and Songs have been written about this.

Twenty two IRA prisoners were playing Football in the prison and suddenly all ran to the wall. They made a human ladder going onto each other's shoulders and climbed over the wall. Sixteen prisoners escaped.

I have said in the previous chapter that Peace in Ulster was not only possible but inevitable.

There were two RUC officers who took me from Enniskillen to Crumlin Road Prison, Belfast, some ninety miles. These decent young men could see I was hanging out for a drink so they stopped the police car at Dungannon and bought me a couple of shots of vodka.

I have met some wonderful people from all walks of life.

CHAPTER TWELVE

I came out of Crumlin Road Prison, Belfast, one morning in June 1976. I had Ten Pounds in my pocket and no idea what I was going to do. I rang Jack Taylor and he wired me Two Hundred Pounds to the main post office in Belfast after going for a haircut. I went to the Europa Hotel my old stomping ground. The Europa had been blown up twenty nine times during the Troubles from 1969, yet still was the favourite haunt of anyone who was anyone in Belfast or people visiting Belfast. All my belongings were in one small suitcase.

I rang Tunney and told him of my plight. Bruce had left the Tunney group to run a Bacon factory in the Republic. This was a step forward for Bruce being the largest Bacon factory and cannery in the British Isles.

Hugh told me he would have a car in Belfast that day and pick me up at the Europa. The car came for me at around four o'clock in the afternoon and we drove to Clones.

Hugh was in financial difficulties and in the process of selling his hotels as well as the factories and farms. He had split up from his wife Irene and was living in the *Penthouse Suite* at the Gresham in Dublin, travelling to Clones daily in his Rolls Royce. It was very embarrassing for both of us but Hugh gave me a working Brief.

My duties were to go around the three plants and recommend improvements where I saw fit. He gave me a new Audi car and I was to live in the Westenera Hotel in Monaghan. The first hotel we had bought together. This was a Friday evening so he gave me a couple of hundred Pounds pocket money and I moved into the hotel.

The same night I met Bernadette, whose father owned the local newspaper and we became involved. It was a wonderful weekend, all my legal troubles were over and I was back with Tunney, albeit at a minor post that had been especially created for me.

Hugh had been offered the Castle of Lord Mountbatten along with one thousand four hundred acres of rough grazing in 1973 when I joined him. At that time Hugh was in no position to take on such a commitment.

As things got better in 1976 we negotiated a twenty five year lease on the castle and the grounds and all possessions with the exception of the month of August. In August, the Royal Family would use the castle for their annual Fishing Holiday in Ireland.

Very sadly, the death of Lord Mountbatten was at the castle in 1978. Lord Louis had a very soft spot for Hugh and invited him many times to Broadlands, his home in England.

Once more, I could see how people change. Hugh was very anti-English and was always coming out with remarks like the *"Bastard Queen"*. However, to see him *"cow tail"* to the Mountbattens was quite sickening. Hugh was himself quite a groveller. This very *anti-English* sentiment is very much based on Jealousy as well as the reality of the hard time given to the Irish over the centuries.

The executives at Clones and Abbey Meats was very very jealous at my return namely John Copass and Ross Reed. These men had been employed during my time at Enniskillen and had both obtained their positions by grovelling and creeping to Hugh. Which, of course, Hugh loved. They resented my position with Hugh again. No matter, I went about my work seeing Bernedette on a daily basis. I brought my ex-foreman, Sandy from Leicester to Ireland and placed him in Abbey Meats and we got the plants to go well. Meanwhile, Hugh was spending his time organising the sale of the farms and hotels.

My drinking was very very bad and I had no time for these executives of Hugh's and let them know my contempt for them. I arranged the sale of cattle to the Israeli government which was a huge contract meaning four Rabbis to be placed in Belfast on a permanent basis to do the ritual slaughter. Dr Cohen, the Israeli Minister of Agriculture told me if my Nanna was Jewish. My mother was Jewish, therefore, by birth I was a Jewish. This was quite a pleasant shock.

I made the peace between Hugh and Gregory Shapiro, an old adversary of Hugh's and we began shipping these cattle again to Nice.

Muerells of Nice were the people I had done business with for Hugh years before. Muerells were the people that sent the limousine for me during my stay in Monte Carlo. Muerell himself was a very successful Jewish meat importer and did a large business with Frans Buitilaar in England as well as Gregory Shapiro and the CR Barron Group, London.

The more successful I was the more resentment I received from the executive staff. Crawford Scott said *"Just hold on there Billy and you will be back where you were"*. I believe today my drinking was so bad this was not possible. Bernadette kept me in some control but I became very dependent on her. I couldn't sleep with the lights out and was a very *frightened drunken man.*

After about two months one Sunday evening a bomb was placed at the factory and exploded. As it didn't go off properly little damage was done but enough to close the plant. I had taken Bernadette home at six o'clock that morning having spent the night together. When I arrived at the factory the police had it cordoned off. So I went to the Leonard Arms in Clones for my Breakfast. The daughter of Jim Meiliff, the Landlord of the Lennard Arms, married Barry McGuigan the World Champion Boxer who is now a Sports Commentator with Sky Television.

About nine o'clock in the morning, the local Police Sergeant came into the dining room and put his hand on my shoulder and arrested me under the *Terrorist Act* for planting the bomb.

At first I thought this was a joke. However, I was taken to Monaghan Police Station and kept there for three days while my clothes were sent to Dublin for forensic checks. Bernedette came to the police station as my alibi. Despite being the daughter of the most prominent man in the town, she was not believed. I later learnt I had been *"set up"* by John Copass, who was then the Company Secretary of Clones, along with Eamon Fergus the Managing Director.

When I was released I confronted Copass who laughed in my face and denied all liability. The following morning I didn't appear for work. I had had enough of *people pleasing* those awful little men, Reed and Copass. Copass rang Hugh the following day saying I was drunk at work and if he didn't sack me all the staff were going to walk out. I should have defended myself yet I was relieved to walk out. I have never forgiven Copass or Reed for the spiteful way they treated me. I recall Ross Reed boasting I would never be as rich as him. My wealth today exceeds the combined assets of Reed and Copass, and I earned every penny myself as a man not *riding on someone else's star.*

Peter Blackburn told me years ago that one must be so careful on the *way up* as you meet the same people on the *way down.*

Ross Reed was from Newbliss in County Monaghan and did accountancy at Queen's University, Belfast. Ross was involved with a Belfast girl and when he graduated she refused to go to Brazil with him, he had been offered a good job there.

Ross took a job with a firm of Undertakers called Browns of Belfast and during his period with them purchased the Transport Business which was very run down. The fact that Browns financed the purchase over a twelve year period allowed Ross to build the company up very successfully and he renamed it *Interland Transport.*

Ross made his first big money on my Portuguese contract and when the contract was over purchased his wife Barbara her first Mink Coat.

Ross and Barbara were both very short and extremely overweight. The image of them copulating would put a lot of people off sex for a lot of years.

We found Copass working in London and he was an old school friend of Liam Marks, a man we had head-hunted from the IDA in Dublin. We secured Copass at Three Thousand Five Hundred Pounds per annum along with a small cottage and company car. His wife was a nice girl, however, Copass was a typical *small minded* accountant. Good at his job and *Very, Very Tame.* He was not, however, a leader of men rather a counter of figures.

I had a long chat with Bernadette and decided to go and see William and Edwina for the weekend. The previous two occasions I had been to see them Margaret had me arrested on both occasions for being drunk. So my previous two visits I had spent in Preston Police Cells for the weekend. I checked into the Crest Hotel in Preston and Margaret brought the children to me there. It was marvellous to see them again and Margaret was surprised that I was sober. I hasten to add I was only sober for the day. The meeting went well and I flew back to Ireland. Margaret was even more surprised I was back with Tunney. I never told her I had just finished with him again.

I went to hospital a couple of times in alcoholic blackouts but soon discharged myself the following day when I felt better. Sandy had told me about one of my ex employees from Leicester, Paul Frangus. He had become a Property Developer in Cardiff and was running around Cardiff in a white Rolls Royce. I rang Paul up and he invited me over to see him.

The white Rolls Royce turned out to be a white Rover, the Property Development was Property Maintenance. However, Paul helped me get a new car on finance and introduced me to George Williams of Anglican Windows. George agreed to train me as a Salesman selling Double-Glazing. His operation was a very good very clever business.

George would advertise his windows and home extensions in all the national press every weekend. The salesman then would call to the responses and sell the windows on a finance package. The salesman then collected 10% deposit. This deposit paid the salesman's commission. The finance company paid George in full for the windows, average price of Three Thousand Pounds per house. George then pocketed this money for two months prior to delivery, the money paying for the windows and leaving a good profit. The finance company then gave George a 5% kickback which paid for all the advertising. This was a perfect way of trading on *O.P.M.* (other people's money). George reckoned I could earn Two Thousand to Three Thousand Pounds per week quite easily so I signed up to go on his course.

George O'Keefe who was in the same business went onto purchase *Pilkington Glass, Royal Doulton China, Warwicke Castle, Madame Toussads, Bangor Racecourse* and eventually the *"Financial Times"*.

George O'Keefe was a very good friend to me in later years.

CHAPTER THIRTEEN

The Sales Course was at Portsmouth about two hundred miles from Cardiff. I stopped on the Saturday at Bath in Somerset and recall buying bottles of champagne for the people in the bar. I arrived at the hotel in Portsmouth on the Sunday evening and went straight for the bar. All the other men on the course were so *very typical salesmen* and all of them *"YES"* men. I got well oiled but was ok for the course the next day. Salesmen can't be taught they are born. All I needed to know was the *Product* and the *Price*.

The Monday night it was back to the bar with the lecturer who was the Top salesman in the company controlling a staff of several hundred salesman nationwide. I drank my usual rations and blacked out. I have no recollection of the rest of the evening. I do recall going to the Hotel kitchen in the middle of the night for food. I pissed my bed and woke up at noon the following day. The bar refused to serve me so I went to the hotel next door.

When I eventually got to the course there was a deadly hush. The lecturer in charge said, *"You ran up a bar bill of Sixty Pounds last night"*. I said *"I thought I drank more than that, the way I feel"*. He proceeded to tell me I had been sacked. They would settle the hotel bill and could I kindly leave. I couldn't get out of there quick enough.

I drove north and eventually come to Arundel in Sussex where I booked into the Arudel Arms. I had a good session of drink and agreed to take the barmaid out for a drive over the Downs that afternoon.

We drove over the Downs and I went to see Doug Clay's brother to borrow some money. Doug was in Belgium and as no one at the abattoir knew me. So empty handed I went back to the hotel with the barmaid. The owners of the hotel were away. The barmaid was a lovely girl whose husband was in prison and we arranged to meet again that night when the bar closed.

I took a gin and tonic and sat in the TV lounge. This rather nice English gentleman came in and sat down talking. We were watching a movie on the television. After about fifteen minutes he said, *"Mr Hayes, I am arresting you for deception booking into a hotel with no money"*. I said, *"I only have to make a phone call to get money"*. He said, *"We will talk at the station"*.

He took my car and sent it back to the finance company in Cardiff and I was remanded to Lewis Prison for two weeks to appear in court. At the court like a fool, to get it over with, I pleaded guilty and received a six month suspended sentence. By now my Criminal Record was building on a monthly basis.

I walked out of the court with not the price of a cup of tea. I rang my mother who sent me Thirty Pounds and I made my way to Bournemouth. It was coming up to Christmas 1976. I stayed with Barbara and David who only had one restaurant left in Bournemouth. One night drunk I left the fat fryer on and the restaurant burned down. Poor David, it was his only source of income. He had lost all his money and the family homes on a failed building development in Cornwall. I felt so very sorry for him and suggested they pack the furniture, move to Ireland and start again. This way, he could avoid bankruptcy.

We contacted Bruce who agreed to put them up and take care of them. We sent all the furniture over on an empty meat truck and they were safe so I moved back with my parents. It was awful, really awful. My father had just got over his operation and had been very ill. I was being treated like a naughty boy.

I got a job as a dishwasher in a Turkish restaurant for Five Pounds a night. I was sacked in the second week for being Drunk. I then used to apply for jobs in the *Meat Trades Journal* as a slaughter man. You always got your travelling expenses and the money was good. I had no transport now, no money, all the money I got went on booze. I recall at various times going to Swindon Wiltshire, Gloucester, North Wales, Norfolk, Essex, Andover, all these abattoirs paid my expenses and about Fifty Pounds per day which was good money in the 1970's, yet I drank it all. I always lived in pubs and the money just went. I was a gypsy going from town to town. I always used a pseudo name, too ashamed to use my own name.

Then one day the police came to the door of my

mother's house. They had driven two hundred and fifty miles over a taxi bill for Thirty Two Pounds and I was taken away in handcuffs, two hundred and fifty miles to court. After two days in the cells, I was Fined and ordered to pay the money. I was then re-arrested and taken to Norfolk, three hundred miles away over a Bar Bill of Seven Pounds and Fined again. Finally I was again arrested and taken to Preston over a Hotel Bill of Thirty Pounds when I had been visiting the children. The reason I didn't pay that Bill was because Margaret had got me arrested for Drunk and Disorderly and I spent the weekend in the police cells.

Despite all of this I again pleaded guilty. Making matters worse I was once again arrested and taken to Birmingham over a Thirty Pound cheque that I had cashed. The cheque had bounced and I had repaid the money so in the years of 1976-1977 I built up a very large police file of my *misdemeanours*. The Police CRA file that doesn't give the details of the circumstances or the amounts of money, merely saying deception. Despite being only Petty Bar Bills, it appears on file the same as *Millions*. The words *"Guilty of Deception"*.

The results of all this drinking trouble was that wherever I was stopped by the police this awful record is on file, no one cares as to the circumstances or events. It's just Bill Hayes, *Con Man*, *Thief*, rather than Bill Hayes, *Chronic Alcoholic*.

I left Birmingham not knowing what to do. I was too ashamed to go to my parents, so I phoned a friend called Edna who was a hairdresser in St. Neots, Cambridge, the first place I had gone on leaving Devon. She was wonderful to me and cleaned me up. Bought me new suits and got me together, weaning me off the booze rather than stopping me. I began to play golf, got my head together and began to look in earnest for a decent job. My problem then was my impatience. I was also feeling very trapped with Edna who was in love with me.

I was offered a good job in Iran with Meile & Co. A good job in Chelsmford with John Hughs, the man who I bought cattle for in Devon. I could have done anything if I could stay off the booze long enough. However, I chose once more to have a go at being a slaughter man at Waltham Abbey in the East End of London. This was the winter of 1977.

I was living in the Royal Oak Hotel run by the father of the England Footballer, Terry Venebles. I was treated well but my body was very weak with the booze. I was thirty years old and a physical wreck. After two days work, I rang Edna to come and take me home.

I had one last go at Baxters Abattoir in Northampton. This lasted only three days then before Edna collected me, I bumped into John Sharkey, my old Meat Inspector from my abattoir in Devon. He was very very kind to me but I was so deeply ashamed of how I had fallen. I declined his invitation to go home and meet his wife and family again.

So after a long talk with Edna, I rang Tunney. Tunney gave me a job straight away as his troubleshooter based in the UK. Despite my failure and my physical mess I still had no idea alcohol was my problem. I honestly believed *"Well, yes. I do drink too much sometimes, but that's okay"*.

I had known so many alcoholics from being a little boy in Devon to all my years in England and Ireland. The previous two years had been nothing but trouble, work trouble and more trouble. Like Mr. Macawber in the Dickens novel I thought *"something with turn up"*. I was going to bed every night praying I would not wake up. This to me was normal. I never expected to reach my Thirtieth Birthday now here I was thirty years old, broke, drunk, with no hope of any future. Making matters worse I had lost the ability to work. I had not got the strength to kill sheep. At least not work a full day. I had seen so many men like me but I couldn't see my own problems. *I was sick and tired of being sick and tired.*

During those previous couple of years I had several times turned up at Bob's office to borrow money, causing some embarrassment to him as I was always drunk and loud. Poor old Bob always paid me. My mother bailed me out on numerous occasions and so had Bruce in my last days in Ireland. The world could see I had become a Derelict yet I couldn't see it at all.

I have nothing but praise for the kindness shown to me by Hugh Tunney. Hugh knew the Real Bill and what I could and should have been doing with my life.

Poor dear Jack Taylor affectionately referred to me as his *Lame Duck*. Jack always believed one day I would come *Good*.

The number of offences I eventually had on my C.R.O. police record exceeded Twenty. The total value of all my alleged Deceptions (95% pertain to taxis fares, hotel bills and bar bills), wouldn't buy a week's cheap package holiday! However, these antecedents were to *Haunt* me for the next twenty years.

CHAPTER FOURTEEN

I found rather a nice four bedroom furnished house in Northampton and moved in. That was the end of my association with Edna. My home was close to the County Cricket Ground in Northampton. This being the nearest pub, became my local. The chief executive of Northampton Cricket Club had a secretary called Terri Crawley. She was a very stunning red haired girl of twenty eight and we became very friendly.

Terri used to organise Rock Concerts every week at the county ground to raise money for the County Cricket Club. Her best friend Sue was an executive with WEA Records. Sue had access to all the top groups, Susie Quatro, Led Zeppelin, Leo Sayer, Manhattan Transfer, Status Quo, Pink Floyd to name but a few. She invited me to one of these Saturday evenings. I had no interest in Heavy Rock but plenty of interest in Terri.

She introduced me to the local wine wholesalers and I filled my house with Whiskey, Gin, Champagne and Wines. The wholesaler was an Irish man and just the mention of Tunney and the Gresham, my credit was unlimited. So there I was in Northampton with all the booze I would ever need, a relatively nice home, car and a wonderful job with Tunney again. The beauty of the job was I had *no rules*, didn't have to mix with his juvenile executives, merely sell the cattle and check the deliveries. It was superb.

I was in love with Terri. She was all the things I wanted, glamorous, intelligent, great sense of humour. Terri had been married at sixteen and had a daughter from this union, Andrea. She lived at the village of Stoke Bruerne, a small stone built country village on the Grand Union Canal with just a village shop and village pub and few cottages.

I was spending more time at the cottage and less at the house. We drank heavily and partied at lot and I would never get to bed until four o'clock every morning. Waking up with a glass of whiskey, I would lie in bed and do all my meat selling from there. I was selling the production of all three of Tunney's factories each day before I got up and dressed.

When there was a problem with meat that Ross Reed had sold or Copass sold, I was sent to re-sell the meat that was already in the UK. Eventually Reed sold Two Hundred and Fifty Thousand Pounds worth of meat to a company called Hawker of Chard that went broke. Then he sold £2 million worth of meat to a German company that also went broke. This forced Tunney to sell Abbey Meats. Reed went with the package. Reed was soon demoted to the job of a telephone salesman based in Dublin with the new owners, Agra Trading, a German firm.

The only travelling involved in my brief was on problem loads. I would sometimes be in London, Bedford or Manchester. All in all it was a very simple brief. I was paid weekly and the money went as fast as I got it. Terri gave up her job at the cricket club, I gave up the house and moved into the cottage.

There was a fly in the ointment. Terri's ex husband Alan. He was thirty two when he married Terri, she was sixteen. Their first child died in infancy. They were divorced when Andrea, the second child, was only a couple of months old. The divorce was very bitter with Alan snatching the baby and hiding it at his mother's until the custody orders were settled. He just wanted to exert his power over Terri. He was always late with the Maintenance Money and generally Disagreeable. It was obvious he was still in love with her and if he couldn't have her he would wreck any new relationship in her life.

I soon put a stop to all of this. The result was that he took Andrea for the weekend then refused to return her. The next thing we were served with a court application for custody. The main grounds of his case were that Terri was living with a drunk, etc. etc.

Making matters worse, prior to the court hearing a social worker came to make a report on Terri. I arrived home half way through the interview drunk. The Welfare Worker said words to the effect *"Did you drive the car in that condition, Mr. Hayes?"*. I replied something like *"Well, it didn't drive itself"*. Terri had brought up Andrea for nine years alone and most of the time with no maintenance. Here I was wrecking her chances of getting Custody.

The court case was in Sheffield some two hundred miles away and we drove up early in the morning. We saw Alan going into the court smirking with his brief case really looking forward to his day in court. Terri turned to me and said *"Take me home Bill. I will not lower myself to answer to him in court"*. So home we went leaving everyone in the court. Alan was awarded custody.

This meant we could have Andrea weekends and even though Alan lived two hundred and fifty miles away, he was happy to bring her each weekend so he could still have his contact with Terri. He was originally from Northampton and would stay with his mother. He told Terri and her parents on more than one occasion all Terri had to do was get rid of me and she could have Andrea back. No one believed our relationship was going to last.

So we carried on alone. Terri also began to drink very heavily although she always had the ability to control herself. Business was good, money was easy and my drinking had increased. At this time I could never have worked in an office. The saving factor was I could sell my cattle from bed. Of course, Hugh Tunney was only looking at the results of the sales and very Happy.

Socially we had a Ball, we mixed with the cricket club crowd of Michael Parkinson, Ritchie Benaue, Henry Bloefield and Collin Milburn. Weekends we would go to London and mix with the show business crowd. Terri was a very popular girl.

The weekends we usually ended up at Danny la Rue's club in the West End. This was a gambling club and Danny always did the Cabaret himself. One Saturday evening I was drinking with Dave Allan the Comedian and Danny said, *"Why don't you come down to my little pub in the country tomorrow for lunch"*. This seemed a good idea so on the Sunday morning Terri and myself found the village near Stratford-upon-Avon where the pub was, but no pub could be found. Asking the locals where we could find Danny La Rue we were directed to this magnificent *"Stately Home"* set in sixty acres of grazing. This was Danny's little pub in the country. He had converted it into a Country Club, Bar and Restaurant. A wonderful time was had and we spent many weekends there. Very sadly Danny lost all of his money the following year and everything was sold. The gambling license was taken from the club in London. Danny was one of the most naturally generous men I have ever met.

I was sat in the chair in the cottage one Friday evening, very very drunk and fast asleep. The next thing I knew there were firemen all over the house and police. I had gone to sleep dropping a cigarette and burnt the lounge carpet. A neighbour going home had seen the flames and called the fire brigade. I was too drunk to move from the chair and was still sitting there in all the debris, water and smoke. When Terri returned home she was so angry and I was so helpless. The police charged me with criminal damage and I was to appear in court in two week's time.

When I appeared in court, I told the magistrate I had no recollection of the events at all. I was sent by the court to see an alcoholic counsellor called Dr. Edwards.

He was a Charming man and a recovering alcoholic himself. He had been struck off the medical register at the peak of his career and placed in a locked ward of a mental home. I always remember he had a chart on the wall in the shape of a "V". The left side going down was the progression of the illness, the right side going up was the recovery.

I read the chart and the left side did not go far enough down for me. I had been passed the bottom of the chart for years. Prisons, Hospitals, drinking in the mornings. He asked me many questions and each time I answered, Terri would say *"Bill"* so as opposed to my usual lies about my drinking I was forced to tell the truth. I owe this to Terri's presence alone.

The result of the meeting was he told me I was a very serious case of a *"Chronic Alcoholic"* and needed hospitalisation urgently. There was a new clinic opened in Oxford called the Lea Clinic. He booked me in for a three week course of Group Therapy. The one condition was I had to go into hospital sober. He said *"Will that be possible?"* I said *"Of course"*.

We were to go to the hospital the following Tuesday so I drank with a vengeance. Terri made me allowances, as at least I was going into hospital. On the Tuesday afternoon I had been drinking all day when we left for Oxford. John Sharkey, my meat inspector from Devon drove the car. Terri in the passenger seat, I was in the back with a full whiskey bottle with a mixture of whiskey and water. When we arrived I was in one hell of a mess. The staff complained I was not sober. Terri promptly told them that was why I was going to hospital to try and stop drinking. I was put to bed and knew nothing until the next day. Terri and John returned home.

I used to ring my parents on a regular basis always telling lies of how well I was doing. I was living on my *past glories* by this time. I would put Terri on the phone to say hello yet they knew my drinking was in a bad way.

I had met my father in London a couple of times. This was very sad for me. He had been very ill in hospital and the shop had been closed for some time. He had been working as a Butcher in Tesco at the time of his illness. He was only fifty five years old. After this illness he decided to take a twelve month college course and become a Meat Inspector. This was ironic after all the years he had been so *anti-establishment*. Now he was going to join them. I remember so well when we killed our first cow *Molly* in 1954 who was riddled with TB.

He actually placed Mr Lethbridge, the Meat Inspector, on the butcher's block in the shop and threatened to cut his head off. Today he would have got five year's prison for that act alone. He was staying at a small hotel in Smithfield, so I took him to the Mount Pleasant Hotel in Clerkenwell where I used to stay on Rugby tours. It was a much more pleasant hotel and he moved there.

My mother had worked her way up from the kitchens of Poole Grammar School to becoming the head of all the catering Poole Technical College. This was a very prestigious position and all done with her hard work and superb intellect, starting at the age of forty seven. *What she could have achieved as a Career Lady* as opposed to a housewife is beyond my imagination.

So here I was in June of 1978 nearly thirty one years of age in an alcoholic clinic. There were six of us on the course and I remember them all well. The stories they had were far worse than mine. I can say in all honesty I had not yet got as bad as any of these people. I had no problem identifying I was an alcoholic but I considered I was different. Most certainly more intelligent and definitely never going to be as bad as these people.

I recall a couple of ex patients coming to give a talk. They were a very classy couple. I thought how nice to grow old gracefully and had visions of Terri and myself being able to do so.

We had group therapy all week and in the evenings we were taken to AA meetings. I didn't drink for the three weeks and Terri came down weekends to be with me. I learned a lot of the theory about the disease, Alcoholism. I also learned about hiding drinks, getting bottles from the local Off License, all the ways to continue drinking in secret. Prior to this I had never tried to hide my drinking, when I was drunk I was drunk and when I was sober I was sober.

The Course was good and we were told to go to AA at least three times a week. I took two of the patients home to Northampton in my car and on the way we called into a pub for ginger ale. Within five minutes I thought one whiskey wouldn't hurt. The result was I got legless, they got legless and we all went home drunk.

The dear old lady Maggie went home to her husband very drunk and also the little Bisexual man my other passenger. There was tremendous alarm that three out of eight patients returned home from Hospital in a worse state than they went in. This was, of course, all my fault.

I told Terri it was the medication I had been given. The whole course was drug free. I also told Terri if I drink any beer it is okay. God Bless her. She believed me and told all her friends and family, *"Bill is cured now, he only drinks Beer"*.

The clinic sent a social worker to see me each week as part of the after care. As I have said it was a good clinic. The first time he came to see me I was in the village pub. They gave me up as one of their failures.

Within weeks the drinking was worse. Hugh now only had the one factory in Clones and it was going to close in August. The fighting began, my violence came into play again. The only difference was I believe I loved Terri as much as I could love anyone. I began to see my children on a regular basis and the relationship with Margaret mellowed. The children got on well with Terri and all was well only my booze. I just could not stop drinking. I recall Terri going out with Andrea one day. I kept a bottle of whiskey all day without taking one drink.

Terri rang to say she would be late home. I had made a nice meal for dinner and was saving the whiskey. By the time Terri got home I had drunk all the whiskey, bought a second bottle and thrown all the dinner in the bin.

I decided to leave and go back to Ireland. Terri used to buy exotic old clothes from the Oxfam Shop then renovate them. She had this lovely Clerical Cloak she had put velvet all around the edges and a gold chain for a clasp. This Friday evening I left for Ireland, I was wearing the Clerical Cloak, White Panama Hat. I looked like Dr. Who. With great drama I left very late at night to drive to Liverpool to the ferry. Just as I got on to the M1 motorway my Big Ends went on the car. There I was at the service station, pissed as a parrot, dressed like Dr Who and had to take a taxi home, knocking on the door *saying "Please open up, I have come home"*. I was pathetic.

Several weeks later I made my second attempt at leaving for Ireland, dressed in a suit this time I may add. I was stopped by the police and breathalysed five miles from home. So again I went back with my *Tail between my Legs.*

The third attempt at going to Ireland I went on the train. Terri came with me just to have a look at the country. We managed to get on the ferry which took eight hours in those days. The Pop Group, The New Seekers were in the bar and Terri knew them so a great party was had on the trip and I was, of course, legless once more. We arrived in Dublin and booked into a small hotel in Parnell Square and I rang Tunney the following day and arranged a meeting.

I arranged to meet Hugh at six o'clock the following morning at the front door of the Gresham. I made a great effort to clean myself up and looked good. Hugh said jump in the car and his driver took us to Clones, ninety miles away.

Hugh and myself talked and he told me all he had left was the castle. We had secured a twenty five year lease on the Castle. Hugh kept the Penthouse Suite of the Gresham for life when he sold the Hotel. He also had the Factory in Clones. I was very fond of Tunney and the feeling was mutual. He could not tolerate my drinking and, of course, I could not stop. I had been back to him time and time again and no one helped me more, only my poor mother.

Hugh's father was an Alcoholic so he had more understanding of the illness than I did.

He told me that he would drop me at the hotel in Clones for if he took me in the factory, all his executives would walk out. That was okay. I told him I needed to get a house in Dublin and he took out his gold money clip and gave me all the cash. He had some Six Hundred Pounds. Having dropped me at the hotel within fifteen minutes the car came to take me to the factory. John Copass was very reserved but terrified of offending his master and quite polite to me.

We agreed that he would open the Plant again. I would base myself in Dublin and deal with him direct and sell the cattle for One Pound per head and carry my own expenses. This was a good Deal for everyone except Coppas who was only on Twenty Thousand Pounds per annum. Jealousy came into play again.

Paddy McQuiggan drove me back to Dublin. Paddy has been a very good singer and represented Ireland in the Eurovision Song Contest, coming second to Cliff Richard who sang the song *"Congratulations"*, written by Phil Coulter an Irish man. Paddy was beaten by the booze and ended up running a small V.G. Supermarket in Clones with rags to his arse and driving a taxi to make ends meet. Paddy's son, Barry, went on to become the wold champion feather weight boxer a couple of years later and restored all the family fortunes. Before each fight Paddy would go in the ring and sing *"Danny Boy"* to the standing ovations of the fans. He was a lovely man who died shortly afterwards.

When I arrived in Dublin I was surprised to find that Terri loved the city. We were lucky and found a nice three bedroom furnished house just off the Malahide Road. I had the phones and telex installed and was again back in business.

I organised one of my meat trucks to bring all the furniture over from the cottage in England and we were up and running.

Within three weeks Hugh realised he was paying me One Thousand Two Hundred Pounds weekly and his executives were all complaining they could do the job themselves. I said quite arrogantly, *"Let them"* and gave my notice. Hugh rang back and Terri let him have it with both barrels. Hugh was so used to everyone *"cow-tailing"* to him he didn't know how to handle Terri who was very, very English.

I was tired of *Pussy Footing* and *People Pleasing*. The result was Hugh went through many many salesmen in the following years but never found another Bill Hayes. One thing I could do well was sell cattle. People bought the man. By being on the phone I could do it from my bed, relaxed in good humour and my clients could never resist me. Hugh was angry but I was adamant I was still very angry over the bomb incident.

I began selling again for John Lyons of Longford on One Pound per head. I also sold for Cunniffes of Balhagadreen in County Roscommon. So every week I was selling one thousand to two thousand cattle and getting One Pound for each in cash every week.

We bought a car and settled down to go the Dublin Clubs every night. There were some very good clubs in Dublin the 1970's around Leeson Street and St Stephen's Green. Barbara and David were living in Portmarnock and had a hotel in Dublin. Whenever I rang them they put the phone down. The first couple of times I thought it was a faulty line. The reality was they did not want to talk to me or know me. I got the very same treatment from Bruce who was very successful in the Midlands of Ireland.

This was very hurtful to me but what could I do. Everyone by this time had turned their back on me. Alan refused to allow Andrea come to Ireland if Terri wanted to see her she had to go to England. This was awful for Terri.

My drinking was worse than ever and a couple of times Terri left me and went back to the UK always returning or I would go and persuade her to come home. By Christmas of 1978 I was doing ok quietly alright in business. I had managed to mail my Christmas money to the children from the post office in Fairview and decided to have a drink on the way home.

I arrived home very drunk and drank more in the house.

After a very bad row I threw Terri out of the house, locked the doors and went to bed. In the early hours of the morning I heard a knocking or banging on the door. It was the police. I remember it was snowing like hell and they had one of their coats over Terri.

They had found Terri nude in a telephone box in the Malahide Road. She was ringing home to get me to open the doors. It was an awful sight and awful mess. I was arrested for assault and taken to Clontarf Police Station. I was bailed to appear at the Four Courts in Dublin that morning at ten o'clock in the morning

I went home. There was no Terri. No booze, so I got dressed, cleaned up and ordered a taxi to take me to the early morning opening pubs in the Smithfield market areas of the Quays. This was about five o'clock in the morning. I asked the driver to leave his meter on and come and join me for a drink but be sure to get me to court by ten o'clock. So off we went and the drinking began. I was *Paying* for company.

Siting in the pub I was soon feeling better when my whiskey hit the spot. The previous weekend we had been to Longford and I was showing Terri the country. I had hired a brand new SAAB car for the weekend. The result was I crashed the car writing it off. I thought Terri was dead in the passenger seat. Leaving the car in the field gateway we got a lift back to Longford town when I heard a voice calling *"Help"*. We had picked up a hitch hiker and I had forgotten him. He was still in the car with the car on its roof. Fortunately as he was drunk, he had slept through it all and luckily was not hurt.

Several weeks earlier I had been invited to Co. Claire to take over a cattle market for a small farmer's co-operative. Having driven nearly two hundred miles, drinking all the way. I went to meet this committee of farmers. I told them *"I don't want the job at any price"* got in my car and drove home.

Despite my love for Terri or love as I knew it, I could not be faithful to her. When she left me I advertised for a Housekeeper-Secretary. I selected the first person who came for the interview. Then while I sat and drank I allowed her to interview all the other applicants. I was crazy. I took love when I could find it and if I couldn't find it I bought it from ladies of the night. I was terrified of the dark and terrified of being on my own. So here I was in a pub, paying a taxi driver for his company.

Sitting in a bar playing to my audience. I have heard the expression many times, *"Sitting on a bar stool, waiting to be Discovered"*. The booze gave me notions of grandeur, I was ten feet tall and bullet proof.

CHAPTER FIFTEEN

I remember going into the court. I was going to cross examine the two police officers and say that locking my wife out of the house did not constitute assault. I felt like Perry Mason, of course, this was the whiskey.

I saw Terri at the court and gave her all the cash I had and told her to go back to England. I believe the Judge was fairly decent and could see my condition and he adjourned the case.

This was not good enough for me. I said, *"Now sir, you will deal with this case today. Here is my cheque book. Make it out for whatever fine you think appropriate"*. That is all I remember flashing my cheque book.

I woke up in Mountjoy Prison the next day. The Judge had remanded me in custody on One Thousand Pounds Bail. I have no recollection of the cells in the Four Courts or going to prison. All I know was my mouth was like the Sahara Desert and I was again in prison.

This was a Saturday morning. The following day the English papers had front page news *"Cattle Baron and Nude in Phone Box"*. Every English paper carried the story for my parents and family to read. The Irish Press had also given me front page on the Saturday.

Because of this all the other prisoners assumed I was a sex offender and I was in great danger. The prison chief who was also called Hayes placed me in the bakery making the prison bread and bread rolls. However, each night when I got my evening cup of tea it was always laced with salt by some prisoner with problems of his own.

Terri came to see me on the Tuesday. I recall her crying and telling me what a waste I had become. She knew I was an intelligent man and here I was in a cage. It was a very sad meeting. She told me Barbara and David as well as Bruce had been in touch with her. I thought at least my family will be able to help Terri.

I received a letter off my father telling me prison was the *"Best Place for me"* and that now I would see some sense.

That was a very hurtful letter but again if I didn't accept I was an alcoholic, how could I expect anyone else to?

I wrote to all of my family and friends for Bail. I wrote to Tunney and assumed in a few days Bail would be put up and I would go home.

Christmas came and went. New Year came and went and then it was January 1979 with no visitors, no letters, only my Mum and no Bail. I later learned Bruce my brother *(based on my father's assumption I was in the Best Place)* had told everyone in the meat trade, the family didn't want me bailed. Bruce and Barbara had not only persuaded Terri to go back to England, they had organised the moving of all our furniture there also. Perhaps my family acted in the way they thought best. It was bad enough them turning their backs on me, it was awful to assist Terri in leaving me.

I had settled into the prison routine with no hope of release when one day in late February I was told to pack my kit. I was taken to the prison reception and there was Eddie Webb, a cattle dealer from Ballyhaunis in County Mayo. He had put up my Bail.

Eddie Webb had supplied me cattle in Longford and then followed me to Clones. I used to purchase some one hundred and twenty Cattle each week from him. His son Ted was a celebrated Gaelic Football player for Mayo County.

Ted the son, was killed by a train that ran into his car on an unmarked railway crossing one evening. He was only twenty one and in the *Prime of His Life*. Young Ted was not a drinker and had his whole life before him as well as a *Charming Young Lady*.

I attended the Funeral and spent the weekend with the Webb Family trying to comfort them in their *Trying Time*. I was because of these actions I later learned, that Mrs Webb insisted Eddie go two hundred miles to Dublin and bail me.

I had only written to Eddie the previous week as a last resort as no one was answering my letters. He took me to lunch at one of Doyles Hotels and booked me into the Phoenix Park Hotel paying the bill for one week in advance.

I had met a social worker in the prison and been accepted to the Rutland Centre at Clondalken. This was a new clinic for alcoholics. Eddie took me there and paid the bill as it was a private clinic and I could go in, the following week. Eddie had told the owner of the Phoenix Park Hotel what a *"Great Man I used to be"* and what drink had reduced me to.

Eddie O'Sullivan was the name of this hotelier. He had spent his life in Australia in the prison service and came back to Ireland and bought the hotel on his retirement. He was a *Charming Man* from County Clare with a drink problem and became a very good friend to me. So there I was with only two friends in the world and one of them a retired prison officer.

I tried to contact Terri but her parents refused to tell me where she was. They had also suffered the embarrassment of the newspapers, of course, Alan the ex husband was *Crowing like a Peacock* about Bad Bill Hayes.

I went into hospital and there I met Mary Bolton. Mary was a recovering alcoholic who had been sober twenty five years. She had spent this twenty five years working with Dr Max Glatt who was now the Chairman of the World Health Organisation. I became a patient of Mary's or client was the term used and I was to spend the next twelve weeks in the Rutland Centre.

The treatment was group therapy aimed at getting to the heart of the problem that caused us to drink. Mary's own theory was that the formative years zero to seven define one's character and the results of these years decide pretty well if we will be normal or have an addiction personality.

When Mary heard of my childhood she was horrified. Making matters worse was the fact that I believed it was normal. I recall her saying "there was that sensitive little boy working in a slaughterhouse all those hours in blood and guts, no wonder you are not normal". This came as a shock to me.

She also told me Margaret's death didn't make me an Alcoholic. I would have been one if she had lived. She said there was a good chance that Margaret had she lived, would have grown to hate me. This was a bitter pill to swallow yet it all made sense.

I met some lovely people in the clinic. We had doctors, priests, businessmen, working men and we even had a nun who became alcoholic in the missions of Africa drinking native beer.

There were school teachers, and people from show business, forty plus patients from all walks of life.

Mary said I was so callous that there was a heart in me somewhere but she would need a hammer and chisel to get at it. After three weeks she was giving up on me. The normal stay there was only six weeks. Mary came up with the idea of locking me in my room with no radio, no books just a pen and paper. I had to write down my life story from as far back as I could remember. This was very hard to do being totally honest. I did my best.

Then Mary got me to talk about Margaret in the end I broke down in tears. I cried and cried and the floodgates opened.

Mary said *"You can if you wish to get better now, Bill"*. She told me I had never grieved the death of Margaret. She also told me that I had covered all my grief with booze. I had never accepted the death *six decks down* and this was why I didn't go to see the body. All she said made sense and I began to get well.

I had dreamed many, many times Margaret was not Dead, that she was still alive and no longer wanted me. I used to see her as clear as day in my Dreams and then as I was approaching her, she would disappear again. It was awful.

My second wife Margaret began to ring me, then one day Terri rang me out of the blue. Mary Walsh, another counselor was in the office when both calls came through. She told Mary Bolton *"When Bill Hayes was talking to those women you wouldn't know which one he was talking to, as he spoke to them both the same"*.

This was quite true yet I was doing it unconsciously and both Margaret and Terri were talking of reconciliation if I got well. I was learning something about myself as last. This was Bill Hayes the actor playing his role, ready to go back and do it all over again.

A very important point to the Rutland Programme was Family Confrontation. This meant your members of the family came into the group, told the group exactly what you were like at home. This was a very painful experience for all my fellow patients when their turn came. I thought well at least I can avoid this as I have no family to confront me. Then after I had been in hospital nine weeks, my parents came to stay with Barbara and David for a holiday. They visited me and Mary lost no time in inviting them to the Family Confrontation.

The benefits of this are painful but immense. It is so easy to sit in a group of people and tell them how you see things, then when the same person is confronted by his family, it's a whole different story. There was one poor man called Liam. He worked for Aer Lingus. According to Liam all he did was get drunk every day, go home and go to sleep. He had been placed in the Rutland by his employers.

When Liam's wife and children gave their account, he used to come up the street from the pub Shadow Boxing. His children were embarrassed as all the other children made fun of their father. He would then proceed to beat his wife, torment the children and go to bed being violently sick all night. This was a Liam we couldn't visualise as he was such a *Quiet Man* when sober as we knew him.

My parents came and my father proceeded to take the blame for me. He said *"I was always his favourite and he never wanted to show this"*, so he treated me the hardest. This was a very sad confession to hear from my father. He mentioned my failing the Eleven Plus exams, so he had noticed this and he also *"nearly admitted"* his blunder when I was in hospital. He admitted that he lost the money but qualified it by saying he believed he was doing right. The result was he broke down in tears. My mother put her hand out to him and Mary Bolton told me after that mother was the strength in the relationship and not my father.

Mary also said what happened to me was bad. *What happened to Bruce was worse as he was the youngest.* I had never thought of Bruce as a victim before. As the years went by Mary was proved to be correct.

On my eleventh week, Terri came to see me from England. I booked her into the Phoenix Park Hotel and Eddie O'Sullivan treated her like a daughter.

Mary then persuaded Terri to come to the Family Confrontation. This was awful. Terri spoke of her fear of me when I was drunk. I could never understand anyone being frightened of me.

The reality was the fear Terri felt was no different than the fear I felt of my father when I was a small boy. Equally, if something was uncomfortable I would fly into a rage rather than be confronted.

Many mornings I would wake and Terri would say, *"Do you know what you did last night?"* Or say, *"Do you know who you rang last night and what you said?"*. I had to sit and allow Terri tell all. I was deeply ashamed. Very humbled and at the end I was better than I had ever been in my life. I was the real Bill Hayes. No Bull Shit. Mary said, *"You can go home Billy. All you have to do is go to AA to keep what you have"*.

Raphael Short, the Director of the clinic said *"Bill, no one has been through what you have been through without a reason. How you have survived is a miracle. You must be on this earth for a purpose"*.

I had been there twelve weeks and was very afraid to go out into the world again. Mary told me when she met me, I was the toughest client she had ever had. She really thought there was no hope for me and only took me on as no one else would. She was the most remarkable, spiritual human being I have ever met to this day. The simple things she taught me made no sense at the time, now I use them every day. Sadly I never grasped the importance of AA. The simple AA Programme just seemed too simple to be true.

One of my fellow patients, Damian, was married to a very successful international singer. They had a lovely small family and were very financially secure.

Damian gave up all his business interests and trained to become an alcoholic counsellor, just the same as Mary. Needless to say, Damian went on to lead a very successful sober life for the last twenty years.

CHAPTER SIXTEEN

I went back to the Phoenix Park Hotel and it was like a honeymoon. Eddie Webb arranged to collect me the following week and take me to Ballyhaunis. Eddie would have no part of Terri and considered her wrong to get me in trouble. I didn't and don't agree with that. Terri had nothing to blame herself for. This was a little bit of Irish chauvinism, *"a wife should take her beating and like it"*.

For the first time since Margaret died I was able to be myself without any shame. It was wonderful. I went to Ballyhaunis leaving Terri in Dublin to find a small house. Note the word small, no more mansions or pie in the sky. Terri found a super little cottage in the main street of Howth, a small fishing village on Dublin Bay. There was no furniture only one brass bed but Terri painted cardboard boxes to fill up the rooms. As long as she had her paints, cigarettes and coffee, she was Happy.

Meanwhile I went to Ballyhaunis to meet Sheir Rafique for the second time in my life. Rafique was a Pakistani from the East End of London, Upton Park. He had purchased a small factory in the West of Ireland for Forty Thousand Pounds. I had met him when I was in Enniskillen and sold him lambs from my farm as Tunney didn't process lambs.

I had given Rafique some of my best lamb and mutton jobs in London and Paris from my days in Devon and my days with John Lyons so I knew the man fairly well.

By 1979 he was building a $4 million factory in Ballyhaunis for beef and lambs. Where he made the money I don't know to this day but it most certainly wasn't all legally. He told me in his first year of business the Governor of Malta's son had caught him for Three Hundred and Eighty Thousand Pounds. He had the choice to pack up and go home or keep on trading hoping he could trade his way out. He kept on trading and was a huge success. He was also building a £5 million Plant in Anglesea, North Wales.

This was the first time I noticed anyone take real advantage of my alcoholism. John O'gara was the Government Vet at Ballyhaunis. He had been the vet in Clones. O'gara was a great mate of Copass.

Rafique was killing one thousand Lambs per day. So each month he had eight tonnes of Lamb's Liver and no market. O'gara whilst still in the government employ, had bought two butcher shops in Dublin and was going to sell all of this liver. So he resented my presence in Ballyhaunis denying him additional income.

Rafique could not carry his position and new power well. He had become an awful *"Show Off"* and had also re-invented his history. As opposed to the real story of his butcher's shop in the East End, he purported to have come from Pakistan where he claimed his family had great holdings of Land and Factories.

I was friendly with the previous owner of the Plant, a man called Hussain who was from Forest Gate in the East End of London. Poor old Hussain couldn't make the plant pay and I introduced him to Yaqoob from Birmingham and took Yaqoob to see the plant. So I knew all of Rafique's history. That was Rafique's business. He was talking to me, trying to impress me with all this Bull Shit, then of course, it hit me between the eyes there were not many men in the meat business with my ability or experience.

Having learnt my new humility from Mary Bolton I said, *"Okay, let John O'gara sell your product."* Rafique said he would contact me in a few months when he opened his new beef line. This was no good to me. I was in desperate need of a job now.

Eddie Webb took me back to Dublin and said *"Just be patient, Bill"*. I was happy to be away from the meat business. Terri was sympathetic to me and we moved to the cottage.

Eddie O'Sullivan gave us bedding, plates, pots and pans and all we needed. He also loaned me money. The ex prison officer was like an *Angel* to me. I had no idea what I was going to do for work or money. We just took every day as it came. Riding on the bus, doing simple things.

The ice cream man came one day and I bought a couple of ice creams for us. I was talking to the Ice Cream Man and he was telling me how good business was. He also told me he had a second van for rent if I wanted to have a go. I agreed and was in the Ice Cream business.

My van was full of drawings of Popeye and the bells chimed *"Popeye the Sailor Man"*. Eddie O'Sullivan loaned me the money for one month's rent. So we went to the Cash and Carry and bought the Ice Cream and all the Ice Lollies and learned the prices. This was a Saturday afternoon.

We plugged the fridges of the van into the main electric of the house via the window and on Sunday morning got up to go and sell Ice Cream. I thought I had better have a *Dry Run* in making the Ice Creams in the cone, so opened up my fridges. The fridge made a noise but didn't keep my ice cream frozen. I had two freezers of liquid that was no use at all. I rang the owner of the van to complain. He said, *"Tough Luck, Bill"*.

This was indeed tough luck as all our money had gone in the stock. I could get no joy from the owner but on the bright side we had transport and we ate all the chocolate flakes which I love.

I sat down that Sunday and pondered what to do as it was a good looking big van. I came up with the idea of getting a small gas stove, frying pan and make Hamburgers and sell them in the evenings. I found a man called Nick Clarke who lived in Vernon Avenue at Clontarf. Nick and myself did the conversion from Ice Cream to Burgers.

Nick was from the North of Ireland and as well as being a *"Naughty Boy"* he was quite a character with a terrible drink problem. He was very politically involved in the North and the South. The van was ready and off go Terri and myself and sat on O'Connell Bridge at ten o'clock at night. That first night we took One Hundred Pounds. We were delighted.

I had purchased two bags of onions from Moore Street market for One Pound. The buns had cost me Three Pence each and the Burgers had cost me Five Pence each. Therefore, the One Hundred Pounds taking was Ninety Pounds profit, so things looked good. The following morning I received a telephone call from Barbara, my father had died.

I rang my mother immediately who was still in a state of shock and said I would come over. God is good. I had the One Hundred Pounds from the Burgers the previous night. However, Barbara called back to say she and David were going over that day with Bruce, and Bruce would buy my ticket if I went with them, so I agreed.

David, Barbara, Bruce and myself flew from Dublin. Terri stayed home. Bruce hired a car from Manchester and we drove to Bob's home in Newbury. This was the first time we had all been together for many years. We went to see my father, a lesson I had also learned from Mary Bolton about not seeing Margaret and the funeral took place.

The initial plan was to have my father cremated but I didn't like the idea and eventually we agreed to bury him with his parents. My father had hardly known his own father, William Hayes, who died in a coal mine disaster when my father was three years old.

My grandmother, Helena, had been disowned from her Society Family in Liverpool for marrying a coal miner that was considered beneath her status and even though she was left a widow with four young children she was never taken back by the family. It was a very tragic story and may have accounted for some of my father's behaviour as a man. He was very devoted to his mother and apparently very spoilt by her.

When the funeral was over we brought mother back to Ireland. I was glad to get home to Terri. Barbara and David who had met Terri, agreed to keep in touch.

I was very secretive about what I was doing, driving a Burger van. Not out of shame, I just didn't want to have to explain all the events in my life. I had spent a day with William and Edwina at the funeral and this was really nice, seeing them when I was clean and sober. So it was back to my Burgers every night on O'Connell Bridge and things were good.

I had been out of hospital two weeks and managed to put a deposit on a Triumph TR7 Sports Car, just big enough for Terri and myself. Nick Clark was building my second Burger Van. Nick then came up with the idea of building trailers that I could pull behind the car so this is what we did. Within six weeks I had five Burger vans and trailers on the road. I also had the franchise to sell food and drinks on Howth Beach from two beach huts. Terri enjoyed running them as she loved the sea and looked the part in her bikini.

We had become socially friendly with Barbara and

David and spent quite a bit of time with them. Terri and Barbara were very close. The work was hard peeling onions all morning, going to the bakery to get my rolls. Eddie Webbs' son was making my Burgers in his shop in Ballyhaunis and I had been able to pay back Eddie O'Sullivan and Eddie Webb.

One morning in June there was a knock on the door. It was Rafique. I had not shaved and just got out of bed and it was about ten o'clock in the morning. I can still see the look of disgust in his face as he must have thought I was back on the booze.

I showed him my Burger Vans and explained I had been selling Burgers all night. Rafique said *"Give it up today and come and work for me"*. Bless him he offered me Four Hundred Pounds per week to set up marketing of lambs in Dublin as well as the liver that John O'gara had failed to sell. He now had fifty tonnes of liver unsold.

I was earning Four Hundred Pounds in two days on the Burgers so I took his offer and kept the Burger business as well.

I rented a yard in Kinsealy and began selling all the lamb that were too heavy for Paris to the Dublin meat trade. Before long, I was doing one thousand Lambs per week in Dublin. Rafique was a very Happy man. I then got rid of all the Burger Vans and was back in the meat business full time.

I was going to AA once a week which was not enough. I was getting *No Benefit* from the meetings.

Barbara and David and Terri were all drinking very heavy and I found life rather difficult. I used to ring Mary Bolton and she would say, *"Keep going to the meetings with your body and the mind will follow"*. This was not good enough for me. I wanted instant Benefits.

I began buying cattle again and killing them at Navan and selling the beef to the same butchers who were buying my lambs.

So I had my salary from Rafique my profit from my cattle and by August 1979 purchased a new Mercedes car again for Twelve Thousand Pounds. Socially, life was good and all was well. So I bought a lease on a five bedroom Bungalow and Farm at Ashbourne, Co Meath. This was big enough for an office, my meat trucks, my two cars. I was back in the meat trade *Boots and All.* I never consulted Terri who was very upset at leaving Howth and Barbara. The new house was out in the country.

Every Thursday Terri and Barbara would go around my butchers shops and collect the money. They made these fun days doing their shopping and having tea at the Gresham Hotel. My butchers liked the idea of two glamorous girls collecting the money and all worked very well.

One day Terri said *"Bill you were more fun when you were drinking".* This was in early 1980 and we had been in business for one year. I had the children for holidays. Bob came to visit. I was seeing Bruce again so I had achieved so much in a short time knowing full well I couldn't drink.

This small mention or a passing remark about drink and I reacted by getting a bottle of whiskey and drinking it in front of Terri. Then going to the pub. Terri left me and went to stay with Bruce and Jane in Longford. Within five days I had smashed the car causing Five Thousand Pounds of damage. I had neglected my business. Butchers hadn't paid for their meat and I had told Rafique to sell his own lambs, that I was too busy. Five days of drinking and I was back to square one. A derelict in my own home. I had called my house *"Bolton House"* after Mary Bolton.

I have a very minor court case coming up for no insurance on one of my Burger vans. Rather than go to court I packed my car, put Kerry my dog in the boot and drove to the North of Ireland and *walked out* on everything. I left my abattoir, farm and home booked into the Killyhavelin Hotel, Enniskillen. I always remember it was the Cheltenham Gold Cup day, 1980.

I sat in my suite drinking gin and tonic watching the races. Then I thought I had better ring home. Sandy, my foreman from Leicester was working for me, so I called him up to Enniskillen and instructed him where to collect monies owing to me and salvaged something.

Terri arrived with Sandy and she was devastated that I had gone back to square one.

I called to see Jack Taylor and paid him the money I owed him and drove to Larne in Co. Antrim with Terri. I booked into the Killwaughter House Hotel and paid the money I owed them from years previously and got drunk. Terri had had enough and got a taxi back to Dublin in the middle of the night when I was asleep.

I took the ferry to Scotland and booked into a hotel in Glasgow, waking up with three hookers in my room. I was back to all my old tricks. Sleazy clubs, slinky women and booze.

I drove to Sterling, a lovely market town in Scotland and booked into the White Lion Hotel. My dog, Kerry the Red Setter, was in the boot of the car so they took care of my dog for me. I then got as drunk as I have ever been in my life. In the early hours of the following morning I rang Mary Bolton.

Mary said, *"I can't help you, Bill. There is only one man that can help you. You are too far gone. That is Max Glatt at Galsworthy House, London. If I book you in, will you go?"* I said, *"I would do anything"*. Mary called back later in the day and said, *"All you have to do is go there, Bill"*.

Recording these events they make no more sense to me today than they did at the time. *Running away, I was always walking out* and *running away*. This is called in AA a geographical escape. Things will be different. What we fail to realise in the problems are all in our heads and we take all the problems with us.

I can only speak for myself but when anything really good happens to me, I think this is too good to last, so I leave it behind before its taken from me. This way, I can't get hurt. Strange as this may sound, it's the way I used to feel.

I had no pressure in Dublin. I was earning as much money as I ever earned but I was still so very unhappy. Had I been happy with Terri I wouldn't have needed other women.

I had sold for Tunney forty of my cattle two weeks before I drank and the cheque came to Fourteen Thousand Pounds. I went to Clones to collect the cheque. Copass told me they were having money problems and finding it hard keeping afloat. Could I wait fourteen days?

I reminded John Copass that day, of what a *"Little Shit"* he was. I walked into Hugh's office and Hugh paid me immediately. I took great pleasure in climbing into my new Mercedes and driving out of the yard with all Tunney's little boys (executives) looking out of the windows. That was the last time I saw Hugh. I was pleased to hear twelve years later he sold out for £10 million.

I remember with great fondness some of the remarks of Nick Clarke from those days. I was going to put up a sign on the road at Howth for my Burgers. I said to Nick *"Where do I get permission to put up this new sign"*. Nick smiled and said as quick as a flash *"The man who tells you to take it down"*.

So Sunday morning in April 1980 the Manager of the Hotel agreed to drive me to London and return on the train leaving my Mercedes in London. I was in no state to drive.

On the way I called into Preston and bought lunch for Margaret and the children and gave Margaret One Thousand Pounds for the children and off we went again.

We arrived at Galsworthy House, Kingston-on-Thames at tea time. This was a beautiful clinic with liveried staff, chef, private deluxe rooms and silver service. The main clients were from show business. I was in hospital again this time with Jimmy Greaves, Peter Cook, Elaine Stritch, Ray McNally. This was the best facility available in England for me to get me well.

My mother had given up her job and with the help of my brother Bob, had moved back to Manchester and Bob had been very successful in his business. However, at this particular time Mum was staying in Dublin with Barbara.

I spoke to Terri and told her I was in hospital. She arranged to go to the house and put all of our furniture in store and ship it to England. We had bought all new furniture for the house at Ashbourne.

Terri also collected the balance of the money owing to me by the Dublin butchers. Poor old Rafique had been ringing every day looking for me. I never saw Rafique again but he went on to build an empire of meat factories and fisheries in England, Ireland, Scotland and Wales. At one point he was worth £100 million. Sadly, in the 1990's he lost it all and moved back to the East End of London.

Terri agreed to come to Kingston-on-Thames and stay in a hotel for as long as it took to get me well. No one had tried harder to help me as Terri in those *black days.* I was in Galsworthy House for one month. Thanks to all I had learned in the Rutland Centre it came easier than on previous occasions.

During my last weeks Terri rented a house in Manchester and moved all the furniture in and set up a home again. What I find so very hard to understand today is that I still *didn't* get the message of the importance of AA.

I would drive to London every week and meet Peter Cook and go to *After Care* at Galsworthy House but did not go to AA.

The house in Manchester was a new four bedroom bungalow. Terri's mum Evelyn had been to stay with us in Ireland. Terri never got on with her Mum but I adored her. We became very close and I also got on well with Terri's father. They were just a nice couple as Terri was adopted as a baby. She was very special to them and Terri was her Daddy's girl.

I met a Merchant Banker called Tyler. He was a decent little man with very big ideas. He had got involved with a meat business in Stockport near Manchester and the result was it was losing him fortune each week. He invited me to take the factory over.

I refused to go to the factory but arranged to open an office in Bolton and do all the marketing. This was agreed and I opened the office. It was very plush and meant I didn't have to get involved with any of the production side. Terri was unhappy. She only seemed to be happy when I was down and out. I moved to Lytham St Anne's right on the seashore. You only had to walk out of the door and you were in the sea.

The move to Lytham meant I had to travel to work every day so I used to commute on the train, opening my office at nine o'clock in the morning and closing at five o'clock in the evening. I had a very good girl in the office, so could nearly come and go as I wanted. From this office I took over the contracts for Burgers and Sausages for all the schools in the North West of England. As we didn't make sausages I used to have ten tonnes a week made for me on contract.

I drank again, stopped again, each time going back to Galsworthy House. Then Max Glatt said *"There is no more I can do for you, Bill"*. I wasn't deterred. I just found a new hospital called St Andrews in Northampton. Peter Cook advised me to join BUPA and they would pick up all the bills. I had paid out over Twenty Thousand Pounds to Galsworthy House. By joining BUPA the same as Peter, I should have known I was going to expect to need more treatment or rather continue drinking. This is how I was fooling myself.

I was given a drug called *Anti-booze.* Your system must be clear of it three days before you drink or you become violently ill. I know because once I drank on the drug. However, I would stop taking the anti-booze, clearing it out of my system. Common sense would tell anyone *the day* you stop taking it is the day you are planning to drink. Yet, I would clear my system, just in case and, of course, always drink again.

By setting up my office so well for the marketing, Tyler made allowances for my drink problem and I would just go away for a few days till I got well. So what I had done, was create a business environment that allowed me to make money, drink, cause havoc at home, then go and get well again. I used to get sober long enough to clear up the mess I had created, in order to drink again.

I have no idea how Terri put up with me. Mum came and stayed for New Year Eve 1980/1981 and we had a lovely time. This was the first time I had danced with my mother at the New Year's Dinner. She went on holiday and while she was away, I had her house all painted as a surprise for when she came home. All in all I was coping, then Terri decided to leave.

I thought what the hell am I doing here by the sea, fifty miles from my office when I only came here for Terri. I bought a house in the Peak District between Stockport and Buxton. It was nice, a small village and I had the canal in my back garden. I bought my first Rolls Royce, speed boat and moved to my new home. I put all of Terri and my furniture in store for her to take at her leisure.

I agreed with Tyler I would base myself at the factory near Stockport as this was convenient to home. So I became Managing Director of British Beefburgers. I had a good staff all the trimmings of success. I met a girl from Scottish Television called Sally. Sally was a couple of years younger than me and had been married twice before. I had not had a drink since October 1980.

At my last hospital I had been diagnosed as a *Manic*

Depressive and given twelve hundred milligrams Lithium a day plus ten milligrams of Librium to pop when I felt the need. So I was permanently high as I took the *Librium like Smarties*. Having said this by not drinking I had *no problems, no violence, no blackouts, no car accidents*. Life was pretty good and Sally was very good for me. Then one day out of the blue Terri rang and said she is coming home. I gave Sally the flick and met Terri at the station.

Terri was in an awful mess either drinking or popping pills. She had not seen my new home and I owed her so much. The first week was perfect only a few complaints about my working long hours again.

So here we were in Spring of 1981 and we decided to get married. I booked a honeymoon at the Hilton Hotel in Istanbul and even Alan, Terri's ex husband seemed content at last. Andrea was staying with us on a regular basis. I don't know how it happened or what happened, but Terri got drunk one night and went crazy, hitting me and smashing up the hotel room we were staying in. I have never seen a woman so wild or demented so the wedding was cancelled.

The result was the Police were called. I explained the situation and they called an ambulance. I paid for all the damage. The doctor said she was having a nervous breakdown so I sent her straight to St Andrews Hospital in Northampton.

St Andrews was Three Thousand Pounds weekly but we were both in BUPA and this was the best place in the country. Terri was kept under sedation for several days and I was not allowed to visit. I felt awful as I believed my years of drinking had caused the breakdown. For the next three months, it was two days home and seven days hospital for Terri as she always needed to go back for treatment.

I took her to Paris and she was ill there and rather than take her home I left her there. The same happened in Spain. On one of her visits home in June 1981 we got married and rather than honeymoon Terri went back to hospital. Terri said it was because all I was interested in was work and making money.

The remark was a shock to me yet, when I thought back to the Family Confrontation at Rutland Centre and I owed her so much. I sold my share of the factories still keeping the Bank guaranties to help Tyler. He was very understanding that my wife came first.

I rented a beautiful Sixteenth Century farm house near Colchester in Essex, only eight miles from the coast so I moored the boat at Brightlingsea for weekends. I opened a small marketing office in Piccadilly, London and semi-retired. I thought Terri was going to pull through and she came good for a while.

So I had sacrificed my business for my marriage. I had been one year with no drink and felt very good about myself. If the love is gone and a marriage is not working, you can't make it work. After a couple of months of this quiet life, the sea, and the lovely home, we went to the Bank one day in Colchester (we banked with Lloyds Bank in those days) and Terri took all her money out of her account, came home, packed her bags, ordered a taxi and said *"It's over Bill, I am going back to Northampton"*. I had just bought a new car for her father and was going to deliver it the next day. So I said, *"Wait till tomorrow and I will take you"*. Terri said, *"No, I am going now"*. I let her go on the Twenty First of September 1981. I had mixed feelings of *Deep Sorrow, Guilt*, most of all *Relief.* That was the end of my marriage. Making the whole thing seem ridiculous was that I was *sober,* not working too hard and all should have been well. But in retrospect, I was *Dry Drunk.*

The wedding had been in Blackpool in June of 1981. We were booked in for three o'clock in the afternoon to get married at the Blackpool Registry Office. We left home late and then became held up in the traffic. This meant we arrived at the Registry Office at four o'clock. The Registrar said we couldn't get married that day, however, he could squeeze us in at half past eight the following morning.

We went to the local church at Lytham St Anne's to have the photographs taken. We then had the small Reception at the Imperial Hotel, Blackpool.

Everyone was congratulating us as we made for the Honeymoon Suite. We then had to discreetly sneak out at half past seven the following morning to actually get married.

This must have been one of the shortest marriages in history, it only lasted two months.

CHAPTER SEVENTEEN

The children were due to come for a holiday and William was going to Boarding school in Ireland for the first time. William was to attend Rockwell College where Bradley, Barbara's son was already attending. The children had met Sally on one of the visits when Terri left the previous time. Now I had no one in my life. I just needed to be on my own for a while. I enjoyed having the children on my own and we had some fun. I had organised William's school fees and pocket money and was again feeling pleased with myself. I spoke to Terri on the phone and put no pressure on her. That was the last time I saw Terri to this day.

Here I was in 1981, thirty four years of age with three failed marriages behind me. I was a failure as a husband and a failure as a father and back on my own again. I knew I would be fine, as long as the children were on holiday. The thoughts of suicide were very strong in my head during those days.

I thought of my father when he died. I believe *he had given up on life*. Without doubt he was one of life's failures in my eyes. He failed at business. When he eventually completed his course as a Meat Inspector no one wanted to employ him so he was living off my mother again. It was very sad. He didn't live a few more years to see my brother Bob's great success in life, equally, my brother Bruce was now running a very large meat complex in Scotland. Barbara and David seemed to be getting on their feet again. Perhaps my father was not a total failure. I recall some lovely words given to me by a very *Special Lady:*

> *If you can appreciate Beauty*
> *If you can leave the world a better place*
> *Whether by a healthy child, garden patch*
> *Loving wife or grandchild,*
> *To know that one life has breathed easier*
> *Because you lived*
> ***This is*** *to have succeeded.*

I had no need to win my father's approval anymore. William was going to Boarding School and would be free and independent.

There was no one who needed me at this time of my life. I loved my mother to death and felt a great pity for her after all those years of work and marriage. Yet my behaviour had only broken her heart even more. I recall her saying when my father was in hospital, *"There is your father fighting for his life Billy, you are throwing yours away"*.

When I was in the Peak District, Alex *"Hurricane"* Higgins lived just up the road in a beautiful Tudor Manor. He had a lovely wife, two beautiful children and was the World Snooker Champion. One night there was a village scandal. Alex had been arrested for assaulting his wife, having smashed all the leaded windows of the house by throwing televisions through them. Poor Alex ended up sharing a council flat in Belfast on the dole having lost his millions and was penniless.

Tony Booth, the father of Cherie Blair and Star of *"Oh Calcultta"* and *"Till Death Do Us Part"* set himself on fire trying to burn his wife's house down drunk. Reginald Bosenquet from ITN News was sacked for being drunk on air and arrested for throwing stones and breaking all his neighbors windows. Jimmy Greaves, the first Million Pound Footballer, ended up on a park bench. I was in hospital with Jimmy and he got well.

James Hunt, the world champion Racing Driver died of a brain haemmorage caused by alcoholism. Alan Lake the husband of Diane Dors was in prison with me again in hospital with me, shot himself drunk. Alan couldn't get well. Poor old Peter Cook never got well and died from alcohol related brain haemmorage.

Everyone knows the George Best story. George ended up in Ford Prison for assaulting the police. Richard Burton died of a brain haemorrhage a very pitiful, sad, unhappy drunk. Today, more and more people have *"Come Out"* with the problem. This was influenced greatly by Dick Van Dyke, the star of Mary Poppins who made no bones about his illness, alcoholism. Dick was and is a great *Ambassador* for AA.

We all have treatment available. Knowing you are an

alcoholic and accepting the fact are as different as chalk and cheese. There was and still is today a stigma with the disease of alcoholism. Thanks to people like *Betty Ford, Joan Kennedy, Liz Taylor, Eric Clapton, Peter Townsend, Barry (Dame Edna) Humpries, Anthony Hopkins, Jim Davidson, Bob Hawke,* and *George Best.* Today people are more compassionate towards the alcoholic. It is a disease and the third biggest killer in the world not including homicides, suicides and road accidents.

Through AA over the years, I have met royalty, doctors, dockers, priests and policemen, nuns and prostitutes. This awful disease has no distinction between race, creed or politics. You can't be nearly an alcoholic, as you cannot be nearly pregnant. You either are one or you are not.

Heavy drinking is what it sounds, *Heavy Drinking.* Alcoholic is when it costs you more than money, e.g. blackouts, car accidents, violence and when you need a drink to function. It is the only illness where the poison which is killing you is also the only medicine that can make you feel better.

Cunning, baffling and frightening. There are only three avenues open to alcoholics. Death through illness, suicide or accidental, Mental Hospital/Prison or Recovery.

The World Health Organisation have produced figures, and I know first hand the profession with the highest rate of alcoholism is the medical profession. This is led by Psychiatrists followed by Pathologists. In London and Dublin there is a Doctors Group of AA with over six hundred active member attendance weekly which goes to show the stigma which is still attached to alcoholism and despite the anonymity, doctors cannot really afford to go to open meetings of AA. Imagine going for open heart surgery knowing the surgeon is an alcoholic.

I was in St Andrews in Northampton on one of my De-Tox visits and there was eleven residents on the alcohol programme which included eight doctors. They know all the facets of the disease. They can prescribe the medicine but cannot get the cure. *"Doctor, Doctor heal thyself".* This goes a long way to showing how complex the disease is.

The addiction is the same whether drugs, alcohol or prescribed drugs. Any mood altering chemical is a form of escape from reality. You could open the prisons of the world and let out half the inmates if it wasn't for alcohol. Far more than cannabis, heroin or cocaine combined. Alcohol is the greatest remover of all. It removes homes, families, business and finally your self-respect. Very sadly there is a story in the **Big Book** from 1938 where the storyteller makes the same analogy about prisons. That has not changed in over sixty years.

If you sit in a barber's shop long enough, you will need a haircut. If an alcoholic hangs around pubs, clubs and his drinking environment eventually he or she will surely drink. You don't go into a *Brothel for a Kiss.*

I personally received in my treatment a great benefit from people like Dr Edwards the first man I saw and Mary Bolton who were themselves alcoholics. Having said this, you don't have to be an lady to be a gynaecologist. There are great doctors in the field who have no drink problem. Dr Max Glatt of the Priory, London and Dr David Curzon of St Andrews Hospital, Northampton, to name but two.

Doctor Curzon was a great help to me. He told me that I reminded him so much of one of his former patients and I was a very bad case. I asked what happened to the patient and he told me that he was found hanging from a tree in Epping Forest. Curzon pulled no punches.

So in the last week of September 1981 the children were going home on Sunday as Margaret was on holidays. On the Thursday I had to go to Northampton and deliver the car I had purchased for Terri's Dad. I had purchased a new Lada car that was very economical. The previous car I bought him was an Austin 1800 and he found it too heavy on petrol. They were a lovely couple and I was very fond of them. Just farming stock, nice village people.

I left early in the morning and it was a two hours drive. I should have been home by lunchtime. A BUPA cheque had also arrived so I put this in the Anglian Building Society whilst I was in Northampton for Terri's account.

I rang William to see if everything was ok at home. He told me someone came to see me. William said they looked like police as he saw them with *Walkie Talkie* radios. This was all I wanted. Police on the door step with my children home alone. I told William to get a taxi to the local hotel. I had booked the rooms there the previous day to take the children out for a meal, breakfast in bed the next morning as a bit of a treat.

I was travelling in the new Mercedes as I had sold the Rolls to an Australian who reckoned he could drive the car for one year in England and one year in Australia, sell it and double his money. I was going to Paris on business when the children went home.

I drove to the hotel first, before I got out of the car police came from everywhere. These guys were Regional Crime Squad armed with guns. I had no idea what it was about. I was taken to Colchester Police Station. I said *"I must go into the hotel and see my children"*. They said *"The kids are at the police station already"*.

The dirty bastards had held my children for three hours. I have hated the actions of the London Police from that day to this. The way they swagger they almost waltz rather than walk. Many of the ones selected for *brawn to intimidate* rather than *brains to investigate.*

They said a car was coming up from London to take me back and that it would be a couple of hours. I was not allowed to see the children, this is all part of the softening up process. I couldn't ring Margaret she was away, my mother was away and Bob was away. In the end we got hold of Bob's nanny, who drove one hundred and fifty miles to Chelsmford and collected the children.

This was an awful traumatic experience for the children and they both still remember it. William was thirteen and Edwina was eight years old. What made matters worse were the three East End Thugs (Policemen) who took me back to London, threatening violence, big talk, yet not telling me what the case was. They were making remarks like *"It will be a long time before you can commit crimes again, as we are locking you up"*, etc. etc.

This was when I realised all my antecedents starting at Devon Assizes in 1970 gave the police the idea they had caught some *Big Fish*. It was all in their minds as each prosecution goes on the file and enhances promotion.

I was taken to Snow Hill and charged with receiving

five tons of stolen meat. They had taken every document from my home some twenty four black sacks of papers. This was all on the desk of the police inspector, Derrick Couling. He was a typical London Secondary Modern school boy with a big chip on his shoulders. They agreed to interview me in the morning.

I was placed in the cells for the night and in the morning when I was given a razor to shave they gave me a *BIC*. I asked for a safety razor saying I had sensitive skin. The Sergeant duly gave me one. I washed, shaved and put the razor blade in my cell. I had written to my mother and Terri as well as a quick note to Sally. I cut the insides of my elbows and cut my wrists. I then cut my throat. I passed out before I could cut my windpipe.

Despite the Librium and the Lithium, I can remember my state of mind doing that awful deed. I woke up in St Bartholomews Hospital, Smithfield, which was only next door. They brought the court to my bed and I was remanded in custody for seven days.

I was handling so much meat I didn't know which five tons was allegedly stolen. After arriving in Brixton prison I was placed in the prison hospital. All murderers are placed in a cell ward as there is always a risk of a murderer in remorse killing himself. It was called the Special Watch Ward. There were eleven prisoners, eight murderers, two arsonists and me. They were a decent bunch of fellows, amongst them was Ronnie Knight the husband of Barbara Windsor. Ronnie was a *"Bad Boy"*, a very nice man but a *"Bad Boy"*.

Ronnie had been there eight months and was awaiting trial for murder, however, because of all the press Barbara got for him and her Appeals. He was acquitted. The acquittal was quite correct as the police had gone *OTT* to frame and catch him. However, saying this Ronnie would kneel in the middle the ward and yell out to the murdered man *"I hope you rot in Hell, you Bastard"*. Ron's guilt or innocence is his own business but a jury of twelve said he was not guilty.

Talking of suicides, thirteen suicides by people in similar situation as mine come to mind. The alcoholic depression causes the suicidal thoughts. If you are Fair Dinkum, you will succeed.

The suicides that came to mind are:

- *The Duke of Bedford at Tavistock in Devon,
  fifteen miles from our own village*
- *Ken Hume, Shirley Bassey's husband*
- *Mary Ure at the opening of "The Exorcist" in
  the West End*
- *Mama Cass of Mammas and Pappas*
- *Ottis Redding the singer*
- *Bob Marley the singer*
- *Harry Finnemore in our village*
- *Keith Moon of "The Who"*
- *Brian Jones of "Rolling Stones"*
- *John Bohnham of "Led Zeppelin"*
- *Reginald Bosenquet of "ITN News", and lastly, poor*
- *Michael Hutchence of "INXS".*

Never believe what you read in the press. The police say accidental overdoes so you think drugs. All the people mentioned were on Heminevrin to get off the booze and substituted it, for booze in the end. Heminevrin gives you a lovely high. There are many many more of my contemporaries who died with drugs and booze. Deaths of Jimmy Hendrix, Sid Vicious of Sex Pistols, Yootha Joyce of George and Mildred, John Bindon the actor, etc.

This disease alcoholism is a great remover even more embarrassing is to wake up and having come so close yet failed, especially having written farewell notes for all to read.

The police realised they couldn't bring a case. However, with all my twenty four bags of papers, produced eleven different charges of attempting to buy goods by deception. In the twelfth week, they still had no evidence, so I was bailed after thirteen weeks. Sally had been visiting me in prison coming two hundred and fifty miles on the train from Manchester to Brixton for a twenty minute visit. She was quite a lady.

This was November 1981 and I had been sober thirteen months. I thought what is the point drunk or sober. *I am in trouble*. I bought a bottle of whiskey at Sally's flat and was back on the booze.

Making matters worse the Bank of Ireland had called on my Bank Guarantee and taken Eleven Thousand Pounds from my account. My house in Essex that I had just received the mortgage cheque for had been foreclosed. All my clothes and furniture were missing. The finance company had taken my car so all I had was a bank cheque with the balance of my account for One Thousand Nine Hundred Pounds. Things looked pretty grim. I had to sign with the police daily as a part of my bail conditions.

Sally had never known me drunk, poor girl. It came as a shock to her but she loved me very much and would have done anything for me. She gave up her job, sold her house. I purchased a false passport and we decided to go back to South Africa. Sally spoke fluent Spanish and French and together we should have perhaps gone to South America but I knew South Africa and knew I could make a new start. This was a geographical escape, running away again. So we bought the tickets and a fourteen day package holiday. We flew from London on the Twenty Third of December 1981 telling no one until we arrived, not even my mother.

The day before we left I spoke to Terri to see if she wanted the furniture that was all in storage. This was from two homes. The Irish furniture we had in Manchester along with all my furniture from house in the Peak District. Terri wanted nothing to do with me so that was ok. I rang Margaret and met her at the warehouse. I told her if she paid the storage she could have it all. This included all my books, paintings, five televisions and two large houses of furniture. Margaret agreed and this also made me feel good for the children's sake.

My brother Bob had taken over the responsibility of William's school fees. Bob in actual fact paid the fees for the next six years and all of William's education thanks to Bob. Bob had proved to be a *"Lion amongst Men"*. He had employed David and Barbara who again got into many problems in Ireland. He paid for the education of Tracey at a very expensive boarding school in Ireland. He financed my mother with a house and a car and changed the car updating it on a regular basis. Whilst doing all of these deeds, Bob made a great success of rearing his own children. Always very quiet and modest, Bob was one of life's great achievers.

Having put my house in order, I signed on with the police early in the morning of the Twenty Third of December. This gave until ten o'clock on that night, the Twenty Fourth of December, before any alarm bells would ring. We took the train from Manchester to London and spent the day at the Tara Hotel in Kensington, leaving from Heathrow that evening.

The flight to Johannesburg took fourteen hours so we arrived in South Africa on Christmas Eve 1981. Sally was adopted the same as Terri. Sally's parents were both in their seventies so the first thing we did was telephone Sally's parents and my mother. Mum was furious that I had not told her, yet she was aware that something was going on. There is no way I could ever fool my mother.

CHAPTER EIGHTEEN

So here I was again in sunny South Africa. In the six years that had passed since my previous visit, I found the apartheid laws were considerably relaxed. The Black Africans were now seen in the best parts of the city. The *Whites Only* signs were beginning to come down at last. Having said this, there was still an air of racial tension amongst the Afrikaners who are tremendous bigots.

The hotel was fine and much better than I expected it to be. The rooms were spacious and well furnished with cable television. Something else new to South Africa, six years previously there were only limited hours per day of television and people used to hold house movie nights in their own home, with videos or even projectors and reels of film.

I rang Cyril Hurwitz, the Chairman of Bull Brand, only to find Cyril had retired and sold the business to Vlicentraal, a large Farmers Co-operative. Monty, Cyril's brother had gone into the feed lot business but their nephew was still the Managing Director. Hans Mohr was the nephew and Cyril arranged me to go and see him at his home on Boxing Day.

The meeting went well. They were having a pool party at their home when I arrived with Sally and obviously had heard glowing reports about me from Cyril and Monty. The plant was closed until the Fifth of January but it was agreed I would start on that date and survey the whole plant. My job was to see where improvements in production could be made and cost cuts. So on leaving the party and having only drunk very moderately, I was already employed at a reasonable salary to start in ten days' time.

Bull Brand was handling about six thousand Cattle per week and at that time the biggest meat works in the Southern Hemisphere. The company produced Corned Beef by the millions of tins a week as well as Bull Cubes which were the same as *OXO* cubes. There was also a new Hamburger Plant and Cooked Meats Department producing ready to serve Roast Beef slices and Meat Balls as well as Frankfurters. They held the Wimpy Bar and McDonald contracts for the whole of the

African continent.

Mohr was in the process of negotiating the Israeli government contract for one thousand head of cattle per week. I asked him who he was dealing with in Tel Aviv and he told me Dr. Cohen. I explained I had done the contract from Belfast a few years earlier and to mention my name. The other company that was tendering was Ecko Meats in Lobatse, Botswana, so when we obtained the contract I received most of the credit.

Sally and myself found a nice little house in Krugersdoorp, the town was east of Johannesburg. The house was only three bedrooms yet had nearly an acre of lawns, fruit trees and servants quarters. Two servants came with the house and a maid whose husband was the gardener.

There was no furniture but we made arrangements with a local store in the village who rented out furniture with the option to buy and we were very organised by the Fifth of January 1982. I managed to buy a new Renault 4 car on finance from Wespac Bank. Anyone who was on the Bull Brand payroll in an executive capacity was treated very well in the town.

There were one thousand employees at the plant all Black African, most of this staff lived in *Male Only* compounds, sending home their money to their families weekly and only going home once a year. I also had sixty school girls or just left school starting on the Twelfth of January to train as packers of Small Goods, Beef slices and Burgers.

There were about twenty five Europeans and Afrikaners in the management team. These were all second rate English and Germans who would at best in Europe be employed as lower middle management. The Works Manager called Hadleigh was an ex Findus Foods employee.

Mohr was the only person who knew who I really was, as I was working under the name in my passport. I explained to Cyril I had some problems in England and didn't want anyone to know where I was. Cyril and his nephew honoured my wishes. The Hurwitz were a Jewish family who had been in the South African meat business for two generations. Cyril had a go at the English meat business prior to EEC in 1972 and left England owing about £6 million.

Sally who had always been a career girl despite her two

previous marriages, settled down to being a housewife and was as happy as a duck in water. I always came home for lunch, having started work at six o'clock every morning and most days I was home by four in the afternoon.

The manufacturing equipment for the burger line was very old and no one really had any idea. The staff of sixty men were producing less burgers per day than I was with twenty men in Stockport, so I began making many changes with great results.

My greatest pleasure was the sixty girls all aged fifteen and sixteen. They were so keen to please and so willing to work and I had the benefit of training them my ways from the start. So this department of freezer meats was a little gold mine. This staff cost no money rather we were paid by the government to employ them. All of this production was for supermarket freezers, e.g. four burgers in a box or one packet of roast beef in gravy per box. Then we had meat balls in gravy, meat balls in bar-be-que sauce, etc. This was all packed by hand by my schoolgirls *free of charge* and a license to print money.

The abattoir itself was a pleasure to work in. The Africans were great natural knife men and I took out the two hide pullers that skin the cattle and went back to the old way of hand skinning the cattle on the line. The results were my kill floor was finished at lunch time each day as opposed to three o'clock in the afternoon. The same staff numbers had taken three hours off the working day under my guidance.

We had our own railway line coming into the plant from the local station, most of our cattle come up from South West Africa or Namibia as it is known today. We also purchased many cattle from the feed lots. With the large feed lots that had been developed in Africa at this time we had supplies of cattle all the year round.

The Boning Halls were the fly in the ointment. This was all Afrikaan supervisors and refused to make any changes. *"We have always done it this way"*, so every morning hours were wasted cutting all the cattle into quarters, that could have been left in sides saving hours of work. I was not going to force the issue as I needed these Afrikaans on my side.

Socially life was good. I loved the climate and lovely

light mornings, most of all I loved the electric storms. All cars were fitted with lightening conductors as the storms were tremendous. Each weekend we were invited out with the European personnel who had bar-be-ques and parties and were all very heavy drinkers. One of the fellow who came from Chelmsford in England had his garden shed which was quite large, done out as an English Pub. Going there on a Friday you would believe you were in England. He had built it all himself with local labour.

Whilst we enjoyed those evenings they were not really our type of people. They were all happy to plod along on very mediocre salaries as they were very mediocre people. I can honestly say there was not one of them I would have employed in my own business. Having said this they were decent people just rather boring.

We were on the edge of the gold fields to the West and the Kruger National Park to the East. It was a very industrial bland part of the world between our town and Johannesburg.

Going into the city one day, we called in to look at Soweto, the shanty town of two million souls. It was not until I got to work on Monday that I realised this was a *No Go* area for Whites. There were Sally and myself driving through, looking at all the sights like a couple of tourists. I suppose everyone was so shocked at seeing is that they failed to do anything to us. We were quite happy in our ignorance. So that was an experience and a half. This was the most heart breaking maze of people and hovels I had ever seen but it gave me the idea to supply all the Shabeens or illegal pub/club/restaurant with meat.

I found a Black Butcher who had the connections and within six weeks I was supplying ten tonnes of beef ribs and steaks to the Shabeens. The five tonne of steaks was all cut from cow beef that had been previously going into the Burgers so this contract alone was very profitable and ripe for expansion.

The more successful I became the more problems I had with Hadleigh, the Works Manager. He was in fear of his own position of course. One Friday evening at a Bar-be-que, he said, *"Bill, I have asked Graham Crisp in Ireland if he has heard of you and he tells me the only person he knows who fits your description is Bill Hayes. He said he has never heard of you which I find strange"*. I laughed it off and changed the subject but the hairs on the back of my neck stood up.

This was on the Friday evening and on the Monday at work he called me to his office. He was like a little Jack Russell terrier not letting go, telling me if I wasn't using my real name, my work permit was invalid and I would have to re-apply to the Department of Immigration. I bluffed my way out of this. At three o'clock in the afternoon I was again called to his office telling me I had to go to Johannesburg and see the Department of Immigration at the same time the following day. I could have killed him and can still see the *false concerned look* on his face.

Hadleigh was in his middle fifties and married to a South African girl of twenty three. He had been only a Supervisor at Findus who were one of my main clients in the U.K. This is why I had never came across him. Graham Crisp was an independent meat broker in Dublin who had formerly worked for Lyons and the Irish Pigs and Bacon Commission. When Graham went into business on his own, he got his first Fifteen Thousand Pounds from my Portuguese contract. I also set him up as an agent for Staburaat, my Norwegian clients. Reg Hope and Harry Madgewick the head men of Findus which is owned by Nestles knew me very well and had been to my wedding in 1967.

I went home and told Sally that I was in trouble and Hadleigh must have been on the phone all weekend checking me out. I had not been home thirty minutes when the lady who had sold us the furniture called around. She had also supplied Hadleigh's furniture and he had telephoned her telling her if I had no Work Permit I had no job.

The delicate thing was Bull Brand. Despite the Hurwitz involvement, was now owned by a Farmers co-operative with a committee of management and they would for sure dot their I's and cross their T's. I explained to the lady this was a personality clash with Hadleigh and if she was concerned about her money I would pay her in full. Sally gave her a cheque.

At seven o'clock that night the local manager from Wespac came. He was concerned about my car on his finance. I had quite a few drinks under my belt and told him to *Go to Hell*, unless he had the power to revoke my agreement. I decided to ring Cyril and tell him I was going to the Immigration the following day and he advised me against it. Cyril said, *"Jump in the car tomorrow and drive quietly over the border to Botswana and re-apply for a Work Permit and come back. This way there is no risk of being deported"*.

The following morning I sold all the furniture at eight o'clock in the morning to a second hand shop. The deal was they pay me 50% in advance, the balance on collection. I only took a small loss.

I told Hadleigh I was not going to work that morning until I had sorted out the immigration. He insisted that if I didn't work I was in breach of my contract. I saw Red and put him against the wall with my hands around his throat and told him *"not to push his luck if he had any concern for his wife and baby daughter, as he was going to be in hospital for a long time"*. He most definitely got the message and I regret not having a got at him before, as he was an awful Coward.

I went to the company Travel Agent and booked two tickets to Botswana that evening and told them to charge them down to Bull Brand, knowing full well they would later ring Bull Brand to confirm the authority. I filled my car with petrol from the company pumps free of charge and went home. We put our cases in the car and just as I was driving out of the drive, the manager of Wespac was driving in.

He had two men in the car with him and told me he had to take my car, as Head Office were freezing my agreement until they had an employment letter from Bull Brand. I told him *"You will have to call back as my wife has to get to the doctors urgently"*. He said he would wait at the house and I said *"That's okay"*. The house looked quite normal, cups in the kitchen, the newspaper on the coffee table and fruit in the fruit bowl. The second hand man had not collected the furniture but we had the 50% deposit.

I drove out of the drive normally and down the road, then when I checked they were not following me, I drove like a *Bat out of Hell* for the border to Zimbabwe, some seven hundred miles up the road. I never took my foot off full throttle until two to three hours had elapsed.

The flight I had booked to Botswana was seven o'clock that evening and I knew full well with the false trail I had laid. No one would ever consider my going to Zimbabwe and as long as I crossed that night, I was safe.

I have no idea what went on in Krugarsdorp or how long the bankers sat at the house. We hit the border at midnight only to find it closed at ten o'clock. This was at Messina in Northern South Africa where Butts Bridge crosses the Limpopo River.

We booked into a small motel and the night seemed forever. The bar and restaurant were closed. There was no TV and sleep didn't come very easily that night. I was up at five the next morning. Then sat in the room for one and a half hours waiting for the border to open at seven o'clock.

We arrived at the Border at five minutes to seven and I was a *bag of nerves*. The customs officers seemed to take forever looking at the passports. Just as we were walking out of the door the telex began. I nearly had kittens. The guard then opened the barrier and I was gone before the telex finished.

The Zimbabwe side was quite simple. This was 1982 and the country was newly independent with all African officers. We stated the nature of our visit was a holiday and visiting family and with no questions we had three month visa stamped on our passports.

We stopped in the village of Butts Bridge at the only hotel, then sitting on the river bank and ate two hearty breakfasts. I could imagine little Hadleigh reveling in all the trouble he had caused me. He had also cost me one month's salary and half the value of my furniture. I would dearly like to meet him again. He was a very spiteful inferior little man.

I knew very little of Zimbabwe. Only that it had been formerly Rhodesia and Ian Smith used to be the Prime Minister. I had met Ian years earlier. On my previous visit to South Africa, I was aware that Robert Mugabe was now the Prime Minister and it was majority rule. Salisbury was the capital and the Victoria Falls were there. Harare was the new name for Salisbury.

I was very moved by the story of Robert Mugabe. First of all, he spent nine years in prison at the hands of the English.

Sally Soames, the wife of Christopher Soames or Lord Soames took care of Sally Mugabe, Robert Mugabe's wife during this time. Sally Soames is, of course, the daughter of Winston Churchill.

Mugabe lost one of his children in a drowning accident during this time in prison and was not allowed to be present at the funeral. Mugabe's story is not unlike that of Jomo Kenyata of Kenya who spent fourteen years in prison then went on to become President of Kenya.

The nearest main town to the border was Bullawayo. This was four hundred miles so it seemed the place to go. I fell in love with the country instantly. It was so lush with lots of grass and many trees for the shelter of cattle. It was a *Cattleman's Paradise*. Our funds were very low but it was not the end of the world, we were still free.

I recall about half way to Bullawayo we stopped at a roadside hotel at the village of *"Todds Saleyards"*. There was a large hotel and bar and there were these enormous wooden pens for cattle and large derelict meat works. Talking to the owner of the hotel, I learnt this meat works had been built by Lord Vestey and closed down during the recent war of independence, the guerillas, who were now of course the government, had blown up all the cattle dips on the white farms. This meant the cattle couldn't be dipped for anti Teste Fly dip and *"Sleeping Sickness"* had killed all the cattle, crippling the white economy.

Whilst I am writing this account today, the same thing is happening in Zimbabwe in order to return the white owned farms to the black majority. It is so very sad the blacks and whites cannot find some compromise and at this time in 1982 many whites were leaving the country and going mainly to South Africa or Australia and the U.K.

The whites leaving could only take One Thousand Dollars Rhodesian and one motor vehicle and their household furniture. This gave them the choice of staying and chancing their luck or leaving broke, some people after two to three generations in the country. It was all very sad and there were valid points on both sides of the divide.

Having learned a little about the country we continued to Bullawayo eventually arriving in the early evening.

Bullawayo was a gorgeous colonial town with the most splendid architecture. The first thing I noticed were the cars. There were cars from the 1950's and 1960's that all looked brand new. We later learned because in Central Africa there is no salt spray from the sea in the air, therefore, no rust. The climate is so very dry.

We found a small family run hotel in Livingstone Road and booked in for a week. I had been working very hard and so we went swimming in the public swimming pool in Bullawayo and generally relaxing. I needed the space and the time to decide what to do. Seeing all the Black and White children swimming together was quite lovely. These lovely pools had of course been built for *Whites* only.

There was a very large meat works in Bullawayo, again built by Lord Vestey. This was comparatively new and set in one hundred acres of splendid gardens all in flower. The plant had been taken over by the government in 1980 and was only working one day a week as there were no cattle. The meat industry was at a standstill.

I met a man in the bar one evening called Jim Carrol. He was second generation rich Irish Rhodesian and in the car business, buying and selling cars. He noticed my car which was only three months old and asked me what I had paid for it. I believe the price was Ten Thousand Rand. He told me if I sold it to him and delivered it back to South Africa, he could pay me the equivalent of Twenty Thousand Pounds but in Rhodesian dollars. This money of course is no use outside Zimbabwe, yet an awful lot of money to spend in Zimbabwe.

I said I would certainly consider his offer and talk to Sally about it. I didn't tell him that I was not in a position to take it back to South Africa.

The following day we went to the Races at Ascot the same name as the English course. Whilst nothing quite the same in size, the facilities were second to none and the whole of the white community had turned out.

I told Sally about the offer from Jim Carroll, what Jim was doing was selling the car to Rhodesians who were leaving the country. By getting car into South Africa and paying on inflated price in Zimbabwe, they were getting around the *sanctions* of only taking out One Thousand Dollars. Everyone was a winner and Jim Carroll must have been earning a fortune. Sally agreed the risks were too great for me.

That evening I got blind drunk and remembered a Dick Francis book where the mother of the hero committed suicide by taking aspirin and swallowing them with Vodka. Apparently very calmly sitting at the kitchen table. I knew for sure that suicide on my previous attempt was a very bloody messy business and the way of the aspirin appealed to me.

I tried to obtain aspirins all over Bullowayo. I must have gone into every chemist shop. I eventually got them in a twenty four hours shop. There were dispirins and other pills but no aspirins anywhere else. I purchased five hundred pills and took them back to the hotel telling Sally of my intention.

We had very little money left. The only asset was the car and I could see no way out. There was no way I was going back to England. I suggested Sally go back and leave me. She said *"If you are going to kill yourself Bill I'm coming with you"*. I then told her of the Dick Francis book and the aspirins.

We booked a suite at the Holiday Inn at Ascot Bullawayo right on the Racecourse. We had an evening of champagne and light dinner and retired to our suite. I began taking the aspirin and drinking. I was washing them down with champagne and vodka and orange. I have no idea how many I took but a good half and Sally perhaps forty-fifty. I was very drunk, very low and very miserable.

Then I was violently ill. When I say ill, I mean *ILL*. I was retching, vomiting and sick, so very very sick. There was no bloody way this was going to work or was working. Thirty minutes after me, Sally was ill. Again no way was it working. We spent the rest of the night drinking iced water and vomiting. I most certainly was not meant to die, that day. I had always believed Dick Francis researched his books well. He most certainly was wrong in this instance. Whilst I am aware I have a strong constitution, Sally got over the attempt as well.

So the next morning, our last money gone on the suite, we moved back to the Livingstone Hotel as we had not checked out and I went off to the car yard of Jim Carroll. Jim agreed I take the car over the border on Sunday morning. He gave me

Two Thousand Dollars cash deposit and made the arrangements in South Africa.

I was to deliver the car to a Greek milk bar in Messina, the first town over the border from Butts Bridge. The arrangements were, the Greek would give me a receipt and drive me back to the border. I was to walk over and make my own way back to Bullawayo four hundred miles. I asked would it not seem peculiar walking over the border and Jim assured me people do it all the time.

So everything was arranged. This was Friday and I was to leave Sunday morning. We agreed Sally would wait in Bullawayo and I would telephone her from Butts Bridge, the moment I was back in Zimbabwe. If I didn't ring by lunch time on Sunday, she was to use the Two Thousand Dollars and fly back to the U.K.

Sally was a very sophisticated lady. She had worked in South America, Spain, Morocco and Malta as well as all over the U.K. She had been married twice and was involved with a couple of men, when I met her. I had no fear that Sally would have any problems, getting back to the U.K. alone, yet I hoped it would not come to this.

On the Saturday evening we had a candle lit dinner for two and danced all evening at the hotel. By the time the evening was over it was time for me to leave for the Border. I had filled up with petrol and had ten gallons of spare petrol in my boot. I was sure to check my oil and water and all ready to set off.

The drive to the border was beautiful in the dark. Then at five o'clock in the morning the sun began to rise and the whole horizon was bright red. The most delightful thing to me were the road signs saying "Danger Elephants Crossing" in just the same manner as Devon, where they say "Danger Cattle Crossing".

I arrived at the border at half past six in the morning so I had half an hour to wait for the opening. I had drunk all my coffee from the thermos flask the hotel gave me. There had been no problem but my nerves were shot.

Messina was only ten miles from the border. We had stayed in a motel there on the previous crossing when we fled South Africa. I was five miles from Messina and ran out of petrol. I couldn't believe it, so near yet so far away. A group of about thirty small monkeys came from nowhere and were all over the car. I was stranded like a bloody idiot. If only I had brought twenty gallons of additional petrol instead of the ten I had used.

I had visions of the South African Security Police coming and asking for my passport and papers. Then going seven hundred miles back to Johannesburg and that little runt Hadleigh laughing in my face. I waited may be twenty minutes trying to decide if to walk to Messina or walk back to the border. I had not seen one car since Bullawayo except a postman on the border.

I saw a red Toyota Pickup coming from the border and flagged it down. There was a Afrikaan farmer and his wife going to Messina to Church. They told me I could ride on the back of the Pickup and this brought back memories of riding on the donkey and cart on my first visit to Ireland.

I was so elated, I felt like the hero from a *Hemmingway novel*, rather than Bill Hayes the boy from the village in Devon. We arrived at the milk bar. I thanked them and off they went to church. Their good deed for the day done.

The Greek was superb. He got a five gallon drum of petrol along with his son drove me back to the car. He inspected the car which was now covered in monkey shit, gave me the receipt and drove me back to the border. I again asked, *"Is it normal for people to walk over the border?"* They answered me, *"People do it all the time"*.

The South African side was no problem then I had the one mile walk over the bridge to the Zimbabwe side, again no problem. I went straight to the hotel and ordered bacon, eggs, tea and toast and telephoned Sally. She was elated and had been praying for me.

I asked the people in the hotel in there was a taxi in the village. They said yes there was one but they did not think he would go to Bullawayo anyway they called him.

The taxi arrived and it was a 1960 Hillman Minx. Hillman cars had been out of business ten years. The driver agreed to go to Bullawayo for One Hundred Dollars and I accepted gladly.

The taxi smelled of petrol. In the back seat there was a hose pipe that took the petrol from the tank into the engine. So I couldn't smoke. I really didn't care. *Third class riding was preferable to first class walking.* The driver was a jolly young man and had never been to Bullawayo in his life. He was so excited, all he did was talk. I reclined my seat and slept most of the journey with a wonderful feeling of calm for the first time in years.

We arrived in Bullawayo in the early evening and we booked a room at the Livingstone for the taxi driver to stay over night. Sally and myself and the driver had dinner together and we all felt pleased, relieved and happy.

The following day, Monday, we went to see Jim Carroll. I had a slightly anxious feeling that he could keep the car and not pay me. This was soon put to rest. Jim took Forty Eight Thousand Dollars from his safe and put it into an old fashioned *"white cloth money bag"* and gave it to me. I had the equivalent of Twenty Thousand Pounds Sterling and the ordeal was over.

Jim then said he could give me a regular job taking cars over the border as the pay was very good. I said *"Thank you but no thank you"*. We agreed to have drinks later in the week.

We spent the next two weeks touring around Bullawayo, drove up to the Victoria Falls and acted like two holiday makers. I rented a BMW car for only *One Hundred Dollars per week*.

We decided to make tracks for Harare, the capital of Zimbabwe where I placed Twenty Thousand Dollars into Gilbeys Bank along with an English cheque for Fifteen Thousand Pounds. We did the same with Barclays Bank account Twenty Thousand Dollars and an English cheque for Fifteen Thousand Pounds. I had no funds in my English account yet was aware the cheques would take six weeks to clear. Having done my banking, we booked the best suite at Meikles Hotel. This only cost One Hundred Dollars per night.

We had one month at Meikles and it was the holiday of my life. The service, the treatment, the food was the best I had ever experienced for Forty Pounds Sterling per day. This type of hotel in London or Paris would be Two Hundred Pounds per day. We were treated like visiting royalty.

After three weeks I went to my banks. I was showing $20,000 in each account. I had my receipt for the £15,000 English cheques which converted at $37,500. Based on the assumption I had brought $37,000 into the country from the U.K. The bank had no hesitation in giving me £10,000 English Traveller's Cheques. I repeated the process at the other bank and there I was still showing a credit balance in my accounts of $37,000 uncleared and in my pocket £20,000 in English Traveller's Cheques.

We could leave Zimbabwe and take Jim Carroll's money with us. We purchased a BMW for Five Thousand Dollars from a white policeman who was going to South Africa and paid him only One Thousand Five Hundred Pounds in UK Traveller's Cheques. So we gained a very cheap car. He gained an extra One Thousand Five Hundred Pounds to take out of the country. *Everyone was a winner.*

We had decided to go north to Zambia formerly Northern Rhodesia. I knew quite a bit about the country from school with the copper mining. The local Doctor in Okehampton, Dr Jones had five daughters, Sally and Leslie were great friends of mine and they were always talking about Zambia as many Devon girls went there as Nurses in the 1960's.

Sally Jones was the nurse in Bristol who put Margaret up during my Plastic Surgery operation in 1967.

I very nearly came unstuck in the last town of Zimbabwe before the border. I had approx Two Thousand Dollars Rhodesian in cash. Greedily I went into Gilbeys Bank at the last town before leaving and I tried the same ploy of showing my English deposit and getting Traveller's Cheques.

The bank took ages and finally gave me Seven Hundred Pounds Traveller's Cheques. The Manager was not *very happy* but the clerk who did the transaction *winked at me and smiled.* There is no love loss between the Indians and the Africans and the Indian clerk knew exactly what I was doing. It was a foolish risk, when I had gained so much. However, it taught me a good lesson not to be greedy.

The capital of Zambia is Lusaka which was three hundred miles from the border. Zambia had been independent for the last sixteen years and the roads were in a terrible state of repair. So it was a long journey and slow, trying to avoid the pot holes.

We arrived in Lusaka in the early evening and booked into the Hotel Zambia. At dinner that night there was a beautiful dining room with dance floor and only seven to eight European couples. The band was good, the food was excellent and the members of the band took it in turn asking Sally to dance as we were the only couple dancing. It was a very lovely evening.

There was no Beef industry in Zambia in 1982 yet today there is a huge Meat industry. There is today a great Irish involvement in Zambia. The Irish Army train all the officers for the Zambian Army. There is an Irish meat company based in Lusaka supplying all the meat to the United Nations forces in Africa, as well as the army in Angola.

We decided to head north to Tanzania and go to Dar es Salaam. This was about a two thousand mile drive but we would see the ocean again. We also had all the time in the world to travel.

We set out for the border at mid morning one day and arrived about six o'clock in the evening. The Zambian side was quite okay, however, the Tanzanian side was a problem.

The first problem we had was, that we both had South African stamps on our passports. This was a *"Political No No"* any part of the apartheid regime.

The second problem was we had no Yellow Fever Card in our passports. The border was in the middle of nowhere and there was no way I wanted to go back to Lusaka.

I noticed a very strikingly beautiful African girl at the border on foot with several large sacks of sugar. She was on very familiar terms with the customs guards and smoking in their office, whilst we were stood at the counter.

She made herself known to us. Her name was Elizabeth Kyuza and she came from Umybeya, three hundred miles up the road in Tanzania. She said in return for a ride with us she could organise the Yellow Fever Cards and overlooking of the South African stamp. So we, of course, agreed. The customs officer gave us the Yellow Fever injection and the card and we were through.

CHAPTER NINETEEN

So there we were in Tanzania with a three hundred mile drive to Umybeya. Elizabeth told us this was a railway junction from Southern Africa to the coast at Dar es Salaam. This was the only route to the East Coast of Africa avoiding South Africa and Mozambique that was in the middle of a bloody civil war. President Michael was the ruler of Mozambique. Today his widow, is the wife of Nelson Mandella.

We thought the Zambian roads were pretty bad after the freeways of South Africa and pot holes in Zambabwe but here in Tanzania we were driving on gravel. The asphalt had worn away and not been replaced in twenty years of Independence. The main crops of Tanzania were sugar and maize. Yet all the sugar refineries in the country were closed and derelict and beyond repair, so all the refined sugar available was what was smuggled from Zambia or Uganda.

Uganda was still getting over the rule of Idi Amin at this time and very little sugar was being refined there. The one thing I noticed was how fertile all the land looked and how healthy the natives living in the country appeared. They were, of course, living off their home grown crops with corn on the cob (mealies) being the main diet.

The little country of Malawi, formerly Nyassaland is nestled in between Tanzania and Zambia. The country is the main grower of tea in Africa. Most of the plantations under the ownership of Tiny Rowland and Lonrho, his London public company based in Cheapside, London. Rowland also controlled all the exports from Tanzania little as they were and he held all the motor car dealerships, mainly VWs and Mercedes.

The country was bankrupt under the dictator President Julius Nyerre. It was so well for those African dictators to preach Communism. Whilst they lived better than the previous Tzars of Russia, 75% of the foreign aid to Tanzania never reached to the shores of the country. Rather, went direct to Swiss Banks in numbered accounts. This all thanks to Oxfam, Save the Children, Care and of course the United Nations. Corruption was a form of life and the black market. The currency was Tanzanian Schilling and they were quite worthless outside the country.

When one looks at the large Charities that operate in Africa, it really is very sickening World Vision in Melbourne takes Sixty Seven cents in every dollar for administration charges. The founder of World Vision, an Indian man, parades around Victoria in a Rolls Royce.

Malcolm Fraser the former Primer Minister of Australia, is involved in many Charities. His daughter Phoebe was a Director of CARE Australia. Poor Old Malcolm was involved in a drinking scandal in America when a Hostess took his trousers and wallet leaving him in a motel very embarrassed.

When we had the elections in Australia in 1995 Fraser was in South Africa for the inauguration of Nelson Mandella, at the cost of Forty Five Thousand Dollars to CARE Australia. He chartered a plane to fly him back to Australia for the election.

Many celebrities of screen and television make appeals for these unfortunate countries whilst travelling first class and stopping in Five Star hotels at the expense of the Charity or rather Donations from *"Joe Public"*.

Perhaps the worse of all Rorts was the former dictator of Zaire who became the thirteenth wealthiest man in the world while his people starved to death and lived in poverty on a wicked, horrible scale. All this wealth was generated from badly run European and American Charities.

When I was at school, Tanzania formerly Tanganiqua, was a prosperous colony and I could see all the potential was still there. Lake Victoria is the largest inland mass of fresh water in Africa and in my opinion Zimbabwe and Zambia could feed the world in conjunction with Tanzania yet all the whites had gone. The Indians had gone and it was just going to seed.

Elizabeth was a very articulate lady about twenty five or twenty six years of age and dressed in traditional native white clothes with a white hat. She could have passed for a princess. She was very regal and tall and carried two fifty pound sugar bags on her head. I have seen Devon farmers baulk at one bag of corn on their shoulders.

We had driven to about one hundred miles from our town Umybeya and I hit a wild dog. It just ran out and hit my grille. It didn't seem too serious but broke the radiator. This caused me to lose water and steam. There was a village only three miles away Elizabeth informed us so I drove on.

By the time we got to the village, I had blown my head gasket with the heat, so the car was finished. Thank God we had Elizabeth as she organised a hut for Sally and myself with the village chief. The chief also agreed that the village landrover could tow us to Umybeya the next morning for One Thousand Schillings or Fifty Dollars. This was good and we accepted graciously.

Sleep came easy once we were used to the smells of animals and cooking or rather boiling. The smell was like overdone cabbage, a very pungent smell. They were a very clean race with giant men and very tall tribal women and the most gorgeous naked children.

Sally and myself curled up on blankets on the floor and felt very close to each other. Once more we were in an adventure movie or novel. This was not us sleeping away in a tribal village and stuck there in the middle of Africa.

The following morning we declined breakfast and had several cups of the most delicious tea and were on our way. The whole village came to see us off. The Chief himself in the passenger seat of the land rover with his driver, Elizabeth and Sally in the back seat of the BMW and me on the brakes and steering wheel.

There were about twelve villagers all sat in a crouch position riding in the back of the landrover and two on the roof of the cab. This was a big day out for all of them.

The one hundred miles took all day and we arrived at tea time paying the agreed price with good tips for the fourteen passengers. We booked into the hotel which was a beautiful old colonial building with bar and restaurant. However, the rooms were an African version of a motel. Behind the hotel and very basic, concrete walls, concrete floor on the negative, yet a giant mahogany bed with mosquito nets on the positive side. We were more than content. Elizabeth promised to come and see us the next day to sort out the car.

We had a charming meal and drinks with some Indians who had come down from Malawi to do their month's shopping.

These Indians appeared very affluent and we learned they were a small group of Plantation Owners and Managers. There are many Indians and Sri Lankans involved in the tea planting in East Africa.

Elizabeth arrived at nine o'clock the following morning this time dressed in a fresh white Kaftan with a different hat but her arms and neck was covered in gold and she had her nails painted and lipstick on. She looked a totally different girl. She explained going for the sugar one has to go discreetly as a peasant girl purporting to get sugar for the family. This kept the prices down. The reality was she had a team of ladies doing this three hundred and fifty mile trip daily into Zambia.

She brought the local garage man who said there was no chance of spare parts, however, he could make a head gasket out of plastic himself, once he got the engine out. We agreed a price and he reckoned it would take ten days maximum and we would have a car like new.

I visited his workshop and my goodness he was a clever mechanic, making all the spare parts of cars himself with a local engineer. They had very little sophisticated equipment.

With the exception of the President getting a new bullet proof Mercedes 500 each year, there had been no cars imported into the country for five years. Even franchise of Tiny Rowland were dealing in second hand cars from Kenya, and cars that originated in Belgium or Holland. There was no money to buy them in foreign exchange. The country was bankrupt.

Our BMW was worth One Hundred Thousand Pounds in worthless Schillings. This was very tempting to me. Elizabeth arranged an Indian taxi driver to come and see me and we did a deal for One Hundred and Five Thousand Pounds Sterling all paid in Tanzanian Schillings.

I had an Aer Lingus Irish airline bag that was quite large. The whole bag was filled and difficult to zip with Tanzanian Schillings. I gave Elizabeth the equivalent to Five Thousand Pounds or 5% and I had One Hundred Thousand Pounds in worthless money but in my mind was the trick I had used in Zimbabwe to get Traveller's Cheques.

The train for Dar es Salaam comes every Sunday morning at seven o'clock and arrived in Dar es Salaam on

Monday night at eight o'clock so we booked a first class sleeping car. I took Elizabeth's address and phone number and this is no doubt I was very attracted to her. Not only her looks but her spirit, get up and go and trying to better herself. Whilst I was careful not to show any signs, Sally picked up Elizabeth's feelings and used to mimic her when we were alone. I must admit Elizabeth was very good for my ego.

We had met Elizabeth's boyfriend who was a very good looking Indian man, so this kept things nice and social with the four of us dining together but I was quite smitten with her and knew I would see her again.

We took the train on the Sunday. The buyer of the car was quite happy for the garage to complete the work on the car.

The weather was hot but breezy. The land like Ireland was forty shades of green. The railway itself was a piece of engineering genius. All steel and concrete for three thousand miles starting in Uganda and built free of charge by the Chinese government to promote Communism in Africa.

The railway was the Lifeline of Southern Africa and the train was massive. It went on for miles or so it seemed. At every station natives sold fruit and cold drinks of sugar cane crushed. This is delicious. I had a customer in London whose wife used to make at the Butcher's shop and sell it to the Indian community in Wembley.

Monday evening we arrived in Dar es Salaam, on the Indian Ocean. For the last one hundred miles of the journey you could smell the sea. The land became even more fertile as we closed on the ocean. This was the great Indian Ocean going all the way to Perth in Australia.

We booked into the Hotel Kenya and had a quiet dinner. All the African hotels from Zimbabwe had a dinner dance every evening and the Hotel Kenya was no exception. I locked my bag in the main hotel safe and was so relieved to have this money out of my hands for a while. We also had Twenty Thousand Pounds Sterling in Traveller's Cheques so all in all we were well off by African standards.

Dar es Salaam must have been one of the most beautiful cities in the world in Colonial days. The architecture of the magnificent colonial mansions, the Arab buildings and mosques. The buildings from the Moors and many other eras. This was, of course, the main slave transporting port of East Africa. The island of Zanzibar only twenty miles off the coast with the slave markets also.

Sadly, so very sadly in 1982 the gardens of all the mansions were derelict. The paint and plaster coming off the walls in chuncks, verandahs broken.

The streets were filthy and full of the most tragic lepers and begging children. This was my first sight of lepers and it has to be the cruelest disease known to man when your arms, legs, nose are dying, rotting and falling off, yet your brain is working normally.

There were many albino beggars. This was with my first experience of them. I had met a white albino in prison but here there were dozens of Black Albinos with the negro features, white hair and red eyes. They looked very strange to my white eyes yet they were considered holy.

Dar es Salaam is like the Tangiers or Morocco of South East Africa. A large sea port, with a constant flow of sailors from all parts of the world and of course with that goes the bars, night clubs and girls, to get every penny they can while they are on shore. Dar es Salaam is a port geared for the single man and not for couples having said this, it is a Paradise for the drinking alcoholic.

This was like the end of a long journey. There was no employment of any kind for a man of my qualifications. So all I did was drink, with the drink came the trouble, the rows, blackouts, and my going off on my own so I could drink without Sally telling me I have had enough.

Sally was concerned about her parents, who had a visit from the police who told them *"Sally has run off with a fugitive"*. They of course went to great details of my criminal record, starting at Devon Assizes. Sally had also seen the very worse of me. I had become an intolerable drunk, everything except the violence. This was only because I knew it would get me in more trouble.

I suggested Sally fly home and see her parents and we call it a day. I was finished in the U.K. and I was on the slippery slide to nowhere in Dar es Salaam. There was no objection from

Sally, only a quiet indifference which was very sad, as she had taken so many risks and given so much.

We booked Sally the air ticket on Lufthansa to fly to Manchester via Hamburg and she flew off on the Saturday afternoon. Before Sally had even gone, I had phoned Elizabeth Kyuza in Umybeya.

Elizabeth was not all surprised at my call and agreed to come to Dar es Salaam on the Sunday morning train arriving Monday evening. *One door closes and another one opens.*

I have no recollection of the farewells to Sally, yet I do recall *making sure* she had boarded the plane. Once more the feelings of *guilt, pity* and *relief.* For someone who never set out to hurt people, I was doing a good job.

On the Saturday evening I found a night club called *"Margaret's".* This was the haunt of all the sailors on leave. I have never seen so many available women under one roof from sixteen to sixty all shapes and sizes for all tastes. I had no difficulty in finding a beautiful half castle girl to take home to the hotel and a different one for the Sunday evening.

I went to meet the train on the Monday evening and saw Elizabeth walking down the platform with her giant suitcase on her head. *It was a sight for sore eyes.* The first thing I asked was how long she could stay and she replied, *"As long as you want".*

I explained about Sally going home and again she didn't seem surprised. Elizabeth did not like the Hotel Kenya so on the Tuesday we moved to the Bahari Beach Hotel about five kilometers north of the city.

This was a magnificent hotel set in sixty acres of gardens with its own private beach of white sand on the Indian Ocean. There was a main foyer, inside and outside dining room, stage and dance floor. Every night there was a cabaret of native tribal dancing followed by a band and dancing for the patrons.

The rooms were all tribal huts with two floors and all modern conveniences, e.g. air conditioning and French windows onto the beach, refrigerator, hot and cold water and of course showers and Jacuzzi. This was and still is the closest I have ever come to *"Heaven on Earth".* If I was not an alcoholic, it's the place I would chose to end my days.

I started the day about lunch time drinking a cocktail from the shell of a green coconut followed by a gin, followed by more cocktails and by mid afternoon I was well in *my cups* and ready for anything.

I would go for a siesta in the late afternoon and early evening and then it was dinner, cabaret and dancing all night until three to four every morning. Drinking vodka and orange endlessly. I have no recollection of even one night going to bed, only being nursed, massaged and loved by Elizabeth.

I got to know Dar es Salaam pretty well and Elizabeth organised changing of money on the black market. There was a fabulous Indian quarter in the city with the most lovely shops, restaurants and dozens of jewelry shops making costume jewelry for export to all parts of the world.

After a couple of weeks we decided to have a week on the Island of Zanzibar. I had heard so much about the place from school days and in the old Hollywood pirate films. It was a beautiful island with all Arab architecture and huge mosques. I remember all the doors to the buildings were like ornate very large church doors. The Arab sailing ships from centuries ago were still used by the fishermen (dhaks).

I didn't see one white person on the island for the first couple of days and the hotel we had pretty much to ourselves. Then on the third or fourth day I met an English man in the hotel. This guy was from Hawker de Haviland and was there to do costing on getting the sugar refinery back into working order for Tiny Rowland. He told me quite candidly it was a non starter as the climate was so humid the rust in all the machinery was quite beyond repair. To replace the refinery would cost millions of Pounds, however, if they had kept a team of two to three men to oil and maintain the equipment over the years, it would have been perfect as the plant was hardly used.

We were having a ball but my tolerance to booze was rapidly diminishing and it took only a couple of cocktails in the morning to put me right back to where I was the previous evening.

After a couple of months, Elizabeth was late with her period so it appeared I was going to be a father again. It was time to sober up, clean up and get my act together. I could make the most marvellous plans in the evenings, yet when morning came and I had my first drink to get me going, I never got further than the bar.

Nothing seemed to fluster Elizabeth yet I believe I treated her very kindly. Anyone with a mind could see I was slowly killing myself. I rarely used to eat anything and it was drink after drink, sleep, drink again. Elizabeth was playing the role of my minder and mother, keeping me out of arguments and protecting me.

Finally, I made the decision to go to North West Africa. I had read an article in *"AFRICA"* the magazine about the French Protectorate of Togo and Timbuktu. My mother always said she was going to Timbuktu when I was a child.

The problem there was no direct flights. East African Airlines were the airlines of Tanzania, Uganda and Kenya. However, they all agreed to disagree so on the day of the Disagreement they all kept whatever planes were in Nairobi, Dar es Salaam and Lusaka respectively. Then it was agreed they could not fly over each other's airspace, e.g. Tanzanian Airlines could not fly over Kenya, Ugandan Airlines couldn't fly over Tanzania or Kenya and Kenyan Airlines couldn't fly over Tanzania or Uganda. All very complicated African politics.

The net result was to get to Togo I had to fly direct to Ethiopia, Addis Ababa, flying past Kenya, change planes to Ethiopian Airlines and fly back to Nairobi, Kenya. Then I could fly direct from Nairobi to Lagos in Nigeria. This in itself was one day's travelling.

I tried the same ploy with the banks that had been successful in Zimbabwe to no avail. The Tanzanian banks would only issue the Traveller's Cheques until clearance of the English cheques.

The only way to get money out was in gold. I had no idea of the values. Tanzanian gold is not *Hall Marked* as the production is so small, it's all used for the Indians in the manufacture of costume jewelry. There was the alternative of precious or semi precious stones. Again, I had no idea of the values. This was also one department where Elizabeth could be of no use to me, all she knew was currency and sugar.

I had taken to wearing a kaftan all day and all evening.

Silly as it sounds there were hardly any Europeans in the city only a few Italians and Swedes who had discovered the delights of the Bahari Beach and the kaftan was so comfortable. In my Devon days and days in Ireland, the first thing I always did when I got home was take off my suit and put on a dressing gown. So this was like wearing a dressing gown all day long.

I decided on gold and purchased rings, necklaces and bracelets in abundance. I even had two very heavy gold ankle chains. I still had my Ten Thousand Pounds in Traveller's Cheques as Sally had taken only half back to the U.K. The balance of the cash I gave to Elizabeth to take home and promised that once I was settled, I would send for her. The pregnancy was confirmed by this stage.

She was a sweet lady to live in Africa with and we were very close. Having said this, I don't know if anyone could live with me at this stage. I was like a *wondering Jew* from hotel room to hotel room, totally irresponsible and totally selfish. I was looking at the world through the bottom of a glass.

The day came to leave and Elizabeth took me to the airport. I don't know to this day why, I was suddenly in such a hurry to leave and going to Timbuktu of all places. This was nothing less than *insanity*. I was flying five thousand miles to Timbuktu. Having to go all around Africa to get there.

The farewells were sweet and I was on my way. It was a Sunday and after three hours in Addis Ababa which was a Moslem country and alcohol free, followed by a flight without booze, two hours to Nairobi, I was desperate for a drink. I spent the night in Nairobi and got myself blind drunk and the following day was on the way to Lagos in Nigeria.

Lagos was the worse place I have ever been in my life. Being drunk didn't help matters much. Thank God I was wearing all my gold. The customs checked all my baggage and took whatever that they fancied. When I complained they put a gun to my head and they were not joking. This was very, very frightening.

When I got out of customs breathing a sigh of relief I went to the taxi rank. There were at least sixty to seventy yellow Peugeot taxis. Three separate drivers took three separate bags all pulling me in a different direction to three cars. I lost my temper and dragged all three bags and sat on them. Then the taxi drivers started to fight, I mean actually fighting with each other punching and pulling.

Whilst this was going on, I took the fourth taxi on the rank and went into the city. The driver took me to the Bristol Hotel and I had no wish to see Lagos after my experience in the airport.

My flight to Togo was two o'clock in the afternoon the next day so I had dinner in the dining room. I will never forget how tribal and primitive as well as hostile the people were in the dining room. The menu was *Chicken* or *Chicken*. The other diners would break a piece of chicken with the bone and put it in their mouth. Chew, Suck and make a lot of noise then spit out these lily white bones with no meat left on them. I have never seen anything like it before or since. At the end of dinner each table was filled with these piles of white bones. How they didn't swallow them I have no idea.

The airport the next day was quite civilised and it was a two hour flight on a very small plane to Togo. I had a drink and thought well I have come this far it must be fate. *It was Fate, all right.*

I arrived in the terminal and showed my passport to the customs and was told I couldn't enter the country as I had no French Visa stamped on my passport. I couldn't believe this. I had just travelled two and a half days, came five thousand miles for nothing. *The insanity of the alcoholic.*

I tried bribing to see the French Consul or to see the English Consul. There was no way I could get in. There was no way I ever wanted to see Lagos again and was not going back there.

I looked at the departure board to see where the international flights were going. I had the choice of Amsterdam via Cairo or Lagos. So it was no contest. I purchased a ticket for Amsterdam. This was Autumn of 1982 and I knew it was going to be bloody cold in my silly kaftan. I was not allowed access to my suitcases to put on a suit.

The plane was due to arrive at nine o'clock in the evening. with one hour stop at Cairo arriving in Amsterdam at ten o'clock the following morning European time. Once I had purchased my ticket, the customs boys allowed me to go to the bar and wait for my flight. However as I was transit I couldn't leave the bar which gave me no problem.

I have no recollection of stopping at Cairo or any part of the journey. I only remember being told to fasten my seat belt as we are now landing in Amsterdam. I walked off the plane and was absolutely freezing, so the first thing I did at the luggage claim was get a suit and jumper from my case and get changed in the toilet. Here I was back in Europe, one hour by plane from London.

CHAPTER TWENTY

So I was back in the cold civilised world again and I took a taxi to the centre of the city and found a small hotel near the Dam. After a shower and shave I realised I had the *mother of all Hangovers* and found a small bar and had a couple of vodkas. Determined to at least cut down on my drinking, I returned to the hotel.

I telephoned Margaret who had collected all the furniture and bought herself a new house. I telephoned Terri who said she had received a couple of postcards and was I still in Africa. I said, *"Yes"*. My mother was very concerned but didn't reprimand me. After making all of these calls, I rang Sally's parents. They gave me a phone number where I could contact her.

This was an awful call, Sally had gone to pieces and was living with a married girlfriend in a council house near Manchester and working in the city. I hadn't realised how important I was to her and she asked me where I was and I told her. Sally had given up her career, home and freedom to go with me to Africa and couldn't settle back in the U.K. I invited her to come to Amsterdam and at least we could sit down and talk. She agreed to fly out that evening.

The meeting was as though we had never been apart. Sally couldn't believe how much weight I had lost and how I had aged. I was thirty five years old going on ninety. We spent a few days in Amsterdam and I agreed to go home, give myself up to the police, face the consequences and Sally would stay with my sister Barbara in Ireland until all was resolved.

Sally flew out to Ireland only to find Barbara in the middle of yet another move. David's hotel had burned down and he had no insurance and they were going to move back to the U.K. Sally flew back to the U.K. and Bob put her up for a while. Here I was acting so irresponsibly and now dumping my women on my family. Today I can't believe my cheek or my appalling behaviour. So Sally was in Newbury waiting for my return as I took the ferry from the Hook of Holland to Harwich in Suffolk.

I arrived in Harwich at about seven o'clock in the morning then I couldn't find a policeman. I eventually found the police office and it was closed. I could have walked back into England as easily as that, I was not even questioned by customs.

I eventually got a taxi to Harwich Police Station, gave my name and told them I was wanted. I was asked to take a chair and wait. This was really wonderful and could only happen in England.

Eventually I was interviewed by CID and all the computer showed was that I was wanted in Manchester over a Twelve Pound bunch of flowers, sent by Interflora and charged to my Burger company. The company had denied the account. As I mentioned earlier, I had paid Eleven Thousand Pounds on the Bank Guarantee and they were so petty over Twelve Pounds.

Losing my patience, I asked the CID man to ring Inspector Derrick Couling at Snow Hill police station, City of London Police. This done, I spoke to Couling and he said he would send a car for me.

Couling came to collect me himself with another officer and he was quite charming, as opposed to the Bastard he had been before. Couling told me he would have passed me on the street and never recognised me. I had highlights in my hair, was as brown as a berry and lost four stones in weight. The result was I was returned on Remand to Brixton Prison. There was no point in my applying for Bail as I had absconded my previous Bail, however, as I gave myself up, I was not charged with this.

Sally visited me from Newbury and I got the prison doctor to put me back on Librium and Lithium for *manic depression*. Sally had been staying for several weeks at Bob's then she got a job in Windsor as the Assistant Manager of a small hotel. She settled into the job very well and fell in love with the Manager and they set up home together.

Sally came to see me regularly until my Trial, then she went her own way. The only solicitor I knew in London was a Jewish girl called Bobbie Tish, who came from Walthamstowe. Bobbie had arranged the mortgage on the property at Colchester. I wrote to Bobbie and she came to see me.

Bobbie had no idea of criminal law and instructed a Jewish barrister called Bob Sherman who I gave the instruction to settle the matter as quickly as possible, do a deal with the *"Old Bill"*. Accept four charges and throw the rest out. This was a foolish thing but to fight the case, I would have to serve longer on Remand, waiting for a trial date. There was a twelve to eighteen months backlog on trial dates at the Old Bailey.

As I came under the jurisdiction of the City of London Police and not the Metropolitan Police, the Old Bailey in EC1 was the venue for the Crown Court. I recalled as a small boy visiting Smithfield and looking at the Old Bailey in awe. The heart of English Justice, never believing I would be visiting it via the cells.

We eventually got a Hearing date at the end of 1982 and the police were very *well pleased*. All the charges could have been easily defended, *as they had no substance*. I had learned an awful lot about the London Police in my time in Brixton Prison. I was back in the hospital wing again and was allowed a twenty minute visit each day.

There was so much public concern about the corruption in the London Police a special task force was set up in 1982 called *"Operation Countryman"*. This was headed by the Chief Constable of Devon and Cornwall. The results of eighteen months investigation were as follows, e.g. ***The force was riddled with deep rooted corruption and it was recommended three hundred and fifty seven Officers be charged with criminal proceedings. Six hundred plus officers be disciplined internally and asked to resign. The result was three Officers were charged with criminal activities, two acquitted and one given a two year suspended sentence. The three hundred and fifty four remaining Officers were given the opportunity to resign quietly. Of the six hundred Officers to be disciplined, the results were never made public. One can only assume they served in the force until retirement.***

If your face doesn't fit you were nailed to the cross. This was just how I felt. To wait one year minimum in prison for a trial with the odds *nine to one* against me, as this is the figure for anyone in a court of law who has been arrested and charged on any offence. The odds are in favour of the prosecution with unlimited resources *nine to one*.

This was the era of the trials of the Guildford Four -

fourteen years in prison; Birmingham Six - *sixteen years in prison*; eight members of the Maguire Family - *twelve years in prison*; Judith Ward – *fourteen years in prison*; the Bridgewater Three - *ten years in prison*; with all these **Malicious prosecutions** the verdicts were only overturned after the mentioned periods had been served.

Despite the police *"fitting up"* or *"verballing"* by way of false confessions, some of the police officers charged with *"Perverting the course of Justice"*, all were acquitted. An English Jury will **_not_** convict an English Bobby (policeman).

Whilst I was in Brixton a fellow called Michael Fagan came into my ward. He had broken into Buckingham Palace, made his way to the bedroom of the Queen, sat and chatted to the Queen who offered him tea and waited for the security to come and arrest him.

Michael Fagan was a nice little man very, very non-threatening and, of course, caused severe embarrassment to all the English Security Forces by his outrageous ploy.

His reasoning was he wanted to tell the Queen in person about his plight with Social Security. People like Michael helped me retain my *sense of humour.*

The Judge listened to my barrister who really had no idea of the case. I was sentanced for periods up to twelve months meaning I served eight months minus the time I was on Remand. I was due for release in May 1983 some five months away. This is the Insanity of the Justice system by Pleading Guilty I got out faster than fighting the case and waiting for a Trail Date with *No Bail.*

I was sent to Wandsworth Prison. Jim Hill, a previous Lord Mayor of Wandsworth and meat wholesaler at Smithfield Meat Market, had given me a character reference at the Old Bailey. The other two character witnesses who I asked, Tony Pike the Editor of the *Meat Traders Journal* and Colin Cullimore of the Vestey organisation failed to turn up. However, Colin Cullimore wrote me a lovely letter of apology. He had go the dates mixed up. I learned recently that Tony had died whilst in France with his author wife.

After the trial I was taken to the Wandsworth which housed one thousand and five hundred convicted criminals.

These were all the *Hard Nuts* of London. The murderers, however, were always sent to Wormwood Scrubs. The day of my trial, Brendon Shute the IRA prisoner tunnelled his way out of Brixton by removing the bricks to the cell next door, then to the third cell which was at the end of the building. He quietly walked out over the roof and jumping down from the wall walked to Freedom.

The governor of Brixton was suspended and later sacked along with eight of his Officers for lack of security. However, Wandsworth was no easy prison. It had a reputation as being a *Hard Prison* and hard it was. The thing that amazed me, was all these London villains with the exception of Frankie Fraser, acted like little boys to the screws. Prison is a great leveler of men. The attitude of the London villain was, you have done the crime, now you do the time. They bow, scrape, and grovel to get an easy job and keep on the right side of the screws.

Frankie Fraser was the exception. He had done sixteen years hard time and Frankie was one of the Richardson gang about ten times as heavy as the Krays. He had his arms broken, his legs broken, his ribs broken by the prison officers and spent all of his sixteen years in the punishment block. Every three weeks he would be *"ghosted"*. This is taken from the prison in the middle of the night and moved to another prison. He was never told where he was going. Manchester - *Strangeways* Liverpool - *Walton*, Birmingham - *Winston Green*, Leeds – *Almany*, *Dartmoor, Durham* Top Security. The reason for this was to disrupt his visits from his family. By the time his family knew where he was, he was gone again. However, Frankie or *"Mad Frankie"* as he was known and loved, never gave up *His Fighting Authority*.

I met Frankie when I was down in *"the Block"* or punishment cells below the main prison. I was there because of my altercation with the kitchen hand and my tray.

Frankie did all of his time in *"the Block"* of sixteen years. Each morning your bed is taken out of the cell and placed outside the door. You are allowed no reading materials or writing materials, then after Tea your bed is returned and it's lights out. This medieval treatment still goes on today.

There were some rough boys in Wandsworth. Bruce Reynolds who had got thirty years for the train robbery was back doing five years for smuggling Krugar Rands and claiming the V.A.T. Bruce was the mastermind of the 1963 Train Robbery and a very articulate man.

Bruce Reynolds was captured by Inspector Slipper of the Yard, the investigating officer in the 1963 Great Train Robbery.

Bruce was in Canada on the run and apparently said to Slipper, *"What took you so long?"* as he was relieved to be going home, albeit to prison. As previously stated, the London villain is lost away from his own *Manor*.

George Ince who was having an affair with Dolly Kray, Charlie Kray's wife, was doing sixteen years for a Silver Bullion Heist at Heathrow Airport. The previous year he had been acquitted of an Armed Bank Robbery on the Bank of Cyprus in Mayfair. Dolly Kray was his alibi and Charlie Kray put a gun down his trouser front and fired the bullet, fortunately missing his vitals and going into his thigh.

The police may be Bad, the prison officers may be Bad, but the London villains are in a league of their own. *Big Mouth, Flash and as soft as Putty.* This is why all the Train Robbers were caught with the exception of Ronnie Biggs. Their world ends at Watford and they cannot live outside their own parish or *Manor* as they call it.

These convicts all want to be the *Best Dressed Man* in prison. They press and iron their shirts and trousers, use after shave and have their hair immaculate, yet on the outside they are just ordinary working class villains living in council estates.

After six weeks I was transferred to Open Prison at Springhill in Buckinghamshire. This was bearable, however, it was again full of London villains. My mother came to visit me, Barbara and David came to visit me and Barbara, bless her, came to the Old Bailey for my sentence.

Charlie Richardson, Frankie Frazer's old boss and the only gang that took on the Kray Brothers, was finishing off his sentence at Spring Hill having been given a category "C" status as non risk after sixteen years inside. With only one year of his sentence left, Charlie escaped and was recaptured and had to then serve an extra eighteen months prior to release back in a top Security Prison.

I was standing in the dock at the Old Bailey and looked up to the Gallery and there was Barbara, sitting all alone and smiling at me. She was allowed to visit me through a glass screen for ten minutes after I was sentenced. This gesture of Barbara's reminded me of my first day at school, holding her hand.

I realised how much I had loved my sister and also how much I had missed Barbara and David in my life during my years in the *Alcoholic Wilderness.*

The prison had a Rugby Team and I was given the job as the coach. It was bearable but I was still on my Librium and Lithium every day. The prison authorities will dish out pills like sweets. Anything for peace and quiet. As the British prisons were so over-crowded a blind eye was turned to soft drugs, cannabis, etc. This again was to keep the peace. You have three men in a cell with no water, no toilet and the cell was built one hundred years ago for one prisoner.

There is no such animal as Rehabilitation. The food per prisoner would cost less than Ten Pounds weekly or Five Hundred Pounds per annum. To keep a prisoner in Jail in 1982 cost the government Thirty Five Thousand Pounds per annum. The officers work sixty to seventy hours a week and were earning Three Hundred to Four Hundred Pounds weekly for getting fat, lethargic and doing time themselves. For the Prison Officer's mentality is that of the prisoners, totally institutionalised. The only difference between officers and prisoners is the uniforms. This is why most officers are recruited from the armed services, Army, Navy, etc.

So there I was nearly thirty six years old, homeless and I was going to be released. I was doing nothing about my problem which was alcoholism. I was taking medication to control it. I was a disaster waiting to happen.

Six weeks prior to my release I was given five days home leave. My mother collected me and took me home. This was very shameful for me, back with my mother at the age of thirty five. My mother was terrified I was going to drink. I was desperate to drink. We arrived home and I went for a hair cut, an excuse to go to the Off Licence and buy a quarter bottle of vodka and drink it from the bottle. That was enough to take the edge off the day, with a second bottle in my pocket.

I decided to go to London on Day three and collect my clothes that were still in Snowhill Police Station as the prison had refused to accept them. My mother was against the idea but in reality I needed to be alone to drink. I was drunk before I got to London, collected all my cases and put them in the left luggage at Waterloo and took the train to Windsor to see Sally.

Sally agreed to see me if I was sober. She took one look at me and turned and walked away. I had some more drinks. I only had one day left before I was due back to prison. I spent all my money and took a taxi at two o'clock in the morning back to the prison one day early. This was the last time I saw Sally in person.

I rang the prison bell and said *"I am back"*. The one condition of the Home Leave was no returning intoxicated. Here I was at three o'clock in the morning ringing the bloody bell *requesting* to be put back in prison. I must be the only bloke in the world guilty of attempting to break into a prison.

The officers told me to go away and come back when I was sober. I made such a fuss, they called the local police who arrested me put me in a Police Cell for the night and returned me to prison the next day. I have to admit the screws were very decent and gave me the chance to leave before calling the police.

The next morning I was told I had lost all my privileges and must return to Wandsworth, the *Top Security* prison. I only had six weeks left so I could live with that.

On my first week back in Wandsworth in April 1983, the prisoners all rioted at Albany Jail on the Isle of Wight. This was a Top Security Prison and the prisoners after a one day siege burned the prison to the ground. The whole of the Albany Jail inmates some five hundred Top Security prisoners had to be re-located all over England. Of course no prison wanted them, but they had to take them.

All he trouble makers at Wandsworth were *"ghosted"* to make room for Albany men as Wandsworth is the most feared prison in England. I was put on the *"Ghost Bus"* being classified as a trouble maker after an altercation with an *"alleged tough cockney villain"* who splashed my gravy on my plate every day. On the fourth or fifth time he did this, I put the tray over his head and gave him some manners. This *"tough man"* then reported me to the screws. I lost seven days remission.

Frankie Frazer was again back in *"the Block"* of Wandsworth. When I told him why I was there he said, *"don't worry son, you haven't got long left"*.

Twenty six of us were put on the bus with no idea where we were going. This is for security. We were all handcuffed in pairs and sat two to a seat on the bus. We stopped at Leicester prison. Everyone by this time was guessing where we were going. It was obviously North.

We were taken off the bus at Leicester Prison, put into holding cells, given tea and sandwiches and we all assumed this was our destination. This was not too bad, two hours from London by car or train.

We were all wrong. The screws all came back and we were put back on the *"Ghost Bus"* still going North. So we all assumed Lincoln, then Hull, followed by Wakefield or Leeds, all Top Security Prisons. After Leeds we were still going North.

At this point we all knew the most northerly prison in England is Durham Top Security Prison. This was the prison in the film *"McVicar"* with Roger Daltrey and Adam Faith. *"The End of the Earth"* for everyone on the bus. My mother was born in County Durham.

Myra Hindley was in the Women's Wing of Durham and also Judith Ward who was Pardoned after serving fourteen years for the IRA M62 bombing of a coach, killing eleven English soldiers. She had been *"Fitted Up"* by police the same as the Guildford Four and Birmingham Six.

We arrived as there we were some *London Big Mouthed Trouble Makers* on the bus. We were greeted by sixty to seventy screws and at least thirty to forty Alsatian dogs jumping at the leash, so the London men very soon shut up.

The prison was full of very petty, small minded screws and small minded prisoners. I served my time very quietly and bumped into poor old Franker Fraser again who has been ghosted there two days earlier. The problem with Durham was it was a local prison as well as a national top security prison all in the one compound. The officers can get away with bullying on local petty criminals but not on the long sentence villains such as Ian Brady or Frankie Fraser.

I was again in *"the Block"* for refusing to work in the Mailbag Shop and refusing to go on exercise. I only wanted to stay in my cell and read. I found I could escape into books.

My mother had always told me how nice the Geordies were or people from Durham. I couldn't stand them or their petty regime. Mum came to visit me and by this time she was an expert at giving me packets of cigarettes on the visits for me to smuggle into the prison later.

This was not the way my mother wanted to return to her home town, visiting her son in the local prison. Mother collected me on my release and we had tea in the local hotel. When we arrived home the first thing I did was buy a half a bottle of vodka and drank it out of the bottle. A beautiful early summer day, the sun shining and me drinking vodka out of a bottle and hiding it from my mother.

CHAPTER TWENTY ONE

I was very nearly thirty six years old, homeless, penniless and a very bad drunk. I needed every penny I could beg, steal or borrow for vodka. I was saving money by not going to pubs. I bought a quarter and half bottles from the Off Licence Sales and drank it out of the neck of the bottles. It was hard to swallow but the effect was almost immediate once you get over the *First Swig*.

I was not only a drunk at this time I was a *Thief, Liar,* and a *Cheat*. I went on the dole for the first time in my life and was claiming rent, which of course I never paid my mother. Today, its hard to imagine unless you have *walked the walk*, yet every moment I was awake my one thought was the next drink and how will I be able to obtain it.

I purchased a Triumph Sports car on finance. I could always get finance. Opened a credit account with Burtons and Hepworths the Tailors, opened a credit account with a department store and purchased all new clothes, so there I was, *"Jack the lad"*, flashy car, good clothes and not the price of a *"pot to piss in"*. Just like the Cockney villians.

I got a job eighty miles away at Buxton in Derbyshire killing sheep three days a week, Monday, Tuesday and Wednesday. I was getting Two Hundred Pounds cash. No matter how much money I got I spent it. I met a lovely single girl of twenty eight and after two to three weeks she couldn't cope with me. I was loud-mouthed so very *anti-English* and *anti-police*, it was almost pathological hate of the establishment.

I blamed everyone for my problems, my parents, my family, not myself. The police, the courts, the prisons, I was so anti-society and full of jealousy and hate. The hate was eating me up. I wanted everything back I had lost and I wanted it right there and then, if I couldn't get it, I drank.

I wrote to Bull Brand in South Africa and got Hadleigh the sack based on my observations of his small fiddles at the plant. I went after the copper Derrick Couling who had caused my imprisonment. I had not one good thought in my head for anyone, only my two children and they, of course, were ashamed of me.

William came to stay for a couple of days and I took him out on the booze. Just a small restaurant and while he had his dinner I was downing vodka and orange, then of course I was going to drive him home. William was fifteen now and he said *"Dad, do you mind if I say something? Please don't drink anymore"*. I replied *"Just one more"* on numerous occasions. I asked William to stay a little longer but he was glad to get away.

Edwina was not quite as bad as she was only ten years old and I could pretend or at least try and pretend I was not drinking. Margaret re-married that summer so at least she had some stability in their lives. I have vague recollections of telephoning William's school in the middle of the night and getting him out of his Dormitory to the phone, just to talk *"Bull Dust"*. This must have been embarrassing for him with his masters. I wasn't even paying the school fees, Bob was.

I was in the Crest Hotel in Bolton near Manchester about three weeks after my release. I don't remember being particularly loud, I was with a girl on our first date. I must have been bad as she asked me to take her home. I was in no state to drive.

There was a local Police Sergeant at the next table who I later learned was also an alcoholic. I must have been big mouthing about Ireland and being in Mountjoy and the Crumlin Road Prison. All I know is the hotel porter came and told me I was wanted in the foyer.

I had no idea who would want me, or even know me. In the foyer there was a white police van backed right up to the front door with its doors open. Two plain clothes coppers handcuffed me and threw me in the van.

I was taken to the Police Station leaving the girl and the car at the Crest Hotel. I was then told I had been arrested under *"The Prevention of Terrorism Act"*. I was going to be held seventy two hours.

I was beaten black and blue and the Police would not believe I was, in fact, an **English man.** On the second day they must have realised the mistake as I was released. However, the drunken Police Sergeant who had instigated the arrest then charged me with not paying the Hotel bill. I said *"How could I* *pay it when you arrested me?"*. He had made as big a fool of himself as me and had to save some face.

By this time the worm had turned. I was sick and tired of all these police cases involving pubs, hotels and taxis. I defended the case and after being kept on bail for six months, the police dropped the charges. I could have done this with every single one of my charges over the years. I always took the easy way out, plead guilty get it over and done with to have another drink as soon as possible.

I met a girl called Jill Ingham. She was a pretty little blonde girl, who had been married three times and divorced. Her last husband was a Male Stripper called *"The City Gent"*. He would do his act dressed in a pin striped suit and bowler hat, like John Steed of the Avengers and end up naked at various Hen Parties and girl's nights.

Jill was from a very good family in Lytham St Anne's and was a short hand typist, she was very wild. The two of us were like the blind leading the blind. She had a little boy from her last marriage who was eight years old and the *City Gent* used to have access at weekends.

The same old saga of Terry and her husband began, He was complaining about my drinking, leading Jill astray, and a bad influence on his son. The *Real Problem* was this guy thought he was *God's Gift to Women* and resented Jill and myself were an item. The result was I found a rather nice flat in Buxton, quite close to where my house was when I had the burger factory, a couple of years previously.

So Jill and myself and her son moved in. I worked my three days a week at Buxton then collected my dole. I received a telephone call one morning from my mother telling me David my brother-in-law had died of a brain haemorrhage. Both David's parents were acknowledged alcoholics so I have no doubt in my mind David was also one. So off I go to the funeral.

This was down in Newbury, Berkshire as David had been working for Bob. Poor David when he lost his inherited fortune on a property development in Cornwall, as previously mentioned. He never seemed to have the ability to get straight again. My sister Barbara had this beautiful manor house in

Devon. One day the Bailiffs turned up on the doorstep to seize everything. David had not informed poor Barbara his wife of his problems. The same thing happened with the hotel in Dublin. The rent had not been paid for six months. When it burned down there was no insurance. Barbara had no idea where the money went. I could well understand David's dilemma. It all went on booze plus all the antics of an active alcoholic.

Having said this I was extremely fond of him and was to me like a third brother. The funeral was very sad. My whole family were very drunk and had quite a wake. I never touched a drop of drink from leaving Buxton until returning. I was very *"put out"* to hear my family saying afterwards, *"Of course, Bill was secretly drinking at the funeral"*.

This was 1983 and the past was now rapidly catching up with my siblings. Two of us with serious drinking problems, albeit one controlled and not causing prison or hospitalisation yet drink problems all the same. They say in AA you have a drink problem only *"when alcohol costs you more than money"*.

I returned from the funeral to Jill in Buxton and received a call from Bruce. Bruce was in Scotland killing about one thousand head of cattle per week and offered me the job of doing the marketing. Whilst the offer was tempting I was content killing sheep three days a week and getting drunk every night with Jill to take care of me.

Jill owned her own house near Manchester and whilst we lived in the flat all her furniture etc was still in her own home. The flat we rented was furnished and very well, I might add. Bruce agreed to find me a house, pay for Jill to move all her furniture and pay my rent plus salary. I bounced the idea off Jill and she was delighted. A new start in Scotland and Billy Boy back on the way up.

So I agreed to take the position with Bruce and drove to Scotland. I again had a breathalyser drink driving case over my head in Manchester. Jill was going to follow on the train after she had sent all the furniture by truck.

Bruce lived in Troone on the West Coast of Scotland with his wife and four children and ran his business from Glasgow City abattoir in the Gallowgate of Glasgow, the markets area in Moore Street.

My job was the usual, selling the cattle. My drinking was worse than ever. I had to drink to function in the mornings. All my drinking was a secret by this time yet the results were there for everyone to see. I couldn't perform and couldn't work under Bruce. I was *Arrogant, Ignorant and Drunk* all of the time.

The net result was Bruce sacked me or I sacked myself. I can't really remember which. All I do recall was I got in a taxi in Glasgow and took it three hundred and fifty miles to Buxton. When I got to Buxton I realised I lived in Scotland, so I took the taxi three hundred and fifty miles back again.

I was out of control. *Totally Insane.* Poor Jill would have done anything for me but I only had **One Love,** and that is **Vodka**. I had to go back to Manchester for my driving case and the Magistrate remanded me in custody for sentancing at Crown Court. The Magistrate didn't believe he had the power to give me a long enough sentence because of my Record or CRO over the previous years.

So there I was in Strangeways Prison, Manchester, awaiting sentence. Jill and my mother *"appealed"* the following day to Judge in Chambers and quite correctly, I was granted Bail. I was only in prison one night but I recall the look of despair on my poor mother's face. We moved back to the flat in Buxton but I couldn't get my old job back.

Jill had sold her house and all her furniture was in Scotland. Life was so very messy and complicated. I had very little money so I sold my sports car for money to drink. The car was a Personal Loan and not HP. I could keep the cash and still make the payments. This money didn't last long.

I went to hospital in Macclesfield on the National Health. The same as my previous hospitals, De-tox and group therapy. Jill found a council house in Leigh near Manchester and my mother paid for all the furniture to be brought back from Scotland.

I had an affair with one the nurses at the hospital and moved in with her. I don't even have any recollection of her name only that she had been working for years in Iran and was a very pretty blonde girl. She, of course, had only known me sober at the hospital. We had a couple of good months. Then the booze began and the relationship was over.

I was again homeless, car less, still the sentence of the Drink case over my head. Jill gave me a home at her little council house. I was a mess. Every morning I would take two milk bottles, go to the shop on this very rough council estate and buy cheap draft sherry from the keg. They would measure it in a jug and pour it into the milk bottles. I recall Peter Cook telling me he used to go to his Off License in Hampstead in pyjamas. Everyone thought he was just *Eccentric* not realising he needed the *Booze to function.* David Willis, my friend in Devon, recently recounted Peter's antics to me.

For anyone who had drunk sherry, taking a small glass as an aperitif is rather nice, drinking two pints of it in the morning to function is a totally different story. Sherry is lethal. I used to go insane on it.

The results were that in the next two months it was Jill's home, hospital, Jill's home again until I found a job as a telephone salesman in Manchester. This was the chance to clear my debts, make a fresh start and clean up my act. I worked for one week then got drunk with the boss and staff at the Midland Hotel in Manchester. The result of that one night was I was sacked, yet didn't realise until I went to work the next day and was asked to leave.

I was earning One Thousand Five Hundred Pounds weekly selling advertising space on Prestel Television advertising. The idea was so good the profit so high I found a partner and started on my own.

We used my partner's office and all of his facilities in Queen Street, Manchester. I told him of my drinking problems and the result was I would sell in the mornings and start drinking at lunch time. I was still drinking out of the bottle at this time to save money.

I had rather a nice flat in South Manchester and was going out with an African nurse for a couple of weeks. My blackouts were so bad I have little recollection of all the events but do recall buying two new Mercedes on finance from London. One car for my partner and one for myself. I was never ever in a state to drive in those days. I had to drink a quarter bottle of Vodka but able to leave home in the mornings.

One day the cars were gone, I was evicted from my flat I still don't know how it all happened. I spent the night in the Nurses Home at Prestwich Hospital with my girlfriend. My partner was one of those weak men hewn from similar timber to that of as John Copass. He took great delight in ridiculing me when I was drinking. I put tens of thousands of Pounds in *his* pockets whilst I spent all my money.

I found a new flat and met a Scottish girl called Naylor Sheridon. She was a lovely creature and very broad Glasgow. She was the Manager of small hotel in Didsbury, Manchester and moved in with me. I set up a Dating Agency called *Euro Club 54* and it was a gold mine. So I had the advertising with my partner and the Dating Agency that Naylor ran having given up her job at the hotel.

My memory is still hazy of this period but I did recall having a blazing row with my partner and head butting him. He was covered in blood and the police were called. I was evicted from my own business.

That night I broke into the office and took the cheque book and the following morning took Twenty Thousand Pounds from the account. The police again were called. I had nothing in writing to say I was an equal partner. After six hours interrogation I was released and told if I went back to the office I would be arrested. We were owed on the books some Sixty Thousand Pounds and were earning Five Thousand to Six Thousand Pounds per week. I walked out on it all yet kept the Twenty Thousand Pounds.

I took the ferry to Dublin and booked myself into St John of God's Hospital for De-tox. I had been there in 1975 whilst at Rathdowney. Naylor assured me she would come to Dublin and help me get well. *Euro Club 54* was running itself pretty well.

Naylor never came so I discharged myself taking the ferry back to Liverpool and taxi to Manchester. I arrived at the flat at eight o'clock. in the morning. Naylor had changed all the locks on the flat. She had also moved in one of the clients from the Dating Agency.

The lease had been changed to her name so like John Larkin, my partner in the advertising business, she took everything and I walked away with nothing. I remember walking the streets of Manchester and having no money then passing out.

I woke up in the De-tox ward of Withington Hospital which was *Skid Row* for *Down and Outs*. I had lost my suitcases, my clothes. I must have telephoned my mother as she came and took me home. All I owned in the world were the clothes I stood up in and, of course, I needed a drink.

The one thing I recall about Withington was being *De-Loused*. This was standard procedure to all *Skid Row Drunks*. You were sat in a plastic container that was sealed to your neck. High pressure water and disinfectant was sprayed over your body for ten minutes to kill all the lice that may be on your body.

My mother didn't know what to do with me. I was aggressive, argumentative and angry. Several times she took me to hospital but the hospitals were now refusing me as a *Hopeless* case.

My court case came up for the drink driving and the Judge in his wisdom came to the rescue and gave me six months in prison for drinking driving. So back I go to Strangeways Prison to serve four months of my sentence. In retrospect, this was a *"Blessing in Disguise"* as I was now in constant blackouts. I have very little recollection of the previous six months and all the trouble that surrounded me.

My mother had been in Intensive Care with heart problems around this time. Perhaps one of the most desperate, despicable acts of my life was to go to the hospital and beg money for booze.

My mother close to *Death's Door* wrote me a cheque whilst crying her eyes out in despair. Memories of that day still haunt me filling me with *Shame and Guilt*.

CHAPTER TWENTY TWO

Sam Lias told me in Devon *"If you are not wanted at Home, you are not wanted anywhere".* Sam was also an alcoholic and a very wise man. The loneliest place on earth is a prison cell when no one wants you. Strange as it may sound, this is my experience.

I saw murderers, rapists, and paedophiles all getting letters and visits. The only contact I had with the world was my mother. I also knew if my father was alive things may have been far worse for me, as my father would see my alcoholism as *Weakness*.

I was eventually moved to an *Open Prison,* again in North Yorkshire to complete my Sentence. Prisons in those days were all staffed by male officers. I believe its different today. However, there was one lady in charge of the kitchen and I got the job as her butcher. It was a good little job with good wages by prison standards and television in the evenings.

She was getting a very rough ride from the male officers especially the ones who were under her. They deliberately sabotaged the kitchen and stealing the produce and meat, etc. making her job impossible. I took her side and one officer was transferred to the prison next door. She was a lady in her early Fifty's and a very good friend to me.

The day before I left prison, she called me into her office and said, *"Bill, I have watched you with interest over the last three months and thank you for all the help and advice you have given me."* The meat came to the prison in carcase form and I used to cut it showing her the cheap cuts, good cuts, bad cuts and how to save a great deal of money on her budget. I also made Black Puddings, Sausages and cooked my own Hams helping her budget considerably.

She went on to say *"I was intrigued by you, so I took the liberty of getting your criminal record and prison record and you know your problem, don't you?"* I said *"yes, booze"*. She said *"you were never meant to be in prison Bill. I pray for you every day and hope you will do something with your life when you are released tomorrow".* These were very moving words from a very tough lady with a big reputation as a tough Chief Prison Officer in female prisons for thirty years.

My mother, once more, collected me and yes the first thing I needed was *Vodka*. I had learned nothing, once more straight out of the neck of the bottle. Nothing had changed except I was now thirty eight years old. Right back to square one.

I knew I couldn't stay with my mother. I had been cleaned up in prison and the four months were all lost with the first drink. I got a job in Hertfordshire, running a Knacker's Yard. I lived in this very grand Tudor house with the boss, his wife and the daughter. My job was killing the horses and running the whole show.

It lasted three days. Started on the Sunday morning living in the house, my own room en suite, company car all my expenses. I was so drunk by Tuesday, I was told to leave or they would call the police. People were now afraid of me drunk. I was very violent and used to fly into rages just like my father.

There was no way I was going back to my mother's so I went to Northampton. I went to the pub that Terri and I had used, perhaps, in the hope I may see her for a *hand out*. I never did. So I rang her father. Ted drove into Northampton and lent me Fifty Pounds. By tea time I had only my couple of bottles and cigarettes left with very little change.

I drank my bottles in the Park in Northampton and within ten minutes there were other men coming out of the bushes asking for a swig. I spent two days in the Park and then took a bus to Birmingham.

I called to see several of my clients asking for handouts. Ted Collins gave me Fifty Pounds, Dennis Eyre gave me Fifty Pounds, and Brierley Hill Meats One Hundred Pounds. I was again living in the Park behind the Bull Ring in Birmingham. The money soon ran out. I woke up twice in hospital during this time in Birmingham having been taken in as an emergency case unconscious, only for the hospital to realise the following day, when I sobered up that I was *just a drunk*.

I remember the warmth of the hospital beds, the nurses bringing my food and never wanting to leave, to go out in the cold again. Yet, on both occasions, I was sent home. Of course,

I didn't have a home to go to.

One of the men in the Park told me that if I was destitute, the social security would give me Twenty Five Pounds to get accommodation. I recall waiting for hours in the Social Security offices only to be told, if I didn't have my National Insurance Number they couldn't help me. So I was back to square one.

I was so desperate just for a drink. I lived every moment just for a drink. I went back to Dennis Eyre, Ted Collins and Brierley Hill Meats and each one told me *"Bill, get a grip on yourself"*. If I had Ten Thousand Pounds it would have been gone as I could never remember anything about where I was or what I was doing.

Lyons of Longford had purchased a Meat depot in Birmingham since my departure. Brendon Flynn, old Matt Lyons' son-in-law was running the operation.

I recall walking seven miles to this depot looking for a handout. Brendon Flynn laughed in my face and told me to Fuck Off. Flynn approached me to do business in 1998. *Poor Old Incompetant Brendon* had gone broke losing Lyons money. He is now running a Slaughterhouse Boning Hall in North Wales. *What goes around comes around!*

I got the bus to London. I knew that in Smithfield Meat Market I was still a legend. I went to Darringtons, Gee and Webb, David Andrade. These people had known me thirty years from being a little boy. I will never forget Peter Andrade telling me no. I said *"Peter, just lend me Five Pounds"*. He said *"No"*. I was so ashamed of what I had become as now I was a beggar, living on a Park Bench.

Peter was the man I brought to my village in Devon and introduced to Morley Guy. Each Summer, Peter would bring his children camping a the village and Morley and himself went onto make a Fortune from my West Country business.

I went back to Smithfield in 1999 and learned that Peter Andrade had suffered a *Stroke* and was still a comparatively young man.

It is strange to recall, that everyone who did the wrong thing by me over the years seemed to come to a *Sad Sticky End.*

I supplied meat to Peter's son, Stephen, in 1998. It was

only a couple of thousand pounds. Andrade wanted me to give them twenty one days credit. I couldn't hold my anger in and told Stephen what his father had done.

I went to American Casings, the owners of Darringtons and no one would believe I was Bill Hayes. I had no ID but assumed everyone knew me. This happened at Gee and Webb as John Brewster the Chairman had gone home and I was dealing with office staff. This was Bill Hayes, the Meat Man, begging for money for a drink. I walked out of Smithfield and didn't know what to do. I hadn't a penny. John Brewster was, and is, a *Gentleman*. It was just unfortunate we missed each other.

I walked from Central London to Hendon. It took me all afternoon and thumbed a lift up to the M1 and back to Northampton. I went to see John Sharkey, my old Meat Inspector from Devon. John gave me Fifty Pounds and allowed me to sleep on the settee for the night. I collapsed the next morning and was back in hospital.

After two days I was allowed to leave and John gave me the bus ticket as well as all the cash he had and I went back to my mother. My tail between my legs, I was beaten. I was in bed for at lest a week and came good, stayed sober. Mum was taking me to AA daily.

I was offered a job to run a large Knackers Yard in Thirsk, North Yorkshire at Twenty Thousand Pounds per annum, cash in hand, company car and accommodation on a local farm with three meals a day. This was a large comedown, however, it was a start.

I went for the interview on the Saturday and was to start on the Monday. So I came back to Manchester on the train. I had been given One Hundred Pounds expenses so I thought a drink to celebrate is the thing to do. I must have had several drinks for I can't remember the journey from Manchester to Atherton and its only a thirty minute trip.

I arrived at Atherton station with no idea of where I had been drinking and I still don't know. Anyway, I fell off the railway platform onto the lines. I was bruised and scratched but I couldn't get up. The passengers were all panicking and the porter came and lifted me off the lines.

The next thing I know the police came and asked me what my problem was. I said, *"I had a few drinks and one of my epileptic fits"*. This was all I could think of. I was leg less.

The police took me to my mother's and heard them saying, *"Mrs Hayes, is this your son?"*. I believe, expecting someone like me to have *No Mother*. She of course said *Yes*. There I was my shirt all ripped, my pin striped suit ripped, my face all black from the soot on the railway lines and only one shoe.

My mother put me to bed and the next day being Sunday I couldn't buy a pair of shoes. I had to go to my Uncle Bill's, my mother's brother, and borrowed his old miners boots that he used for the garden. So dressed in pin stripe suit, overcoat and miner's boots, I set off for Yorkshire again to start my new job.

I looked like the children's puppets *"Bill and Ben, the Flower Pot Men"*, nice suit and giant boots!

The Sunday night I was booked into the Black Bull in Thirsk. This is the home town of James Herriott, *All Creatures Great and Small*. I kept myself under control that night and was just glad to get to bed.

Alf White was the vet in Thirsk and, of course, came to my yard almost daily to do post-mortems. He was a lovely man so very quiet and refined. Using his nom-de-plume, James Herriott, he relayed all the years of his veterinary practice in the market town of Thirsk known as Darroby in his books.

Since the success of the program *"All Creatures and Small"* on television and the book in America, Thirsk has now become a huge tourist town for visitors looking for Darroby. They have even changed the name of one of the pubs to *"The Darroby Arms"*.

I began the job like a new broom, sweeping clean. I got the whole place running well. I only had a staff of ten men and six lorries driven out on the road all day collecting animals. The local squire's daughter worked in the office. She was a lovely girl of twenty and we soon became involved.

So I would take her racing at York or Wetherby, Ripon or Thirsk. There are many fine racecourses in Yorkshire. We always went to the pub for lunch and I was again out of control.

I was banned in the village pub, went off with one of my lorry driver's wives who was also an alcoholic and was asked to leave the farm where I lived. All in all, Bill Hayes was **Trouble.** I was eventually sacked and my car taken off me.

I had returned to the Plant drunk from Leeds with a street girl. Driving the company vehicle in this condition was Bad, however, I couldn't find the keys to the safe to pay the girl. I got a sledgehammer from the yard and was in the process of knocking out the safe door when the boss walked in with his wife and his *hoity toity* daughter.

I would love to have the scene on video as it was one of those situations where I was only left with my wits and sense of humour. The boss said, *"What the Fuck are you doing, Bill? Have you gone mad?"* I said, *"No. I have lost my key"*. He was decent enough to get a taxi to send the poor girl back to Leeds, sixty miles down the road.

I took the train to Middlesborough. Stayed the night in a hotel. Spent all my money and hitchhiked home to my mother.

This was an awful walk. I called into York to see Jo Mulihul, the horse trainer. Joe was from Malahide in Dublin. He lent me Twenty Pounds reluctantly which I spent immediately.

I booked into a hotel in Leeds stating *my wife was en route and would settle the bill*. I drank all the booze from the room mini bar and walked out not paying a penny.

I was now entering my *lowest days* of all time and would not wish those experiences on my worse enemies. *I was a walking corpse living in Hell.*

I had two more Breathalyser cases against me. I was charged with receiving stolen pet food and in trouble yet again. My poor mother didn't know what to do. So I opened an office in a derelict builder's yard, installed two telephones and drink day and night, sleeping in the office.

I came up with an answer. I would go to Portugal. I was very *"well got"* with the Minister of Agriculture and I would start again in a new country and never return to England. This was the plan and my mother and myself put it into action. *My Poor Darling Mother* was at the end of the road with me. This was December 1985 and thank God, my mother has never seen me drunk from that day to this.

I purchased a package deal to the Algarve for two weeks including hotel, car and my plan was to use this as a base, drive up to Lisbon. I would find my way around the meat business again, if not there, Brazil. This was a sensible plan and I was very optimistic. My mother took me to Manchester airport and kept sober in those days and flew off.

My cousin Kevin Crowther and his wife Phil were very kind to me in those days. I recall turning up at their house in Manchester several times very drunk. I always had a different girl with me. Despite my condition they never turned me away, never ridiculed me. They always treated my girlfriends with respect and humored me. Kevin was a genuine Police Officer and I mention him because there is *Good* and *Bad* in everyone. I must have compromised Kevin professionally with my drink driving. I owe this couple a very *Special Thank You.* Kevin is retired from the police force today and they have built a very successful chain of Rest Homes in the north of England.

I never got further than the hotel bar and a little bistro about one hundred yards from the hotel. I became totally infatuated by a little Gypsy girl and that was that. I met several English couples at the hotel bar and one particular couple from Lincoln were really good fun.

The Gypsy girl's father was an alcoholic and I used to drink with him each night. Very early in the evenings he would be *"Out for the Count"*. My Gypsy girl's brothers would lift him into a motorcycle sidecar and take him home to the Gypsy camp.

The couple were Richard and Margaret Karpinski. He was about twenty four years of age and a giant of a man, six feet four inches and twenty stones, she was a couple of years older than me. They were great socialites and had purchased a large manor house outside Lincoln City which they were renovating. I was the life and soul of the party but have no recollection of ever going to bed or even my room. I was drinking for oblivion.

When the drink really takes over your life you find yourself mixing socially with people who are socially and intellectually inferior to yourself. I have had this explained to me, it is so that you can feel good about yourself. I had *Notions of Grandeur* and was living off my past glories for at the time I had *nothing* and was *nobody*. I was just a *Hopeless, Helpless Drunk.*

By the end of the second week my money was running low. I had not the energy or the inclination to get any further than the bar. I thought when the money runs out I will *Hang myself.* I had attempted suicide on three previous occasions. The driving into the bridge in Devon, cutting my throat and the aspirins and vodka in Zimbabwe. I had never heard of anyone failing with hanging themselves. Once I made the decision life became quite bearable.

There is a funny sad story about an Irish man I met in Brixton Prison. This poor soul was at the end of the road with booze. His wife had gone, his daughter's all grown up. He tried to hang himself and the rope broke. So he closed all the kitchen doors and windows and put a pillow by the gas oven and lay down to kill himself by gas. His daughter came home and said, *"Don't be so silly, Dad. You can't gas yourself on North Sea Natural Gas".*

Feeling very dejected, he sat down at the kitchen table and lighted a cigarette. Well as you can imagine, *"BANG"*. The house exploded as the gas ignited. His daughter's fiancee was injured and the house was wrecked by the explosion.

He was charged with Arson and Attempted Murder when I met him. I never did find out how his case went but it was a very sad funny story. The depths to which we alcoholics can fall!

The night before the Karpinski's left Margaret gave me her card saying *"Keep this safe, Bill. One day you may need it".* I put it in my pocket and the following day they left.

I had a few more days left and by the Saturday, my money was all but gone. I could still charge to my room though. I decided to do the deed *(Hang Myself)* on the Sunday morning as my hotel booking was finished on the Sunday night.

I have no recollections of the Saturday only I was with my Gypsy girl and sent her home rather than stay in my room that night. I woke up Sunday morning with a dry mouth, dry retching and was feeling very very rough. I showered, put on clean clothes and a suit, wrote letters to my children and my mother and went to the bar for a *Hair of the Dog.*

One drink became several and going through my wallet, I found Margaret Karpinski's card and it just said her name and **Clairvoyant,** along with her address and phone number. I went to the phone in the bar and rang her in Lincoln, England, reverse charge.

Basically I said *"What is going to happen to me, Margaret?"*. She said *"I see Australia. Cattle and Horses and you will go there and be very successful"*. She then went on and pretty well told me my life story. I was amazed, drunk but sober enough to be shocked. I said, *"If I fly to England, I am wanted by the police. Will you help me get to Australia?"* She called Richard her husband and he came on the line and said, *"Fly back to England and I will collect you from the airport and you can stay with us till you go to Australia. Do you have any money?"* I said, *"I don't have a penny"*. Richard said *"That's okay. Ring me when you know your flight times"*. I hung up, booked a flight that evening as my ticket was a return ticket and informed Richard I would be in Manchester at nine o'clock that night. Richard told me it was snowing like Hell, but he would collect me.

I checked out of the hotel and went to the airport. I was very, very drunk. On the plane I ordered vodka and more vodka and the bill came to Twenty Six Pounds. I had no money to pay. The Hostess called the Chief Steward and the Bastard rang Manchester Airport for me to be arrested when I arrived in Manchester. I was informed, when the plane landed, *I was to stay in my seat or they would restrain me.* This was dear old British Airways.

So again I was so close yet so far away. I knew if I was arrested and taken to a police station in Manchester, I would be kept in custody on the other charges. I had got myself again in a spot, just for the sake of a few drinks on the plane. It was crazy, *insane.* I sat in my seat and resigned myself to the fact I was now again in Big Trouble.

Some people are very *Strange.* The male stewards seemed to take great delight in all the drama. I stayed in my seat and all the other passengers left the plane. The two police officers were very very good and said to me, *"Mr Hayes, we will have to arrest you. We can see you are very drunk. We have to take you through the airport, collect your baggage, then take you to the station. Do we need handcuffs or will you behave yourself?"* I was very grateful and said, *"Yes, I will behave".* They said, *"Okay, we won't use the handcuffs".*

We collected my bags and I walked between the two officers out of the doors of the International arrivals. There I saw Richard and Margaret waving at me. I told the coppers, *"These people have driven two hundred miles in the snow to collect me. Can I please speak to them and explain my plight?"* They agreed and I told Richard what had happened. Richard agreed to pay the Twenty Six Pounds immediately and the police let me go. I thought *"All my Birthdays had come at once".* I was so resigned to my doom at this stage as I realised that, as in all walks of life, there are good police and bad police. These two young men did their job, arrested me, when they were paid they released me. They most certainly did not have to do this. They restored my faith a little in the English Police force.

I was grateful, relieved and embarrassed and desperate for a drink. It was snowing like Hell and we had to drive over the Pennines to get on to the M1/A1 for Lincoln. I was desperate for a drink so Richard stopped at the first pub and bought me a couple of vodkas and I was fine.

I agreed that during my stay with them I would try not to drink. They were kind to me and I believe also afraid of me. This was Richard's second marriage and the brother of his first wife was a Police Detective Inspector in Yorkshire. Richard had a copy of my C.R.O. with all of my previous convictions. I believe to make sure I was not wanted for Murder or Rape or Terrorism. This couple were two *Angels* sent by God to help me and guide me. Even writing about this incident I feel a glowing warmth towards them.

The following day I came off the booze *cold turkey,* rang Barbara my sister who ran a travel agency for my brother, Bob and she booked me a flight to Australia. However, I had to *"Pay up Front".* I rang Jack Taylor and borrowed the airfare for Nine Hundred Pounds and probably would have saved Two Hundred Pounds using an agent in London. I paid through the nose and up front to my own family.

My flight was booked and Richard took me to the

station at Lincoln and gave me some cash. He was in financial trouble with his business and I had spent two days advising him how to liquidate his company and avoid bankruptcy. They were most definately two angels sent by God, this I am sure, and even then I nearly blew it on the plane. In fact, I did blew it and was rescued by some *Divine Hands*.

I was going to spend two days with my sister Barbara as my mother was staying with her. On the train to London from Lincoln, I met an Australian fellow and asked him about Australia. All I knew of Australia was that Menzies was the Prime Minister or so I thought. This was from thirty years previously at my Primary School.

The Australian man told me when I arrive in Sydney to get the 'Sydney Morning Herald' on the Saturday and you will find pages of jobs, pages of accommodation. I thanked him. In London I called to Australia House and got a three month Business Trip Visa. The Vestey organisation had given me details of their meat interests in Australia and the address of their head office in Miller Street, North Sydney for the visa.

I took the train to Newbury, spent three to four days with Mum and Barbara and they took me to Gatwick to see me off. Both were crying as they thought they would never see me again. I never took any drink for those days and had a wonderful time with Barbara, really getting to know her again. Everything was *very, very Twee* and quite sad.

The moment I got into the International lounge and waved goodbye to them, I purchased two bottles of duty free Vodka to take on the plane. I only had Four Hundred Pounds and cash was short. I was not going to get caught on a plane again with no booze or no money to pay for booze.

I have no recollection of the flight. I was awake but drunk until I arrived in Bali. We had a three hour delay in Jakarta and I have no memory of this. Bali, I remember well as I was high as a kite and drinking my vodka out of the bottle.

*Village Carnival. I am the Prince
at Front Right 1954*

*Eggesford Hunt Meeting outside
"Tumbles House", our Family Home
1948*

Barbara, my sister as a Teenager

*Mum relaxing at Devon and Exeter Races
22 August 1963*

*Terri and Mum on New Year's Eve 1980
The first time I danced with my Mother*

*Margaret and myself in Monte Carlo 1974
awaiting results of my coup in Ulster*

GLAMOUR GIRLS

Amy with MGB Sports Car

Edwina on Stage, 1994

Priscilla, 1998

Amy at Windsor Hotel, 1997

Priscilla at Kinsealy Hall, 1997

Priscilla and Siobhan at the Vineyard, 2001

Amy and Rangoon in front of
Ashleigh Hall, 1996

Amy and Ruth, our pet Ewe, 1996

Children at the Cattle Yards on Farm, 1995

Amy, Mum and children
at Ashleigh Hall, 1996

Children cleaning the Swimming Pool, 1993

Priscilla and young Larry the Ram, 1995

Amy and Mum in Australia, 1996

*Charles, my father-in-law and myself
at home, 1997*

Playing Cards with Mum, 1996

*Chatting with Mum and saying Goodnight,
1996*

*Siobhan, Daniel, Robert and David
in our Four Poster, 1995*

Amy, Siobhan and Mum, 1996

Amy Relaxing, 1997

Priscilla and Siobhan, 1995

Amy in the Garden, 1997

Priscilla and one of her Rabbits, 1995

Robert and Siobhan, 1992

Robert and myself, 1993

Robert and myself, 2000

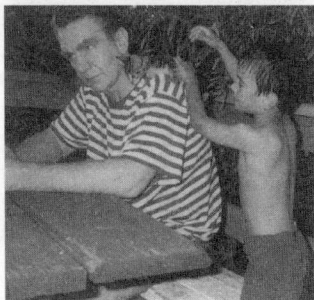

Daniel and myself, 1995

David and myself, 1996

Siobhan and myself, 2000

Amy and the Whole Gang, 1993

Boys ready for work on Farm, 1994

My farm staff, Anthony, Tommy and Paul,
myself and Charles, my father-in-law, 1996

Mum and myself on Farm, 1996

Larry, my pet Ram, 1997

Priscilla in foreground
Shearing Time, 1997

Me killing a Pig, 1997

Keeping my hand in with knife
skinning a calf. Mum in background, 1996

My Wedding Day in Prison
13th July 1994

Dancing with my Mother
New Year's Eve 1988

Amy and myself
Windsor Hotel, Melbourne

Caulfield Cup Day
Caulfield Races 1997

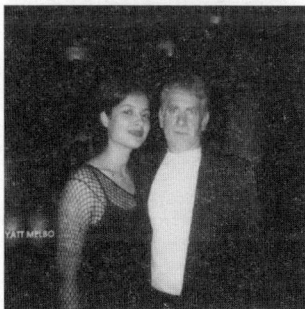

Priscilla and myself
Grand Hyatt, Melbourne, 2001

Paul, my Farm Hand at Ashleigh Hall, 1997

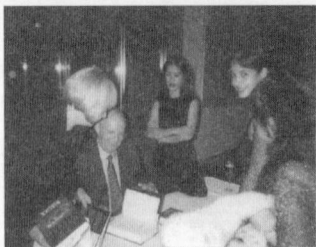

*Priscilla, Amy and Wilbur Smith
at the Grand Hyatt, Melbourne, June 2001.*

Wilbur Smith Night at Grand Hyatt, 2001

Wilbur Smith Night at Grand Hyatt, 2001

*Mercy Ball, Melbourne at end of
my Drinking Days 1993*

An Evening Out with Amy, 2001

*Amy at our table,
Lillian Frank Charity Night 1995*

DADDY'S GIRLS

Edwina 1998

Priscilla 2001

Siobhan 2000

CHAPTER TWENTY THREE

I arrived in Sydney ten o'clock on Saturday morning, the Twenty Sixth of January 1986. It was Bank Holiday weekend for Australia Day. I purchased the *"Sydney Morning Herald"* and went to the bar at Sydney airport to read it exactly as I had been instructed by the Australian on the train.

I can still remember the cold beer in a chilled glass as I was so dehydrated from all the vodka. So after a couple of schooners of beer I read the paper. I couldn't believe my luck. There was a job advertised for a slaughter man at Richmond in New South Wales. There were two phone numbers one was after hours.

I rang the number and spoke to an Irish man called Joe Carroll. I had known Jim Carroll in Bullawayo but they were no relation. Joe told me if I was any good the wage was about Six Hundred Dollars weekly and he could also arrange accommodation.

The job was killing mainly sheep and some cattle. I said, *"I will come over on Monday morning"*. Joe told me Monday was a holiday but to be there at six o'clock Tuesday morning. He gave me directions from Central Station, take the train to Windsor about fifty minutes. Get a taxi to the abattoir, about five miles from Windsor in the village of Wilberforce.

So there I was thirty eight years old, drunk been in Australia less than one hour and got myself a job. I had no fears or reservations about my ability with a knife. As long as my strength held up, I knew I could manage one day.

Then back in the bar I found the accommodation section and booked into a small hotel opposite Central Station which was Forty Dollars per night. I needed three to four nights accommodation so the money I put to one side, and took a taxi from the airport to my hotel.

My first impression of Sydney was like a very beautiful South African city. The climate was very similar perhaps more of a dry heat in Sydney. The taxi driver was talkative and charming. There I was in my Pin Striped Suit with collar and tie and he said, *"How was your flight from England"*. I said, *"How do you know I am from England?"* Of course, everyone in Sydney was in shorts or slacks with thongs or canvas shoes and T-shirts. It's amazing how sometimes you can't see yourself or how you appear to others.

The hotel was fine, small, clean and cheap. I showered, shaved and went straight off to have some more of this cold beer. The pub also had chilled glasses for the beer. I had never seen this before and thought what a wonderful idea. I enjoyed the beer so much. I never missed my vodka and as I was low on cash, it served my purpose. *Escape from Reality.*

I asked in the pub where the *"action"* was, clubs, girls and bars I was directed to Kings Cross. I immediately fell in love with the Cross everything for a drinking alcoholic. Walking from Kings Cross Station to find a pub I was propositioned two to three times by lovely girls in shorts and t-shirts. They were out of my budget yet I have always been at home with slinky women and sleazy bars.

I spent the evening at a Club called the *All Nations Club* in Bayswater Road. There I met an Australian girl who took me off to the Journalists Club followed by the Taxi Club and she left me at breakfast time. I slept all day Sunday then went back to the *All Nations Club* Monday night.

Today I have an office in the building next door to the old *All Nations Club* or where it used to be.

This time and I met a Mauri girl and we had a ball. She took me to Central Station at four o'clock in the morning to get my train to Windsor as I was starting work at six o'clock. I arranged to meet her that evening and booked one more night at the hotel.

I got a taxi from Windsor Station to the village of Wilberforce and still can remember walking into the plant in my Pin Stripe suit. All the men were looking at me as they thought I was an official of some kind. This man came up to me and said, *"G'day. Can I help you, Mate?"*. I said, *"Yes, I have come for the job"*. He said, *"The job is for a Slaughterman"*. I said, *"Yes, I know, but I need to borrow some knives, boots and clothes"*. I saw he was looking at me very apprehensively however he fitted me up with one knife, boots and shorts.

The majority of the staff were Mauris and when the kill began, I realised they were not very good slaughter men. They were skinning sheep with *Green River* Beef Siding knives. There was no way you can go fast with Big Knives, it was like eating a yoghurt from the carton with a desert spoon.

I was put on the back legs of the sheep the most skilled job on the line and within twenty minutes the line was blocked up, as I was going too fast. I thought, *"Right, you Buggars, I will give you a day to remember"*. I began putting on a real pace, then getting down from my stand and helping them clear the line. I saw several people came onto the kill floor to watch me. Then walk away. I was loving every minute of this and the sweat was pouring out of me.

We stopped for breakfast at nine o'clock and Joe came to me and said, *"I have spoken to the local caravan park and you can have a caravan for One Hundred Dollars per week and move in tonight"*. I explained I had to go back to Sydney for my clothes and would move in the following day. I didn't mention I had a date that night and was exhausted.

I was going to keep up this pace until lunch time if, or when I got too tired, I would make an excuse to go to Sydney early. As it worked out by three o'clock in the afternoon we had killed all the sheep on the plant some five hundred and fifty sheep. The normal working day was till four o'clock and the most sheep previously killed in one day was four hundred and thirty. So we had done one hundred and twenty sheep over the tally and finished one hour early.

I was physically wrecked yet very very sober. I must have sweat gallons of booze out of my system. I told Joe that I would skip the Wednesday and come over and move in and start on the Thursday. He was a little disappointed but I knew I would not be able to get out of bed the next morning. This was my first real manual work for six years.

I organised Two Hundred Dollars cash as a sub on my wages and took the train back to Sydney. I was so hot I realised my suit had to go. I was wearing shorts and t-shirt which I had been working in and I could see the wisdom in the Australian dress.

The village of Wilberforce and the town of Windsor are

on the river plains of the Hawkesbury River, sixty kilometres west of Sydney. It was a very pleasant train journey back to the city and as I sat looking contentedly out of the window I was well *pleased* with myself.

All the farms we passed on the train seemed to be either grazing cattle or market gardens. I was amazed how lush and green everything was. I later learned this was because the Hawkesbury River floods every winter and can rise as high as forty feet leaving the land saturated for the summer grass.

So back in Sydney, my girl didn't turn up for our date and I slept right through until lunch time the following day, I packed my bags and took the train back to Windsor to move into my caravan. *How the mighty fall*, yet I was free and having a go if only I could stay off the booze.

I arrived at the caravan park on the Thursday morning and apart from the heat it was okay. The park was situated on the banks of the Hawkesbury River and there was a small boat club, utility building, shop, showers and toilets, etc. I could walk over two fields or paddocks as they call them in Australia and be at the back of the abattoir in ten minutes.

There was a telephone extension from the office to the cattle pens, that used to be switched through when the office was closed at five o'clock in the evening. Every morning when I arrived, I would make my phone calls to the U.K. and use the cattle pens as my office. I rang Margaret Karpinski and told her there I was actually in the cattle pens with two stock horses in the paddock within my view. So her prediction of Australian cattle and horses was bang on the nail.

The English Meat Industry, has very little Union problems as the men are treated with Dignity and Respect. This cannot be said for Ireland in the large plants. In Australia the owners and top management treat the staff with Contempt and Cruelty and this is the reason the Trade Unions have such a hold on the country. The owner of the plant, Ian Stewart was a Prize Bastard. Just a little jumped up cattle dealer killing perhaps two thousand five hundred sheep per week. Talk about *notions of grandeur*, he made himself known to me and said, *"Can you do any job on the line, Paddy?"*. I said, *"Yes, Mr Stewart, and yours as well"*.

I had been working three weeks and every day doing the job of three men which was ok only I was getting the same wage as the rest of the men. I had also started to go to the local hotel on my way home and was getting a reputation as a Heavy Drinker. I drank beer only. Thank Goodness I stayed off the vodka as it would have been fatal. Then it got to the point I would go to the hotel for my lunch hour and have four schooners of beer for a liquid lunch.

I was asked to leave the caravan park as I made too much noise coming home at night or when the hotel closed between one and two o'clock in the mornings. I recall getting a couple of warnings and then finally telling the owner *"To go to Hell"*. They were not a nice couple, small minded second generation Australians. I recall the owner's wife showing me the paper and Lindy Chamberlain the Seventh Day Adventist whose baby was taken by a dingo. She had been released from prison, whilst serving a life sentence pending Appeal. The venom with which this lady told me that *the Chamberlain girl was guilty* was awful. As it happened the Appeal proved she was innocent and the forensic evidence was worthless, a total Miscarriage of Justice. The Australians knock anything they don't understand. The fact she was a *Seventh Day Adventist* and the media stating she was linked to the *Occult, Voodoo and Devil Worship* meant she was guilty in the eyes of the majority of Australians. I had no idea what a Seventh Day Adventist was but I know no one could be given a *Fair Trial*, with the likes of this caravan park owner serving on a Jury.

I was told to leave on the Sunday morning so I had to walk five miles to Windsor with my knives in one bag, my clothes in two suitcases. I was carrying one and pulling the second one on its wheels. This was a really hot February day and I tried every pub in Windsor looking for accommodation to no avail.

I was told to go to Richmond one stop on the train down the line and try the Royal Hotel. This I did and was given a super little room, en-suite with a small verandah and phone and to make it just perfect, two bars down the stairs.

This was a good little pub and was owned by some *villains* based on the Gold Coast, Queensland. They had seven pubs in the Sydney area all used for laundering money. The Manager, Graham Scott, was a Melbourne man, *ex-con* with tattoos all over his arms and neck that had been made with Indian ink and a needle in prison.

One of the men from work lived in Richmond and gave me a lift every day. So I had been working about three weeks and was earning Six Hundred to Seven Hundred Dollars weekly. I said to Joe Carroll, *"Joe, I should be getting a little extra as I am carrying the line"*. Joe agreed and told me he would speak to Ian Stewart on the Thursday when he came to the plant.

Friday was Pay Day and I got the same wages yet again. Joe told me that Ian Stewart said, *"Paddy is getting a good wage and his share"*. I asked Joe how many sheep we had on Monday and Joe said *"About six hundred"*. The kill was now five hundred and fifty to six hundred sheep every day, prior to my starting the biggest day was four hundred and thirty.

There were nine of us on the line so my share of six hundred sheep was sixty six sheep. So on the Sunday night I stopped drinking at midnight. Graham took me to the plant at twelve thirty in the morning. I began killing on my own. I killed seventy sheep and was finished by six o'clock all cleaned up. The sheep were dressed perfectly. So I was having a shower ready to go home when the men came to work.

Joe said, *"What have you done, Paddy?"* I said *"Killed my share of the sheep, Seventy"*. In fact, I had done four extra. I told him, *"I get the same money as these other men, let them do their own share"*. I went home to bed. I learned the following day that plant had only killed four hundred and twelve extra sheep from mine. I said to Joe, *"You can get Ian Stewart on the phone and if he doesn't amend my wages, I am leaving"*. Joe rang Ian Stewart who said he would not pay any extra money. So I walked out and went back to the hotel and got drunk.

I spent two weeks on the booze and my money was running low, so I took a job on the beef line at Riverstone Meats, part of the Vestey organisation. I used the name Ross Reed as I didn't want to use my own name with Vesteys. We were killing seven hundred cattle a day finishing by two o'clock in the afternoon each day. The money was about Four Hundred and Fifty Dollars weekly. So I was on Three Hundred Dollars less per week but the work was so easy and I was in the bar each day at half past two in the afternoon.

Some of the boys at Riverstone left every year in March to do seasonal killing in North Queensland or the Northern Territory. Vestey had three plants in the Far North, Rockhampton, Townsville and Katherine in the Northern Territory.

There was a plant in Alice Springs owned by George Whittaker, Chairman of Wales Meat Company and the slaughter men could earn One Thousand Four Hundred to Two Thousand Dollars weekly. The season was only six months and people went to mann these plants from all over Australia.

I decided to contact George Whittaker of Wales Meat Company and phoned him from the hotel. George had already heard of the *"Speed Machine"* who had been working at Wilberforce. Everyone knew about the night I went and killed the sheep myself. This was the talk of the Australian Meat Industry. This was spread by the Meat Inspectors and drivers from plant to plant. Very few men in Australia can do all the jobs on the line. They can only do one back leg or one front leg or skin the head. So I had an interview with George Whittaker in March 1986.

Wales Meat Company was based in Pitt Street, Sydney right next to Townhall Station. I went into the city on the train and was appointed Killing Hall Supervisor for the *"Alice Springs Meat Works"*. This was a two year old $14 million Plant. I was given a basic salary of Eight Hundred Dollars weekly, house and car. However, I was to get the same salary as the men on the kill floor One Thousand Five Hundred to Two Thousand Dollars weekly once the season began plus a loading of 20% bonus.

I liked George Whittaker and George gave me One Thousand Dollars cash and one way air ticket to Alice Springs for the following week. So off I go back to my hotel, the Royal at Richmond like a *dog with two tails.*

We had dances at the pub on Friday and Saturdays and I was going with a girl called Susie Brown whose father was the Hairdresser in Richmond at the RAAF base. Susie was a secretary in Concorde, Sydney and she had a drink problem.

Every night she would have a bottle of Champagne and sit down with the bottle and pay Five Dollar Corkage. This was a very pleasant, very cheap way to get drunk as Champagne or Sparkling Wines in Australia are very cheap and very palatable.

I was sad to leave Richmond and the Royal Hotel, my first real home in Australia. They gave me a farewell party and I caught the plane to Alice Springs in my evening dress, having not been to bed by seven o'clock in the morning when the plane left.

I arrived in the Red Centre at lunch time in my evening dress and very drunk. George met me at the airport and the last thing I must have looked like was a slaughter man. George showed me the house which was a four bed roomed bungalow in Smith Street, Alice Springs, then took me to the plant.

The plant was superb. I can honestly say the neatest meat plant I have ever been in. We had beautiful cattle yards, cattle wash, cattle showers to keep the cattle cool. Large meat plant and by-products plants as well as facilities to dress our own hides. I have never seen a plant so totally self-contained. Of course, being in the desert one thousand kilometres from Adelaide or Darwin, *self-contained*, we had to be.

The cattle all came in on road trains with two hundred and forty head of cattle on one truck. This was a cattle/meat man's dream. Alice Springs is as the name suggested an oasis in the desert.

The town is a lovely spot complete with racecourse, camel racecourse, casino and several five-star hotels. As well as the constant stream of tourists visiting Alice Springs and Ayers Rock. The local farmers from as far as eight hundred kms came to town once a month to shop. There was a large Aboriginal community and they all drank in the Todds Hotel. This also soon became my watering hotel.

Todds Hotel had a piano bar, lounge bar, music bar as well as a public bar. When the plant opened we had a staff of two hundred as well as the skilled men we had some sixty girls packing the meat. These were Backpackers from all over Europe as well as Australian girls. They all drank every night at Todds Hotel.

I was made General Manager in our second week of

production but my social life was taking its toll. I shared the house with a man called Ralph Brown. Ralph used to own one of the largest meat plants in Australia at Inverell in North New South Wales.

Ralph and his family had gone broke and the banks sold his plant to the Smorgan Family for Four Hundred Thousand Dollars, less than one tenth of the value. Inverell was killing one thousand Cattle per day. Ralph had lost his farms, aeroplanes and cars, all to the Receiver.

Ralph was a very devout Salvation Army man and would live every day by the Bible. I learned later he was too honest to be in business. His job in Alice Springs was to purchase all the cattle. He was a good Buyer and good judge of cattle. Ralph knew immediately I was an alcoholic and did all he could to get me off the booze.

I had money in my pocket. The hotel was happy to look after me as the more the plant did, as the more staff were employed the more money they were getting over the counter. I had no shortage of girls and mainly went out with Aboriginal girls.

The drink began to take its Toll. I was now working one day, sleeping one day and working the next. When I was organising the plant, I enjoyed it. Once the plant was running itself, I became very bored and only wanted to go to Todds Hotel and be with my girls.

George begged me to *get a grip.* He would do anything for me and made tremendous allowances. I just could not get off the booze. Then one night I was arrested for being Drunk and released without charge the following morning. I went home and spent three days in bed.

George was furious. We were shipping beef to Taiwan and very very busy. The following Saturday we lost our engineer who ran the boilers of the plant. Without an engineer with a *"Boiler License"* the plant couldn't operate.

We found a man in Brisbane. He was Indian and I was sent to collect him at the airport on Saturday afternoon. To get to the airport, you have to go past the racecourse. So on the way back I called into the Races. I had been drinking at lunch time and soon became very drunk.

The poor little Indian engineer was terrified of me and kept asking to go and see Mr Whittaker. The result was I forgot him and left him at the Racecourse and went back to the plant. George said, *"Where is the engineer, we have been closed all day, Bill."* I had no idea what he was talking about and no recollection of collecting the engineer. Then, of course, it all came back.

I had a vague recollection of going to the airport. I was, of course, in an *Alcoholic Blackout.* A Blackout is when you have no recollection of the events of a drinking evening. This can happen to social drinkers. You can't recall going home after a Party. However, with an alcoholic, we can lose days on end with no recollection of where we have been or who we have been with.

George went to the Race course and collected the little Indian man who had flown two thousand miles at a rush to operate our boilers, only to be left lost at the races all afternoon. George sent me home to *sober up*.

I went to Todds Hotel drank all evening and have no recollection of the next few days. I reported for work the Thursday of the following week. George said, *"Bill, if you could only see this season out, I will build you a plant anywhere in Australia or Europe, but you must get off the booze".*

I could not get off the booze and became worse and worse and George finally had to replace me. He was very decent about it but by this time the men I was drinking with, were losing or had lost all respect for me as a man. I was *The Town Drunk*. There were very many men with drinking problems in Alice Springs many of our men were heavy drinkers, but they could all perform at work. It soon became the talk of the town *"Bill will not be in tomorrow, look how pissed he is".* The men then began taking days off and what could George say? *"Its okay for Bill Hayes but not for you?"*

George gave me a week to get out of the house. I saw a job for a slaughter man in the *"Weekend Australian"* and the phone number was 087 code. As Alice Springs was 089 code, I thought it must be somewhere local. I rang up and it was killing on my own in a small slaughter house in the Claire Valley, South Australia about one thousand four hundred kilometres away. I took the job and arranged to travel on the Greyhound Bus to Adelaide.

I had spent all my money, was borrowing money off the staff at the plant to buy my drinks, and the bus fare I borrowed off a man called Captain Watt of the local Salvation Army. I had met Captain Watt one night at AA which was run from the Salvation Army office in Alice Springs.

When things had got *Really Bad* in Alice, I went to a couple of AA meetings at the Salvation Army Headquarters in the town. I didn't like the people and took only the negatives from the meetings, causing me of course to continue drinking. I considered myself a *"Better Class"* alcoholic than these people.

I left Alice Springs with two bottles of wine and two packets of Marlboro, my suitcases and my knives. The journey was thirty hours on the bus and half way to Adelaide I sold some of my knives to buy more booze and the Truck Stop.

I met an Irish girl on the bus who was Back Packing around Australia. I was very lonely and very attracted to her but by this time my life was in such a mess I had nothing to offer. I recall writing down her address in Ireland never believing I would ever have any use for it.

I got off the bus at a junction twenty kms from Claire which was about one hundred kilometres north of Adelaide. I thumbed a lift to Claire, went to the local hotel and had two to three beers and phoned my new boss to collect me. He said he was busy but would be there within the hour. When he arrived he had to pay Thirty Dollars to the hotel for my booze and he took me to the plant. Drink was my God in those days. I didn't care how I paid for it as long as I could drink it.

He was a nice little man and always wore this funny woollen hat. I later learned he had spent Forty Four Thousand Dollars on a hair transplant that had gone wrong. So instead of a head full of new hair, he had a head full of scars.

I had to kill three sheep the same afternoon and my knives did the *talking for me*. I also had to kill two pigs by hand with a twenty gallon boiler of water and one Jersey cow. He was *"wrapped"* with me and showed me the accommodation. I was to share a farm house with his cousin who he employed this in the village of Saddleworth. The money was poor but it was a pleasant job, nice house and use of the company ute (pick up truck).

The Clare Valley was one of the most famous wine growing areas of Australia and this being May, was harvest time for the grapes. The main population were all of German extraction and, in fact, many of them had been *"interned"* during the last war. All the shops had German names. It was a lovely part of Australia.

The boss, I later learned, had a large manor house in Adelaide and a chain of butchers shops. He had given the business to his sons, walked out on his wife and given her the Manor House and moved onto the farm with his Filipino girlfriend.

They were now married and she was away on holidays when I arrived. We worked out the routine for the week. I would do all the killing. He would run the butchers shops and wholesale market and everything should have gone well. However, on the third day we both got Drunk and had a lovely evening. The wife returned home and I learned this was his *first drink in six years*. He was also an alcoholic. His wife was furious with him and with me for leading him astray. She made it clear I had to go.

The Boss had sent his Cousin down to the village for a slab of twenty four cans of Beer and a bottle of whiskey liqueur.

After many drinks he decided we would fill his twenty thousand gallon water tank *Free of Charge* by bypassing the water meter. Water is very expensive in certain parts of Australia.

Having called a plumber friend of his, we cut the main pipe at the meter having turned off the main tap, placed a polythene pipe to bypass the meter and turned the mains back on.

It all appeared to be working well. This was a high pressure two inch water main. We went to bed drunk but the next morning all Hell Broke Lose as the pipe came off in the night and flooded the village at the bottom of the hill.

The police and fire brigade were called and I don't know to this day how the Boss *squared* it all but I gather some money had to change hands. Once again, the *insanity of the drinking alcoholic.* He didn't need the money and was so busy *Chasing the Mice*, he was *Missing the Elephants.*

The boss came back from the cattle sales in Salisbury, Adelaide, a couple of days later and informed me that there was a considerable sized plant at Anguston in the Borossa Valley about sixty kms away. The boss told me he had agreed to lend me to them as they were very busy and their Best slaughter man had cut a tendon in his wrist.

I said, *"Okay, this is fine, when do I start".* He said *"I have agreed to take you over this afternoon as they have a very big day on".* So I packed my bags and he drove me to Anguston.

I was booked in the local hotel and taken to the plant. This was a nice small modern plant with only four slaughter men and five when the Top Man was working. I began work immediately.

We were killing sheep till about eight o'clock that night and caught up on the day. I was quite pleased with myself and ready for a beer. I learned then they had a pig killing hall across the yard and we had to kill one hundred and twenty pigs that night. I was a real speed machine as I was trying to get finished before the pubs closed.

The boss got me to the hotel by eleven thirty that night. He was also a very very bad alcoholic so we drank together until three o'clock in the morning. *This was just what the doctor ordered.* When the bar closed he told me he was having *"a lie in bed"* the following day but not to worry, his son would collect me at seven o'clock.

So at seven o'clock the following day his son collected me and we had a big day of work, yet were finished and back in the pub by four o'clock in the afternoon. I asked the boss how long he needed me for. He said, *"Need you? I paid One Thousand Dollars to get you and your job is permanent".* So I had been sold in Salisbury saleyard for One Thousand Dollars, I imagine, at the instigation of the wife of my previous boss. I still find this incident very amusing.

The job was okay, quiet and average wage of Six Hundred to Seven Hundred Dollars weekly, enough to drink on. The local police sergeant's ex wife ran an *Introduction Agency* and put me on her books as she was short of eligible males. In the hotel at night everyone seeing me, assumed I was in the management of the meat works and not just a *lowly Slaughterman.*

The drinking became worse and I recall being invited to a Country and Western evening by the police sergeant's wife. I met a rather nice divorcee who kept horses. She was telling me she had a problem with one of her horses with a soft mouth. I told her to get surgical spirits and bathe it daily and it would come hard.

She said she would pick me up in the morning and take me to see the horses. I didn't get to bed until four o'clock the next morning *well shot* and had a drink, of course, to surface. By the time the girl had arrived I was well on. I asked her for a vodka when she offered me morning coffee. I sat in her home and got wickedly drunk. She had two lovely children all dressed up for this visitor to call. I just sat in the chair talking *Bull Dust* and living in my past whilst telling them what a *Great Man* I used to be.

I eventually looked at the horses and fixed the mouth of the horse with problems. I then took the horse for a ride and took it all around the paddock at full gallop, jumping the gates, racing back to the stables, and fell out of the saddle drunk. The poor little girls were crying thinking I was going to hurt the horse. By this time the woman was upset and eventually ringing for a taxi to take me back to the hotel.

This was a bad drinking bout, as that night I went to work when the bar closed at four in the morning. The boss's son was there loading meat on the lorries as we didn't start killing until seven o'clock. I sat in the office drinking vodkas. Telling the son, all the things they were doing wrong.

The result was by seven o'clock when it was time to start work, I was *legless* so I went back to the hotel and slept for two days. I was, of course, sacked. There was no second or third chances like George Whittaker in Alice Springs.

I took the bus to Adelaide and was *Flat Broke.* I had only Four Dollars. I didn't know whether to buy a bottle of wine or a packet of Marlboro. The wine won. I called into a newsagent telling the girl at the counter I was waiting for my wife. Could I have thirty Marlboro and my wife would pay when she arrived. I lighted one and it was delicious. Then I went through all the pretences of looking for my wife up and down the road and going back into the shop saying, *"I don't know what has happened to her"*. Eventually I ran away down the road stealing the cigarettes.

I spent that night in a hostel for the homeless. It was awful, no money for drink. It was the worse memory of this time. I walked to the local Salvation Army to borrow Five Dollars to buy a bottle. They were not like Captain Watt of Alice Springs. They told me to go away, like the police there are good and bad in the Salvation Army also.

I found a job in the local paper as a *Table Hand* in a sausage factory at Two Hundred and Forty Dollars per week. This was linking sausages from six in the morning to six at night, five days a week. I was to start on the Monday morning. This was the longest weekend I have ever known. *No money, no bus fare, no booze and no fags*. I had no idea what to do, then came up with an idea.

I put on my best suit, washed and shaved and rang the Hilton Hotel in Adelaide saying my name was George Whittaker of Alice Springs Meats. I told the manager I had a meeting there at two o'clock that afternoon and was running late and would not be there until six that evening. I also told the manager, *"This man I was meeting is a Mr Bill Hayes from Ireland. A very important client. When Mr Hayes arrives can you please take care of him, drinks, meal, etc. Put this all on my account and I would settle the account when I arrive"*. The manager was most helpful and told me, *"Not to worry"*. He would take care of Mr Hayes.

I walked several miles into the city centre and arrived at the Hilton. I was given red carpet treatment declining a meal and drinking vodka. I spent all afternoon sitting in the foyer of the Hilton getting quietly drunk. All would have been ok if I had stayed sober but no, *big shot Billy* went *OTT*. I was ordering bottles of French Champagne and mixing with the other people in the Foyer making a Bloody nuisance of myself, as well as drawing attention to myself.

I should have realised that whenever I got drunk in

those days, I lost complete control of my actions. I used to go back to my days in Ireland and England buying what I want, when I want and charging it down. I was now constantly *Blacking Out*.

At around eight o'clock that evening the manager came to me. He was a Black African from Mombasa in Kenya and we had a long chat about Africa and the Hilton group. The drink was still flowing and all appeared to be well.

The manager eventually came back and said he had been on the phone to George Whittaker of Alice Springs Meat *(George used to switch the phone from the plant through to his house at weekends)* and Mr Whittaker had not telephoned, nor was he going to Adelaide. The manager was quite ok but could I settle the account, some Three Hundred Dollars. I had not one cent on me even my cigarettes were charged down to George.

The police were called and I was arrested. I was in a terrible state of drunkeness and can only recall waking up in the cells in the morning. I was bailed at ten o'clock to appear in court at a date to be fixed.

I should have been at work at six o'clock that morning so I rang the factory to see if I could still come. They told me yes. They also told me the police had been on the phone to them, to check if I worked there. I must have given the factory address as I had *No Fixed Abode* which is essential to get Bail.

I arrived at work at midday. If I had the money I would have been drinking as I felt awful. The work was hard. There was a staff of about ninety Vietnamese and Cambodians, one Italian and the owner was an Irish man, Brendon Connolly from Athlone in County Westmeath.

They knew all about me as they were great friends of my previous boss in Claire. The word was getting to towns in Australia before me, *the Irish drunk who was a Great Butcher but couldn't get off the booze*. I collected a day's pay at six o'clock that evening when I was told to be early the next day, and went to the local pub. I met an English man, a fellow alcoholic who said I could stay with him for a couple of days until I found some accommodation. So I fell on my feet yet again.

The flat where I stayed was rather a nice building.

Dave the English man had a very serious *Drink Problem* and had resigned himself to the fact he would never stop, nor did he want to stop. I have never seen so many empty bottles in a private home in my life. The verandah was stacked with bottles like the back door of a pub.

Dave, the alcoholic worked every morning driving a delivery van. He finish at two o'clock leaving his van at home. He then walked to the pub and drank until eleven o'clock each night. He would get a pizza on the way home and do the same the following day. The routine never varied, weekends were different as he drank all day.

This man had been an officer in the R.A.F in England, was married with four sons, then his wife had divorced him. He took over the family business from his father when he retired from the Air Force and he drank the business and family fortune away in five years. This proves once more that alcohol is a *Great Remover*. It removes everything.

I met a Scottish girl at the Singles Dance called Trish Davey. She was Broad Glasgow and had been in Adelaide twenty years. Trish was a nurse. We had a relationship and eventually I moved into her home. Trish had rather a nice house at Goodwood in Adelaide.

My drinking became worse and the *"days off"* started again. I was again sacked. I got a job with a company called KIMCO *Kangaroo Island Meat Company*. They had a new plant on the island, off the South Coast of Australia and wholesale depot in Adelaide. My job was selecting the meat for the orders, checking the weights and general *Dog's body*. I began work at four o'clock in the morning and finished around lunch time. Trish took me to work and collected me each day. Everyone at the depot was on the fiddle from the Manager to all the employees. Each morning they would arrive in their cars, load the cars with meat, then do their day's work and drive home with their boots and back seats full of stolen primal cuts. The Manager himself was taking full carcasses of meat.

The boss arrived one day and when we were talking he asked me would I like to move to Kangaroo Island and run the abattoir. It has cost $8 million to build the previous year and they were having great problems teaching local people to become good operatives. I agreed and was furnished with a package of house, good salary and percentage of profits. The house was, in fact, built for the Managing Director who had decided to move to the mainland if I took over the plant.

I purchased a car on finance and was ready to move. Trish was going to follow if things worked out ok for me. This was a good relationship and she did all she could to restore me to my *former glory*.

I met the Company Chairman on the ferry going to the Island and got very very drunk. I can't remember the end of the conversation or getting off the ferry but I told him about the thousands of dollars going out of the plant each day in stolen meat.

I arrived on the Island went to my hotel that had been booked for me and this was all I can honestly remember. The following morning the local Police Sergeant very quietly took me to the airport and put me on the plane to Adelaide telling me *never to come back to the Island.*

It transpired the Island is a very close community and I was very drunk in the bar of the hotel, sharpening my knives, demonstrating how to kill sheep, making a general nuisance of myself. I also was heard to say if the Islanders didn't improve their performance at the plant I would sack them all and bring in my own staff from Alice Springs. This I could have done, but was politically incorrect as the plant was owned by a co-operative of local farmers. Equally, the staff were all local farmers and farmers' sons. Thus the Chairman was called and asked, *"Who is this mad drunk you have brought to the Island who is going to put us all out of work?"* etc.

The result was the local Police Sergeant who was also a small farmer was given the job of sending me packing. They would put my car on the ferry the following day.

I arrived back at Trish's home in Adelaide the following day. She was aware of all I had done as the Managing Director had telephoned her and asked if I was always as bad as this. So, of course, I needed a drink and went on the booze.

I have no idea how it happened but on the Thursday, I had been off the drink for nearly a day and went into the D.Ts. I was walking in Adelaide and thought everyone was chasing me so I ran and hid behind a wall. It was dusk time also pouring with rain. I have no recollection of the rest of the evening. Only at six o'clock the following morning I walked into the Hilton Hotel and asked for my key. I was *Stark Naked.*

The night porter went and got me a towel to cover myself and told me I was not booked in the hotel. I believed I was on the film set of *"Far From the Maddening Crowd"* with Alan Bates, Terence Stamp and Julie Christie. *So I asked where the crew were.* This, of course, made no sense to the porter and he called the police. I still have vague recollections of this morning albeit I was in D.Ts.

The police were very decent and they had no idea where the film crew were either. So they took me to a Salvation Army Hostel for *Homeless Men* and got me some clothes. I was told to stay there. I remember walking out the moment the police left and went to find the film crew. I had no idea where I was or where I lived so I thought I would go and see George Whittaker at his home. This was Adelaide and George's house was three thousand miles away in Sydney and his second home fifteen hundred miles away in Alice Springs.

I found what I thought was George's house and walked in the door, went to the kitchen, put on the kettle to make coffee. I then opened the fridge and began to make a sandwich. This man walked in wearing his pyjamas. It was about eight o'clock Sunday morning. He asked me what I was doing. I didn't like his tone so I said, *"What do you think I am doing, I am waiting for George".* This man got quite aggressive and tried to get me out of the house. I sat down on a chair after giving him a piece of my mind.

The next thing was the same two policemen came, who were at the Hilton and said *"Not you, again!"* I asked them to take me to the film set and they agreed. They, in fact, took me to the Angus Park Mental Hospital where I was certified under the Inebriate's Act of 1972.

I was kept in hospital for a week with alcohol withdrawals. This happens when you come off booze after many weeks of abuse. The body cannot stand the change to the system.

I remember looking out the window at many potted

plants on the verandah and seeing Jill from Manchester. She was no more than eight or nine inches high but it was her. She kept hiding behind these plant pots and then she grew a shell like a tortoise. This is all still so very clear in my mind. This was, of course, D.Ts.

Trish came to see me and eventually I was allowed home. I had apparently walked out on Trish and moved into the Seven Stars Hotel in Adelaide. This was where all my clothes were. I have a small recollection of getting out of bed and the ceiling was being lowered on me, not broken, but coming down like a lift. I also have a vague recollection of banging my head and seeing sparks, not just seeing stars but actually sparks. This was all my *Hallucinations* or *Delirium Tremors*.

So I will never ever really know what happened. I only know that I was a very "S*ick Boy*" and the worse I have ever been in my life. I decided to go back to New South Wales. I had no idea what I was going to do or where I was going to live. I made up my mind. Trish took me to the airport. I would never have recalled my clothes being at the Seven Stars had Trish not come to see me.

I arrived in Sydney, only a three hour flight and couldn't find a taxi who would accept a cheque so I hired a limousine from Hugh's Cars based at the airport and told the driver to take me to Richmond. We stopped at the first bottle shop and I drank from the bottle in the back of the limo and was going back to where I had started, having pretty nearly been around all of Australia in the previous six months.

I was told in AA there were many *YET's*, that come to us all if we continue to drink. This was my first serious D.Ts. The tremors are very frightening yet despite all of this, I couldn't stop drinking nor did I want to stop drinking. This was also the first time I had been *certified*.

Writing about these events, it is as clear as crystal. My problems were all being caused by my drinking, yet I could delude myself that things would get better. Bad things would eventually stop happening to me. I was full of self-pity, *Poor me, Poor me, Pour me a Drink*.

Trish had been in touch with my mother and the two of them who loved me so much, could do nothing to help me. In my clear moments, when I was not drunk, people got a small glimpse of the *Real Bill* or as much of me as I could to show.

All I had left was *Front and Show*. I was afraid to tell people who I really was. A *Failure*, a far greater failure than my father knew how to be. I had nothing, was going nowhere, so I lived in my Past as my Present was far too painful to live in.

Everyone who came in contact with me did so at great expense to themselves. By now I had lived with *Margaret, second Margaret, Anne, Mary, Lisa in South Africa, Terri, Sally, Elizabeth, Jill and Trish Davey in Adelaide*. All Serious relationships causing the ladies involved great financial hardship, loss of face and bitterness in the early days of separation.

I recall a lady at AA saying we alcoholics are incapable of having relationships. We *"Take Prisoners"* or *"Hostages"*. Once people are wise to our weakness we feel threatened and when there is talk of cutting down on the booze let alone stopping, we feel threatened. When a normal person sees a bottle of whiskey, it as *Half Full*. An alcoholic would see it as *Half Empty*. Then become concerned what am I going to do when it's gone.

I was made very welcome at the Royal Hotel and given my room back. The driver told me if ever I needed him again to give him a call.

I got very very drunk and saw Susie Brown that evening and the following day everyone was going to the Hawkesbury Races just two miles up the road. I recall going to the Races then telephoning the car hire company again for the limousine. When he arrived I asked him to take me to Riverstone Meats, the Vestey plant where I worked on the kill floor under an assumed name.

The car waited and I met the General Manager and introduced myself as Bill Hayes, told him of my life long connections with Vestey and asked if they had any management positions. The Manager telephoned Scott Benton, the Vestey Australian Managing Director, who invited me to Head Office in Miller Street, North Sydney.

The driver took me there and I told him to wait. The Vestey headquarters was a twenty storey building in Miller

Street and Scott Benton was on the top floor. We had a long chat and I had my bottle of sparkling wine in my hand and swigging from the bottle. This was perfectly natural for me by this time yet it must have looked very strange to any normal businessman. I could hold my own with anyone in conversation regarding the meat business and my arrogance was second to none. The result was that Benton said he would write to me. I knew by my behaviour alone, *I couldn't fit into any Corporate situation.* I was really just spending the day, enjoying *Talking Meat* to people.

The driver said, *"Where to now?"* I had no idea where to go. My money was gone. I had no employment in Richmond so we went to a pub. The driver loaned me money to put on my account. After several drinks I could see the driver was getting very anxious and was making several phone calls. I later learned he was ringing his boss. The account was about One Hundred and Twenty Dollars and the driver could see the state I was in and getting worse. So back we go to the car. I said, *"Back to Richmond"* the driver said, *"We have to make a call first".* So off we go and he drives straight into the yard of Waverly Police Station, behind Bondi Beach.

I was charged with hiring a car with no money to pay the fare. I was placed in the cells and slept right through until court the next morning. My case was adjourned and I was bailed for One Hundred Dollars or remanded into custody to Long Bay Jail if I couldn't raise the Bail.

The Police Sergeant said, *"Have you anyone who can post Bail?"* of course I had no one. I was allowed one phone call and rang Graham Scott the Manager of the Royal Hotel. Graham said he would come into the city and bail me. So Graham drove seventy kilometres and bailed me out.

Graham gave me Fifty Dollars and told me I couldn't come back to the hotel. He had brought all my clothes in his car with him. Apparently the previous evening I had made quite a bit of trouble in the bar and one or two of the locals were going to give me a *Good Hiding.* Only Graham intervened and saved me. I would love to see Graham again sober and thank him in person. He was a lovely man. *Very much a Man's Man.* Just a *Really Nice Guy.*

I found a Bed and Breakfast at Strathfield and got the Saturday's Sydney Morning Herald and looked up jobs for a butcher. Every day there are always ten to fifteen jobs for shop butchers in Sydney to work on a casual basis. I found a job starting at seven o'clock in the morning on the Monday and Roselands Shopping Centre and went to bed for the day.

The Guest House was owned by a Polish couple on the Sunday morning. I was *awakened* with the smell of Bacon and Eggs. So up I get to have a good breakfast then spend the day in bed. I sat down in the dining room and ordered a *Double Breakfast*, Double of everything. I was served coffee and the owner said, *"Are you staying tonight?"* I replied, *"Yes, I start work on Monday"*. The owner said, putting my breakfast on the table, *"Breakfast is Five Dollars per day Extra"*. I said, *"Okay, this is Fine"*. I was just about to cut into the delicious Bacon and butter some toast when the manager said "Five Dollars". I said, *"Yes, that is no problem"*. He said, *"NOW!"*. I told him I can't pay him till I come home from work on Monday. So the Bastard took my breakfast away. I was starving and he took my coffee as well and told me to get out of his Guest House.

This was perhaps the most *Despicable Act* ever done to me and typified the abuse a drinking alcoholic faces daily.

I can never walk past a drunk or beggar with their hand out for money. I always give them whatever change I have in my pocket. I have been there and know the *Pain*, *Suffering* and *Humiliation* of being *Penniless, Alone* and *Suffering*. What goes around, comes around. What I have today I can only *keep* by giving it away. This is *Truly Beautiful*.

I found digs at a pub in Petersham and went to work on the bus the following morning. I never stuck a job more than two days. I was always paid daily and must have worked in twenty to twenty five butcher's shops in Sydney, moving from pub to pub as I usually got *barred from drinking in the bar*. I can think of two to three pubs where I lived and by the second day it was made a condition I could live there but drink elsewhere. I can't recall one of the incidents that caused the ruling but know the Hotel managers always had to help me up the stairs to bed. This *could have been worse* as I was at least allowed to live there.

I ended up in a pub in Ashfield and the owner was a nice man called Mr King. I later learned he was a *Recovering Alcoholic* and had been sober twenty years. The room was clean, small verandah and a private entrance at the back of the pub.

I remember going for a job at Blacktown one morning, pissed and really nasty. The manager gave me Thirty Dollars to go home rather than have trouble in his shop, especially me with a knife.

I came home in the early hours one morning and had lost my key. So I put me elbow through the glass door to lift the lock from the inside. The glass must have been reinforced as initially it wouldn't break then with all my force I got my elbow through and opened the door.

As I got to my room I saw blood everywhere. I looked down the corridor and it was the same. I didn't realise the blood was coming from me. It was in fact my elbow. I had a massive cut on my elbow and the flesh was hanging off. I must have cut a vein as the blood was running like a tap. I went back into the street and got a taxi to the nearest hospital.

I passed out in Casualty and remember this doctor shining a torch in my eyes. I had already been stitched and bandaged and I was in Canterbury Hospital. The doctor said, *"You are in real trouble, Mr Hayes. Do you want some help?"* I asked him what he meant and he told me I was in acute alcoholic withdrawal and he could get me into hospital, if I would go. I readily agreed and an ambulance took me to the McKinnon Unit at Rozelle Hospital, Sydney.

This was a De-tox Unit with an optional three week course of Group Therapy along with AA. I was de-toxed for three days and accepted on the course. I rang Mr King and told him I would pay for the window, he said he would bring all my clothes himself. This was when he told me he had been sober twenty years. He also said that I was in the right place. He knew I was a serious alcoholic the first evening I stayed with him when he saw me drinking.

The McKinnon was very similar to my first hospital in Oxford. The treatment was very intensive and we had to go to AA every day. I met some *Charming* people and every Sunday morning we went to the Matthew Talbot Hostel in Kings Cross. This is a hostel for about five hundred to six hundred Homeless men. I recall one of the staff telling me this place was going to *open my eyes.*

The Matthew Talbot was a very sad place with *Wino's and Derelicts.* Inside and outside the building but it didn't open my eyes as I already had been much worse off than these people. The Sunday morning AA is the largest group in Sydney with may be two hundred members each week. It was a *"great"* meeting, straight talking and people who had *"really recovered"* as well as the usual play actors and hangers on. Many people with contented *sobriety* also.

I became *very well* and was ready to leave and Lisa, one of the counselors, told me not to go back and live in a pub but that McKinnon could arrange a half way house. The conditions were no drinking and attend AA at least twice a week. This was relatively simple as one meeting on Thursdays was actually in the half way house itself.

I was advised to go to ninety AA meetings in ninety days as a preamble to my recovery. I thought this was also a good idea. Australia, without any doubt was the most foreword country I have lived in regarding alcoholism, the *Disease* and the recovery. The police will arrest a drunk and give him a chance to sober up. The magistrates can implement the *Inebriate's Act* and place a sick alcoholic in hospital rather than in prison. I must hand it to the Australians. They do care about alcoholics. Rather like the Irish, most families seem to have one or at least know one.

The half way house was in Concorde, Sydney and I moved in with six other men. The other men were very sick men. They had no intention of working or even making an attempt to get well. We each had a chore in the house, three days cleaning the kitchen, or three days cleaning the showers etc. We had a communal meal at seven o'clock each evening.

The other men were fine. They could claim dole or Sickness Benefit. I was at this time an *Illegal Immigrant.* I went back to butchers shops working. This time I could hold a job. I was working at a butcher shop in Mona Vale, fifteen kilometres north of Sydney. The owner was a Greek about my age thirty nine and he had a girlfriend who was about twenty four years old. He was *showing off* to his girlfriend and said, *"Get rid of the Old Man, he looks Too Dirty to work in my shop"*. He was dressed in a mohair suit, immaculate shoes and gold all over his hands. I didn't wait till the end of the day, I said to him, *"I will see you again one day Son, so take a good look at my face and remember it. Maybe life won't always be as kind as to you as it is now"*. Four years later the same man was begging me to supply him with meat and, yes, I did supply him and charged him plenty. *Don't get angry, get Even.*

I drew my pay and took the bus home. When I got home there was a phone message for me from a garage where I had done an application for car finance. The car I had seen was Eight Thousand Dollars but the dealer said I had been approved for Twenty Thousand Dollars, so I could get a better car. He was, of course, a Good Salesman. So I purchased a Holden Calais and that night had transport.

I still went to AA on a regular basis when I saw a job in the Sydney Morning Herald for a telephone salesman, based in the city. I went for the interview and was given the job, selling calculators to the schools of Australia. The senior schools all take about three hundred calculators each year for students going into senior years, also students going from Junior to Senior. The average price of these machines was Eighteen Dollars to Thirty Dollars each so it was a good little business.

The business was Japanese owned and we were the New South Wales main agents for Casio. The records were all available of the schools, when they last purchased and when it was anticipated they would require supplying. So it was a *"Doddle"* of a job. There were two other companies in Australia doing the same thing. Our prices were all pretty much the same and of course I was allowed to Discount. I was selling six thousand to eight thousand machines per week. I later learned the profit was up to Ten Dollars per machine. It was a *license to print money.*

I was initially paid hourly then negotiated a deal of Eight Hundred Dollars per week plus garage for my car during the day. I worked from eight o'clock in the morning to four o'clock in the afternoon. I had plenty of time for AA. No pressure, small bank account, cheque book and credit cards. I was getting well and felt better than I had in years.

Initially shared a house in Glebe with a girl called Nicky Ferguson. House sharing is a very common thing in Australia and it worked out well except I took Nicky out one evening and she wanted a serious relationship. I had been told at McKinnon to avoid serious relationships for at least two years.

I found a flat in Victoria Street, Potts Point in a building called the Gemini Building. These were Twin Towers, swimming pool on the roof, tennis courts, security parking and Gym. The rent was reasonable and it was fully furnished as the owner was going to Queensland for six months and would be returning.

From my balcony I could see the Harbour Bridge, the Opera House and it really was *Heaven on Earth*. Whilst it was very small living room, one bedroom, bathroom and small kitchen, it was just perfect for me. I was reading my AA Big Book and enjoying meetings. I had three to four casual relationships with girls, a Chinese nurse I had met, an Australian girl from Adelaide who was a money broker and a Colombian girl who worked in a hotel.

AA came first in my life and I never missed a daily meeting. Sometimes lunch time, sometimes evenings and I always went to Kings Cross Matthew Talbot every Sunday morning. Life was good and I was writing to my mother. She was *Happy* and sent me out the balance of my English suits I had left with her.

I met some lovely people at AA and really believed I was going to make it this time. This was the end of 1986. I went to see Mr King at Ashfield, the owner of the pub and paid for the window. I sent money off to the children for Christmas and began going to the Theatre and having a *nice, dignified, quiet social life*.

I was doing very well at work and the company were very good to me in all respects. I was counting the days of my meetings, still aiming for *Ninety Meetings in Ninety Days*. I loved living in the Cross. Drunk or sober I still enjoy sleazy clubs and slinky women. I could shop twenty four hours a day. I could collect the morning papers at midnight every night, come home to my flat read the papers looking over Sydney Harbour lit up at night. Life could not have been better.

Finally I made it to the meeting number eighty nine one Friday evening. The following Saturday was my ninetieth day. So I went out Saturday lunch time and *bought a bottle of vodka.*

This was a prime example of my getting sober long enough tog et straight enough, clean up the mess I had created, then celebrate my achievements by having a drink.

When I look back, my life was like a child building sandcastles on the beach, then the tide comes in and washes them all away.

I couldn't see it was the first drink that caused the damage. Just as night follows day, the other drinks follow.

CHAPTER TWENTY FOUR

I remember bringing the bottle home very secure in the fact I was in my own home. My own car parked downstairs. I was going to my work on Monday, so of course, drinking was only going to make me feel better. I was so *Seriously Deluded*, kidding myself as I had never really accepted the fact I was an alcoholic. Yes, I had a drink problem, yes, drink got me in trouble but I was different from other alcoholics. Namely I was too intelligent to be typecast, too smart to be the same as the people I had met at AA.

I remember drinking and on the Saturday evening, Jenny the Chinese girl came over. She had never seen me drunk and used to say to me, *"Why do you have to go to these AA meetings, Bill?"* Well, now she saw first hand.

I remember walking up to the Cross for a second bottle and I was so drunk a young fellow walked up to me as I was paying the Off-License of the Rex Hotel. He took my wallet and ran off. I was too drunk to even attempt to chase him. This was my money, cheque book, Bankcards and Driver's License gone. I went home and have no more memories until the Monday.

I went to work and was feeling very very rough so at lunch time, twelve noon, I went to the pub next door and *got on the vodka*. I came back to work and proceeded to tell the boss, a little Japanese man called Eddie, everything he was doing was wrong. The result was he was so afraid of me he sacked me. So I went back to the pub. I don't really know what I said or did but I imagine the old old story of *how great I had once been*. I knew when he settled my account the following day he chose to meet in the cafe next door and asked me *not* to go to the office.

I met poor Eddie many years later at the Ritz Carlton in Double Bay at a dinner dance. I was able to apologise and he could see my life was going well. Making amends where possible gives one a really good feeling. *The Rewards of Sobriety*.

On the Tuesday I met two young fellows and a girl at the Off-License of the local pub. They were admiring my car. In retrospect they were *lining me up*. I said, *"Would you like a drive?"* I gave them the keys to have a spin and that was the last I saw of the car. It was burnt out and wrecked that evening.

On my lease agreement it was insured inclusive and under the insurance, I could hire a car for fourteen days until my stolen car turned up or was written off. I can still remember going into Kings Cross Police Station to report it stolen. Of course, I said I left my keys in the car at home and the car was stolen. My suits that Mum had kept for me were in the back seat as I had just collected them from the cleaners. When I reported the car I was Case No.39,700 and something. In other words, thirty nine thousand cars had been stolen in New South Wales that year. I never dreamed anyone would steal *my* car.

I was given a Volvo 740 GLE by Budget Rent-a-Car whilst the insurance was going through. On the Wednesday I crashed this. Not only crashed it, I hit a stationary truck normally parked on the side of the road and wrote the Volvo off. The finance company cancelled my agreement and refused to re-finance me. This time, I was charged with drink driving and because of this, the insurance was invalid, so I owed Budget Twenty Four Thousand Dollars.

I went back to my flat on the Thursday having spent the night in the police cells and found an *Eviction Notice* pinned on the door for the previous tenant. It transpired the man I rented the flat off did not, in fact, own it. He had sub-let it off one of his mates who had done a *Moonlight Flit* owing six months rent.

By the Friday, I was back in hospital at the Cumberland Hospital in Parramatta right behind the Parramatta Prison. The oldest prison in Australia, so there I was in a Mental Hospital, with the view of the prison wall directly outside my window.

After four days the staff said to me I was to be discharged. I had been de-toxed and they considered any further treatment a *waste of time*. I borrowed some money off Jenny and got drunk again and collapsed in the street in Sydney. This time I was taken to the Langton Clinic, another De-tox Hospital with a very good Reputation.

The Chief Counsellor was called Pat McGarry or known as *Pat the Rat*. She was a *Strange Lady* with no compassion at all. What Max Glatt would have called a *"Lady gratifying her own inadequacies by dealing with people less fortunate than herself"*. Having said this, I have met many many people she has helped get well, just as many who went back on the booze because of her.

I had been de-toxed and Jenny was coming to see me daily and I had my first day in group therapy. Pat turned to me and said *"Bill, how many times have you been in hospital?"* I sat and counted up and it was about forty times, so I told her. Pat said to me, *"Well, if that's the case, there is no point in you staying here. We can't help you. You can only help yourself"*. I said, *"If that's the case, I will go home then"*. I got up from the group packed my bags, borrowed Twenty Dollars off a fellow patient called Andy and left.

Andy was several years my senior and came from Deniliquin on the Victorian border. He was a writer of rather good children's books doing all of the illustrations himself.

It was so amusing to listen to him. He was a *Very Clever and Very Funny* man. The local AA in his town only had two members who had been business rivals and enemies for years. They refused to speak to each other and only through Andy.

The result was, of course, all three of them went back on the booze, however, Andy had the ability to *laugh at himself*, which is a wonderful thing.

When I got outside the hospital I realised I had *no home, no job, no car, no money*. I had lost everything in two weeks. This was on the Twenty Third of December 1986 and I was in the same position as I had been exactly one year ago in Portugal. I walked to Oxford Street and bought half a bottle of vodka and drank it out of the neck of the bottle.

I will always remember that day. The hate I felt for Pat McGarry yet of course she was so very right. All I was doing was using the hospital for a rest and get well enough to go for a drink again. I recall seeing people driving cars, sitting in restaurants and they all looked so *Happy,* so I was very, very jealous of everyone. I had the *Poor Me's* again.

One memory very clear on that day was all the restaurants in Oxford Street, Sydney and people sitting down eating their meals, without wine on their tables. I thought *"What a waste of money"* going for a meal and <u>not</u> even having a drink.

My meals were always several bottles of wine and no interest in the food. So there I was full of anger and jealousy. Two of the ingredients to guarantee I would drink, to drown my sorrows.

I rang Jenny who was nursing at the Prince of Wales Hospital and asked her if she could put me up until I found somewhere to live. She was a nice girl and very much in love with me and told me to come over. She was on her way to work but she would leave the key under the mat.

I had ripped up a Twenty Dollar note in small pieces a couple of days earlier saying, *"This is what I think of money"* when I arrived in the flat. The pieces of the Twenty Dollar note were in Jenny's fruit bowl on the dining room table, so I sat down with a roll of cellotape and put the note back together again. It took me ages but I did it. So off I go to the local pub. They reluctantly accepted it and I could buy a full bottle plus quarter bottle of vodka. I don't recall Jenny coming home as I was passed out in the bed.

The following day was Christmas Eve, so I told Jenny to leave me Fifty Dollars and I will go shopping and make her an English Christmas Dinner, Turkey, Yorkshire Pudding, potatoes and Christmas Pudding, etc.

Jenny had extracted a promise from me that I would not drink if I was staying at the flat and gave me the Fifty Dollars for the food. I remember her going to work at lunch time and my running down the road to buy a bottle of sparkling wine Three Dollars and Sixty Cents and drinking it immediately out of the neck of the bottle.

I went shopping and bought a large chicken, bought the vegetables and flour and really was *shopping for value,* giving me enough change for three more bottles of sparking wine. I duly prepared the Christmas lunch basting the chicken with the butter and bacon and to account for the money spent on the booze told her it was a *"Guinea Fowl"* I had bought from the butcher at triple the price the chicken had cost.

Christmas lunch was splendid and Christmas Day was good. I got off the booze and for New Year's Eve bought two tickets for the New Year's Eve Dinner at the Wentworth Hotel, a five-star hotel in Sydney. The tickets were One Hundred and Twenty Dollars each. The format was a sit down dinner in the

Ball Room, the tables were cleared and the room divider taken down and dancing began. I can still see all the bottles on the table and thought this is going to be a good night.

Jenny was in evening dress and I was in Dinner jacket. All I can remember is being woken up in the hotel foyer at four thirty in the morning by Jenny. I was so bad I had made a scene at the table and proceeded to get drunk. Prior to New Year's day at midnight, Jenny was so embarrassed that at some point of the evening she had gone home and left me. Then waking up and finding I wasn't home, felt guilty at leaving me and phoned the hotel who told her I was asleep drunk in the reception.

I must have had a couple of days in bed and tried various jobs, only most of Australia was closed from Christmas Eve until the first week in January. I remember selling cars and also a job Buying cars.

I saw an advert in the Herald for telephone advertising salesman at Bondi and went for the interview. Jenny took me there and my drinking was *well out of control* by this time. My drink driving case came up and I was banned for one year and fined.

The job was selling advertising in a Navy magazine called the White Ensign. The pay was commission only of 25% paid in cash every Friday. Peter Templer the owner of the publication was a nice fellow and we both took to each other. He asked me about my previous experiences, of which I had none but I was aware of advertising space by the television advertising I had sold in Manchester.

The first day of work I listened to all the other salesmen who would make four-five calls, go for a coffee and all go to the pub for two hours at lunch time. I picked up very quickly how to sell this product and worked every minute from nine o'clock in the morning to four o'clock in the afternoon making fifteen to twenty calls an hour, drinking coffee at my desk.

The first week I sold Twenty Two Thousand Dollars worth of advertising space so my pay was Five Thousand Five Hundred Dollars. I thought there has to be a *catch in this*. They will never pay me. We finished at lunch time on Friday and Peter brought in cartons of beer and prawns for all the sales staff. Then he gave me a cash cheque for Five Thousand Five Hundred

Dollars to take to the bank and draw cash over the counter.

Jenny collected me and I gave her the money to keep for me, telling her to take out all the money I owed her. The next week was the same. I never sold less than Twenty Thousand Dollars and so I decided to rent a five bedroom house in Carringbah complete with a Philipino Maid. I thanked Jenny for all her help and moved to my new home and bought a car for the maid to drive me as I was banned.

The house in Carringbah suited me down to the ground. My girl would take me to the station each morning and I had twenty minutes train journey straight to Bondi. I could read the paper on the way to work, have a coffee and sell until four o'clock in the afternoon. Then straight to the pub and travel home. My fridge was full of vodka and it was *vodka all evening*.

The house was so large it was quite silly of me to live like this and I spent every penny I earned with no thought for the future. I had this idea in my head I would never see my Fortieth Birthday so I lived every day as thought it was my last. Jenny had helped me furnish the house, then one Saturday morning after a blazing row over my drinking I threw all her clothes out of the front door and told her to leave.

Jenny went off in her car and returned with the police to retrieve all her clothes. I have no idea why she called the police as I had no idea why people were so afraid of me when I was drunk. I later learned my Philipino maid used to barricade her bedroom door each night with furniture as she was also terrified of me.

Peter brought back his previous Sales Manager, a man called Barry Holland. This man was a very good salesman but also a drinking alcoholic. As the Sales Manager, he was getting a 5% Rider on all of my sales. There was a personality clash mainly caused by his envy of my sales figures. Prior to me he was the *King of Advertising Salesmen in Sydney*. The result of this conflict was a stand up row. I walked out.

I was so angry over losing my income that I sent him several telegrams, telling him what I actually thought of him. I also sent the local Undertaker to his office telling the Undertaker he had died at his desk. The result was the police came one morning with a Search Warrant. They believed I was an IRA

Terrorist. The Bondi firm of Undertakers were *Not Happy* either!

My little Philipino Maid answered the door at seven o'clock in the morning and was making cups of tea for all the police when I was woken in bed. This was quite amusing as I had told her that if anyone comes to the house, the first thing she must do is offer them tea on *Silver Service* or drinks. The last thing on these policemen's minds was drinking tea.

Having searched the house and realising this was a false alarm, I was charged with sending malicious telegrams. Having said this, the police were very decent to me and they had found seven bottles of vodka I had hidden in the house at various times and forgotten where they were hidden.

Peter's biggest rival was a man called Eric Reynolds. Eric had a publication called *"Wings"* which was for the Royal Air Force so I joined Eric a couple of days after leaving Peter and took a lot of my leads and clients with me. The selling was more difficult and the money not as good yet I was still earning Three Thousand to Four Thousand Dollars weekly. Eric was a drinking alcoholic and would have been very nearly as bad as me.

Eric's wife was also in the business and this was his saving factor. Lynn the wife, was not very Happy with a second drinking alcoholic in the business so I decided to sell from home.

I converted one of the five bedrooms into an office and hired a secretary a local girl called Belinda and was away again. By working at home I had a routine of starting so sell at nine o'clock every morning. I would sell until one o'clock in the afternoon and start drinking. Belinda would type up the sales and fax them all to Eric's office.

I kept thinking of the words of Pat McGarry at the Langton Clinic *"There is nothing we can do for you"* so I was resigned to the fact I would never be able to stop drinking and, therefore, I prepared my life in such a way I could maintain my drinking and still earn money. Most mornings Belinda would get me up, put me in the shower and ensure I begin to sell.

Every Friday, Belinda would take me to Bondi and go over the weeks sales figures with Eric and his wife and collect the cheque. I would then draw the cash, pay my wages and drink until Monday.

I was still involved with my Colombian girlfriend, Jenny would also pop over from time to time. I let the Philipino girl go and had an Australian girl called Josie take over doing the house on a daily basis. Josie was a friend of Belinda's, so everywhere I went I used to have these two very glamorous girls taking care of me. My girlfriends realised the relationship was purely business as well as good friends and I needed them to support me as by now I was a man living on the edge of sanity or rather insanity with my drinking.

I found a house at Gray's Point on the coast. This was a lovely old colonial house so I moved six miles down the road. I used to hate the weekends, hate being alone. I was afraid of the dark and slept with the lights on. I hadn't read a book for years now as I was always too drunk to focus on the pages. I went to bed every night praying I wouldn't wake up. I had now provided the necessary people to help me function and was living from drink to drink.

One Saturday morning in July of 1987 I took the car out to buy vodka from an early opener in Sydney. On the way back I have no idea what happened but on a straight piece of road, President Avenue, Carringbah, I hit a garden wall and rolled the car on its roof onto some one's front lawn caused by booze, yet I needed another drink.

This couple came to the door as I was climbing out of the car, around seven o'clock in the morning and asked me, *"If I would like a cup of tea"*. I said, *"You wouldn't have a drink by any chance"*. There was my car on its roof on their lawn.

The police came and were very decent. I think they were about to go off duty. These two young men could see my state, yet drove me home and I was never charged, yet I was drunk and driving whilst banned.

My birthday came and went on the Twelfth of July. I had several commissions to sell on other publications as well as *"Wings"* and by tea time most days I was out for the count until the following morning. I remember thinking to myself if I have reached forty and not died, just imagine if I live to be fifty. I knew I couldn't take ten more years of this way of life.

Thursday, Twenty Seventh of August 1987 came. It was just another day of the same old format. A friend of mine called Samantha came over on the previous evening and had stayed the night. That evening Samantha was still there. Belinda and Josie also when Jenny turned up and within five minutes my Colombian girl had also turned up as well. So I had five separate women in the house all sat politely chattering to each other and deciding how they were going to help me.

I found on this day I couldn't drink. I was dry retching and couldn't swallow my booze. I had slept very badly on the Wednesday night. I was continually in the *Twilight Zone*. Couldn't stay awake, couldn't sleep, couldn't stay sober and now I couldn't get drunk. I was sick and tired of being *Sick and Tired*.

I have no idea why, to this day. I asked Jenny to give me a lift to the local AA meeting at Carringbah. When I arrived there were only three other people. Michael a Barrister, Barry a car salesman, and Bill an Irishman from Co. Down. I was so annoyed. There I was going to AA and only three people had turned up for the meeting. So we ignored the normal format and each in turn told his story for about twenty minutes. I left the meeting thinking this was a waste of time. However, I agreed for Bill to collect me the following day and take me to another meeting at Crunella.

Jenny collected me at the end of the meeting and I thought I really ought to buy her something as she had been very kind to me. We called into a Chemist on the way home and I bought her a little Mickey Mouse Teddy Bear with the last of my money. When we arrived home I was relieved to find everyone had left so it was just Jenny and myself for the rest of that evening.

I recall going to bed and couldn't sleep and wasn't really awake and for the first time in years made an attempt to read again.

I found a job the following day, Friday, selling advertising space on commission and was able to start on the Monday. I went to AA that night with Bill and on the Saturday and Sunday, Jenny took me to the local AA in the area. There is no reason for anyone not to go to AA, in Sydney alone there are over three hundred meetings a week. This is the some the world over.

I still had my court case looming over me of the malicious telegrams. The case didn't concern me, it was the fact that I appeared in court so drunk on the first occasions, the Magistrate had ordered a Probation Report. My fear was that the fact I had overstayed my visa by eighteen months may come to light.

This anxiety over my illegal Immigrant status was the most difficult part of my staying sober. Jenny moved into the house with me and still retained her flat which she owned in Arncliffe and my work went quite well. The money wasn't great only about Two Thousand Dollars weekly. Some weeks Two Thousand Five Hundred Dollars but, of course, my cost of living was zero without drinking. I found for the first time in my life, I was saving money and saving quite a bit of money.

All I did was go to meetings and listen, taking the positive points and leaving *with difficulty*, all the negatives. Things were going so well I invited my mother for a six week holiday in the October of 1987. She was overjoyed to see me getting well and we both had a wonderful time and I took her to the airport to go home a *Very Happy Lady*.

By the end of October we had purchased a house on the central coast of New South Wales. This was a large mansion built in the side of the mountain that was overlooking the central coast and Brisbane water. It was a beautiful home and I had saved One Hundred Thousand Dollars on the price because of the *Black Monday* Stock Market Crash on the Twenty Ninth of October 1987.

I had no idea. How I was going to pay for it but the rewards of AA began to happen. Too many good things were happening in my life to be a co-incidence. Jenny realised she was pregnant, my mother had gone home happy, we had the house and I was working with a publishing company based on the central coast and earning Two Thousand Five Hundred to Three Thousand Dollars weekly.

I had cut down my AA but was still going a minimum of three times a week. I couldn't see any change in myself at all but I knew I was getting well. My court case came and I was

Bound Over to keep the peace for twelve months. My being sober in court of course helped my case. I was paying my bills and living a respectable life.

Socially we were going to the theatre weekly and dining out a couple of times a week. I saw an enormous change in Jenny or perhaps the change was me, seeing her through sober eyes. We traded in Jenny's car and bought a brand new Ford Falcon for Nineteen Thousand Dollars. I was still banned from driving and I religiously took this seriously as a Recovering Alcoholic. I stayed very close to the three members that I met at the first meeting and I have no idea who was most surprised at my recovery. Them or myself for this was surely a miracle. Although I sometimes had the desire to drink, my common sense told me I had nothing to go back to.

So we came to Christmas 1987 and this year I bought a *Real* turkey. We went to the New Year's Eve dinner at the Regent Hotel. I didn't need a drink and remembered the whole evening. We were going to move into the new house on the Twenty Sixth of January 1988. I would have been in Australia exactly two years. I was earning good money and had a Half a Million Dollar house and was expecting a baby in the August. *Life was pretty good.*

I decided over the Christmas holidays to work for myself. I was getting 30% commission and could be getting 100%. I used all the money I had saved for the Deposit on the house to set up my office. I purchased a fax machine, photocopier, computer and stationery and started on the Second of January 1988.

My first publication came off the press on the Twenty Fifth of January 1988 and we mailed one hundred and eighty advertisers copies. I had Sixty Three Thousand Dollars in the book in revenue and by the time printing, some Sixteen Thousand Dollars had been already paid up front. My second publication was ready for the printer on the Twenty Ninth of January with Twenty Nine Thousand Dollars in revenue. I had just enough money by Twenty Ninth of January to pay the deposit on the house and Advance Bank had given me 90% mortgage for the balance.

The last thing to go on the furniture lorry was my desk

and it was the first thing to come off. I only lost half a day's business whilst moving house. I now had confidence to employ a couple of girls in the office based in Gosford and was selling Thirty Thousand Dollars every single week. By March 1988 I was receiving Nine Thousand Dollars weekly by April Fourteen Thousand Dollars weekly and by June of 1988, I was getting Twenty Thousand Dollars weekly, *week in week out* and never less. I had at last made it and made it *Big Time* and was still going to AA three times a week.

I was finished work by two o'clock in the afternoon every day and my girls finished off the work in my absence.

I organised my *Permanent Residence* through a man called Les Hardy in Sydney at the cost of Ten Thousand Dollars cash and married Jenny in June of 1988. William my son had decided to come for a three month holiday with his girlfriend having made it quite clear, if I was drinking he would rather not stay with me. This was okay.

I organised a little VW Beetle on a three month lease for William. Jenny and myself traded our Ford in for a Volvo 747 GLE. In August of 1988 my daughter Siobhan was born. I was elated and absolutely *Rapped* with my beautiful daughter. *I was a Blessed man.*

I spent every weekend on my garden and built a swimming pool on top of the mountain at the back of the house. The rock we dug out to build the pool was used to terrace the mountain and on the summit I built a lawn by craning up soil and turf. I could look out at the whole of the central coast on my recliner at the top of the mountain. I even had a phone extension there as mobile phones were still quite primitive in 1988.

I recall *fantasizing,* so very often, about sitting on top of my mountain with an ice bucket and a bottle of *ice cold* champagne. So I was still thinking of drinking with Euphoria.

However, I didn't drink. *One day at a time.* I couldn't picture the rest of my life with no drink, but I could handle one day. I often would take Siobhan to meetings at weekends in her carry cot to give Jenny a break.

We had good girls in the office, good domestic staff and a full time gardener. I spent One Hundred Thousand Dollars on my garden alone with Palm trees, fencing, the pool, the lawns and some six hundred square metres of tiles, fountains and bar-be-que. I had an Irish lady, Rosemary Kelly, do all the curtains for another Thirty Thousand Dollars and all the furniture was hand carved mahogany from Indonesia. I found a small man in Gosford who used to import the mahogany direct.

I had an excellent lawyer in Sydney, Bill O'Brien, and a good accountant on the central coast, Graham, so I could handle *anyone or anything*. Bill, my solicitor was probably the sharpest legal brain that has ever worked for me and Graham, my account was very tame and followed instructions. All in all, I was very well off and my mother was coming out for three months holiday in December 1988.

Jenny's brother had decided to come from Malaysia to Australia in 1988 and he stayed initially with us along with his wife and small son. More credit to Danny, he got a job with Wespac within a week and his wife, Kiki, also got a job at the University of Sydney and they were up and running within two weeks. I was happy for Jenny that she was in a position to help her family. Then her parents came on holidays and they were a nice couple. Jenny 's father spoke no English and like me, used to chain smoke. We got on very well yet could only communicate in sign language.

It was a marvellous Christmas. Siobhan's first Christmas and on New Years Eve, we went to a masked ball in Sydney, staying in the hotel for the night. I was forty one years old and this was the second time I danced with my mother. It was marvellous.

In January of 1989 I purchased a farm of one hundred and ten acres in Richmond, the first town I had lived in Australia. I chartered a plane and flew with my mother to Gunnedah in Northern New South Wales to buy sixty cows and sixty calves to put on the farm. The farmer met us at the airport and after buying the cattle gave us a farmhouse lunch. I could see the pride in my mother's eyes that I had really had *come good* this time.

Just before my mother went home in March 1989, I took her to Richmond to see my first Racehorses. I had bought seven mares all in foal to very good stallions. As well as my own farm I was renting three farms and all the orange orchards in Richmond to graze sheep and cattle.

I bought myself a new BMW top of the range car and a new four wheel drive for the farm as I had got my driving license back. So these were all the rewards of being sober eighteen months. I so very often thought of Margaret Karpinski and her prediction for me as by January 1989, I had my house valued by the bank at Eight Hundred Thousand Dollars, my farms a further Two Hundred Thousand Dollars. I had seven Racehorses, a Stock horse and two hundred head of cattle. Margaret Karpinski saw *"Horses, Cattle and me being very successful"*.

I paid every penny back I had borrowed from people in the UK and Ireland by enclosing cheques in Christmas cards at Christmas of 1988. I still remember people saying at AA how they had paid monies back they owed and I used to think how *Bloody Stupid*. There I was doing the very same thing myself. I began to ring Mary Bolton about every two weeks. She had retired from counseling and bought a small Guest House in County Tyrone, Northern Ireland. Very sadly at the end of 1989 she was suffering from *Dementia* and when I rang initially would have no idea who I was. This became so sad at the end I gave up calling, as my calls seemed to confuse all the more.

By Winter of 1989 or July, Jenny realised she was pregnant with our second child. Jenny was thirty nine years old so had all the usual tests that are available to check on the pregnancy, praise God, all was well. Business was good and I was still getting Twenty Thousand Dollars every week doing all the selling myself.

Life could not have been better yet there was a huge *"void"* in my life. The *"void"* was caused by no alcohol in my system. I used to dream I had been drinking and wake up with cold sweats, yet I never felt guilty about having been drunk in my dreams. My only fear was someone *would know*. I suppose, six decks down this was checking my motivation.

I met some amazing people at AA and some people from those days I still think of kindly today. I also met some very *Sad* people and some very Funny people. We all made the same mistakes. I recall one man at a meeting in Carringbah who was very concerned about his son going to University.

He didn't know whether he should go to University in Melbourne or University in Sydney. I was listening to this man and his problem and just to make conversation I said, *"When does your Son have to decide?"*. He then told me his son was only three years old. It may seem crazy, but this is how we alcoholics project into the future rather than living in the day.

There was a lovely old Scottish man in Woy Woy AA every Thursday. This was my local group. One evening there was a lot of boasting going on. One man had been sober twenty years, one fifteen years, etc. all patting each other on the back. This really is the last thing an alcoholic in the early days wants to hear. Jock got up and spoke. He said, *"I never mention how long I have been sober, but for the record it's thirty three years. Yet, the most sober person in this room is the first one that got out of bed this morning. This is a daily program and we are all only one drink away from a drunk"*. Well, that shut everyone up.

There was another man who had been sober fourteen years and going home to his wife one evening, she said *"I hope you told all your mates at AA what a Bastard you are at home"*. That stopped him dead in his tracks. It is easy to be good at meetings and a Bastard when you get home.

When it came time to sell my cattle for meat, I took them to Homebush Saleyards. This is now the site of the *2000 Olympics*. The buyers at Homebush all worked in a clique, governing the prices of the cattle, so I took my cattle home and then had them killed myself and sold the carcasses to Sydney wholesalers. So I was back in the meat business.

There was a new company starting in Australia called *CALM, Computer Auction Livestock Markets*. The way they operated was go to the farms, select and weigh the livestock. Then put the description on computer and hold an Auction twice a week. This wonderful way of marketing meant the factory owners did not have to leave the office to purchase their livestock, very similar to shopping on the Internet. *CALM* became huge with perhaps one hundred thousand sheep and thirty thousand cattle for sale each week.

I began to use *CALM* and purchased sheep each week

and started a small wholesale meat business in Sydney. Before long I was killing one thousand sheep per week. Having them slaughtered at Wollongong and Mudgee Abattoirs. The cost to kill my sheep was Eight Dollars per head so it was costing me weekly Eight Thousand Dollars to kill my few sheep each week.

In August of 1989 I had the chance to buy a meat works at Kempsey in northern New South Wales. This was an abattoir and a By-Products factory. The by-products plant was making Tallow and Bone Meal. With the plant went the business of every butchers shop in northern New South Wales and South Queenlsand taking their *Fat and Bones* on a twice weekly basis as raw materials for the plant.

I had no problems in getting finance to buy the plant, however, I had to spend some Two Hundred and Fifty Thousand Dollars to bring it up to standard. The main expense was a new boiler for Fifty Thousand Dollars as the previous boiler was wood burning and this was very labour intensive as well as too small for the production I had anticipated.

The plant was in the small village of Toorooka, thirty miles west of Kempsey right out in the Bush. There was a village pub, village garage and shop and the whole village was dependant on the meat factory for employment.

I bought a twenty acre site of parkland set in trees with outline Planning Permission to build a large colonial home. So it was my intention to develop the plant and build a large home and spend the rest of my days doing what I love the best, farming, with my own meat works and living in the country.

I had the plant opened by September 1989 complete with cattle lorries to collect the livestock and meat lorries to deliver my meat into Sydney which was four hundred kilometres south of the Plant. I had a staff of about thirty men and three lorries collecting the Fat and Bones from some three hundred butchers shops.

I rented a small farmhouse and furnished it, all in colonial style until we had the new house built. There was only one drawback with the plant. We were on the banks of Macleay River, one of the biggest rivers in New South Wales which was liable to flooding in winter. As the banks were forty feet high, I saw no danger in this and was assured by the owner and the locals the river had never in *living memory* reached the meat works.

Things went very well and at Christmas of 1989, we closed the plant for two weeks and went to Malaysia for Christmas Holidays. The second baby was due in late January or early February 1990. So Jenny, Siobhan and myself flew off a couple of days before Christmas.

We had a wonderful holiday staying at the Rasa Saya Hotel in Penang also having a couple of days in Kuala Lumpur and Singapore. I met all of Jenny's brothers and sisters who were all in the banking industry in Malaysia.

Jenny's sister introduced me to one of her clients who was buying sheep from Australia so I had a very good connection for the supply of one container of sheep per week of six hundred *rams*. The holiday over it was back to New South Wales.

I gave up the publishing business and devoted my time to the meat plant. We lived in Kempsey at the farm during the week and came back to Gosford for the weekends. Every Friday Jenny spent the day in Sydney collecting money from all of our clients. Our main client, a Lebanese meat wholesaler took one thousand two hundred Sheep per week and paid every Friday in *Cash*. Things were wonderful, the work was hard for Jenny and myself but the rewards were good.

Harry and myself became good friends and Toddy Belmore Meats is the largest producer of domestic mutton in Australia.

Then on the Seventh of February 1990 Jenny gave birth to our second child, Robert and all went well with the delivery. Siobhan stayed with me during the confinement and it was marvellous fun. My young daughter and myself running the meat plant. Siobhan had no fear of the animals, the blood or the guts. I have a habit of putting my right hand in my belt and pulling my trousers up. One of the wives of my men came to me one day and said, *"There is no doubt whose daughter she is"*. I asked, *"Why?"* and she said, *"We were looking at you outside the window yesterday unloading the sheep. There you were with your stick, your hand on your belt and there was Siobhan doing exactly the same, yet both unconscious of each other"*. I had no idea until that day that I ever had this mannerism.

We had a lovely bunch of men and used to hold bar-be-ques for their families. We had our own cricket team and used to take on local villagers. I treated all my staff with *Dignity and Respect* and in turn expected maximum performance from them.

Jenny worked very hard in those days even though we had domestic staff. She drove many miles each week and was a very hard working loyal wife. I adored my two children and was still going to AA but only once a week as this was the only meeting available in Kempsey. Then I would also skip meetings.

1990 was a good year until the winter when the Macleay River flooded. It flooded with a vengeance rising some sixty feet taking my meat plant in the water. This meant all my Blood Tanks, Tallow Tanks, bones, grease and fat were all washed down the river for some thirty miles. This tallow which is rendered animal fat caused slicks similar to oil slicks at sea, polluting the river and the river banks and leaving the most awful mess.

The local TV picked the story up also the fact we were killing very plain very old sheep. So I was subjected to a *Boots and All* expose of how we were polluting the local environment and should be closed. The Meat and Livestock Commission told me that a government environment impact study would cost me $7 million and I would have to pay the bill.

There was a world glut of wool in 1990 and the sheep industry was in turmoil. I was getting thousands of sheep each week given to me *Free of Charge*. Things were that bad for the farmers and now my plant was closed until the water subsided. I had no Insurance covering the flooding which is classed an *"Act of God"*, *(force majeure)*.

When the water went down, I was told by the Meat Authority I had to:

    (A)   Get a Government Environment Impact Study $7 million

    (B)   Build a new drainage system $600,000

    (C)   Reduce Production to four hundred head per day from 1,000 per day

    (D)   Failing this, my license would be suspended.

I had spent $2 million on the plant to date in building, equipment and Trucks. There was Eighty Thousand Dollars in concrete alone. This expenditure was not removable so without my Full License, it was a total loss. I was devastated, angry and bitter.

I made a *Foolish* mistake with my meat works. I should have lobbied the New South Wales Politicians, become a member of the New South Wales Meat Authority. As it was, I was an outsider and had put considerable *noses out of joint* by my taking over the Sydney Mutton Trade. With the exception of Mulligans who had been established for fifty years and Peters Meats, I was the largest wholesaler of Mutton in Sydney and as previously stated, this mutton was costing me Production cost only as I was getting my sheep *Free of Charge*.

The head of the New South Wales Meat Authority, John Carter, was a great friend of Mulligans and he told me that even if I spent this projected One and a Half Million Dollars there was *No Guarantee* I would get my license. In his opinion, there were too many Meat Plants in New South Wales not running to full capacity. In hindsight, I was acting just like my father and *fighting City Hall* as opposed to *cow tailing* to them, something I regret to this day.

John Carter was a prosperous New South Wale farmer with interests in various meat companies and used his position as Chairman of the New South Wales Meat Authority as his own personal fiefdom to enrich his own lifestyle. Carter was a man who preferred power to material gain.

My Plant was not viable on four hundred sheep per day so I was forced to close. This was a second mistake as my *license was withdrawn* and I had to now spend the money on the plant in the hope I would get my license back.

This was the same mistake my father made in 1961 letting the Licence go and closing. History repeating itself. I was *my Father's Son*.

This was a very very sad day for me. Paying off my staff and leaving my plant idle, all my dreams were shattered. I was holding Personal Guarantees to all the finance houses and this was eating into my capital. I was Thirty Thousand Dollars over my overdraft limit at Advance Bank and this had been authorised by the Manager, on his own back without Head Office consent. My Bank Manager told me he had had a visit from a Mr Bob Reid of Consumer Affairs and I was going to be charged with twenty counts of breaching the Trade Practices Act of New South Wales. in connection with my publishing business. This, of course, frightened my Bankers.

I contacted Bill O'Brien, my solicitor and he dealt with Consumer Affairs, stating this was the liability of my Limited Company, *Counsellor Press* and, therefore, the Company not myself was charged and fined Forty Six Thousand Dollars. I liquidated the company and avoided the Fine. This caused Bob Reid from Consumer Affairs to *haunt* me for the next eight years as there was nothing legally he could do to me personally.

I paid my Bank Manager the Thirty Thousand Dollars in Cash that I was over my limit and the following day the Bank foreclosed on my mortgage on the house in Gosford. The house was valued Eight Hundred Thousand Dollars and I only had a mortgage of Two Hundred and Sixty Thousand Dollars as Jenny had paid One Hundred Thousand Dollars off the mortgage with the proceeds from the sale of her flat.

I was *snookered.* There was nothing I could do. All I was now concerned with was avoiding bankruptcy. I salvaged the refrigeration from the meat works and put this into my small factory in Sydney. I still had two Butchers Shops in Sydney and the Factory at Earlwood. This was no use to me without my abattoir. I made arrangements to slaughter all of my livestock at the plant of Nick Peters at Harden in southern New South Wales. So there I was, paying Nick Eight Thousand Dollars weekly to kill my stock, my own Plant was *lying idle.*

I contacted a firm of accountants called Nelson Wheeler and Arnold and Tom Arnold was the accountant in Newry, County Down, Northern Ireland when Dalgetys owned the Plant during my days in Clones.

Tom specialised in Liquidations and Bankruptcies. I paid Nelson Wheeler & Arnold some Forty Thousand Dollars to avoid Bankruptcy to no avail. My banks and finance houses were *running scared* because of Bob Reid and Consumer Affairs.

I lost the house, the meat works and was now renting a

house in Sydney on Six Hundred Dollars per week with all the furniture from home. Jenny had lost One Hundred Thousand Dollars of the money from her flat in Arncliffe and was *not a Happy Lady*. The revenue from the shops and factory in Sydney were not enough to keep us so decisions had to be made. This was September of 1991. I had been sober for four years. I went back on the booze initially *slightly controlled*, eventually totally *out of control* again. I was now married with two lovely young children and drunk. However, I did salvage my racehorses and Mercedes.

I handed my Buyers over to Harry at Belmore Meats and decided to give up the shops altogether. I gave my shops away for a *Song* and then went back into publishing. I made a Deal with Peter Templer that we would become partners on the New South Wales Tourist Directory and several Soccer Magazines. I put Twenty Five Thousand Dollars cash into the business but I went to the office very drunk one day and frightened Peter so much he got a *Restraint Order* against me banning me from my own office. History again repeating itself, the same as Manchester in 1983.

We had Three Hundred Thousand Dollars to collect on the New South Wales Tourist Directory and my Twenty Five Thousand Dollars cash so I lost One Hundred and Seventy Five Thousand Dollars in one day, e.g. 50% of Three Hundred Thousand Dollars. I later learned from Peter that if he hadn't got rid of me, Bob Reid was going to close him.

Australia Post closed all my mail boxes and in a period of six months, this happened with *five different Banks and seven different Post Offices.* I couldn't collect the monies for my Sales. Bob Reid of Consumer Affairs had effectively closed me. I paid a *Private Investigator* to investigate this fellow Reid and why he was pursuing me with such vigour, almost pathologically. Like the Lieutenant of Police in *"The Fugitive" closing Richard Kimble.*

The investigator's report showed that Reid was in *Cahoots* with Percival Publishing, the largest printer of Free Association Publications in Australia. The report also showed Reid had ties with Consolidated Press. The magazine business is very *Cut Throat.* There is a story of when Rupert Murdoch went to Sydney having bought the *"Daily Mirror"* from the Packer family. Sir Frank Packer stopped Murdoch from printing in New South Wales. So Murdoch purchased the printing works of the Catholic News in Surrey Hills. After spending an awful lot of money Murdoch had his own printing works in Sydney. Kerry Packer and his brother Clyde took a group of men with *Iron Bars* and smashed up the printing works one night. Murdoch had got wind of this and had his own photographers there to photograph the Packer boys in the act of doing this. He then, of course, put the photos on the front page of his own newspaper. This will give you some idea of how competitive publishing is because it is so lucrative.

I was effectively prevented from going back into publishing so I rented a large mansion out at Richmond with stables and land which was adjacent to my own farms. Having paid all my finance houses, my Banks, my accountant Four Thousand Dollars, Bill O'Brien Twenty Thousand Dollars to fight Consumer Affairs, I was eventually bankrupt by AGC for the paltry sum of Eighty Thousand Dollars on finance on the Boiler and Blood Drying Plant at my meat works. So having paid everyone I was still bankrupt. This meant three years of staying out of business in my own name.

I would have been better to pocket half a million cash and go bankrupt for *the lot* as the penalties are the same. I had saved my Racehorses, my Yearlings and Mares and had these at the country house and went back from *whence I came*.

One girl in the office and selling myself. I completed a Backpacker magazine in one month with revenue of Fifty Thousand Dollars printed the book and distributed it, when again, my bank which was Barclays Bank at Blacktown had a visit from Reid, and my post office box in Windsor was closed. I lost all the revenue from my magazine, Fifty Thousand Dollars.

I could have sat down and wept. This was January 1992. Jenny had gone to Malaysia, followed by England with the children to a wedding of my niece so I was home alone. This was bad in itself, then I had a knock on the door one morning from Derryn Hinch, the TV Current Affairs Programme, doing an *expose* on why I was still in business when bankrupt. My company had been fined Forty Six Thousand Dollars and in their opinion, I was not a *Desirable* character. The information given to Hinch was from a *Reliable source*. Bob Reid of Consumer Affairs, New South Wales.

When the program went to air and all the locals turned against me. So there I was in a eight bedroom mansion, Mercedes, four wheel drive, racehorses, no bank, no money, and exposed Australia wide as a *Con Man, Crook, etc. etc*. Little did they know how bloody hard I had worked. My drinking was in *fits and starts*. I would drink for two to three days and stay sober for one week. I had guilt about my drinking but I had lost all *Hope* of ever getting back on my feet.

Hinch was a fellow from New Zealand who left school at the age of fifteen to join the local newspaper. He came to Australia and worked on numerous newspapers but made a name for himself on radio in Melbourne in the early days of Talk Back Radio.

Hinch used to create the image of being a Battler and get the working man *on side* based on the assumption *"Derryn was a Mate"*. He would expose wrongdoers, fight politicians, etc. The worker's *"alleged"* friend.

This was all, of course, a front rather like:

> *The folk singer came from America*
> *To sing at the Albert Hall*
> *He sang his songs of Protest*
> *For a Fairer share for all.*
> *He sang the Rich were much too Rich*
> *The Poor too Poor by far*
> *As he went back to his Penthouse*
> *In his Chauffeured Rolls Royce Car.*

This was Derryn Hinch, a *Man of Straw* and not even a good actor but good enough to fool the ill-educated Blue Collar workers.

The disgraced Christopher Skase, who is on the run in Majorca, gave Hinch his first go at Television in the Eighties on Channel Seven which Skase owned at that time.

The most amazing thing about Hinch was during the end of the interview I said to the Reporter, *"Tell Derryn Hinch, thank your mother for the Rabbits!"*

I had picked up this saying from Syl Higgins, my alcoholic Dentist during my Ruby days at Longford. This is just a silly old saying. Hinch now uses the expression as his by-line. *Very Little* is original in *Show Business*. Current Affairs are more Show Business than Journalism today.

Jenny was very bitter about the loss of her money and quite rightly. She was very angry, very hurt and the marriage was over by March of 1992. I couldn't trade in my own name and didn't want to work for anyone else.

I moved to a small flat in Sydney on my own leaving Jenny and the children. Jenny had had enough of me and rented a small house in Rockdale, Sydney. I got a job on a Business Directory at the wage of One Thousand Five Hundred Dollars weekly, with this money I opened a small office in Rockdale and rented a nice five bedroom house with swimming pool for Jenny and the children.

I was working for Simon and Ben Tilley who also ran a Debt Collecting Company called *"Brodies"*. These two yuppies were the sons of Ben Tilley Senior who was Kerry Packer's gopher in those days.

I began to trade on my own Directory and within weeks was back on Four Thousand to Five Thousand Dollars weekly again. I had to trade with Jenny's brother, John Ford, a fellow publisher as I couldn't bank the money myself. Just as things were going well, I was subject to two more *Hinch exposes* on the Directories, again served papers by Bob Reid from Consumer Affairs. I did a deal with Consumer Affairs. They would drop all charges if I agreed to stay out of publishing in N.S.W. for a period of ten years. This applied to Jenny also. I negotiated *five years* and signed the agreement.

In all my dealings with Consumer Affairs, Reid would be personally involved in the Serving of Papers, etc.

The marriage was over. Jenny had organised herself a flat for herself and the children without telling me. So as it was over, I decided to go to Melbourne in Victoria, a new State, a new start, away from the jurisdiction of Bob Reid and New South Wales Consumer Affairs. This was February of 1993.

The decision to move out of the State of New South

Wales was done very reluctantly. Having failed as a father with my first two children I wanted so much to have a family and be a real father to Robert and Siobhan. Jenny had made this impossible whilst I have the greatest sympathy for Jenny and the loss of her money, she wanted for nothing during our marriage and I believe I was a good father to my children. I am first to admit she had six months of hell with me prior to our marriage and six months of hell at the end of our marriage in 1992/93 caused by my alcoholism. However, she was a *Volunteer.*

Jenny had met me at my worst, then left me when *the wheels came off and the roof caved in.* She had called the police on me in Carringbah prior to our marriage. She also called the police one evening in Sydney in 1992 and I was arrested and locked in the cells for the night with no charge. This was not for being violent I might add, merely for being drunk.

At the end of the marriage and rather than upset the children I put a bed in my office and if I was very drunk I slept in the office. This was *awful for me* but at least I didn't take my trouble home. One evening Jenny called the police to the house just because I was drunk again. There was no trouble, no violence, but I was drunk. So I left the house and slept in my office. The next morning Siobhan said to me, *"Daddy where were you when the police man came 'cos we couldn't find you".* Poor little Siobhan, there was no way I wanted her to witness what William and Edwina witnessed.

Robert my little boy I believe suffered the most at missing me as a father. I hope in the years to come I can make amends to both my young children. The final straw with the marriage was Siobhan said to me one day, *"Daddy, you told me you know everything".* I said, *"Yes Darling, I do"* and she said, *"You don't know where Mummy's new flat is 'cos that's a Secret".* To say I was deeply hurt was an understatement. Jenny had come from a poor background and was a material girl and yet she was not the only one who had lost. I had lost Two and a Half Million Dollars albeit my own fault, it most certainly was not on purpose.

Jenny had proceeded to have a go at my mother about my behaviour, the amounts of my phone hills as the phone was in Jenny's name because I was bankrupt. She sent the phone bills to my mother telling my mother to pay. There was a very cruel streak in Jenny. I have no idea today if she ever really loved me or saw me as a *meal ticket*.

The most hurtful thing in our whole relationship was in 1987 long before we were married. I got very drunk one night and was arrested and granted Bail of One Hundred Dollars. Jenny was living at Arncliffe and I was living in my house in Carringbah. Jenny was holding Five Thousand Dollars cash of mine for *safe keeping* so I rang her when I woke up in the cells on Saturday morning telling her I needed One Hundred Dollars to get out. If I didn't have the money I would have to stay in the cells till Monday. *Jenny refused to bail me saying I was better in the cells and that I had put myself there.*

I had to call Peter Templar to come and bail me. On the Monday, I took the Five Thousand Dollars back off Jenny and of course squandered it all. Jenny having met me at the worse, she had no illusions about me. The night I stopped drinking on the Twenty Seventh of August for four years, there were three other ladies quite happy to *take me on*, yet Jenny got rid of them and took control of me herself. *As I said, she was a Volunteer.*

I have not any great anger or bitterness today suffice to say yes, I was hurt probably as much as Jenny. I was not a good Husband and I will always be grateful to Jenny for my beautiful children and the help in getting me sober in 1987. Having said this my obligations today relate to my children only and not to Jenny. We were both Volunteers and it wasn't meant to be. I have no regrets or remorse over this chapter of my life. I believe I serve the role as a Father better living away from Jenny.

Today, I am extremely close to Siobhan and Robert. We talk on the phone almost daily. I pay regular maintenance, pocket money and I am always there for them. The children stay with me on school holidays four times a year, so yes, we have reached a compromise.

I thank my God of my understanding for giving me this chance.

CHAPTER TWENTY FIVE

I organised an accommodation office in Melbourne. I had visited the city twice before and rather liked the *Old Worlde* charm and the trams in Melbourne. I rented a small four bedroom house with swimming pool in the suburb of Mount Waverley. It was big enough for me to work from home with plenty of room for the children to come on visits.

I spoke to the children daily and Jenny and myself seemed to get on better with a thousand miles between us. From Day One in Melbourne I found AA and began going three to four times a week. I went on a diet and lost some weight and began to take care of myself. I found a housekeeper to come in the mornings, as it worked out she could also type and use the fax. So *albeit small*, I was self contained and started again and chasing money.

There were monies owed to me in New South Wales which I gave to Jenny. I began in Melbourne with exactly Seven Hundred Dollars. I was working from day one on my *Business Directory* and the money soon began to roll in. I organised a friend of mine in New South Wales to do the typesetting and invoicing initially then I moved the whole operation to Melbourne. I lived a quiet life with many girlfriends and enjoyed dining out and dancing, however, all this was done sober.

When any of my girl friends asked about my drinking, I told them I was an alcoholic whilst they may like me sober, they most certainly would not like me drunk. I began to play Rugby for the Harlequins *Golden Oldies* and all in all I settled into the role of a Single Man. I was forty five years old.

I met a Burmese girl called Amy who lived about six to seven miles from me. I was in love with her from the start. Apart from being unusually beautiful she shared many of my interests, jazz music, loved to dance and read. She was a *Pisces* just like my first Margaret, perfectly matched for me, *Cancer* the Crab.

I could quite easily have gone head over heels with this girl. However, with my track record I was afraid to get seriously involved and was content playing the field. I was friendly with a Hong Kong Chinese girl, a Malaysian girl, a South African girl and was spoilt for choice. I recalled the words of my brother Bruce's wife Jane, who said *"Bill Hayes, you could have your pick of any girl in the world as long as you stay off the drink!"*. This was said to me in 1976.

Having put my small business together, I knew Bob Reid only had authority in New South Wales and I was quite safe to trade in Victoria. However, I still had Derryn Hinch who had gone on a *Personal Crusade* against me. I always reacted to his reporters and, of course, this made very good television viewing, *"Bill Hayes kicking the reporters out of the door, or Bill Hayes grabbing the TV camera, etc. etc."*

Edwina had decided to come for a holiday at Easter and I was quite looking forward to this. Life seemed to be going well when one Friday evening Bob Reid arrived at my door with a Summons to appear in the Supreme Court of New South Wales for breaching the Court Order, agreeing not to trade in the State of New South Wales. This Summons was quite worthless and today seven years later is still being *set aside*. However, this goes to show the veracity of Reid's relentless pursuit of me at the request of his publishing paymasters. The large publishing houses in New South Wales all had *Protection* if they paid enough to Bob Reid.

And, of course, it made good television for Derryn Hinch in his *Boots and All* expose, yet again. I organised a local solicitor, Paul Vale of Ringwood, to act for me and after paying some One Thousand Five Hundred Dollars, the solicitor was not worth the *Price of Piss*. So I had the matter adjourned myself.

The last thing I wanted was my past to follow me to Victoria. It was the old adage of *"give a dog a bad name"*, plus all the boring details of having to explain it to my new friends and girlfriends. I had made yet another large mistake in my life. I should have turned and fought back Bob Reid there and then. Prior to his three years of chasing me, he had *not nor has to this day* managed to bring a prosecution against me let alone a conviction. I recall today two stories in my life.

Once when I was sixteen and chasing a very Nasty Sow. This was a large sow that had escaped from the slaughter pen belonging to Lord Vestey. I know no fear of animals yet after nearly a mile of chasing this pig in Devon, down country lanes, the sow *stopped turned and gave chase of me*. I was shocked and terrified and ran like hell, *straight up the nearest tree*.

The second time was a little rat came out of the drains at my meat works in Devon. I had a stick and chased the Rat. The Rat was hit twice with my stick and then the rat stopped running, *turned and jumped at my throat*. I avoided it and never stopped running until I was in my house and the door closed. The *Rat* and *Sow* both evaded their fate. They were brav*e* enough to face their enemy.

I should have stopped and chased Bob Reid and proved to the authorities he was Corrupt and Dishonest and had acted *Unprofessionally* if not *Unlawfully*. I leave the punishment of Bob Reid to God today. Had he acted out of belief no matter how misguided he was, I could live with this. However, I believe he was acting for financial reward and *abusing his position* as a government official.

I had left New South Wales because Bob Reid had made it impossible for me to trade. I should have let the Consumer affairs proceed with the case, but like all alcoholics, I took the *easier, softer* way out of this situation and moved States. I tried to explain the case to Amy, my Burmese girl, but she never realised the full implications. She did, however, point out to me that *I should have dealt with Bob Reid from the beginning instead of running away*. People will believe a government official rather than the individual and nine times out of ten this would be the sensible thing to do. *My case was the exception to the Rule.*

I felt very persecuted and I started drinking again. This was April 1993. All the AA went out of the window. Edwina was staying with me and hadn't seen me for ten years. There I was *drunk as a skunk*, my children came down from Sydney and there I was drunk. Amy had never seen me drunk. She had never ever met an alcoholic prior to me and she was in for the shock of her life and decided to call it a day.

I managed to get along nicely without Amy as I had plenty of replacements. However, they all reacted the same upon seeing me drunk. I let the incident with Bob Reid slipped from my mind to all intents and purposes until the day I had to appear in court. I took Amy to New South Wales for the court case and it was adjourned to the following day mainly as Reid had not *expected me* to turn up. Jenny too had to be there for the court case. So the twenty four hours in Sydney was a total disaster.

I took Amy to the Sebel Townhouse to stay the night before the case. I was exceedingly drunk and then took her to the Irish Bars down at the Rocks in Sydney, my old haunts. Poor Amy by this time was terrified of me as I was so unpredictable. I told Amy to go back to Melbourne and the following day it was adjourned for six months so the whole case was *not a case* at all.

The court case was enough for Derryn Hinch to air it on television. Hinch, since this time has been divorced by his wife, gone personally Bankrupt and has been sacked from *all the TV Channels in Australia,* with the exception of the ABC and SBS who would never employ such an ill educated low life. I have no time for this awful *Badly Bred, Common* little man. However, his source was the impeccable New South Wales Consumer Affairs, so I can't blame Hinch totally as much as I would love to.

With the sixth Hinch Programme exposing me in a period of eighteen months, everyone in Victoria now believed all they and seen on TV, especially Amy's ex-husbands and family. I saw no point in defending myself and became the typical *arrogant drunk.* Amy's ex husband had taken her twin boys who were only three years old. Her first husband had taken the daughter who was only twelve years old. So there I was, back to a Terri situation yet again or a Jill situation with concerned ex-husbands.

I told Amy of my moving to a new home in Donvale and she agreed to move in with me. It was only eight to nine miles away but far enough to live in peace as *Mr Unknown* or so I thought. This is my thirteenth live-in situation with wife or common law wife (de facto as called in Australia). I knew from the start there was little hope for us as drinking was again my first love, sleazy clubs and sleazy women.

The relationship was *doomed* from the start as I was only sober for one month with Amy before Bob Reed came to my door. My values had changed. The time of sobriety I spent with Amy was Heaven, then of course, drink got in the way. I packed Edwina off to Queensland. She saw enough in the time she was there. Jenny was popping back on the scene and I think then she would have considered a reunion but I didn't want this.

Amy had given up her house and her children were taken off her simply for the fact that she loved me and wouldn't give me up. She was just like Terri and Jill. But I had *lost the fire* I had when I was sober. I was back on sparkling wine buying twelve bottles at once, vodka as well, then the violence came back.

Amy couldn't handle my drunkenness or my violence as she had been physically abused by her ex husbands and it was the last thing she wanted in her life. She had nowhere else to live so with the help of a friend, went to live at a Women's Refuge in Geelong for battered wives and their families.

I got back with Amy after a couple of weeks and I said to her, *"If it ever happens again, call the Police and get me arrested"*. This *proviso* gave Amy the confidence to come back but things were never the same again, too much damage had been done.

Then on the Fourteenth of September 1993 at seven o'clock in the morning, fifteen Policemen came to my home. The Hinch Program were there with the police and after my house was searched, all my documents were taken. I was arrested and taken to Glen Waverley Police Station. All this happened in front of Hinch TV cameras. The arresting officer was a *Uniformed Sergeant* from Mount Waverley, who was a *Frustrated Detective*. He had believed Bob Reid's story that I was trading unlawfully now in Victoria.

The raid was aired on Television by Hinch nationwide that evening and, of course, my Bank foreclosed on me yet again. My printers, typesetters refused to work for me and even Joyce, my domestic help left me in disgust. This is the power of the Media.

I was kept in the Police Station all day and released at seven fifty that night when my piece on the *Hinch Program* had been televised. Gover, the arresting officer had received his *Fifteen Minutes of Fame* and I was again disgraced.

Bob Reid rang Amy at her old house in Nunawading. Reid spent fifteen minutes on the phone telling Amy what a *Bad Boy* I was and telling her she should not work for me.

Amy, of course, was involved with me unknown to Bob Reid and repeated the conversation verbatim. This was how I knew first hand what he had been doing. My Banks and friends were a little too afraid to tell me, all for fear of repercussion from Reid. Sergeant Gover used the same *modus operandi*. This abuse of authority is the *Bone of Contention* that really stuck in my throat.

I agreed to go back to the Police Station on the Second of October and answered questions for the whole morning. The arresting officer, David Gover then gave me 110 Charges of *"selling advertising space in a non-existent publication"*. These charges were typed up prior to my interview or my answering any questions. So Gover had appointed himself *Judge and Jury* prior to the event. I can only assume in concert with Bob Reid.

I was taken to court and the Hinch Programme were at the court. This time I overheard Gover on the phone stating, *"We will be at Oakleigh Magistrates Court at two o'clock"*. At the previous raid Gover denied all knowledge of informing Hinch.

Gover asked Twenty Thousand Dollars Bail and brought up all of my large *Drink related English Criminal Record*. This all made terrible reading to the Magistrate and Bail was granted for Five Thousand Dollars. It may as well have been $5 million as I had no money. I later learned Bob Reid obtained my English Criminal Record from a detective hired by Percival Publishing. This detective was a London Cockney who had been a useful heavyweight boxer in his day. He is now one of the leading investigating and security consultants in Australia. His name escapes me, yet this is another man I would like to meet one day.

Amy went to all my people in Melbourne and Sydney as well as to her own family to raise the cash but, of course, no one wanted to know me. She put up half the bail money from her own pocket and had to ask Jenny for the other half and after three days in custody I was bailed.

When we arrived home Amy said she didn't want to be involved with the police or the media and that she wanted *out*. Like Terri she was now on pills so I let her go. She went to share a house with some friends. Once she went Jenny came to stay.

I had to get my publication printed as the allegations against me were that I was *"selling advertising space in a publication that was non-existent"*. This again was Reid's doing so I warned poor old Gover that he was going to be left with *egg all over his face*.

I printed my publication with the help of Jenny doing the typing and Amy lending me money to get it printed. The only pleasant thing about this time was that I had the children staying with me.

Amy called in one day to tell me she decided to have the operation of reversal tubal legation to enable her to conceive our child. It was the *most wonderful news* I have heard in a long time as this issue was a *bone of contention* between us. After three children she didn't want to have any more but she loved me enough to have this done. I was so proud of her and felt a *Very Lucky Man.*

So with Jenny staying in the house I was visiting Amy in hospital. Jenny told me then I would never give Amy up. Yet, as much as I loved Amy I couldn't even handle myself and I knew full well I was drinking in such a manner trouble was sure to follow and follow it did. Two breathalysers in one week.

The second one was when I was stopped for speeding initially. I got out of the car and said to the police officer, *"I am as Pissed as a Parrot, so you may as well take me in"*. These police officers in both cases were very *Decent* to me.

I recall being breathalysed after the English Derby in 1976. I was travelling on the road that runs parallel to Tattenham Corner on Epsom Downs. The Lotus being so very low to the ground and myself being paralytic, there was *no way* I could get out of the car. The police officer said, *"Have you been drinking, sir?"*. I said, *"Don't ask Silly Bloody questions. Lift me out of the car"*. I was taken to Epsom Police Station. My car parked by the Police for me and the Police very decently drove me back to where I was staying.

Jenny went back to New South Wales and Amy moved back to the house. I had told her before that if I got seriously drunk to call the Police. I reiterated this to her and changed the name on the lease of the house into her name, so that she has a home to stay in future. I got my publication out to my clients, so *effectively* the police had no case at all. The 110 charges were, *"selling advertising space in a non-existant publication"*. The publication was now in the hands of all my clients. I also sent Gover a copy by hand.

Feeling very pleased with myself I had thwarted Bob Reid in the Supreme Court of New South Wales and Gover was thwarted in Victoria. Despite all the damage and trouble, I had won, so of course, I had a drink to celebrate. Amy was quite hysterical as I wielded an axe on the four poster Mahogany bed, and she called the police. This time I was arrested and charged with *Attempted Murder, Assault, and Criminal Damage*. I could remember none of these things taking place as I don't even recall Amy being in the house, however, the four poster bed was damaged quite badly.

The result was I was bailed and told *"Not to go near my home"*, a condition of my Bail. The previous Bail from Gover I was already on stated *"I must reside at the home"*. I was so sick and tired of the whole situation. Amy had effectively evicted me from my own home. My two Bails were *contradictory* and I had to breach one or both of them. So I took the first plane to New South Wales and *Ran Back* to Jenny, walking out on everything.

I went to Jenny's flat and told her what had happened. I couldn't possibly adhere to both Bails. The charges the Bail's related to <u>never</u> to this day materialised in a Court of Law. I was again snookered, *Lock, Stock and Barrel.*

To say I was angry was an understatement. I didn't want to go back to Brisbane, Alice Springs, Adelaide or stay in Sydney. So I chose to go to Perth in Western Australia, the only State I had never visited.

Jenny took me to the airport with the children and it was a sad occasion for them as they knew they would never see me again. It was like a nightmare as everyone was crying including me. Money was very short and now I was a *Fugitive* all because of Bob Reid and his new found friend, Sgt David Gover.

As previously stated none of these *trumped up charges* ever saw the light of day in Court. So the only crime I had committed was to jump Bail on charges that would not convict me. Morally and mentally I believe I was quite correct. However, legally I was in the wrong. This police officer was desperate to become a Detective and Bob Reid the corrupt Government Officer had *made me a Criminal*. To make matters worse, Derryn Hinch had been sacked by Channel Ten so his TV Program could no longer do me *harm*. The day of my leaving Victoria, Twenty Ninth of November 1993, I had served a Writ on Hinch for Defamation.

Should Hinch ever regain any assets or obtain any material wealth, I will without doubt pursue him through the Courts.

I arrived in Perth and went straight to the Red Light District to my usual sleazy clubs and slinky women and then telephoned Amy. I was surprised that on the phone she was acting as though nothing had happened. I don't believe *she had a clue* of the damage she had done to me, or the trouble she caused. She had taken me at my word and called the Police. After five minutes chat I invited her to Perth. I was so shocked that she agreed to fly the following day.

Poor Little Amy was so very naïve in so many ways but I had no doubt at all she loved me very much. I had been drinking heavy the two previous nights and had several beers in Sydney at Jenny's yet was not drunk. I was bored in Perth and the beer was doing me no good. I was afraid to go on the vodka so I booked into a motel and slept well that night collecting Amy at the airport the next day.

I had no idea what we were going to do and it was very nearly Christmas 1993 so I searched all the papers for a job selling advertising. I found a job selling space on AFL Australian Football league Score Cards. I went for the interview on the bus. This was like Wilson Coulter going to meet the Libyan delegation at Belfast Airport.

The little man was called Pat Mullens. He was a

charming little man, a homosexual alcoholic but nice. He gave me a job with an immediate start. I worked in Perth under the name of Peter James.

Within days, I had built his sales to figures he could only dream of. As opposed to being grateful he resented paying me the high commission, so as I usual I started on my own with his idea. I found a small flat opened an office, Amy hired a computer and a fax machine and we were up and running. The money was all *"Paid Up Front"* so we were cash liquid from day one.

We spent a very quiet very strange Christmas and managed to purchase a small car, a little Holden just big enough for the two of us. Amy flew to Melbourne and packed all the furniture into storage and came back to Perth. I had under-estimated little Pat Mullens. An *Angry Homosexual* is like a *Woman Scorned*. He had contacted Gover in Melbourne and gave him my address and on Saturday the Eight of January 1994 I was arrested on an Extradition Warrant for jumping Bail. This was Bail on *charges that never materialised.*

I was taken to Perth Police Station and remanded in custody to await the arrival of Gover. My first morning in the prison I was borrowing a cigarette from one of the officers. He said, *"Surely Bill, you can afford a cigarette with all of your money?"*. I thought it strange or he was just a *friendly Screw* as he gave me a packet of cigarettes. At lunch time I saw the *"West Australian"* newspaper and the headlines of *"$7 million Fraud"*. There was my photo and a photo of Pat Mullens and David Gover, the Victorian uniformed police sergeant. Gover had obtained the extradition on the basis of $7 million fraud. Gover had perjured himself. I bumped into Tony Locke, the Kent and England Cricketer from my schooldays who had been arrested the same day. I believe Tony has since passed away.

I later got the transcript from the Extradition proceedings and low and behold in Gover's papers to the Court, he told the court that *"Hayes was wanted in Victoria in connection to over $1 million of Advertising sold in Bogus Publications"*. This was enough for me to be like my *Sow* and my *Rat* and Turn on Gover and Reid. The stakes were very high and the price I paid was very high. Yet, I was now going to

Turn the Tables on Gover and Reid.   *The Fox was going to become the Hound.*

At this point, on the Eleventh of January 1994, Gover was guilty of:

1)   *Bringing 110 charges of selling advertising in a publication that did not exist.   When he realised the publication "did exist" he refused to withdraw the charges.*

2)   *Brought the charges without contacting one of the alleged complainants.   Therefore, he was guilty of bringing a **malicious prosecution**. The charges were typed and ready prior to my Statement on 2nd October 1993, prior to my being questioned.*

3)   *Instructed the Hinch Program of his proposed raid on my home, which is contrary to Section 5 of the Victorian Police Code of Ethics.*

4)   *Contacted the Hinch Programme on the Second of October 1993 to attend the Court in Oakleigh when the 110 Trumped Up charges were lodged with the court contrary to Police Code of Ethics Section 5.*

5)   *Deliberately misinformed the Western Australian Police and Perth Magistrates Court of charges to the value of $1 million. Even the 110 Trumped Up Charges only came to $21,000 and this was a **Malicious Prosecution**.*

6)   *Informed the "West Australian" of $7 million fraud when there was no fraud of any kind.*

7)   *Verballing me and Slandering me with by*

Banks, Friends, Business Associates over $7 million fraud which was non existant.

8) *Raided the furniture store in Clayton where Amy had placed our furniture on a warrant based on Deception stating $7 million fraud.*

9) *Deliberately lied and misled the reporter of the "West Australian" newspaper in relation to my alleged offences and gave them a copy of my passport photo, contrary to Section 5 of the Victorian Police Code of Ethics.*

10) *Took mail from my home in Donvale without a warrant and refused to return it.*

11) *Took audio recordings and mail from Canning Vale Remand Centre without a warrant.*

12) *Took mail from my home in Perth without a warrant as well as mail from Australia Post, Perth.*

13) *Leaked the news of my court case on the Second October 1993 and the case at Perth in January 1994 to the "Waverley Post" newspaper contrary to Section 5 of the Victorian Police Code of Ethics.*

This was on Thirteenth of January 1994 and only the most serious of my allegations against Sgt David Charles Gover. He acted *Unprofessionally* and *Unlawfully* and with *Malice*.

When Gover realised I was going to nail him, he continued to *lie, perjure himself, and pervert the Course of Justice* in many ways which we will come to later in the story. This was a corrupt, malicious government official from New South Wales who was in the payroll of a publishing house and a *frustrated uniformed police officer* from a small station who was going to *Ride to Glory* on my back to achieve his dreams of being a detective.

Gover came to Canning Vale Remand Centre to take me back to Melbourne. I was amazed that he was on his own when normally in such matters, there are always two officers. On the plane trip back to Melbourne, Gover made *certain propositions* to me which I declined.

We arrived in Melbourne and I was taken to court the following morning, the Fourteenth of January 1994. Gover applied to have me released into his custody. I objected and the request was denied by Nick Pappas who was then the Chief Magistrate of Melbourne, and I was remanded to Pentridge Prison until March of 1994.

It was at this point in January that Gover contacted all the alleged complainants. I have seen all the statements and many of them are in Gover's own handwriting. Gover's *"modus operandi"* was this; ***"Hayes is now in prison for selling advertising space in a publication that does not exist. Hayes has made over \$7 million profit from ripping off small businesses. "Had you known the publication does not exist would you have paid for the advertising?"*** and my clients, of course, said *"NO"*. So Gover was twisting all the facts and the evidence to make them fit the charges. One must remember the charges were drawn and typed on the First of October 1993, one day prior to my interview. This was February/March the following year before they were interviewed.

I personally wrote to my clients from prison and explained to them what Gover was doing. I also explained how he had *lied* and *fabricated* and *perjured himself* in order to make the charges stick. *Many concerned alleged complainants have spoken to me in relation to these events and are prepared to swear affidavits as to this paragraph of events.*

Gover was given an office in the Detective Unit of Glen Waverley Police Station in order to conduct this \$7 million inquiry along with an assistant, a uniformed constable Raelene Byron. The result was none of the one hundred and ten charges could be validated. There was a wicked little Detective called Gregory Palmer assisting Gover in all of this. Palmer would be one of the most Evil men I have met and yes, I have met a few. He was like Frankie Abbott in the Television series

"Please Sir!".

Gover then charged me with not paying my phone bill, not paying my electricity bill and not paying my gas bill, the charge *Evading the Debts by Deception*. He failed to mention the *Police themselves* had banned me from going to my own home to do these things.

I made my allegation against Gover to Police IID (Internal Affairs) and the Chief Constable himself. The result was they believed Gover so the file was sent to the Serious Fraud Squad at St Kilda in Melbourne. A *Special Task Force* was set up of four police officers including two Sergeants from the Serious Fraud Group to check on this $7 million fraud.

The task force called *"Operation Stack"* was headed by Sgt Alan Compte and then by Sgt Chris O'Mallon. They travelled four States of Australia, interviewed some three hundred clients, friends, business associates and could find *no fraud* or *no wrong doing* of any kind. They spent six months and many hundreds of thousands of dollars and realised Gover had got it all wrong.

Sgt Jorgensen of Police IID Internal Investigation Division, rather than investigate Gover, took Gover's side against me. So the whole of Police Internal Affairs was used to validate Gover and, of course, *they could not.* The result was all the officers investigating Gover were later put back into Uniform and lost their Detective status. The Victorian Police IID was disbanded and replaced by a new Police Ethical Standards Unit.

The head of *"Operation Stack"* Compte, was disgraced in the County Court of Victoria for Unprofessional conduct in relation to a firm of solicitors and falsely imprisoning the staff at their office. He was reprimanded by the Judge and fined $10,000. The Task Force was then headed by Sgt Chris O'Mallon.

There is a *"Bully Boy"* cult in the Victorian Police. They all help each other. The scandals that came to light over the following years would make one's *hair stand on end* from murder to fabricating evidence to drink driving and one case of a drunken Police Officer being killed behind the wheel of his car with three other Police Officers also drunk. Then his body being put in the back seat so that his wife would receive her Pension.

The biggest scandal was the *"kick backs"* paid to the force from Glazing Companies in relation to Vandalism. Perhaps the worse rort was their own publications. The Police Association of Victoria had an arrangement with a Publisher called Bill Douglas based in Hawthorn.

Bill Douglas would produce the *Police Journals* and *Diaries* earning his revenue from small businesses. These books would gross $4 million a year in advertising revenue.

The *"modus operandi"* was the Salesmen would call small businesses, mainly Vietnamese, Greeks and Italians purporting to be from the Police looking for Donations. No one in their right mind was going to *refuse the Victorian Police.*

Bill Douglas would then invoice between Two Hundred and Fifty Dollars and One Thousand Dollars for the space.

Everyone supplying the Police in Victoria from Ford to Holden, Telstra and all the major Banks felt obliged to contribute. This lucrative business was exposed by me in one of my publications, *"The City Reporter"* and Bill Douglas was given the flick by the Police Association.

Then guess what? Percival Publishing took over. One can only assume through Bob Reid. This lucrative publication is still produced in Victoria today.

Bill Douglas received some Fifty Thousand Dollars in advertising revenue from me and, in fact, paid me Twelve Thousand Five Hundred Dollars for my services so I am talking *first hand* about the Victorian Police Association Journals as I sold space in them on Commission.

"Operation Stack" came back to Victoria with no evidence of any wrong doing against me, not even a parking ticket in October of 1994.

This task force with an unlimited budget cost the Tax Payer more money than the investigation into the Wash Street Police murders. Compte and O'Mallon were so frustrated they charged me with Criminal Defamation against David Gover.

When my case was due to come to Court, the Prosecution said that based on evidence of Chris O'Mallon, Bill Douglas had *Dementia* and could not be called. The reality was I had opened a *Pandora's Box* the Police didn't want spoken of in an Open Court. Everyone was *Wetting their Pants* especially

Danny Walsh, the Secretary of the Police Association.

The case against me was crumbling and as I had predicted, *Gover* had *egg all over his face*. Rather than admit defeat, perjury on a grand scale commenced which we will come to as the story unfolds.

Gover's strategy was if he couldn't get me, he would get Amy. Then by putting pressure on Amy, force me to do a *Deal*. Amy was arrested on her return from Perth and charged with:

1) *Stealing her own car*
2) *Stealing my phone handset*
3) *Failing to return two library books, therefore, charged with Possession of Stolen Property*
4) *Failing to pay her electricity, phone and gas bills.*

With all of these cases, Gover called witnesses and went through the whole procedures of bringing the charges to the Magistrates Court at Melbourne. Amy had to sign on with the Police three times a week and surrender her passport. These ridiculous charges formed three separate trials, and of course, at each trial *Amy was acquitted with a clean record*. Gover was furious and now began to make serious mistakes because his very *Career was on the Line*.

The Police raided Amy's home in April 1994 and again in October 1994. This was after I published my allegations against Gover, mailing them to the Judges, Magistrates, Clients, and the Commissioner of Police. I did this as the corrupt officers were in the Police IID was failing to investigate Gover. The *"Operation Stack"* task force knew Gover was wrong but were going to *"Cover"* him. I, therefore, took the matters into my own hands.

"Operation Stack" under the instigation of Sgt Chris O'Mallon brought forty four counts of Criminal Defamation against Amy and against me. The Hand Up Brief was thirteen volumes, some three hundred witnesses were going to be called, however, I stuck to my guns. I knew that if these charges ever got to court, I could expose *the corruption in Public*. I had no

doubt I would beat Bob Reid and Gover *Fair and Square.*

This was where Gover and O'Mallon both *Lost the Plot.* They proceeded with the charges relying on Police Officers to perjure themselves in the County Court, which of course would have caused serious repercussions. They did, in fact, get numerous Police Officers to perjure them selves in the Magistrates Courts. There was one Police Officer Detective Gregory Palmer who perjured himself on four separate occasions in four separate court appearances and seemed to *enjoy doing it.*

One example of the police officers perjuring themselves was as follows.

I instructed Amy to print five hundred copies of my allegations and take them to Mount Waverley and Glen Waverley suburbs. She is to place them under the doors of each Business and Shops in those towns. Amy was very reluctant to do this, however, I pointed out to her that:

1) Gover and Reid are allowed to go to anyone and say what they want about me, knowing this to be Untrue.

2) What is wrong with me telling the Truth about Gover?

I explained to Amy I only need *one fair minded person in authority* to read my case and I will be released.

The criminal defamation charges were *"Police Payback"* and nothing more.

Amy and myself were the only people who knew when these leaflets were delivered and how. As it happened, Amy delivered Mount Waverley on the Tuesday and Glen Waverley on the Wednesday, therefore, two suburbs on two separate days.

Chris O'Mallon persuaded three officers from Nunawading Police Stations to claim *they had Amy under surveillance and they followed her first to Glen Waverley, then to Mount Waverley and watched her deliver the leaflets.*

Constable Raelene Byron was persuaded to say she was sat in Glen Waverley Police Station and was called to the town center by someone who had received the leaflets. Byron went onto say she witnessed Amy delivering the leaflets.

These four police officers perjured themselves in the extreme at Melbourne Magistrates Court at the Committal Hearings. Apart from the Perjury, they had the story all wrong stating all the leaflets were distributed in one day.

If the surveillance had really taken place, it's amazing the four concerned police officers were not falling over each other. *The whole police evidence was fabricated.*

Gover under oath *Perjured* himself in relation to Hinch, the "West Australian", and the evidence in Perth Magistrates Court in relation to Bob Reid. Gover even accused me in court on the Fourth of December 1994 of threatening to kill Bob Reid. The Magistrate said *"If this was the case, why was Mr Hayes not charged?"* Gover was getting in deeper and deeper, having to perjure himself now to cover his previous Perjury.

I applied for Bail on six separate occasions each time denied as the Victorian Bar, the Barristers in Melbourne were terrified to go up against the Police. The main reason was they were aware of the camaraderie of the Police and the *"Rambo"* style cult. The barristers did not want to be breathalysed on their way home from Chambers or *Open Season* being declared on their families by the Victorian Police.

I was eventually granted Bail in December of 1994 on a $10,000 Surety and surrender of my passport and not leave the State of Victoria.

The sixth application for Bail I conducted myself as I have stated the Melbourne legal fraternity would not attack the credibility of the police officers.

Magistrate Martin, after three days of my application in Melbourne Magistrates Court, granted Bail. When it looked as though I was getting the *Better* of the Prosecution, Sgt. Gover claimed that I was guilty of threatening the life of Bob Reid.

Gover even produced a *Bogus Police Incident Report* from Mount Waverley Police Station fabricating the *alleged Attempted Murder charge.* Magistrate Martin, in his wisdom, found in my favour.

I had married Amy in prison on the Thirteenth day of July 1994. This was the best day's work I had ever done and she visited me every single day for eleven months, not only did she visit, she wrote every day also and we had numerous telephone calls each day. I will always be in Amy's debt if I live to be a hundred years old.

Amy had prepared my full Defense on all the charges and with her help by staying and fighting, I not only *"Put Manners"* on the corrupt N.S.W. Government officer Reid, but the *whole of the Victorian Police Force*. The matter took three and a half years to get to court.

I was released from prison and immediately began my Business Directory, from exactly where I had left off in 1993. Reid was powerless to stop me. Gover, if he had any conviction in his actions of course could have stopped me. So for the next three and a half years, my main income was from the same book I had been wrongfully imprisoned eleven months for previously publishing. I had them all *"on the run"*. I was now in the same situation as the *Sow* that chased me or the *Rat* that jumped at my throat.

The money rolled in and we moved from the small house that Amy had rented whilst I was in prison to a *Grand Colonial House* on a hundred acre farm, complete with Rolls Royce, Mercedes, a string of Racehorses, peacocks in the garden and all the trimmings of a lifestyle of a Country Gentleman.

We heard on the grape vine that many of the Police Officers in the Gover case were now *quietly leaving the force*. However, poor old Gover was relentless in his attempts to get *Revenge* on me, starting with contacting the New South Wales Immigration Department and trying to revoke my Citizenship. The case was thrown out by the Federal DPP who decided not to prosecute everyone was aware that Gover was on a *Personal Crusade*. The police action caused me great anxieties and my drinking escalated.

The money kept running into the business and Amy took a very active role in all the administration, typesetting and getting the books ready for the printer. Whilst life was good, we had the children four times a year on holidays and I could afford to pay regular maintenance. Amy still had to go through the ordeal of all the ridiculous court cases. The *Library Books* case, was Hilarious as Gover was going to fly the Librarian three thousand five hundred from Perth to give evidence. The Commissioner of Police himself must have now begun to wonder if Gover was, in fact, *Mentally Stable*.

We were subject to unauthorised phone taps and police surveillance. O'Mallon tried on three occasions to revoke my Bail unsuccessfully. However, this cost me some Thirty Thousand Dollars in legal fees. I was charged with driving whilst disqualified and Gover tried to introduce my U.K. antecedents that were over ten years old. Of course, the magistrate would not allow this.

O'Mallon was a *Vindictive Bully* who had only reached the lowly heights of Sergeant, in his police career spanning twenty years. He was selected for *Brawn to Intimidate* rather than *Brains to Investigate*.

O'Mallon was perhaps one of the most *Frustrated, Bitter, Jealous* men I have ever met. I recall him standing on the steps of Melbourne Magistrates Court after he had been verbally *horse whipped* by Robert Richter, Q.C. and chastised by the Magistrate. O'Mallon was saying, *"It's not fair. Hayes has the money to employ Richter"*. The bully seemed to forget he had unlimited resources to convict me had I done anything wrong.

So much sensational scandal was now coming out from Police *Whistleblowers* and victims of Police corruption. I found the press began to change sides. Far from the likes of Derryn Hinch who was now bankrupt, the genuine Press and Television came to realise *my complaints were valid* and I began to receive sympathetic Press. The DPP kept adjourning the defamation and whilst Gover and O'Mallon subjected me to three years of relentless intimidation as opposed to getting weaker, this only strengthened my resolve.

I would have sued Derryn Hinch for slander, however, as he was a bankrupt, it was a futile exercise. The most *despicable* act of Gover and his buddy O'Mallon was making Amy's two previous husbands witnesses for the Crown as they thought by a character assassination of me prior to the trial, a Jury was bound to convict me. How wrong they were.

The two Police Officers, Gover and O'Mallon, were instrumental in taking away Amy's twin sons by helping Amy's ex-husband get custody, stating that *"Amy was a woman of*

Disrepute living with Hayes who had been in prison and facing charges of Defaming the police", etc.

My stepdaughter, Priscilla, was now fourteen years old and she lived with us. Her father, would ring my home and be quite abusive to Amy and myself of many occasions. Of course, I told him *exactly* what I thought of him. O'Mallon and Gover then flew him two thousand five hundred miles from Queensland to give evidence against me in Revoking my Bail, based on the false allegation that *"I had contacted Crown Witnesses contrary to my Bail conditions"*. Robert Richter, Q.C. acted for me. As the foremost legal mind in Australia, Robert publicly ridiculed O'Mallon and Gover and they ended up apologising to the Magistrate for bringing a *Frivolous case*. One can only assume *out of spite*.

This happened to Amy also. They tried to revoke Amy's Bail on an equally Trumped Up charges. This time the Magistrate *publicly chastised* O'Mallon and Gover for bringing a frivolous case to the very busy court. The more Gover and O'Mallon lost, the more Personal their vendetta became and, of course, *once you get personally involved in a legal matter you are going to lose*. Never go to court on a matter of principal.

I must admit I took the great pleasure in publicly ridiculing O'Mallon and Gover as what they had done to me was *Wicked* as well as *Unlawful*. It takes a *Brave Man* or a *Mad Man* to take on the might of the whole Victorian Police Force. I think I was a bit of both. However, I believe I cleaned up the system for *weaker* and more vulnerable people than myself. After the last incident of *Unlawful* surveillance by O'Mallon. I reported this to the Commissioner, O'Mallon quietly left the Force. O'Mallon was a Bitter man caused by his own failure to rise through the ranks of the Victorian Police.

This last incident was a car parked outside my farm. I had no driving license and the police were trying to catch me driving the Rolls Royce whilst disqualified.

I asked the young man what he was doing. He told me his car was broken down and he was waiting for the RACV. When we arrived home he was still there. I rang the RACV on my mobile phone giving his car registration number. The RACV had no report of this car.

I had the car registration number checked. The car belonged to a company in Oakleigh who rent Undercover Cars to the Serious Fraud Group in St Kilda.

I reported the matter direct to Neil Comrie, the Commissioner of Police quoting the car registration number. *O'Mallon left the force.*

Life was good for Amy and myself. We ran cattle on our farm and a few sheep. We had chickens to give us fresh eggs every day and I began a small meat wholesaling business of one thousand calves as well as three hundred cattle a week. I specialised in the Vietnamese market in a similar manner as I had the Indian market in London or the Lebanese market in Sydney. We used to go to the cattle auctions three days a week and Amy came with me. I taught Amy how to *"Bid"* at the auctions and she became involved in the Pig Industry. We fattened Sows for slaughter and breeding.

We had a full time handy man on the farm called Paul who was an Italian. He could turn his hand to anything from building sheds to changing a pane of glass in the house window. We also purchased two five tonne truck loads of bread each week from a local bakery to feed all the animals. We had sixteen mares and our own Stallion fed on bread as well as cattle, sheep and hens, ducks, peacocks, pheasants and turkeys. This was a marvellous way to feed animals as the best wheat normally goes for bread and the second and third grade for animal feed. Our animals were getting all Grade One at very little cost to me.

Socially, we went to many Charity Balls, each Sunday we would go for Tea at the Windsor Hotel. Amy had never been in a Rolls Royce until I bought her one from the charming David Eckberg. David presented Amy with a Bouquet and a Bottle of Champagne when he delivered the car. Equally, one day in Melbourne Amy saw a Mercedes sports car she liked. The following day, I bought her one. This girl of mine deserved everything I could give her.

Amy's father came on holidays from India. He was in the Diamond business so Amy took a course in Diamond Grading with a Jewish friend of ours, Rueben Fischer of Crown Diamonds. Sadly Rueben passed away this year. Amy just blossomed. She had been under the thumb of her previous husbands who were both failures and both violent but didn't drink. Amy was now *"Queen of the May"*. Exceptionally *Well Dressed*, *Very Mature* and the *Lady of the Manor*. "Ashleigh Hall" our home was the foremost house in the area and Amy was the Lady of the Hall. *I loved her more as the time went on.*

I did nothing about going back to AA in the three and a half years I was waiting for my court case. Had it not been for my strict Bail conditions, *I had to sign on at the local police station every day for three years*, I would have got up and gone. My gut instinct is to run away rather than face trouble, therefore, have to *thank* Gover and O'Mallon for making me stay and fight as I so very badly wanted my day in Court. I needed the public arena to *"Out"* them for what they were. I was going to act myself and prepared my case with the guidance and help of Mr Alex Lewenberg who is today my legal advisor and our family solicitor. Alex is one of the most *Decent* human being I have ever had dealings with.

When the police raided Amy's home on the Third of October 1994, Amy was arrested. At ten o'clock in the evening O'Mallon and Compte refused Amy Bail and called in a visiting magistrate. I was in custody at the time. Alex Lewenberg drove to St Kilda Road Police complex and made a case to the Magistrate for Amy to be bailed.

The wonderful Alex, of course, succeeded in putting all the points *Honestly and Fairly* and Bail was granted as Amy only had public transport, Alex and his lovely wife drove Amy home.

This man, Alex Lewenberg, was yet another *Angel* put in my path by the God of my understanding.

My drinking was in bouts. I would go one to three months and never drink. Then perhaps drink for one-two days. Each time I drank I became *Legless*. There was no way I could have one drink or drink socially. One of the Balls we went to I drank and succeeded in making a public fool of myself. My drinking was very embarrassing. Every time I drank, I blacked out with no recollection of events.

I was *Dry Drunk*. This is when you go through all the motions of being drunk without the booze. This was very hard on Amy, my wife and Priscilla my stepdaughter. I never drank when the children came though. Today, I can live with my past and have no regrets. I believe had I stopped drinking totally, I wouldn't have had the *courage* to take on my enemies - Bob Reid, David Gover, Chris O'Mallon, Alan Compte and Mick Jorgensen of Police Internal Affairs and the *Evil* Gregory Palmer.

My mother came for a six week visit and this went very well. She taught Priscilla to drive and really had a lovely time. Amy and my mother got on very very well. So my life was good, my children were getting many benefits and fabulous holidays. They also loved Amy. I was getting on well with Jenny and paying my weekly maintenance.

Edwina and Jenny had become quite friendly after the divorce and this was okay as I encouraged Edwina and the children getting to know each other. Also Margaret, my second wife visited Australia and stayed with Jenny. This I thought was quite strange yet they had the children in common so that was none of my business.

The court case was scheduled to take six months if the Police brought all the three hundred witnesses. I demanded they do so. We were booked to commence trial in October of 1997. The Prosecution then wanted to call the witnesses. I would not allow this. I was aware the witnesses had been verballed which I was going to prove in court.

Our case was the only case in fifty years of legal history in Australia, the other one related to the famous author Frank Hardy. Criminal Defamation is an unusual case as it can be with Malice which is under the Crimes Act or by Recklessness which is a lesser charge under the Wrongs Act. To say my eight year battle with Bob Reid and David Gover had not taken its toll on me mentally would be wrong. It had drained me, exhausted me and very nearly *Broke* me.

Had they not tried to *Revoke my Bail* and my Citizenship, I may have been more lenient. However, I went all the way until the day of the Trial. The prosecution wanted to *Try* Amy and myself together. I fought this for three days and demanded separate Trials. The Judge in his Wisdom agreed to this.

The Prosecution then brought Amy's case on first. This was a problem as I didn't want to waste my defense and give the Prosecution a *Trial Run*. I, therefore, instructed Amy to plead guilty. Amy had, in fact, mailed some of the correspondence in relation to Gover and she may even have typed some of it. So we had no problems in *Pleading Guilty*. At least Amy and myself were *Fair Dinkum* and *Honest*. I was told many years ago *"If you look the Truth in the Eye long enough, all will be revealed"*. Judge Duggan, in his wisdom, gave Amy a twelve month conditional discharge and recorded *No Conviction*, so Amy to this day, has no criminal record. I had every confidence and faith in the legal system and every confidence in *Judge Duggan who is recognised as a Hard Judge but a Fair Judge*.

My case was due the next day. The Prosecution intimated they wanted to deal. Judge Duggan suggested we adjourn for two weeks to negotiate and this was done.

The Prosecution agreed to bring six counts of Criminal Defamation on the Wrongs Act and withdrew thirty eight charges on the Crimes Act if I would plead guilty. I prepared a Statement for the Press and Televison outlining again my allegations against Gover, e.g.

(1) *Perjury*

(2) *Attempting to collect a Bribe*

(3) *Perverting the Course of Justice*

(4) *Bringing frivolous charges against me constituting a Malicious Prosecution*

(5) *Bringing frivolous charges against Amy constituting a Malicious Prosecution*

(6) *Defaming me*

(7) *Contacting the Hinch TV Programme (contrary to Section 5 of the Police Code of Ethics)*

(8) *Contacting the "West Australian" newspaper (contrary to Section 5 of the Police Code of Ethics)*

(9) *Contacting the "Waverley Post" newspaper (contrary to Section 5 of the Police Code of Ethics)*

(10) *Attending the Family Court out of Malice*

> *against my wife, Amy*
>
> *(11)*   *Attempting to revoke my Citizenship*
>
> *(12)*   *Taking my mail without a Warrant*
>
> *(13)*   *Working in conjunction with Bob Reid, a corrupt New South Wales government official, who was in the pay of various publishing houses and working in conjunction with Bill Douglas, the publisher of the Victorian Police Association Journal.*

I gave this written statement to all Television Reporters and Newspaper Reporters who attended the case. I did notice none of them had the courage to print my allegations. However, I proved my point prior to the trial. No matter the outcome, I was telling the *Truth* and going to retract nothing!

The Prosecution were not going to call officers O'Mallon and Byron who had left the Force and Jorgensen, Walsh and O'Sullivan who were back in Uniform. Bill Douglas a key witness who for years had made millions of dollars by publishing the Police Diaries, Police Journal in conjunction with the Police Association had *dementia,* making him unavailable to give evidence. The ironic thing was that Percival Publishing from New South Wales the paymaster of Bob Reid was producing the Victorian Police Journal. That speaks for itself on the *Real Motives* of Bob Reid.

Detective Greg Walsh deserves a mention here. Walsh was a detective at City West Police Station in Melbourne. Walsh was a *Gung-ho, Yuppy* type police officer and brought a charge against me on his own.

Later I learned this was done in concert with Gover. The object of the exercise was Walsh to prove that a second police officer had grounds for complaint, therefore, trying to validate the actions of Gover.

The charge was frivolous in the extreme and related to my employing Amy via an employment agency early in her time working for me. Walsh tried to claim I deceived the Employment Agency by virtue of the fact I knew Amy personally.

This charge never materialized, of course, and Walsh

disappeared from Gover when things became *Hot.* I often wonder what happened to this *Dishonest Police Officer.*

Perhaps the most amusing charge Gover brought was on the Second of October 1993. The charge was *"Obtaining employment by deception with Douglas Publishing"* (yes, the publishers of the Victorian Police Association magazine). I put Fifty Thousand Dollars in Bill Douglas's pocket. Bill paid me Twelve Thousand Five Hundred Dollars. Like all people in the commission publishing game, I was working under a nom-de-plume.

I have kept all the original charges laid by Gover. I also have all the statements in his own handwriting where Gover verballed the alleged complainants in the manner previously stated, e.g: *"Had you known $7 million fraud, etc."* By virtue of the fact Gover had me unlawfully in custody, my clients would assume I had done something wrong.

I have also preserved all the papers of my defence of this case of Defamation. I know the DPP knows and the Prosecuting Counsel knows that had I elected to defend the case, I would have **Walked.** The police were guilty of so much *Unprofessional* if not *Unlawful Conduct* .

On a serious note, perhaps the greatest *Miscarriage of Justice* was on the Third of October 1994. O'Mallon raided Amy's home taking all my Defence papers for my forthcoming trial.

This was a cold, calculated, dishonest attempt at *Perverting the Course of Justice* by *"Operation Stack".*

Fortunately, Amy had been warned by me and secreted copies of all documents in the one place the police did not have access. This was my cell at the Melbourne Remand Centre.

I was determined to go into the witness box and reiterate my allegations against Gover as they were my *Honestly Held Opinions.* I published the aforementioned list of alleged offences and gave this to all of the media prior to the trial.

The only thing I would not deal on was Gregory Palmer. This was a Dangerous, Vicious, Victorian Police Officer who was a *Corrupt Pathological Liar.* This was the man who *enjoyed* Perjuring himself. I demanded all charges in relation to Palmer be withdrawn as I would repeat my allegations until the *Cows Come Home*. Palmer who is still a serving Victorian Police Officer is the most *Evil* man I have ever met.

Gregory Palmer can destroy all the *good will* of five thousand decent Victoria Police Officers.

I have never stated that all the Police are *Wrong* or *Bad*. Rather, *Flies attract flies, Flies become Maggots*. The worse element of all this affair was the <u>*COVER UP.*</u>

Joe Public, if in the wrong, should and does stand trial. The police must also be accountable and not abuse the *Power of the Law*. They are *Public Servants* and should serve the Public.

So in Court, I qualified my pleas on the six charges by stating to the crowded court I will not withdraw one of my allegations. Equally, I believe Gover had acted *Unprofessionally* if not *Unlawfully*.

The six times I had applied for Bail, Chris O'Mallon and Alan Compte packed the Magistrates Court with uniformed police officers for days on end. This is, of course, a form of intimidation. The Magistrates Court with Police Prosecutors are *Playgrounds* for the Police.

One particular Police Prosecutor, *Constable Williamson*, a large loud individual successfully prevented my Bail on four occasions by these tactics.

Williamson even brought his Mum and Dad to the Magistrates Court to watch their *Little Boy* in action.

I noticed in the *Real World* of the County Court, these Thugs were conspicuous by their absence. They would not have the *Balls* to try to intimidate a County Court Judge.

I have said in the *Author's Note* to this Book that the people who set out to do me harm will realise I have been factual in the Book and written it as it was, without malice.

I feel very sad that so many men should rally around one officer because he was a *Mate,* a *Buddy*. What goes around comes around or at least it has in my colorful life. You cannot defend the *indefensible*.

Having said all of this, the Prosecution said, *"Mr Hayes is showing No Remorse in his actions and this should be taken into consideration by the Judge in Sentencing"*. The Judge, in his wisdom, said, *"It's been quite apparent throughout all of these proceedings Mr Hayes 'Feels No Remorse' in his allegations".*

Judge Duggan fined me One Thousand Five Hundred Dollars on each of the six counts and the case was over after three and a half years. I had won. I had stood my ground and told the *Truth* and the *Truth* prevailed.

Gover was furious, Palmer even more furious. O'Mallon had more sense than show his face. Compte was also *conspicuous by his absence* on this the Eighteenth day of January 1998, some eight years after Bob Reid began his *Campaign of Terror* against me by exploiting his position as a New South Wales government official.

Gover was so angry he demanded the DPP to Appeal the Sentence. The DPP said *"If you want to Appeal the Sentence Mr Gover, you pay the costs yourself".* Gover had cost the State of Victoria in excess of $4 million in his quest for promotion and ruthless pursuit of me. He was transferred as a Detective to the Transit Police in Melbourne and now serves still as a Sergeant at Ringwood Police Station in Melbourne, Victoria. He must have the *Skin of a Rhinoceros*, yet the case restored my faith in the legal system.

As for Palmer, he is also back in Uniform and was recently in the headlines for releasing a prisoner on Bail, it was alleged, in order for him to be shot by the Victorian Police. *What goes around comes around.* I recall Palmer strutting around my home in Donvale saying *"He get his Rocks Off dealing with people like me"*. He also said he was going to break me and freeze all of my assets. Like all bullies, *Rats hunt in Packs.* On his own, Palmer is a *very Insecure, Insipid Little man* with many of his own problems.

When the telephone rang in my home at Donvale, Palmer grabbed the handset saying *"He was the Victorian Police raiding my home"*. Little did he know who he was talking to. This man would have come forward had the Criminal Defamation case proceeded.

Palmer picked up my AA *"Daily Reflections"* book from my bedside table and stated *"Oh yes, who's the Fucking Alcoholic then?"*. Palmer would be called a little *Gobshite* in my home village.

I have memories of Gover laughing in my face at Perth Airport in front of the Perth Police saying, *"What are you going to do about it, Hayes, write me a letter?"*. This is what gave me the idea to force him out into the open. I wrote him not one but several letters and he had to prosecute me, giving me the opportunity to cross examine him in Public. If you can't take it, you shouldn't give it. I forced the Prosecution in the same manner as the Marques of Queensbury did to Oscar Wilde in 1896.

I don't suppose Gover has ever heard of Oscar Wilde.

CHAPTER TWENTY SIX

So in January of 1998, I was old enough and wise enough to realise that by attacking my persecutors, although many had left the Force, I was always going to be at risk. *Who polices the Police?* – to quote Oscar Wilde.

I decided to move back to Ireland taking a long lease on a $5 million Country House and Farm in north county Dublin called *"Kinsealy Hall"*. This property complete with stables and excellent grazing was the ideal spot for me to breed racehorses.

I began a publication called *"TAXI TALK"* for the Taxi Driver's Union of Ireland and negotiated a deal with Esso Petrol Company ensuring all Taxis in Ireland run on Esso petrol for a period of five years. The taxis as well as running on Esso Petrol would advertise Esso Products and a limited number of taxis would be painted in *Esso Livery*. The Esso deal alone was to pay me $5 million over five years.

In 1998 the Irish Pig Industry was in crisis so I offered my services to the Irish Farmers Association (IFA) to market all the surplus pigs on the home market thus culminating in marketing some six hundred pigs a week.

We imported a Stallion from Paris called *Califfe Dore* bred by Sheik Mohammed. *Califfe Dore* was the grandson of the *Great Northern Dancer* and I put together numerous thoroughbred mares from all over Ireland. Once more we had our Peacocks on the lawns and our daughter, Priscilla finished her Final Year at school in Portmarnock.

I found Ireland had changed quite a lot in my self-imposed exile of twenty years. The country was now riding on the back of the *"Celtic Tiger"* and enjoying tremendous prosperity for the first time in the country's long tragic history.

I was fifty years old when I returned to Ireland and my life has seen many changes in the twenty seven years I had been away from my village in Devon.

Today, I am a *Happy* member of AA and go to meetings never less than twice a week. I still don't know how AA works and care even less. All I know is that the only years of *Peace* I have known in my adult life have been the years I attended AA on a regular basis.

William, my son, lives in London with a wonderful girl Tanya who simply adores him. We went for his birthday in 1999 to *Simpsons-on-the-Strand* in London and had a rather nice Roast Beef Lunch. Amy, Tania, William and myself. I have never been a Father to him the way I would have wished, yet I was there in the vital seven formative years according to Mary Bolton and I have yet to find anything Mary said wrong.

Edwina, my daughter, is a Professional singer and recently performed at Ronnie Scott's in London. She is doing really well in what she loves. I hope in the *Winter of my Life* to get to know Edwina as a young woman as I missed all the years of her childhood. I am extremely proud of both my eldest children and owe a deep gratitude to my second wife Margaret for all she has done for them, most of all, always being there for them as I was always absent.

My mother is now eighty years old and lives in a luxury apartment on the beach at Sandbanks near Poole, Dorset. Whilst she is very badly crippled with arthritis, she is mentally still as *Sharp as a Razor.* She has been there for me all my life in my very *Bad times and very Tough Spots.* Without her love and support I have no idea were I would be today.

My brother, Bob, is retired in Guernsey and has three grown up children. He built a very successful Insurance business with branches all over the South of England. Bob was always a *Quiet Achiever.* I recently spent an afternoon with him at his family home on the cliffs in Guernsey overlooking the sea and had one of the nicest afternoons of my life, just talking about nothing. I think one of my greatest regrets was losing the friendship of my brother Bob for twenty five years. He was the first person to try and get me into hospital in 1974. He rings my Mother every day and is a Wonderful Son.

My brother, Bruce, lives on the Isle of Man and has a very successful Property Business in the North of England that is controlled by his eldest son, Jason. Bruce has four grown up children as well as a young son. Mary Bolton told me that no matter what I suffered as a child, Bruce suffered far more than me and this will all come out in later years. This is my story. I believe both of my brothers have stories of their own to tell that would make *even more interesting reading* than my story.

Barbara, my sister, now has three grand children. Her own three children being all very successful as well as very loving to her. Barbara lives in Bournemouth and is at Peace with the World enjoying a long term relationship with Michael, a charming English Officer and a gentleman.

David, my brother-in-law would have been so very Proud of his daughter, Tracey, who has two beautiful daughters and created a business empire second to none.

Tracey has restored all the family fortunes with a bonus and recently purchased a new luxury home on the Avenue in Sandbanks. This is the most valuable real estate area in the United Kingdom. Despite all this success, Tracey like my brother Bob, has retained her humility and remained the same lovely person she was as a child. I am extremely proud to be her uncle. This lovely child has made her father's sad life so very worthwhile.

Amy, my wife and myself have recently celebrated seven years of marriage having been together now for seven and a half years, the *Longest and the Best Relationship* in my current life. Amy supports my going to AA and after many years of trying has finally succeeded in getting some *Religion and God* into my life. I will love my Amy until I die and Priscilla is as beautiful as her mum. I am very proud of my wife and my daughter.

Siobhan and Robert live in Sydney with Jenny. I talk to them weekly and see them at School Holidays. I hope God allows me to be a Real Father to them, support them and always available to them as I was absent to William and Edwina.

There are many stories I have left untold in this book. I could write a book on each situation I got myself into. I have counted thirty hospitalisations, seven times in prison totaling some three and a half years, sixteen serious car accidents resulting in total write-offs, twenty seven drink driving charges and twenty one convictions all relating to alcohol, not paying hotel bills, taxi fares, bar bills, etc. etc. along with perhaps twenty to thirty arrests and Police cells.

The whole story is not a *"Pretty Picture"*, yet it's the *Walk I had to Walk*. Today I am able to *Talk the Talk*.

Alcoholism is recognised by the World Health Organisation as the Third Biggest killer in the world today. This figure does not include *Homicides, Suicides, Traffic Accidents* or *Accidents at Work*, all caused by booze, easily making it the *biggest killer* in the world today. I have no fear of Death today but I am sick and tired of all the Rehearsals.

The Twelve Promises of AA on Page 83 of the *Big Book* of AA says:

- ***We Will Attain*** and maintain sobriety.
- ***We Are Going To Know*** a new freedom and a new happiness.
- ***We Will Not Regret*** the past nor wish to shut the door on it.
- ***We Will Comprehend*** the word "Serenity" and we will know peace.
- ***No Matter*** how far down the scale we have gone, we will see how our experiences can benefit others.
- ***That Feeling*** of uselessness and self-pity will disappear.
- ***We Will Lose*** interest in selfish things and gain interest in our fellows.
- ***Self-Seeking*** will slip away.
- ***Our Whole Attitude*** and outlook on life will change.
- ***Fear Of People*** and economic insecurity will leave us.
- ***We Will Intuitively Know*** how to handle situations which used to baffle us.
- ***We Will Suddenly Realise*** that God is doing for us what we could not do for ourselves.

It is not my job to sell AA as AA is based on an *Attraction rather than Promotion.* The door is a two way door. You can go out and try drinking again and still be welcome back and no one to question you or criticise you.

How I have survived is a miracle in itself. How I have become sober is a bigger miracle. I keep my programme very simple. I go to meetings, take the cotton wool out of my ears and put it in my mouth.

The alcohol is in the bottle, the *"ism"* is in the person. I believe my *formative years* followed by my father losing all my money in 1966 escalated my alcoholism or at least allowed me to *"justify"* my drinking resulting in becoming an alcoholic. You can't be nearly an alcoholic as you can't be nearly pregnant. *You are or You are not.*

Alcoholism is the only illness I know where the patient needs more of the poison that's killing him or her in order to feel better. I cannot be cured my disease, but it can be arrested on a daily basis.

Finally, I come to my dear departed Margaret who I loved so very dearly. I was already an alcoholic when I married Margaret in 1967. She used to call me her *Michael Henshard* as in the *Mayor of Casterbridge* by Thomas Hardy. I know that one day we will be united as well as my baby daughter that I still have yet to meet. I wonder if when I see her she will recognise me. I have prayed quietly for her soul every day for thirty one years and carried the burden of guilt for the same length of time. I not only deprived myself of a beautiful wife and loyal friend but I deprived William of his natural mother and I hope my God as I understand him will forgive me as I will *never be able to forgive myself.*

I am closer to my Father in his death than I ever was in his life. I dream about him frequently in a lot my dreams I am still afraid of him. Despite all the things I didn't approve of in my father, I find myself doing the self same things myself today. This is because I am *my Father's Son.* Today, I understand him as I never could when I was a young man.

EPILOGUE

CHAPTER TWENTY SEVEN

It was October of 1998 and I was sat in my Study at Kinsealy Hall, our country mansion complete with racing stables, in north county of Dublin, Republic of Ireland.

This had been a good year. We had returned to Ireland from Australian in March. We had been fortunate enough to find this exquisite Gentleman's residence in the heart of the country, yet only one mile from the beach at Portmarnock and seven miles from the centre of Dublin.

The property had been purchased for Five Millioin Dollars by Fyffes, now a public listed company. Yet, previously the company of Lord Vestey, so once more the Vesty organisation had come into my life. Fyffes had purchased Kinsealy Hall with the long term plan of developing the ninety acre farm into redevelopment land, if and when zoning was approved. This enabled me to enjoy the facilities for at least the next five years minimum with a full option.

I had been running a publication for the Taxi Driver's Union of Ireland and the previous Tuesday we had finalised a deal, whereby all the Taxis in Ireland would run on Esso petrol, the drivers all having an Esso Charge Card. The Union would receive Five Pence per gallon *Kick Back* and I would receive the same. This meant some $5 million over the next five years. The Directors of Esso, Amy and myself shook hands on the deal in the Esso Boardroom over morning coffee and blueberry scones. The deal was finished.

A couple of months previously I had purchased a refrigerated meat lorry along with a new Jaguar car and was wholesaling some six hundred pigs a week in Dublin on behalf of the I.F.A. as well as some three hundred ewes a week on my own account.

Each Monday, I would go to livestock market at Maynooth and purchase my sheep and I was finally living the life I believed I was born for.

We only had a staff of three people, one man Alan who

was a handyman took care of the horses and fed some thirty to forty pigs that we kept. We had imported a new stallion called *Califfe Dore* from Paris. This fellow was the Grandson of the Great *Northern Dancer* and had excellent potential.

We had a boy called Emlyn and I was teaching him the whole of my business as well as selling on the *"Taxi Talk"* publication and a second salesman called Tony Crook. Crook was an English man who was one of the *Best Advertising Salesman* I have encountered, yet did not fit in with our family business. *"Taxi Talk"* was a nice little earner of Three Thousand Dollars nett per week.

I had sold a publication to a local company and Tony Crook went with the publication as part and parcel of the deal. I believed Crook was quite Happy with the situation, but I was wrong. I sold the publication for One Hundred and Fifty Thousand Dollars and *life was pretty good.*

It transpired that Tony Crook was a Closet Transvestite and met Des Ekin the journalist, at an illegal club for Bisexual men in Dublin. Crook had a child born to an Irish girl and the child at six weeks old was taken into care by Welfare Officers. Ekin killed the story as a favour to Crook.

Life is very difficult in Ireland for Homosexual and Bisexual men and despite all they did to me, I have a great pity for Ekin and Crook, living in the closet and not only the fear of being found out but also the fear of arrest as this is still *Unlawful* in Ireland.

Amy had visited my mother in Bournemouth for a few days and stayed at the *Ritz in London* with Priscilla to entertain some friends from Australia. I had arranged a tour of Harrods by the personnel of Mohamed Al Fayed and a good time was had by all, crowning it with lunch at *Fortnum and Mason* of Piccadilly. As I reflect on that time, October 1998, things were pretty good all round. I can only speak as I find and despite all the adverse publicity, Mohamed Al Fayed has always been extremely *Helpful and Charming* to me.

Priscilla was attending the local school in Portmarnock and in her Final year and seemed at last to be settling down to life in Ireland. In fact, Priscilla was becoming more Irish than the Irish and she loved Dublin.

Socially, we went Racing a few times, the Irish Grand National at *Fairyhouse*. We were at the Curragh for the unveiling of the Bronze life size statue of *Nijinski*, the marvellous son of *Northern Dancer* that won every classic race on the Calendar, ridden by Lester Piggot.

Lester Piggot was there with Robert Sangster and Vincent O'Bricn along with the Aga Khan and many other racing notables. We were on television that day and Priscilla saw us from home with the Aga Khan and his lovely new German wife.

My sister, Barbara, had been to visit and so had Edwina, my daughter. I was in touch with my brother Bob on the telephone and also my other brother, Bruce. All in all, it seemed a Right Decision to return to Ireland, yet I didn't like the changes in the people's attitude or the speed at which the economy was growing.

Ireland had been very fortunate in Europe since 1972 and with only three million people and twelve million cattle along with thirty million sheep, soon became the *Larder of Europe*. Ireland was feeding France, Germany, Belgium and Italy with prime beef and lamb, and having the smallest population of any EEC State was the beneficiary of enormous EEC grants in subsidies to farmers. Grants to build new roads and factories . All in all, Ireland was *"Riding on the Pig's Back"*.

This was not a true economy as it was based on nothing more than charity. However, the young people of Ireland I noticed in 1998 were taking all the credit for the rise in the economy as they were the educated generation. Companies such as Citibank were employing two thousand and five hundred young people (Yuppies) as they moved the European headquarters to Dublin, taking advantage of the grants and subsidies as well as the tax advantages available.

When an economy goes into decline the first companies to close are the paper shufflers. My own opinion was that in 1998 not enough was being done in the manufacturing quarter to build a permanent secure economy.

I was shown figures in Brussels in 1974 stating that by the year 2000 Ireland, France and Norway would lead the

European economy. This was well before the unification of Germany who formerly always lead the economy with the Deutch Mark.

Corruption in Ireland was still rife in 1998. There were several tribunals going on into money laundering, politicians and tax evasion, etc. The biggest *"scam"* in Ireland was Insurance. This was controlled by several English companies all with their subsidies in Ireland and still goes on as I write this book.

Charles Haughey was my next door neighbour and I hadn't seen Charles since my Clones days. Charles invited me over for morning drinks saying, *"What are you doing in my little Parish, Bill (Kinsealy) without my Permission?"*

I have a lot of time for Charles who was, and is, a *Great Irishman* despite all the recent scandal over his days as Prime Minister and alleged tax evasion.

I purchased a Mercedes 500 and for insurance I was quoted Two Thousand Five Pounds, Two Thousand Pounds and One Thousand Seven Hundred Pounds, and eventually became insured for the sum of Seven Hundred and Nine Pounds. This was ridiculous, yet shows the *sub serviant* Irish were still open to gross exploitation of their former English masters.

The Taxi Driver's Union ran insurance for the drivers of which only a few took advantage. Bruenes of Cork were Brokers for the N.T.D.U. and each year received $3 million in premiums from the Union. The claims for 1997 were Three Hundred and Sixty Thousand Dollars, so this was a nice $2.6 million profit for a small group of Lloyds Underwriters.

There was only one Irish man with the sense to do his own underwriting. This man was called Quinn and based at Cavan. Mr. Quinn was in the Truck business and was sick and tired of the variations in the quotes to insure his own lorries. So he formed his own brokerage and insured the lorries himself. He soon realised the *Big Money* was in the underwriting. He then underwrote his own insurance. 1998 saw Quinn Insurance as the third biggest in the country doing many of the private cars and they were coining in millions of Pounds every week, all money up front. I have never seen Profits of this magnitude in any business.

The Federation of Insurance Brokers had a strangle

hold on the industry and constantly fed the Irish Press with stories of how much money car insurance was *losing*. The result was that for anyone under twenty five years of age in Ireland to insure, their car would cost more than the car value itself. Once more <u>*no one*</u> did anything about the situation, they paid the English masters and kept quiet.

I was so incensed at the One Thousand Eight Hundred Pounds difference in my top insurance quote on my Mercedes and the bottom one that I became a small time Insurance Broker. This was so difficult to do as the Insurance Brokers Association for obvious financial reasons ran a very **Closed Shop** and will do anything to prevent any new players coming into the market, yet against *Impossible Odds*, I began.

I found initially I could quote for insurance to High Risk drivers and place the cover myself with the Irish Insurance Companies and Brokers. This is quite legal albeit unusual. I was getting anything from One Thousand Dollars to Two Thousand Dollars profit per client. By getting paid in cash up front and paying my Insurance monthly over twelve months. I soon became very cash rich in this small business. I had young men coming to the door with bags of cash, anything from Three Thousand Dollars to Six Thousand Dollars and *Happy* to pay me.

Like Mr Quinn at Cavan, the obvious next move was to form my own underwriting group based in the U.K. and underwrite the Risk myself. By October of 1998 I had only one claim of One Thousand Dollars out of perhaps Four Hundred Thousand Dollars in Premiums. Then the Insurance Brokers Association *"Got Wind"* of what I was doing and *"Closed Ranks"* on me and I couldn't get facilities anywhere in Ireland to take my cover. When I think of how *Infantile* the Irish mentality still is after the seven hundred years of raping and pillaging, it makes me quite sad.

I met one insurance broker who offered to take over my business. He was based in Swords and said to me, *"It's wonderful to sit in my office each day and see the long queues of people all with paper bags of cash and knowing I can use this money for the next two months interest free and still get my commission from the underwriter"*. He was right, of course, it was very easy money in the most enormous amounts. This man was taking in Four Hundred Thousand Dollars *Daily in Cash*.

So sitting in my study one Friday in early October, I had just finished for the week having been offered the lease on my own meat works at Killbeggan in County West Meath where I was killing my Pigs and Ewes. *The world was bright and gay.* I had in my own mind made a good decision to bring my wife and daughter to Ireland. I loved my home, my horses and my family and my lifestyle.

The telephone went as I was sitting contemplating my *good fortune*. It was a guy called Des Ekin from a very grubby little newspaper called the *"Sunday World"*. This paper gets its advertising revenue from Sex Phone Calls and Mutual Masturbation. Yet its *"alleged"* editorial pages are full of expose of Prostitutes with such Juvenile headlines as *"Sex Slaves night with Doctor Death"*, etc. etc. The paper is very badly written by a bunch of working class *(Hinch stereo type)* journalists out at Rathfarnham, *gratifying their own inadequacies* from their by-lines. There was a reporter like Des Ekin in one of Harold Robbins' books, *attack being the best form of defending his own Sexual Peculiarities.*

The result of my phone call from Ekin was he had been in touch with Gover of the Victorian Police and Bob Reid of New South Wales Consumer Affairs and was going to publish their allegations about my business in Australia. Fourteen thousand miles away from Ireland, of course, in the view of the *Sunday World,* this was in the *"Public Interest"*. I told him I had no statement to make, however, I suggested to him that he get his facts correct as I was aware of the laws of Libel. I did not allow for the Irish mentality, on this occasion, to my cost.

Amy and myself collected the newspaper at nine o'clock on Saturday evening and there was my photo on the front page under the headline *"King Con"*. The paper stated I was a multi millionaire having made my money from bogus publications. The photographs used were direct printouts from my own Publications. Gover was quoted as saying, *"If I set foot in Australia, I would be arrested on sight"* yet didn't qualify on what charges. Equally, he said the Australian Police *did not* want to extradite me, once more a total contradiction.

It appeared the salesman, Tony Crook, I had sold with the small publishing business had put the story together, gleaning information from my Australian Publication *"The City Reporter"* where I exposed Gover, Reid, Hinch and company. Tony Crook got hold of David Gover who was only too pleased to assist and once more got a little revenge. This time I went to Neil Comrie, the Commissioner of Police yet again and informed him of Gover's activities.

Gover denied everything since that time. I have received a letter written by Des Ekin to Gover at Ringwood Police Station. This letter conclusively proves the involvement of Gover.

David Gover provided newspaper cuttings and video film of the Hinch Program, I can only assume from his *Personal Scrap Book.* These documents were copied at the *Sunday World* and given to me.

The three page article with photographs was quite Horrible and there was a good case for a *Libel Suit* against the *Sunday World* so I instituted proceedings that are still pending in the Four Courts of Dublin, seeking damages of $6 million. The case is relatively simple and pretty cut and dried. This is *another* matter for *another day.*

This result was the Taxi Driver's Union pulled the plug on me with the publications and worse of all, the Esso Deal. I was down $5 million over five years in one morning. The IFA panicked and went to all my customers in Dublin asking them to pay the IFA Direct and not myself for Pork to the value of Six Hundred Thousand Dollars.

Everyone who carried insurance with me came for a refund within three days and I had to pay out One Hundred and Twenty Thousand Dollars in insurance premiums. So the whole of Ireland, always happy to cut down a *"Tall Poppy"* isolated me completely. I had also negotiated a beautiful Manor House with forty stables with the all weather race track and one hundred acres of land in Co. Tipperary on a ten year lease and the deal *Fell Through* as a direct result of the article.

The following Sunday there was a follow up story and three weeks later yet another, so it was a *Boots and All* character assassination by this fellow Des Ekin and the *Sunday World.* I cannot *"comment"* too much on the case as its still before the Courts. Having said this, I am quite confident of a rich *Cash Settlement* at the end of the day. They also published allegations of me with Prostitutes at the Quays of Dublin on a regular basis, etc. etc.

What surprised me most of all was the veracity of the attitude of my alleged business colleagues and friends. The men who I considered *Real Men* or *Tough Men* were the first to run from me. I suppose in retrospect the NTDU were afraid of an expose on themselves, equally, the IFA. I still had my four luxury cars, a string of racehorses, manor house and farm as well as my wholesale meat business but I was very low mentally.

I had just had eight years of this in Australia and now the same two men had caused this in Ireland. It was a *Big Body Blow* but I decided to carry on regardless.

Within a couple of days of the articles I received the mobile phone account for two mobile phones that I had no knowledge of. These accounts exceeded Two Thousand Five Hundred Dollars. This fellow, Tony Crook had taken two phones in my name or rather my company's name and the calls all being itemised gave the full history of the expose.

He didn't realise I was going o receive the itemised account from Telecom. This showed a pattern of Crook ringing several of my advertising clients in Melbourne then calling the Police at *St. Kilda Road Police Station* and *Ringwood Police Station*. Even calls to *Gover's mobile telephone*. We had all the evidence against Crook. I have taken no action against Crook at this stage, yet I believe he had a *Good Smack* by a friend of mine one evening. I was once told by a very reliable Arab businessman *"The man who takes Revenge after ten years, is a man who has acted in Haste"*.

Mr Tony Crook will keep. Des Ekin will have to pay me via his masters through the Courts and we will see then how I deal with Mr Ekin. I imagine like Sgt David Gover. He can hand punishment out to improve his own By-line. We will have to see how he can take it himself. I have the rest of my life to deal with these people, if I deal with them at all. I would rather be like me, *Warts and All* than poor old Des Ekin dressed in ladies underwear, all dressed up and nowhere to go.

The one thing I had not done in Ireland was come to terms with my drinking. I had good staff, plenty of drivers, good friends in political organisations and I recall the first time I got drunk. This was followed by going to the local pub daily for four to five pints of Guinness. I did stay off the vodka and spirits. This caused problems at home not because of my behaviour but rather because *I Drank*, full stop.

I had a visit from Barbara my sister and while I was serving Wine and Sherry to Barbara and her daughter, I was drinking Scotch in my coffee cup. So even Amy *didn't know* I was drinking. I got very drunk the night Edwina came. I was very protected by good staff and this enabled me to drink and get away with it, yet with the drink came the *Unknown* fears as well as the *Real* fears and the insecurity. I played with AA but not *boots and all*. I was playing with fire, of course. Half measures avail us nothing.

The day we paid all our Insurance clients out, one young man called back to return his Insurance Disc. He seemed a nice young fellow and he promptly left. That evening as I went out to see my horses, I was assaulted by three masked men with knives. They had balaclavas on their heads and all I could see was their eyes.

It was so quick I thought it was all over and that I was a dead man. My life literally flashed before me as they knocked me down in my hall with a large window box from the front porch.

Amy was in the kitchen downstairs and Priscilla was upstairs. We were ushered into my Study. I realised at this stage they were the same three young men who had visited me in the afternoon. They knew where the safe was so I opened it and they took Twenty Three Thousand Dollars cash and various documents as well as Priscilla's jewellery.

I could tell they were frightened and hysterical so I knew, all I had to do was stay calm. They eventually left and we called the Police.

The nice young man who had returned his Insurance Disc was in fact caught by the police. He was kept for twenty four hours then released. As I knew who they were I made *contact* with them and arranged for them to return the papers and documents along with Priscilla's jewellery. In return I would not complain about the cash.

They, in fact, handed the documents and passports with Priscilla's jewellery into a Police Station in Dublin stating they had found it in a Park, but the cash was never returned. The local police showed me photos of the three men and knew who they were but in Ireland we have the presumption of innocence and I don't believe charges will ever be laid.

The local police had also read the articles in the *Sunday World* and were *not going to go overboard* to assist a man, who has been charged with Criminal Defamation against the Police, so I again had to cut my losses.

This raid had a devastating effect on Amy, Priscilla and myself. Had it been anywhere else but Ireland where violence has been *Par for the Course* for the last thirty years, it may have been a little easier. To say it was unsettling was an understatement. The police officer investigating the case seemed more interested in my business and activities after the *Sunday World* expose than he was in apprehending my assailants.

I immediately thought enough is enough. I have lost my cash flow business all because of Gover and Reid yet again. Now the police are looking into all of my activities. The Insurance Broker's Association were not giving me a *"Fair Go"* getting into the insurance market. It was the old adage of *"Give a Dog a Bad Name"*, yet again. I really didn't want to leave. I didn't want to stay. I didn't know what to do so I rang my brother Bruce in the Isle of Man and decided to pay him a visit. Bruce needed some short term assistance in his business and this would at least keep me busy.

Amy had met William, my eldest son in London as well as Tanya his charming young lady and they had spent an evening together when Amy was at the Ritz.

Alan my general handyman was quite competent to take care of the Horses and Pigs in my absence so it seemed a good idea to get away for a while. I flew to the Isle of Man and was met by Bruce. I was drinking Gin and Tonic and so was Bruce. We both went to a party that evening so very little business was spoken of.

The following day I had a splendid day with Bruce. He drove me all over the island. We saw all parts of it and Bruce told me the history of the place. I had visited it once before with Terri in 1979 for a couple of weeks. Bruce had lived there for several months as a Tax exile.

Bruce complete with his new top of the range Mercedes, was a very unhappy man. His second marriage had broken up and he was being treated as a *Manic Depressive,* taking Lithium on a daily basis. I could see myself in 1980, nineteen years earlier. Bruce had many problems and none of them were being dealt with. I tried to discuss his problems with him just like me in 1979, he was so callous. I could not reach him. My heart went out to him and I recalled the words of Mary Bolton that *Bruce had suffered far more than me* in our childhood.

My father never went to his wedding in 1969. There was no bloody reason for that. No matter if he approved of the Bride or not. He went to my wedding and he went to Bob's wedding. Bruce was the hardest worker and best knife man that ever walked this earth for my father and for many people after that. I wished I could have helped him but I couldn't reach him.

I raised the question with Bruce if there were any opportunities for me in his business. It appeared there was but nothing specific. He also would have to consult with his son, Jason. I believed any assistance I could be to Bruce, I would be better doing it from a distance. I missed my home and missed my Amy and Priscilla so on the Sunday, Bruce was playing golf all day, I flew back to Dublin.

By the Old Moulmein Pagoda, looking eastward to the Sea
"a Burma girl a'sitting", and I know she thinks of me
"Road to Mandalay" - Rudyard Kipling

Amy in Paris on my Houseboat
September 2000

Two Cabins of the Houseboat
2000

My Swans comes for Breakfast – Paris 2000

Sydney Harbour from my apartment
Elizabeth Bay, 2001

My return to Devon after 25 years, 1999

Amy and me at the Savoy,
London, 1998

Myself with my Sheep
Victoria, Australia 2001

Ray Gall with his "Hong Kong"
a Champion Mare

Robert Richter Q.C.
alias "The Red Baron"

Gerry Adams and Martin McGuinness
Belfast 1999

Amy & myself at the Premiere of
"The Man in the Iron Mask", Dublin 1998

The late Reuben Flescher and his lovely wife
Enjoying a quiet evening at
Ashleigh Hall, 1997

Kinsealy Hall, Dublin, 1998

*Henry Shannon, my Accountant
and myself in my study at Kinsealy Hall, 1998*

Priscilla at top of stairs, Kinsealy Hall, 1998

*Alan cleaning Amy's car at the
Stables, Kinsealy Hall, 1998*

*Priscilla and friend in Dublin
Premiere of "The Man in Iron Mask" 1998*

*Tracey my niece and her daughter at the
Stables, Kinsealy Hall, 1999*

Barbara and myself in Dublin
in 1998

Edwina and myself
in Dublin 1998

Priscilla, Amy and friend from Australia
at Fortnum & Masons, London 1998

My daughters, Priscilla and Edwina
Dublin 1998

Priscilla, Mum and Amy
Bournemouth 1999

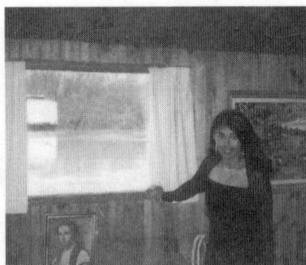

Amy on my Houseboat
Le Paniche Black Moon, Paris, 1999

*William and Tania and myself
at the Savoy, London 1999*

*Amy, Tania and William at the Ritz
London 1998*

*William and myself at the Lyric in
Soho London 1999*

William and myself at Savoy, London, 1999

*Amy, Priscilla, and William at the Ritz,
London 1998*

*Myself, Barbara, Tracey and Barbara's new
grand daughter at Fitzpatrick's Castle
Dublin 1998*

Priscilla and Siobhan at home in Victoria 2001

My five younger children: Priscilla, Siobhan, Daniel, David and Robert
Victoria 2001

Woodpas, my Stallion
Ireland 1998

Amy and Priscilla at Ashleigh Hall
with Racehorses, 1996

Daniel with a Racehorse
Victoria 2001

One of my Best Mares
Australia 2001

Daniel, David and Priscilla
with Broodmares 2001

David with a Racehorse
Victoria 2001

Courtesy of the "Records of the Week", The Tip Sheet, London

Original Song of the Week 8 May 2001

THE ROAD
Edwina Hayes

▶▶ Edwina is a young, London-based singer songwriter without publishing, label or management.

▶▶ She's another talent we discovered through the A&R Network CD (see Peter Whitehead's Forum).

▶▶ The Road – one of her first compositions – won *Song of the Year* at London's Virtually Acoustic Club last August.

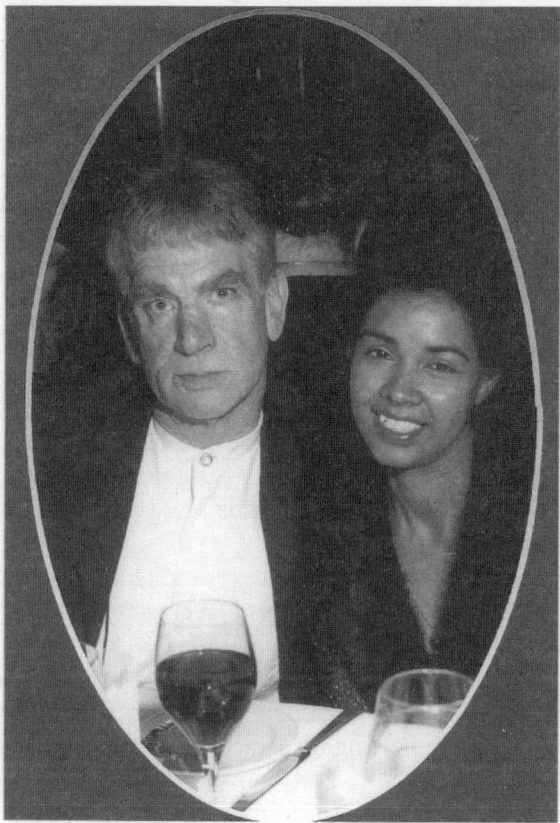

Amy and myself at Grand Hyatt Hotel, Melbourne
An Evening with Wilbur Smith – June 2001

CHAPTER TWENTY EIGHT

I decided for the New Year I would take a week and go down to my village in Devon. I didn't want to linger only to see the grave, look at the house and show it all to Amy. We also decided that on the way home we would call to Banstead in Surrey and Amy's old school, also her home in Plaistow in the East End of London.

I booked us in at the *Jamaica Inn* near Launceston. It had been twenty five years since my previous visit to the village and I still was not ready to meet anyone. The Jamaica Inn is a Fifteenth Century Coaching Inn and the basis for the book of smuggling by Daphne Du Maurier. I decided to take the Jaguar which was less conspicuous than the Rolls and quietly do my trip and face my ghosts.

Then the day before we were leaving Jason, Bruce's son, telephoned to say that he was bringing Bruce for a Fiftieth Birthday trip on the Thirtieth of December to stay in Dublin along with a couple of the company executives. This was fine but there was no way I was going to cancel my trip to Devon.

I arranged meeting for Bruce and Jason with some Irish Accountants, gave them a party on the night they arrived then handed the house and keys over to them to do with as they pleased as we took the ferry to England.

Much as I would have loved to spend a couple of days with Bruce, my plans were made weeks previously and his visit was on such short notice. Today, I wonder if poor old Bruce thinks I was deliberately shunning him but this was far from the case. I would do *anything* for him at his asking.

The trip to Devon and Cornwall was very brief but *"just nice"*. I showed Amy my village school, the church, my home and even the field gates I had built and the posts I had sunk were still in place after thirty five years. This was our own meadow at the back of the meat works.

I went to Larry House's farm and showed Amy the *"Little Well"* on the side of the road. We then visited the Crockers at Deckport, one of my first memories was going there to kill pigs during rationing days with my father. We were given a Royal welcome.

I showed Amy Okehampton, my senior school is now the police station. Then I took her to Dartmoor and Lydford Gorge. We spent New Year's Eve very quietly at the Jamaica Inn. The whole thing was partly spoiled by my problems in Ireland I knew I was going to have to face.

We came back via Clovelly and North Devon which is still very beautiful. Amy could not see the best of Devon at Christmas/New Year. It has to be seen in the Spring, however, we will go again.

We decided to call and see my mother in Bournemouth. I did not tell my mother of my visit as I knew she would wonder why I didn't visit various people and this was a very private visit for my wife and myself alone.

On the way to Bournemouth we stopped for Tea at Dorchester which, of course, was *Casterbridge* in the days of Thomas Hardy. My first wife Margaret's *Henshard* was, of course, the *Mayor of Casterbridge*. The visit to Bournemouth was brief and beautiful. I had never seen my mother's apartment before.

My mother's flat was situated right on the beach at Sandbanks, Poole in Dorset and the verandah opens out onto the water. It really is a beautiful spot. My brother Bob purchased one for my mother and one for his wife's parents. They are huge apartments with security parking in the basement and security doors as well as lifts between the floors. My brother Bob is a *Wonderful Son* to his parents, seeking no praise or reward. He just quietly does anything they require to make life pleasant.

We spent the Friday evening all day Saturday and Saturday evening with my mum. It was nice. I had not seen her since her previous visit to Australia at Christmas of 1996. We met Barbara's grandchildren who also doted on their Nanna, and all in all, it was very pleasant.

Sunday morning we made an early start for London and by ten o'clock we were in the village of Banstead where Amy had been taken as a small child from Burma. She lived there with her family. We visited their old home, school, and library. It was so lovely to see the excitement on Amy's face. We took several photos for Amy to show and give to her family in

Australia.

We were booked in the Savoy for the evening. This has always been my favourite hotel in London and I am always given a *River Suite*. Nothing to me is nicer in London than looking out over the Thames in the evening from a *River Suite* at the Savoy. No matter how long you are away, the staff at the Savoy always remember you.

The Savoy make all their own furniture and you can purchase this for your own home. The beds and Down pillows to me are second to none. The showers are like fire hoses. Everything is the *"last word"* and yet it is so very unassuming.

On the way to the city we were driving from Surrey through Clapham and *"low and behold"* we passed the very street where my son, William lives. This was twelve noon of the first Sunday of 1999. I decided we would call in and see him.

Tanya, William's fiancee was home and William had gone to Heathrow to return a car as they had just come back from their Christmas holidays in the North of England. Tania refused to let us go until William returned so we sat and had coffee and cigarettes until he arrived.

I had not seen William for ten years in 1988 when he came to Australia. When he came in the door I could only see my father in stature as a young man as well as his mother. He was a big man, small waist and massive arms and shoulders. It really was a very moving moment for me. He had filled out into a *Giant of a Man.*

We had many dealings on the telephone over the years but never sat down together or seen each other. It was arranged that Tanya and William would join us at the Savoy that evening and we would have dinner and drinks so that was an unexpected bonus to my trip. Amy had in fact met William for the first time on her previous trip to London at the Ritz.

Amy could not get over how similar we were, the way we slouched in a chair, held our cigarettes, even the bushy eyebrows, yet I was not conscious of this. I find today I have many of the mannerisms of my own father. You can pick your friends but you cannot pick your family.

So Amy and myself left and checked into the Savoy. We only threw our clothes into our suite and went off to explore the East End where Amy had been a Teenager and gone to her Senior School. We found the house, found the school and we couldn't believe that it was only a stone's throw from all my Indian clients from my days in Devon. How many times I must have gone past the school when Amy was a girl, I thought.

The Hogs Head is the favourite Watering Hole of Richard Harris. The last time I had seen Richard was at Gatwick Airport in 1970 when I was on my way to the Canary Islands after my Devon Assizes case. That day Richard was very drunk in the Departure Lounge. I was with Barbara and David at the time and this was prior to my first visit to Ireland.

Richard who was a giant of a man in those days was dressed in Dirty Jeans, unshaven and wearing the most amazing leather coat that almost touched the floor. This was the height of his *Hell Raising* days.

Damian, Richards' son went to Rockwell College a couple of years before William, my son. Richard never stopped drinking but was fortunate enough to be able to control his drinking to a point.

The evening at the Savoy went very well, only I had too much to drink. Mainly nerves and partly obsession and knowing I only had to go upstairs for bed. We went for drinks in the Hogs Head next door to Savoy Place and then being Sunday most of the restaurants were closed. Back in the hotel the same applied, the restaurants were closed also. London is a *Bad Place* to be on Sunday evenings yet wonderful on the other six nights.

William was quick to organise things. He told the night porter to get the room service menu and set it all up on tables in the foyer. The way William organised all of this was marvelous. Bu then, of course, I could see so *very much of myself* especially the way he had all the staff quite excited and keen to assist as though we were all going to a party. The whole evening was very enjoyable and I was very impressed with his young lady, Tania, who obviously thought the world of him. What I liked most of all was the way she was always touching William. Patting his shoulders, holding his hand.

The following day, Amy and myself set off for Liverpool and took the ferry back to Dublin. We called into Stoke Bruene, the village where I lived with Terri and had a couple of drinks on the canal. I showed Amy the White Pheasant that Bill Griffiths, one of my sheep buyers had shot in the 1970's. The bird was so unique it was stuffed and placed in the Plough Inn in a glass showcase.

At Liverpool we stayed in the Adelphi Hotel which is supposed to be the Best Hotel in Liverpool and was the subject of a long series of television documentaries called *"Hotel"*.

This was without doubt the worse service I had received on any hotel in my life. It began with having to park the car myself some half mile from the hotel. The Porter refusing to carry out bags in until I made a fuss. The Receptionist was disgraceful whether Racist as my Amy is Burmese or just bloody rude I don't know, or may be a lot of both. People were coming to the desk after us. She was talking over our shoulders at the other customers as though we were not there.

We eventually took the best suite available and it was dark and dowdy with a double bed, a small canopy classed as a *Four Poster*. It was a joke and very expensive joke at that.

We went to the Restaurant or rather the Bistro and whilst there were two staff at the counter, no one come to our table. After ten minutes I walked out in disgust. We were too tired to walk half a mile and get the car and change hotels, so we ordered two meals from Room Service. Amy got cold congealed Spaghetti and I got a cold, bland, Burger with cold French Fries, and the most awful coffee.

We thought may be the staff were just having a *Bad Night*. It takes an awful lot for me to complain but in the morning they were worse. I still have no idea why, we will never stay there again even Free of Charge. The main attraction of a holiday or a break is to be a little *pampered* and *spoilt*. This was just the *Pits*.

The ferry trip home was nice and quiet and I made my decision to quit Ireland and move back to the U.K. I knew all the damage that had been done by the Sunday World, yet what hurt most of all was the small minded attitude of all the people who read the articles. They branded me Guilty of all the allegations without the benefit of any Hearing.

So on the ferry I made some plans with Amy. Our

main concern was Priscilla being in her last year at School. Fortunately, Priscilla was in Australia for Christmas, so she was also going to be in for a culture shock when she returned home. Amy had pledged to see her through school so we had to honor this pledge Amy had made to herself.

It was with great sadness I drove home to Kinsealy Hall that day as we approached our wrought iron gates and the gate lodge at the end of the drive. We had made this place our little Heaven on Earth. I drove up the drive and looked at my horses, all the stables were newly painted and the house was literally the *last word* inside.

The finishing touches to the interior of the house were floor to ceiling mirrored wardrobes taking a full wall in each of the bedrooms. My coat of arms *"Hayes"* on the gates at the front of the drive, everything about Kinsealy was Bill Hayes.

It would be easy to say it was my alcoholism that caused the move but this would be Untrue. It was the attitude of the Irish people. *"The small minded people with their Churches and Steeples"* to quote Winston Churchill.

We organised a beautiful small flat in the suburb of Clontarf for Amy and Priscilla for the next six months while Priscilla finished school. I sent my Rolls and Amy's Mercedes across to my brother Bruce at Hull and we loaded all books, paintings, private papers, computer equipment, etc. into my own meat truck. I got a squad of some six men to give a hand and it was done in one day. I placed all the furniture into store and selected seven of my best Horses and the Stallion and had them transported to the U.K.

CHAPTER TWENTY NINE

Bruce had storage space for my truck and private goods and chattels. When I say goods and chattels, we had a further twenty foot lorry load of books and paintings. Amy drove the Jaguar and I drove the lorry complete with Priscilla's two cats, my small dog. We said farewell to our beautiful home for nine months, Kinsealy Hall. It was snowing and freezing in the evening so when we got off the ferry in England, our destination being Hull, we stopped overnight at a roadside hotel on the M62.

I could handle this but for my poor darling Amy. It was Hell once more, the sense of insecurity with me. At least we had enough furniture for two houses and paintings for six houses and each other. My God how I loved my wife that day in January 1999.

Like Naomi in the Book of Ruth in the Bible, my Amy would have followed me to the ends of the earth. We arrived in Hull the following afternoon and Jason, Bruce's son, very kindly put us up for the night.

On the Sunday not wishing to impose on these young people we took room at the local hotel in Beverley. I had arranged temporary accommodation for my horses at the Beverley Racecourse, which being a flat racing course, was closed for the winter.

I was very impressed with Jason my nephew and his lady, Caroline, who is now a Barrister.

The warmth and kindness they showed me that day and the time since have quite honestly overwhelmed me. I knew I could do business with Jason but we were too much alike to work together.

We left Alan to take care of the Kinsealy Hall until I handed it back to Ffyfes and I have never been so disappointed or shocked as I was with that young man. He stripped Kinsealy Hall of all the gates of the farm, some Twenty Thousand Pounds. He stripped all the mirrored fitted wardrobes Twenty Thousand Pounds and even stole the cooker, fridge and the beautiful antique mantelpiece. He of course denied it yet he was the one left in charge and knew every inch of my Property.

This was a *Savage Blow* by a man who had spent most of his life in prison and to whom I had been more than Generous. I leave God to deal with Alan as he sees fit. What really annoyed me was that I was placed in a very embarrassing spot with Fyffes.

We settled into the hotel and had a couple of weeks prior to Priscilla's return from Australia. It was quite obvious that Jason did not want me involved in the business that was okay. So we looked for a farm property in North Yorkshire to get started again.

We found the perfect farm with stables, farm buildings and twenty five acres through Strutt & Parker, the Real Estate Agents. So I sent the horses on ahead.

We drove to the small village of Grewelthorpe, some three miles from the farm and had lunch in the local pub. We inquired about accommodation in the local area.

We were fortunate and found a Sixteenth Century furnished holiday cottage two up and two down, right in the pub yard or car park and could have possession immediately. So of course we took this and settled in. Amy then had to go back to Clontarf and await Priscilla's return. Poor Priscilla left a *country mansion* and was coming home to a small flat. No matter, it was the best we could do at the time.

The Monday after Priscilla's return home I had problems with Strutt and Parker. They refused to make certain improvements on the house as agreed. I received a very *High Handed* phone call on my mobile phone driving from Hull to North Yorkshire and the result was I told Strutt and Parker to put the farm where the *Monkey puts his Nuts* (up their Jumper!).

So I had eight horses in the stables, feed purchased and now had to vacate. The manager of Strutt and Parker called me back, apologised and said he would meet my demands. I am a great believer in Fate. I was not comfortable with the deal and *let it go*. That was that.

I organised a lorry and moved my horses and found Livery for my Stallion with two girls, who were very good with horses in the village. Then I was fortunate to find the most beautiful Barn Conversion Cottage I have ever set foot in.

The cottage had everything, Tudor Beams, right down to the Hunting Scenes on all the Crockery and even the Ash Trays. It was *Divine* and just big enough for the three of us. I couldn't wait to tell Amy. The next weekend Amy came over and she also fell in love with our little Holly Tree Cottage. We even had Peacocks in the garden again. It was all I could have wished for and with two phone lines and fax, I was ready for business.

I assisted Bruce in preparing the sale of his Property Portfolio. *Then came up with the idea of doing Refugee accommodation for Asylum Seekers. I made overtures to the Home Office in London and various councils in Yorkshire to find the man responsible in Bruce's town of Hull. He knew Bruce well and played golf with him. I made all the introductions from London to Leeds and gave it all to Bruce. This was January, February and March of 1999.* I was delighted to learn within less than a year Bruce had succeeded in signing contracts with various councils and now has all his properties, formerly Student Accommodations, full of refugees and asylum seekers.

I knew I could be of assistance to Bruce more so from a distance than working in his company. Bruce was very generous to me financially and this gave me enough to go on. So to quote the Baird of Stratford, *"It's an Ill Wind that Blows no Good"*. I am very Happy for Bruce.

I couldn't hack being alone without Amy and was spending lunchtimes in the village pub, sleeping in the afternoons and my evenings in the village pub. I was drinking cider and not spirits by the end of the evenings I was always *"well on"*. With drink comes *Trouble*. One weekend in late February on a Friday I was drinking until about three o'clock in the morning in the Pub as I was going to collect Amy at Leeds Airport on the Saturday morning at nine o'clock. I was stopped by the Police for not wearing a seat belt.

These were two nice young officers and even I could smell the booze on me. I was running late having overslept. I hadn't shaved, wore the same clothes as the previous night obviously with booze spilt on them and of course was arrested.

I was taken to the Police Station. The Police were very decent, called Amy at Leeds Airport and she came to Harrogate by taxi. I was Bailed to appear in Court some time in March. So I had been back in England only two months after an absence of fifteen years and back to my old tricks, drink driving, etc. etc.

Making matters worse, less than a month later, I flew from Leeds to Belfast and *couldn't even see my car let alone drive it*. This was one o'clock on that Saturday afternoon. I tried to drive to the border, got lost, and was seeing *double*. Why oh why I didn't stop I still don't know. I have *never* been so drunk. I managed to get to Lisburn and was pulled by the Police. They had seen me on the motorway cameras for the last fifteen miles.

I refused to take a breathalyser knowing full well I was three to four times over the legal limit. No matter what anyone says about the RUC, they treated me so **Bloody well**. It was a credit to them. I again rang Amy who came by taxi and had to drive me home. I was so ashamed yet I knew I could have killed many other people as well as myself. The insanity of driving on the motorway, seeing double. No matter what I did, slap my face, bang my head, I saw double all the way from Belfast City to Lisburn. *I deserved five years imprisonment* for that and I am the first to admit it. *I was a very stupid, wicked, selfish man.*

My drinking was now well out of control. My stability gone. My Big House gone. My staff gone. My protection gone all because of *Tony Crook, Des Ekin, David Gover* as well as *Bob Reid*. These four men had stripped me of everything once again.

I had furniture in store in Dublin, also in store in Hull, cars in Dublin, Hull and North Yorkshire. A cottage in North Yorkshire, flat in Dublin. I was all so very very confusing and costing me a fortune. I broke down and put by hands up in despair to Amy. I couldn't go on alone much as I loved my cottage, without her I was so wretched and alone. We had been as one for six years. She was a part of me yet we had only three to four months to wait to finish Priscilla's school.

I decided to move into the flat in Clontarf. Even now I have to *laugh at myself*. We put a single bed in the kitchen and I slept there whilst Priscilla and Amy had the bedroom. It was *rough and ready* but it was home with my two girls. I dread to think what poor old Priscilla thought. The whole flat was the size of our drawing room at Kinsealy Hall but it was home. This is all I could say.

I went back to AA on a regular basis and got a job with the Advertising Company in Dublin. Everyone jumped on the bandwagon at Kinsealy. Partners in horses accused me of stealing their horses, my Insurance clients who had been repaid accused me of not having them covered at the time I had insured them. The investigating officer of my break-in at Kinsealy Hall when I was robbed at knife point now wanted to question me. Never mind he hadn't arrested my assailants, despite the fact he knew who they were.

My bankers, trades people all believed the *Sunday World* story and now were all jumping on the band wagon of my *"Moonlight Flit"*. There I was, this **mega rich multi-millionaire** (Sunday World) *"King Con"* living on a single bed of my wife's kitchen, rather than in my cottage alone. This is the insecurity, insanity, fear of the drinking alcoholic. *Poor me, Poor me, Pour me a Drink.*

I was coming home from work in my second week. I had earned about Six Thousand Dollars in Commission selling advertising space. I knew I was only *treading water*. I called into the Irish Permanent at Fairview and filled in a form to withdraw some money as my account was held at Malahide. The transaction seemed to be taking too long a time, the cashier talking to his seniors and making phone calls. I left without my money and climbed into the Jaguar with Amy. I can small *Trouble* today at *one hundred paces.*

I told Amy something was terribly wrong. I believed they were trying to delay me in the Bank, the way you see in the movies. On the way home I happened to ring Henry Shannon, my accountant to see how he was getting on with my VAT claim. Henry told me how he was proceeding and said, *"Oh, by the way Bill, a Police Officer from Malahide was on the phone looking for you. I said you were in England but gave him Amy's address at the flat".* I said, *"Okay, Henry, that's fine".*

I turned to Amy and said, *"The reason for the delay in the Bank was to do with the Police. We must not go home, take me to Clontarf Castle and drop me there. You go home and I'll ring you".* Amy followed my instructions and I sat in the

Clontarf Castle Hotel with a pot of coffee.

Amy had been home fifteen minutes when the investigating police sergeant from Malahide duly arrived at the flat, looking for me. Amy told him she had just taken me to the Bank in Fairview and driven me to the airport. I was well aware now of the reasons for the delay at the Bank. The police had visited the Bank and said, *"If Bill Hayes comes into any of your branches, telephone me and hold him there until we arrive"*. This was again a police officer in his own private *"Quest for Glory"*. Now I had become the centre of his investigations once more based on the *Sunday World*. So I got out of Ireland by *gut instinct* and fifteen minutes to spare.

I telephoned two members of a *"Political Organisation"* to come to the Hotel and assist me. They arrived within thirty minutes. I had made some very strong allies in Ireland over the years.

These men went back to the flat and collected two suitcases and my brief case and I drove for the border that night. I was aware no general alarm was going to be out at this stage, yet it was still a little nerve racking. The Boys escorted me in a tail car all the way to the Border.

I hit Newry in Northern Ireland about nine o'clock that evening and pulled into a roadside pub. I had no idea what I was going to do, go back to the cottage in Yorkshire was the obvious choice. Yet I knew I was going from the Frying Pan into the Fire with my drinking problem.

I rang Amy and told her I was safe and booked into the Canal Court Hotel in Newry. This hotel had just been completed as a £7 million project and was a beautiful hotel in facilities and services everything about it. I had always known Newry as a *"No Go"* area in the Troubles starting in 1969. From my first visit to Ireland in 1972, Newry was a *Blocked Off* town. It was really wonderful to see all the barricades gone and people prospering and getting on with normal lives. I have always loved the openness of the Ulster people. Comparing Belfast to Dublin is rather like London to Manchester. In Belfast, they call a Spade a Shovel. It's very endearing.

Amy agreed to get Alan to bring her and Priscilla up the following morning and we would all breakfast together. As I write this and think of all the things my poor Amy had to do, it fills me with a great *Tenderness and Love* for her. I am really so *Very Proud* of her as a *Woman of Substance*.

We had a wonderful breakfast and booked into the hotel for a week while we decided what we were now going to do. The only thing that was vital to us was that we get Priscilla through the next four months of School to take her Final Exams. It was wonderful to be in a luxury suite with my wife again after two weeks of my single bed in the kitchen.

CHAPTER THIRTY

Amy fell in love with Newry immediately. It was so wonderful to see the town fully open. County Down is one of the prettiest parts of Ireland with the Mountains of Mourne and the beaches of Down. *"Where the Mountains of Mourne come down to the Sea".*

I managed to find a brand new five bedroom house in the small village of Rostrevor. Rostrevor is a coastal village that sits underneath the Mountains of Mourne and a beautiful little quiet spot. My house was next door to the Financial Controller of ABP. This was the very man who had sacked Copass from Clones on behalf of Larry Goodman.

Amy and myself brought enough of the Kinsealy furniture to furnish the house and the rest we left in store. We had decided that we would give up the flat in Dublin, place Priscilla in a Hotel on Monday to Thursday nights and Amy would deliver her and collect her in the car, to be home at weekends. Priscilla had the comforts of the Hotel by night and School by day.

We settled into village life quite easily. All in all it was a good move. There seemed no point in keeping the cottage in Yorkshire that we were hardly using by this stage. So we decided to give this up also. Priscilla settled back into school and whilst this was not Kinsealy, at least it gave us a chance to make some plans and decisions.

I was contacted by a *"Political Organisation"* to help them move a large shipment of cash to the U.K. This money was to be laundered in England and returned to Ireland within two years. I contacted Bruce initially but he didn't really have the facilities for a transaction of this kind so I set up an operation in London to deal with the money.

I travelled to London a couple of times in order to arrange offices for the money deal and on my return home one day in April, I was accosted at my home by two Dublin villains.

Pierce Moran, one of these men was six feet four inches tall and weighed about twenty stone. The other man, Kevin McGarry, was a flash little back street Dublin boy. The result of this visit was they were going to take me by force back to the South of Ireland rather like Bounty Hunters. Pierce Moran was executed in August of 2000 with a bullet in the head for an alleged contravention of rules laid down by the Provisional IRA.

I called the Police or the RUC who warned them off. However, they stayed parked at the end of our road and followed us wherever we went. This was quite a horrendous experience in view of all we had already been through with the armed robbers at Kinsealy Hall.

I contacted my Political friends who had these two men removed physically and they were sent back to Dublin pronto with their tails between their legs. The only person who knew the address of our house was Alan, the handyman from Kinsealy who we suspected of plundering Kinsealy Hall. With this latest event, I had no doubt he was no longer to be trusted.

Whilst we could live like this with twenty four hours *Protection*, it was not the life I wanted or needed and I made the decision with Amy that we would quietly drive to England, take a look around and find somewhere to settle down. Yet in retrospect, each time I moved, I was going *down the rungs of the ladder* as opposed to going up.

I had been shipping horses to the U.K. and was very interested in getting back into the sheep and calf industry which was going through a bad time. So the trip to London was a two fold trip.

We took the ferry from Belfast to Liverpool and drove to London. Stayed for one night in the city and started looking for properties with London prices and the small apartments for Big Money, plus parking our cars and giving us the space we needed, London was a *No No*.

I had heard a lot about Kent being the *"Garden of England",* yet had only had dealings there in the 1970's when I was flying calves to Italy from Manston.

Amy and myself decided to drive down to Kent and have a look around. I think also why Kent was in my mind was the television program *"The Darling Buds of May"* which was set in Kent in the 1950's. There is no doubt why they call Kent the Garden of England, it really is a beautiful County.

We drove to Maidstone, Ashford, then Canterbury.

Canterbury was beautiful and I remembered my father had been there during the War. My father was called up in the Royal Marines at Deal in Kent and was also stationed at Canterbury.

We found a nice house in the village of Ash between Canterbury and Dover or, in fact, very close to Sandwich Bay and Deal in Kent. We were four miles from the beach with a lovely old Kentish house, nice gardens and swimming pool and the weather to most certainly enjoy all the facilities.

The village of Ash was small and only a couple of shops, couple of pubs, Rugby Club. Just a nice small Kent village. Once more we had no trouble settling in and Priscilla flew home at weekends as her school year was very nearly completed.

Amy lost no time in setting up an office and I set up a network of livestock buyers to buy Calves from Cornwall to Scotland. The Government Scheme to purchase calves was coming off on the Thirty First of July 1999 so Calves were going to become worthless.

By setting up a marketing and slaughtering network, I saw the opportunity to make an awful lot of money.

The lovely thing about my calf business is that I was now buying calves from all my cattle markets in Devon and Cornwall where I began as a Boy. So now I really had gone *Full Circle*. Atlantic Meat Company within a very short space of time became the leading Calf Buyers in England, Wales, Scotland and I was buying calves for One Pound to Four Pounds, less than I paid thirty five years previously as a Boy. The same calves in 1963 were costing me Six or Seven Pounds.

I spoke to my Buyers every night from Devon, Somerset, Wales, Cheshire, Scotland and recorded the numbers they had purchased and gave the instructions for the following day. This was a *Big Gamble* yet I was at least doing what I had always wanted from being a small boy.

I took Amy to Smithfield Meat Market early one morning. Smithfield was where I had begun. After a recent £20 million face lift there were only two to three of the original traders left in the market and it was definitely *No Good* as a sales vehicle, only as a dumping ground.

I met John Brewster who had handled my first sheep

and calves thirty five years earlier when I was a boy. John put me in touch with some of the current London Boning Halls and Transport Companies. He was now the President of the Market Association, still the same *Smart City Gent* he was when I was a Boy. John had been a guest at my first wedding in 1967. It was good to be back, nice to be back and I was now **back in style** and back with a Vengeance. I was confident with Amy by my side, life would turn out well.

The largest and most reputable Indian/Pakistani meat company in London were based in Wembley. Amy had met the Company Accountant at the Ritz and try as we may, they would not handle our sheep. The main reason being they were inundated with suppliers from all over the country as their reputation for *paying* was very good, also very unusual in the Pakistani community.

We drove to see them one morning after visiting Smithfield and whilst driving through Willesden, Wembley, Ealing, I was amazed how the Pakistani community had not only grown in thirty years but became so very Prosperous. In Southall, it is like being in Karachi or Lahore, even the underground station is signed in Arabic.

I asked Amy to write down the names of all the butchers shops as we drove past and by the time we had left London, we had a list of some forty butchers. Based on the assumption each shop would use thirty to forty sheep per week, there was a ready market for one thousand Sheep per week. So when I got home I rang them all.

Telephone selling meat has always come easy to me and getting back into the business after twenty eight years was no great difficulty. I began to purchase live sheep from Wales and the West Country, have them killed on contract and supplied the Pakistani community. We soon built a good business in West London and North London. So as opposed to using a contract transport company, I purchased my own Mercedes Truck to do all my own deliveries followed by a second truck.

Amy took care of all the administration side of the business and every Friday she would go up to London and collect the payments, mainly in cash and all in all, we had again built a successful little business. I was again selling my Hides and Skins to Exeter Hide and Skin Company. This was part of the Vestey organisation in my early days in Devon. John Ross, the Managing Director, had been a very good friend to me and was, in fact, my son William's Godfather. He also carried Margaret to the grave as one of the pallbearers. John's son Paul was now the Managing Director and since the demise of Vestey, they were now a Private Company and the largest private Fellmongers in England.

Once we had the North of London completed it seemed obvious to go back to the East End where the very large communities of working class Pakistanis still live in Upton Park, Ilford, Dagenham, Walthamstow, and Bow. Ironically, Upton Park is next door to Plaistow where my Amy went to school and Upton Park Market next to the West Ham Football Ground was where she used to go shopping as a girl. Now here she was back selling meat.

One Saturday we went to Green Street and Queens Market, again taking shop telephone numbers and bumped into Cyril Mallon from Ireland. Cyril had been in the Indian mutton business for about two years. Cyril was also a Recovering Alcoholic and a very genuine man. Cyril's story is not unlike my own.

We had coffee with Cyril and it was agreed I would market sheep for him as well as my own sheep. Cyril was in a *"Big Way"* of business handling a couple of thousand sheep each week. Cyril also put Amy on the payroll to keep the records and collect the payments, so again, we were back on our feet.

I purchased a new Mercedes and took delivery. This was financed by the N.F.U. (National Farmer's Union) Finance. *Life was pretty good.* The job was exhausting as Cyril's trucks arrived from Ireland in the early hours of the morning and I had to meet them with my truck, select my orders, write the delivery notes, returning to Kent by eleven o'clock each morning. Then conduct my own business.

I did these hours for three months and eventually built a good business for Cyril as well as a good business for myself.

Amy's job was also exhausting doing three days in London driving through the London traffic, collecting the money from our clients and giving receipts. The Pakistanis are all natural *"hagglers"* and this was a long winded job but all in all it was very exhausting.

The strain of all the moves, all the Trouble in Ireland began to show on Amy and, of course, tell on the marriage. Making matters worse I was doing nothing about my drinking. Cyril being an alcoholic himself could tell when I had one drink let alone a skin full. I got to the point I was terrified to take his phone calls, so at least, I was feeling guilty about my drinking.

With Amy being gone three days a week, my being at work five nights a week, I began to drink at the village Pub and went straight back on the vodka. I was a great procrastinator in my drinking. I had not drawn one penny off Cyril from day one. I had wanted to build the business first. Then my past began to catch up with me yet again.

Cyril was an Undischarged Bankrupt and, therefore, I was handling all the money. I arranged to get a second Mercedes from N.F.U, the finance was granted and I was awaiting delivery. Cyril couldn't get finance because of his bankruptcy. I agreed to give him my Mercedes and he would make the payments via myself.

With this arranged we duly met Cyril and gave him the car *(worth Seventy Five Thousand Dollars)* one Saturday in late August 1999. Cyril drove home with a friend of his. I received a phone call two days later from Cyril who told the man driving the car had no License and had been stopped by the Gardai in Kells, County Meath. The car was impounded pending investigation of the vehicle.

At the mention of Bill Hayes, *Red Lights began to flash across Ireland.* In no time at all the Investigating Officer from Malahide was talking to N.F.U. Finance telling them about the *"Sunday World"* and Australia, etc. etc.

The net result was that N.F.U. cancelled my agreements on both cars. Worse than this, put me on a ***Bank Black List*** so I was told by my bankers, Midland Bank and Barclays Bank to close my accounts, despite being more than Sixty Thousand Dollars in credit in both banks. This was followed by American Express cancelling my Credit Card. So there I was, fifty two years old in September of 1999 and could no longer trade.

I had by this time opened a depot in Barking, my staff were all Pakistanis. I no longer had to go to London each night as the business was running itself. I handed the whole business over complete with my two trucks to Cyril. I just gave it all away. I had a lot of time for Cyril and being a fellow alcoholic had no problem in giving him a lift in his business.

Amy was to stay employed by Cyril and I decided to move to Paris, once again for a *"Fresh Start"*. This time I was going to go alone. Amy had had enough of following me to no avail and was now considering either staying in London or going back to Australia where her family and her two sons reside. So effectively, Amy and myself had *Run out of Road* and I was very quietly *Running out of Countries.*

I was tired physically and mentally, grossly overweight and drinking yet again. I gave all the furniture to Amy and kept the Rolls Royce and two suitcases and walked out on everything. I was secure in Amy's future as she had a job with Cyril, and all the furniture and the Mercedes Sports. It seemed the decent thing to do.

I had a meeting at the Savoy in London or rather three meetings on the same day to split up my business. I also met a Buyer for a considerable amount of my stocks of veal. The results were as follows:

Cyril was to have the depot in Barking along with all the Pakistani clients, my trucks, staff and ten tonnes of Veal I had in stock. The price would be fixed at a later date as Cyril also owed me for three months work setting the business up and I owed Cyril some Twenty Five Thousand Dollars in cash I had taken from the business.

Ted Haste, a Calf Dealer from Devon, I had done business with in the 1960's as well as in 1999 was to take over the calf business using the slaughtering facilities at Hatherleigh, four miles from my village in Devon.

Routley and Brown, two young men from Devon who had been supplying me sheep, I introduced to Karachi Halal Meats of Luton. This introduction was at the Savoy and they were to supply Karachi Halal with some four humdred ewes and two hundred lambs per week. I organised the slaughtering facilities and was to get One Pound per head for each sheep giving me One Thousand Five Hundred Dollars weekly.

There was a company of Kebab manufacturers from Essex prepared to take a further ten tonnes of my veal stock and pay me c.o.d.   This would give me a small capital to help in Paris with starting again.

The negotiating took all day and the drinks bill exceeded Three Thousand Dollars of which I did not pay one penny. Everyone was happy. Only Cyril, as I was not going to take Cyril into my confidence until I had completed all my negotiations. Everything going well I had been on vodka all day. I took a taxi to my depot in Barking for a final look and then got leg less drunk. *Poor me, Poor me, Pour me a drink* and arrived home in this state by taxi from London some eighty miles.

Amy now had a habit of going very cold when I was drunk or drinking and she just switched off and very little was said.

My Rolls Royce was in Guernsey. I had sent it to my brother Bob in July, not realising the roads of Guernsey made it impossible to drive. Bob agreed that I pick it up and booked me the ferry from Guernsey to France.

We hired a Bentley for the week and Amy drove me to Exeter in Devon to take the plane to Guernsey. I had booked a room at the Royal Clarence Hotel in Exeter and would depart England for the final time from my home County. Many times Margaret and myself had afternoon tea at the Royal Clarence as our bank was only around the corner. I also have memories with my meeting with James Black, at the Royal Clarence during my Devon Assizes case.

The business of Atlantic Meats took an awful lot of controlling. We received phone calls on our mobile phone on the way to Devon from Ted Haste, our man in Cheshire could no longer kill our calves, a phone call from young Brown that the first load of sheep for Karachi Halal had been rejected. A phone call from Cyril he needed cash for the Bank. *"What could I do?"*. I turned the mobile off and thought that like learning to swim the first thing you need to do is go in the water. These men all had to now manage without me. Atlantic Meats could run without me.

The trip with Amy and Priscilla was most unpleasant. Amy was very bitter that our relationship had to end up this way with my going off yet again and she couldn't see any future in us any more. She was *Bitter* having to leave Australia and now she would have to go back and start again alone. Priscilla was desperate to get back to Australia. For my own part, I could not get away from both of them fast enough. I was tired of the past, tired of trying to cope with the present and very apprehensive about the future. All I really wanted was to be alone.

We arrived at the hotel in the middle of a blazing row. I was flying at nine o'clock the next morning. The atmosphere was so bad I left half way through the meal and went to bed. The next morning the girls left and I flew to Guernsey.

The taxi driver who took me to Exeter Airport was an ex Butcher and was telling me he used to work for the Vestey Group. I asked him could he remember George Downes. He told me George had taken over the Vestey Farm and Abattoir at Longdown and was still involved in the meat business.

I was delighted to hear this and wished I had the time to call and see Mr Downes after all these years.

Bob collected me and took me to his home. This was our first meeting in seventeen years and we had a wonderful time talking of old times. His home is perched on the top of a cliff with a lovely meadow running down to the Channel and the views are magnificent. It was just the sort of place to spend the winter of your life in retirement as Bob was doing. Here was I, heading off for yet another new adventure.

I took the ferry to *St Malo* that evening and I arrived in France about ten o'clock at night I found a small hotel and went out for drinks that evening. I was not too bad in drinking moderately, the mobile phone never stopped so I kept it switched off.

The following day I drove to Paris and a hundred kilometres from Paris, the Head Gasket went on the Rolls Royce. This was the last thing I needed so I got the car towed to a garage and took a taxi to Paris and found a small a hotel in Montmarte.

I rang Amy and there were more problems. Cyril was frantic and wanted to know where I was. He had not stopped to realise how much I had given him and thought I had run off with all his money, rather than given him a considerable amount of my money. He turned up at the house friendly at first but then turned nasty and demanded that Amy take money out of the account and give it to him. He took the mail from Ash when Amy was not there and *Terrorised* Amy.

So she got a removalist to come over and organised to have the furniture stored at a warehouse. Then Young Brown turned up at the house in Ash and was demanding to wait on the door till I came home. Poor Amy, after all the problems in Ireland was again terrified and fled to my mother in Bournemouth. All the plans I had made for her went down the drain.

People say how can a man walk out on a business, home, beautiful wife, Rolls Royce and Mercedes. The answer is I was again a drinking alcoholic. I believed now I would never get well.

Amy agreed to bring me the Mercedes Sports Car to Paris and I met her from the Ferry in Cherbourg. We drove to Paris at leisure taking two days. When Amy saw Montmarte the Red Light District and me living in the heart of it, she saw Red also, *pardon the pun.* I was also drinking. All Amy wanted to do was leave. I had been on the booze for three to four days and was very haggard from it. I ordered Amy a taxi to the airport and she flew back to my mother's home in Bournemouth, eventually moving to London and going back into the workforce.

This was like 1987 again. This time, the Seventeenth day of September 1999. Whilst I was driving through Montmarte and I saw a sign saying *Drugs and Alcohol.* I drove around the block and parked the car. This was in the eighteenth district of Paris. I went into this office that dealt in drugs and alcohol rehabilitation and asked for a list of AA meetings. This was *not* the sort of thing I have *ever done before*. I was given a phone number of the Secretary of the American Church in Paris and told they have meetings every night of the week.

This again, was a *miracle*. How I spotted the sign, why I went to the meeting, all I know is from that first meeting I have never had a drink to this day. I know and knew AA worked. I can't say why that day I was ready to quit. I had plenty of money, good cars, I could drink if I wished. I also had *No Hope* of getting well. It was as easy as that. Once again, I surrendered to AA, the simple program for complicated people. Then the second miracle, thanks to AA, yet again. I was *Home* at last.

I went to the American Church on the Saturday evening at the usual time of half past eight and there was no meeting. On my way back to the car I picked up an American (French) magazine and reading this in my hotel in the early hours of Sunday morning, saw a five bedroom Houseboat advertised that was moored on the Seine at Port Marly. I thought to myself this is worth following up.

I rang the advertised number the next day and made arrangements to look at the Houseboat that day. The owners were an Australian couple and we negotiated a lease and I duly paid three months rent in advance. The telephones, fax could be installed the following Tuesday. Subject to this I would move in on the Wednesday.

The couple who owned the Houseboat had done an excellent job on the main structure. The main saloon or living room was thirty feet long and as wide as the craft. There was a laundry room, shower room, toilet, everything one would find in a very large flat in Paris with five bedrooms. I converted two of these into offices and still had two guest rooms. My bed was a double bed built in the same position as a top bunk with a ladder leading to it and wardrobes underneath.

I installed cable television, Internet, E-mail, fax and phones and had the most unusual but wonderful little office in Paris. I could be in the city in twenty minutes. Plenty of space to park my car. No neighbours to trouble me and water all around me. I was visited every morning by a couple of Swans and their two young Cygnets for morning bread.

I very quickly fell into the French lifestyle of collecting my daily baguette from the local Boulanger and set out to do some regular exercises, lose some weight, go to AA a couple of times a week and rebuild my life. There is no doubt I missed Amy yet I was not prepared to go back down *Memory Lane*. My only hope of getting well was to be alone.

I set about exploring the Paris meat trade again and

found a nice little niche for myself supplying the Black Community with English and Irish Mutton. I opened a depot in Rungis Market and contracted all of my transport.

My working week was ten o'clock at night to three o'clock in the morning, five nights a week or twenty five hour week and I was soon handling one thousand head of sheep per week, then two thousand. Just enough to keep me in the manner to which I had been accustomed, e.g. my Rolls Royce and five-star hotels and always have cash in my pocket.

Amy came to stay prior to Christmas and spent some six weeks on my Houseboat. This was a very sad time for her. She did not want to be involved in yet another business, nor did she want to stay in France. She made it very clear that she was considering returning to Australia.

I decided to let her have the master bedroom and I moved into one of my guest rooms. Priscilla went back to Australia for Christmas and Amy and Priscilla made their own plans to return. They eventually left from Paris in early February 2000.

There was no *Big Drama*. The furniture was already en route from the U.K. I took Amy to Charles de Gaulle Airport, kissed her goodbye and that was the end of that. Driving back to Paris I had a mixture of feelings, Sadness and Relief. I believe the relief outweighed the sadness.

Madame Bacardi, formerly Madame Charles de Galle was extremely helpful to me. Sandra had a male secretary called John Murphy, who was originally from Ireland.

John is one of the most cultured men I have ever met and now works for me full time running the Meat Business and liaising with my clients as he is bi-lingual.

I can be found most lunchtimes at Fouquets on the Champs Elysee or at George V Hotel in Avenue George V, usually having coffee with members of AA or my business colleages.

Some American friends of mine and myself opened our own small AA group in St Germaine En Laye. Prior to having a meeting room we held the meetings on my Houseboat. I got a great kick from this and now it's a very successful group up and running every week. So this is, of course, how AA grows based on *Attraction* rather than *Promotion*. Had someone told me twenty years ago I would have starting my own AA group, I would have said *"Yes, and Pigs might Fly"*.

Regarding the allegations against me in Ireland, I wrote to the Officer concerned and quoted the words of poor old Brendan Beehan who died of Chronic Alcoholism at the age of forty two.

Brendan wrote to the Bow Street London Magistrates Court from Dublin where he was wanted for Breaching Bail on a Drunk and Disorderly charge.

"Your Worship, you have found me Guilty in my absence, and Sentanced me in my absence. Therefore, will you kindly **Serve the Sentence** *for me in my absence. Yours, Brendan Beehan"*.

God grant me the Serenity
To Accept the things I cannot change
The Courage to change the things I can
And the Wisdom to know the difference.

It's hard to put the Cork back in the Bottle

APPENDIX

I sent a Draft of this book to John Morris who was the Electrical Contracting son of Mrs Morris mentioned in my earliest memories.

John reminded me that Joe Skinner's taxi was a Hillman and not a Humber. He went onto say he thought I was rather hard on my father.

John recalled my father moving to Devon after the war. He believed the war had a great effect on Bob, my father.

My father's Brigade of the Royal Marine Commando's had to live off the land in remote Snowdonia preparing for the Norwegian landings in 1940.

My father also told John that any man who panicked or couldn't handle the strain of these landings, had to be thrown overboard, to protect the Operation. This was a very sobering thought, having to murder your own comrades in the interest of King and Country.

John went onto relay many amusing stories of Bob, my father, and the village people, all engaged in the Black Market of meat during Rationing days. John mentioned the various ways they avoided Constable North, whilst moving contraband. There was one butcher who sent a hearse to London each week with the coffin full of prime cuts of meat for the best London's hotels.

John suggested my father's business failure was caused by being in a hurry to catch up in his six missing years of the War. There was no way he could make money, selling ten pence worth of meat per customer which were the Meat Rationing rules.

I thank John for enlightening me to these facts as this information was new to me despite my knowing my father had a *Bad War*.

John also informed me that Richard Bendyshe, the local young squire, died early in the year 2000. I would dearly loved to have seen Richard again after thirty years and thank him personally for his support to Margaret and myself.

WILLIAM HAYES
Paris, France
13 November 2000

CONCLUSION
Where are they now?

LARRY HOUSE, *my School Friend as a little boy, is farming in South Devon.*

DAVID WILLIS, *my School Friend, in Secondary School has led a very successful life in business and now lives in my own little village of Exbourne with his beautiful Canadian wife and small son.*

GEORGE DOWNES, *the South West Area Manager for Vestey is living at Longdown, Exeter and still involved in Meat and Farming. I was in a taxi going to Exeter Airport and the driver being an ex Vestey employee told me how he had taken all George's Staff home at Xmas after working late at night with the Xmas orders in 1998.*

LORD VESTEY *opened the Yarra Valley Hunt in Victoria, Australia in July of 2000. I now have farming and horse interests in the Yarra Valley myself.*

THE VICTORIAN POLICE OFFICERS *involved in the Criminal Defamation case have either left the Police Force or back in Uniform without one exception who is a Detective at Ringwood, Victoria.*

JOHN CARTER *was sacked as Chairman of the New South Wales Meat Authority.*

JAMES BLACK, *my Barrister from Devon is now a Judge in New South Wales, Australia.*

MICHAEL *the Barrister I met at my first AA Meeting in 1987 is also a Judge in New South Wales Australia.*

BOB REID *of Consumer Affairs, New South Wales, was given Premature Retirement by the Carr Government. Reid was not formally charged with Corruption.*

DES EKIN *is still with the "Sunday World" writing his weekly column exposing the seedy side of Dublin Night Life that he knows so very well. Ekin has been ostracised by all the reputable newspapers in Ireland and London, as his Dual Standards and Hypocrisy are now an Open Secret in the Newspaper Industry.*

LIAM MARKS *is On the Run from his creditors in Ireland and residing in South Africa.*

ROSS REED and JOHN COPPAS *are both managing separate Cold Stores in Ireland, very suitable employment for them.*

CRAWFORD SCOTT *died a couple of years ago. **Homer**, his eldest son, is one of the most successful Racehorse Trainers in Ireland today.*

BRUCE REYNOLDS *was flown to Brazil by the "Sun" newspaper to bring Ronald Biggs back to England in 2001.*

FRANKIE FRASER *is a Free Man and his de facto has recently published his autobiography.*

RICHARD BENDYSHE, *the Local Squire who sold his estate to Noel Edmunds, died in 2000 and was buried in his own under an Apple Tree in his orchard in Devon. Richard was a Beautiful Human Being.*

HUGH TUNNEY *is living between the Penthouse of the Gresham Hotel and his Castle in County Sligo.*

JACK TAYLOR *died on a golf course in Spain in 1989. He was Godfather to my daughter, Siobhan. Daphne, his wife, was tragically murdered in Bangor, County Down in 1994.*

JOHN ROSS *is retired and living in Exeter. Paul, his son, is now Managing Director of Exeter Hide and Skin Company.*

MARGARET HAYES (2) *is living in Yorkshire and we share the Pride we have in Edwina and William.*

TERRI *still lives in Northampton and is now a grandmother of two small children.*

JENNY *lives in Sydney, Australia. Siobhan and Robert spend School Holidays with me.*

THE INVESTIGATING OFFICER FROM MALAHIDE – *I sent him the draft of this Book and spoke to him on the telephone and he said "Well Bill, the allegations in Ireland are no more serious than **Traffic Offences".***

SALLY, JILL, MARY – *I have no idea where you are. Should you ever pick up this book, I apologise from the bottom of my heart for any Pain and Suffering I caused you.*

JOHN SHARKEY – *John left the Meat Inspection Industry and now works with Northampton Rural Council at Towcester. John has thirty grandchildren and three great grandchildren. He is still happily married to the lovely Mary.*

ALEX LEWENBERG – *Alex would be the most famous solicitor in the Melbourne CDB. His beautiful solicitor daughter Vivian, has made him a very proud **grandfather.** Lewenberg and Lewenberg are not just a firm of solicitors. "They care about People".*

ROBERT RITCHER, Q.C. – *The wonderful Robert or the "Red Baron" as he is endearingly called is still the foremost legal mind in Australia. He recently considered defending a War Criminal from World War II. Robert who is proudly Jewish is not only a gentleman but the epitome of a **"Fair Minded"** advocate.*

BILL O'BRIEN *is still proudly practising law in Sydney, Australia.*

DANIEL AND DAVID – *My Step-Sons. David was Australian National Karate Champion in 1999. Daniel then became Australian Karate Champion in the Year 2000. David was again Champion in 2001. I assume it will be Daniel's turn next year. I have no doubt they will be taking me to Athens for the Olympics in 2004. I am very proud of my sons.*

DERRYN HINCH *was sacked from a Melbourne Radio Show in 2001. This would be comparable with being sacked from British Rail.*

ALEX HURRICANE HIGGINS *is still living in a council flat in Belfast. I saw a photo of him recently in the British Press and thought there but for the Grace of God, go I.*

FRANS BUITILAAR *died of Cancer in December 2000 aged Sixty. His son and daughter will continue the Cattle Dynasty in typical Buitilaar style.*

JOHN MORRIS *is retired in North Tawton, Devon and Seventy Three years old. John's two sons operate the large electrical contracting business that John created.*

JENNIFER AND JOSIE RICE – *My two favourite ladies from Exbourne village. I had drinks with Jennifer in the Plume and Feathers, Okehampton, twenty five years ago. I hope to see you both in Paris or Australia in the near future. Jennifer's beautiful daughter with the angelic voice is going to put the village of Exbourne on the Map!*

<u>ACKNOWLEDGEMENTS</u>

First and foremost I thank Amy Hayes for her *Patience* in transcribing my shocking handwriting into a legible form of English.

Jane Mays, Literary Editor of the "Daily Mail" for her *Help and Inspiration.*

My Darling Mother who read and re-read the manuscript checking my spelling mistakes. *My mother was deeply hurt at the first reading of the draft and apologised to me. I explained to my darling mother that there is no Hero in this book. At best, I am an "Anti-Hero".*

There is, however, a *Heroine* and that is my mother. She has always been there for me over the last fifty years despite my *Breaking Her Heart*, time and time again.

I recall her so well telling me to get some **Will Power** and resist the *Temptation to Drink.*

The first step of AA is to admit we are **Powerless over Alcohol** and our lives have become unmanageable. All the will power in the world will not stop an alcoholic from drinking.

I wrote this story from memory and had no notes or diaries for reference. Each chapter could be re-written as a book in itself. However, I merely told the story as it was. Should my Book help one **Struggling Alcoholic**, then it has not been in vain.

I would like to say to my siblings that they may have totally different recollections of our days as children. This is my story, **"Bill's Story"**. This is how I saw my life albeit many years through the **Bottom of the Glass.**

Mary Bolton was the greatest inspiration in my life. The many things she taught me twenty years ago are paramount in my life of Sobriety today.

Mary was twenty five years sober when I met her in 1979. She had everything that I want and will always aim to achieve.

I would like to thank all members of AA that I have met over the years for their story that have helped me.

I recall a very young lady at AA in Paris saying we must **"let go"** of the Past or it will surely drag us back to the Booze.

The length of one's sobriety is quite immaterial, it is the **Quality** that counts.

Finally I would like to thank Hugh Tunney for ***always being there for me.***